Teenage Pregnancy in Industrialized Countries

Teenage Pregnancy in Industrialized Countries

A STUDY SPONSORED BY
THE ALAN GUTTMACHER INSTITUTE

Elise F. Jones, Study Director; Jacqueline Darroch Forrest,
Noreen Goldman, Stanley Henshaw, Richard Lincoln,
Jeannie I. Rosoff, Charles F. Westoff, and Deirdre Wulf

Yale University Press
New Haven and London

Designed by Susan P. Fillion
and set in Baskerville type by Keystone Typesetting,
Orwigsburg, Pennsylvania.
Printed in the United States of America by Edwards
Brothers, Ann Arbor, Michigan

Library of Congress Cataloging-in-Publication Data

Teenage pregnancy in industrialized countries.

  Bibliography: p.
  Includes index.
  1. Pregnancy, Adolescent—United States.
2. Pregnancy, Adolescent—Canada. 3. Pregnancy,
Adolescent—Europe. I. Jones, Elise F. II. Alan
Guttmacher Institute.
HQ759.4.T432 1986   304.6'3'088055   86–9237
ISBNs 0–300–03705–8 (cloth)
        0–300–04325–2 (pbk.)

*The paper in this book meets the guidelines for permanence
and durability of the Committee on Production Guidelines for
Book Longevity of the Council on Library Resources.*

10 9 8 7 6 5 4 3

Contents

Tables and Figures

TABLES

FIGURES

Preface

The relatively high adolescent birthrates and abortion rates in the United States have well-documented serious and adverse consequences for the teenagers themselves, for their progeny, and for society; the determinants are many and complex and are only partly understood. Because few teenagers report that they want to get pregnant, it should not be difficult to develop interventions to prevent adolescent pregnancy. However, despite considerable publicity given to the problem, and the development of numerous programs designed to deal with it, adolescent pregnancies have continued to increase. This book describes a study that attempts to cast some light on the determinants of teenage pregnancy in the United States, and the means to prevent it by comparisons with the experience of other developed countries. The primary purpose is to gain some insight into the determinants of teenage reproductive behavior at the national level, especially factors that might be subject to policy changes. The study is limited to industrialized societies because the nature of the problem appears to be different in developed and developing countries, and because there is typically much more information available for the more developed countries.

The project was carried out by the Alan Guttmacher Institute with the collaboration of members of the staff of the Office of Population Research at Princeton University. A 1983 article by Charles F. Westoff, Gerard Calot, and Andrew D. Foster reported that although adolescent birthrates had been declining in the United States, and in virtually all the countries of northern and western Europe, teenage fertility is considerably higher in the United States than in most other developed countries (see Appendix 1). There is an enormous differential in the United States between the birthrates of black and white teenage women, but even if only whites are considered, the American rates are unusually high. The excess fertility of U.S. teenagers is much more marked among women below age 18 than among those aged 18–19.

Whether the differences in birthrates extend to pregnancy rates (births plus abortions) and, if so, whether they result from variations in levels of sexual activity or quality of contraceptive practice, and how and why such adolescent behavior should differ from country to country were believed potentially revealing and useful subjects for study. The results of such a study stand to be of immediate value to those concerned with the problem of adolescent pregnancy and childbearing in the United States. Chapter 1 presents the results of a quantitative analysis of the determinants of adolescent fertility in 37 developed countries. Chapters 2–9 are devoted to in-depth case studies of teenage pregnancy and its antecedents in six selected countries including the United States. A final chapter draws the lessons from the entire study that appear relevant to policy formulation in the United States.

Although all of the investigators collaborated on each aspect of the study, Elise F. Jones, the study director, was primarily responsible for chapters 1, 2, and 9; she wrote chapters 6 and 7 with Deirdre Wulf and chapter 8 with Charles F. Westoff; Jacqueline Darroch Forrest was the major researcher and author for chapter 3; Stanley K. Henshaw for chapter 4; Noreen Goldman and Richard Lincoln for chapter 5; and Jeannie I. Rosoff and Richard Lincoln for chapter 10. Richard Lincoln also edited the final manuscript. Ellen E. Kisker collaborated in the multivariate analysis in Appendix 7. The authors are grateful to Lynne Brenner and Karen Fuller for the research assistance they provided.

The project was fortunate in being able to enlist in advance the services of a strategically placed professional to act as a liaison during the preparation for visits made by the investigators to the five countries chosen for comparison to the United States. The major responsibility for identifying and contacting appropriate individuals for interview and for arranging the program of the visit rested with the liaison person. Not only did each one fulfill this crucial task most admirably, but all were very generous with their personal time and attention during the visit, and several have continued to provide guidance during the report-writing stage. The project participants wish to extend their sincere thanks to Judith Nolte of Canada, Joanna Chambers of the United Kingdom, Henri Leridon of France, Evert Ketting of the Netherlands and Eva Bernhardt of Sweden. They also wish to emphasize that the final content of the country reports, including any errors therein, is entirely the responsibility of the authors themselves.

Teenage Pregnancy in Industrialized Countries

1

The Determinants of Adolescent Childbearing In Thirty-Seven Developed Countries

THE STUDY

In 1983 Charles F. Westoff and his colleagues summarized data assembled by the Institut National d'Etudes Démographiques which showed that fertility among American teenagers was higher than that of 27 out of 30 other developed countries for which there was information; among younger teenagers, the U.S. level was higher than that of any industrialized country except Hungary (see Appendix 1). Other research on abortion showed that the legal abortion rate among U.S. teenagers was also higher than that of any other developed country for which there were data (Tietze, 1983, table 7).

The first part of the research on which this book was based was undertaken to see whether a cross-country statistical analysis could shed light on the reasons for the exceptional reproductive behavior of American adolescents and for the overall pattern of disparities among countries. The initial intention was to focus on pregnancy, including abortions as well as births; since both follow from conceptions, and neither is without consequence. In addition, it was planned to focus the analysis on women under age 18. Not only is the contrast between the United States and other countries greater for the youngest women, but the adverse socioeconomic, emotional and health consequences of pregnancy are also more serious for them than for older teenagers. Moreover, earlier research indicates that an even greater majority of pregnancies experienced by younger teenagers are unintended (Zelnik and Kantner, 1980). Finally it was planned to carry out a cross-sectional analysis based on data from the period around 1980.

This investigation is essentially exploratory. It was hoped that if the

1

theoretical framework were not rigid, new perspectives might emerge. Certain underlying ideas nevertheless played a significant role in the conceptual organization. One is the notion that young people's perceptions of their future opportunities affect their motivation to avoid early childbearing. A second is the general impression that the way the subject of sex is treated in a society as a whole can encourage or discourage the development of responsible attitudes among adolescents. Yet another issue is the possible impact of ethnic, cultural, and socioeconomic diversity within a society. A particular effort has been made throughout to pursue topics of possible policy relevance such as sex education and teaching about contraceptive methods, the access of young people to fertility control services, and paternal financial responsibility for children born out of wedlock.

It was recognized from the start that many kinds of information pertinent to adolescent pregnancy would not be widely available. Nevertheless, it seemed worthwhile to examine whatever data could be assembled for developed countries as a group in an attempt to identify possible determinants of this phenomenon. Such an approach would permit at least limited quantitative evaluation of relationships. Any generalizations that emerged would be of interest in their own right and could also serve as a guide to promising areas for further attention in the case studies of individual countries to follow. Moreover, the scope and limitations of existing resource materials would be clearly established in the process.

SELECTION OF COUNTRIES

Two criteria were established to define developed countries. These were a total fertility rate below 3.5 children per woman and a per capita income of more than $2,000 per year. A minimum population size of one million was also imposed. It was necessary to impose these limitations in order to exclude both countries that have achieved relatively low fertility but cannot be considered as developed in a socioeconomic sense (e.g., China), as well as wealthy countries where traditional ways of life still prevail (e.g., Saudi Arabia). Thirty-seven national entities that also had information on the fertility of women under age 20 were identified by these criteria (see table 1.1)[1]

1. Cuba was included despite the fact that its per capita income was not known because of its low overall level of fertility (total fertility rate 1.9) and its possible relevance for Hispanics in the United States. Argentina, Trinidad and Tobago, and Uruguay were also identified as eligible but were dropped because no information was available on the fertility of women under age twenty. In the case of the United Kingdom, some items of information proved to be available for England and Wales only or for England, Wales, and Scotland, while others related to the United Kingdom as a whole or, occasionally, to

Table 1.1. *Developed countries selected for the study*

Australia	German Democratic	Portugal
Austria	Republic	Puerto Rico†
Belgium	Greece	Romania
Bulgaria	Hong Kong†	Singapore
Canada	Hungary	Spain
Chile	Ireland	Sweden
Cuba	Israel	Switzerland
Czechoslovakia	Italy	Taiwan
Denmark	Japan	Union of Soviet Socialist
Federal Republic of	Netherlands	Republics
Germany	New Zealand	England and Wales*
Finland	Norway	Scotland*
France	Poland	United States
		Yugoslavia

*United Kingdom.
†Not independent countries.

MEASURES OF PREGNANCY AND FERTILITY

The data on births and abortions necessary to calculate pregnancy rates were available in varying degrees of detail for individual countries. Bearing in mind the twin goals of focusing on pregnancy and on women below age 18, eight dependent variables were considered. Data for 1980 were used whenever possible, but if necessary figures from as far back as 1978 were accepted. The first section of Appendix 2 indicates the sources used for the eight variables, and the data themselves are shown in Appendix 3.

The number of live births per 1,000 women aged 15–19 is the most basic measure of teenage fertility. It can be obtained from routine statistical sources in almost all developed countries. Although widely available, this measure is imprecise in that it treats only births rather than pregnancies, and it covers all teenagers as a group rather than looking at younger and older teenagers separately.

An extensive collection of data on births by single year of age of mother and corresponding estimates of the female population by single year of age, covering 30 of the 37 countries in this study, has been assembled by Gérard Calot at the Institut National d'Etudes Démographiques. The availability of these data makes it possible to calculate single-year birthrates, which can then be summed to form cumulative

---

Great Britain. It was decided to use separate observations for England and Wales and for Scotland insofar as possible, counting them as two countries. It should be noted that the set of countries finally included constitutes a universe rather than a sample, albeit one that is something less than complete. Thus statistical inferences based on sampling theory do not apply.

birthrates across any desired subgroup of age. Intercountry comparisons of the resulting rates are free of possible influence by differences in the age distribution within an age range, in the same sense as the total fertility rate is free of major distortions due to variations in the age distribution of women aged 15–50. Three such variables were constructed: for all women younger than age 20, for women below age 18, and for women aged 18–19.[2] Thirty of the 37 study countries were covered—all except Bulgaria, Chile, Cuba, Hong Kong, Singapore, Taiwan, and the USSR.

The remaining measures of fertility relate to pregnancies rather than births. Numbers of pregnancies were estimated by combining abortions with births for each age group. However, abortion data that were judged to be reasonably complete, or that could be adjusted for undernumeration, proved to be available by single years of age for only 11 countries and, for the 15–19-year age group, for only 13 countries. Pregnancy rates were calculated for these countries, but their very limited coverage severely restricted the possibilities for their use in statistical analysis. The pregnancy rates used here are the sum of births plus abortions tabulated by age at time of outcome; they do not include an estimate of miscarriages and stillbirths and are not adjusted to age at conception.

It was decided to proceed using as dependent variables two measures of the birthrates: the cumulative birthrate for women under age 18 and that for women 18–19 years old. This approach allowed the desired age breakdown. Although it was not possible to focus directly on pregnancies, calculation of the pair-wise correlation coefficients among the eight potential dependent variables suggested that the relationship between births and pregnancies is quite close for the subset of 11 countries for which the pregnancy rates could be computed. The correlation between each birth measure and its corresponding pregnancy measure ranges between 0.90 and 0.96, indicating a very strong positive correlation between births and abortions. It is not known whether a similar association holds in all the developed countries; nevertheless, it appears that the birthrates may provide some insight into the underlying issue of pregnancy.

The cumulative birthrates for women under age 18 and women aged 18–19 were also highly correlated with the birthrate for women aged 15–19 (0.90 and 0.98, respectively). Hence the latter rates could be used to estimate the two cumulative rates for the seven countries where they were missing. (These estimates are shown in Appendix 3.)

2. It should be kept in mind that, precisely because of the social and possible legal significance of achieving age 18 that lies behind the choice of this age break, there is some probability of bias due to age misstatement involving women below age 18 stating that they are 18 or older.

THE INDEPENDENT VARIABLES

A search was made for national-level indicators relating to all topics that might have a bearing on adolescent pregnancy and childbearing. With the exception of the country survey, which is described below, the data were taken almost exclusively from published sources. The target year was 1980, although information going back to 1975, or in exceptional cases even to 1970, was considered acceptable. A large number of specific items were considered in the course of the data-collection process and eventually dropped because the information was of manifestly poor quality, was not comparable across countries, was available for only a very few countries, was distributed in a highly distorted manner (i.e., a very large majority of the cases fell into one category), or it overlapped excessively with other items.

It became obvious at a very early stage that there was very little information of a comparable nature on either sexual activity or contraceptive use among adolescents. Such data are usually derived from large-scale surveys of individuals. Consideration of these two central topics thus had to be deferred to the second phase of the project, when case studies of individual countries would be carried out (see chapters 2–9).

Few data concerning several other factors believed to be related to teenage fertility have been published that involved information that might be known to observant country residents. Examples of such topics are the prevalence of sex education, the availability of fertility control services to unmarried minors, and some aspects of societal attitudes concerning sex. A country-level survey was undertaken, therefore, based on a questionnaire drawn up for this purpose. It was sent to the public affairs officer of the American embassy in each country included in the study, to the embassy of each of these countries in Washington, D.C., and to the family planning organization or other agency responsible for family planning services in each country. At least one response was received from every country except the USSR. Substitute information for the USSR was supplied by a life-time resident recently arrived in the United States. A questionnaire for the United States was filled out by one of the project members, bringing the coverage to 100 percent.

The information acquired from the country survey was accepted for the most part at face value. Simple, ad-hoc rules were devised for the processing of the data. Although the quality of the information was difficult to evaluate, comparisons were made whenever more than one completed questionnaire was available for a given country in order to ascertain the extent of disagreement, to see which questionnaire appeared to have been filled out with most care, and to learn whether there were any specific items that regularly caused difficulty. The overall level of agreement was reassuring, and many conflicts that did occur could be resolved by selecting one set of responses as clearly superior to another. Where there was no obvious basis for decision between differing responses, the item was coded as missing data, along with others where no reply had been given.

Forty-two independent variables were identified as being potentially useful for analytical purposes, including 10 derived from the country questionnaire.[3] The external sources from which the data were taken are listed variable by variable in the second part of Appendix 2, and the actual figures are shown following the dependent variables in Appendix 3. The variables derived from the country survey are given in Appendix 4. The questionnaire appears as Appendix 5.

BIVARIATE ANALYSIS

The first step in the analysis was to examine the bivariate relationships between each of the 42 independent variables and the two dependent variables. Table 1.2 shows the pair-wise correlation coefficients, with the independent variables grouped under eleven headings that indicate in a general way the nature of their presumed link to adolescent fertility. The categories serve only as a way of organizing the material; they are not viewed as definitive, and frequently a given variable could have been examined under some other heading.[4]

Marriage

The proportion of women married at ages 15–19 is different from the other variables for two reasons. In the first place, marriage could be involved in a circular relationship with the dependent variables, whereby it would be partly determined by, as well as be a determinant of, teenage childbearing. Although it may be less true now than in the past, in some societies premarital pregnancy has tended to precipitate a marriage before the birth of the child. In the second place, marriage plays the role of an intermediate variable through which the effects of

3. With the possibility of multivariate analysis in mind, variables that were ordinal in form were converted to interval measures by whatever means appeared most suited to the particular data.

4. In addition to the correlation coefficients, plots of the two-way relationships were systematically examined at this stage to check for nonlinearity and other possible idiosyncrasies. In exceptional cases, where there was an outlying point that either exaggerated the appearance of a relationship or else obscured a relationship that was clearly present among the rest of the countries, the correlations were recalculated excluding that country on the basis that it was not desirable to use results that were unduly influenced by a single observation.

other independent variables, such as sexual activity and contraceptive use, could be expected to be mediated. Hence the strong positive association between adolescent childbearing and marriage is not surprising. The minimum legal age for marriage without parental consent may to some degree affect the number of teenagers who marry, but it is probably more properly viewed as an expression of social attitudes toward youth and women's roles. The legal age for marriage is fairly strongly negatively related to the cumulative birthrates for both age groups.

Childbearing

It was assumed that the prevailing fertility climate in a given country would have some bearing on the reproductive performance of teenagers. The total fertility rate for women aged 20 and over (summed in the usual fashion across five-year age groups) is rather closely associated with teenage fertility in most countries; but there are enough exceptions to reduce the overall correlation virtually to zero. The principal outliers are Ireland and Israel, which have low levels of teenage fertility given their high rates for older women, and Cuba, which has the lowest total fertility rate for ages 20 and older of any country and the next-to-highest age-specific fertility rate for women aged 15–19. National policy to influence fertility was coded in three categories: to lower fertility (only Taiwan fell into this category); to maintain the present level or not to intervene at all; and to raise fertility. Having a policy favoring higher fertility was found to be moderately and positively associated with teenage birthrates. (The correlations hold even if Taiwan is excluded.) Policy regarding maternity leaves and benefits was represented by an index that was coded as representing low, medium and high maternity support. Young women tend to have more births where these policies are generous. Because of the variety of governmental programs helping to ease the financial burden of raising children, government expenditures on income maintenance and family allowances were combined in one variable. This information was available for only 17 countries, and there is no evident relationship with the teenage birthrates. The correlations do not suggest any noticeable effect on teenage birthrates of the availability of paternal financial support for the children of unmarried mothers. However, the two items in the country survey on which that variable was based (see Appendix 5, items 13 and 14) may not have covered it effectively.

Contraception

The first two variables under this heading refer to the pattern of use among married women, which could influence what teenagers know

Table 1.2. *Zero-order correlations between independent variables and cumulative birthrates*

Group and variable	Cumulative birthrate for women, by age		
	<18	18–19	N
Marriage			
Proportion of women aged 15–19 who are married	0.83	0.84	37
Minimum age for marriage without parental consent*	−0.33	−0.39	24
Childbearing			
Five-year total fertility rate for ages ≥20	0.06	0.13	37
Government policy to raise fertility*	0.25	0.36	35
Liberal policy on maternity leaves and benefits*	0.35	0.48	28
Percentage of government expenditure on income maintenance and family allowances	−0.19	0.09	17
Paternal financial support (Q)	0.07	0.21	31
Contraception			
Percentage of all currently married using the pill	−0.18	−0.17	20
Proportion of all currently married using condoms	−0.63	−0.58	13
Policy favoring provision of contraceptives for young, unmarried women* (Q)	−0.50	−0.49	36
Policy favoring teaching contraception (Q)	−0.21	−0.06	37
Proportion of female students taught contraception (Q)	−0.27	−0.16	36
Age at which contraception taught (Q)	0.12	0.17	28
Abortion			
Abortions per woman aged 15–44†	0.67	0.77	24
Least restrictions regarding parental consent (Q)	0.03	−0.08	33
Public subsidy of abortions (Q)	0.05	0.26	29
Sex			
Open attitudes about sex* (Q)	−0.49	−0.52	37
Minimum age for consensual intercourse‡ (Q)	0.26	0.18	34
Proportion of female students in coeducational schools (Q)	0.00	0.04	36
Health			
Population per physician	0.12	0.05	34
Maternal mortality*	0.43	.51	35
Per capita government expenditure on health care	−0.13	−0.11	19
Education			
Percentage of secondary-school-age women attending school	−0.13	−0.27	31
Percentage of women 15–19 attending school	−0.21	−0.12	14
Per capita government expenditure on education	−0.44	−0.38	18
Social Integration			
Total marital divorce rate	−0.26	−0.27	19
Mortality rate from liver cirrhosis*	0.34	0.35	34
Incidence of suicide ages 15–24	−0.17	−0.15	30
Proportion foreign born*	−0.35	−0.28	19

Table 1.2 (*Continued*)

Group and variable	Cumulative birthrate for women, by age		
	<18	18–19	N
General Social Conditions			
Log of population density	−0.18	−0.13	35
Percentage in cities ≥500,000*	−0.12	−0.32	34
Percentage of labor force in agriculture*	0.60	0.66	34
Religiosity	0.66	0.67	13
Employment			
Labor-force participation rate for women 15–19	0.28	0.11	15
Labor-force participation rate for men 15–19	0.11	0.02	15
Proportion of labor force female*	0.22	0.39	33
Labor-force participation rate for women 35–44	0.35	0.42	18
Overall unemployment rate‡	0.15	0.16	27
General Economic Conditions			
Gross national product per capita*	−0.51	−0.61	33
Average annual growth in gross domestic product	−0.06	−0.06	28
Percentage of total household income to top 10% of population	0.06	0.00	14
Percentage of total household income to bottom 20% of population*	−0.41	0.14	19

Source: Appendix 5; Appendix 2.
Notes: N = Number of countries in 37-country study for which data are available; items marked (Q) were taken from AGI country questionnaire.
*Included in multivariate analysis.
†Excluding Japan.
‡Excluding Puerto Rico.

and do about contraception. It is notable that the teenage birthrates appear to be lower in countries where the condom is in more common use, but the relationship is extremely weak for the pill. Since the condom is well suited to episodic sexual activity and is often more available to young people than other methods, this result makes some sense. Information on use of the condom was available, however, for only 13 countries.

The remaining four variables in this group have to do directly with young people, and all were derived from the country survey. A set of questions was included on legal and practical restrictions that might hinder the access to contraception of unmarried women under 18 as compared to older women (Appendix 5, items 1–3). The replies were combined in an index of contraceptive policy for young unmarried women, and less restrictive policies are clearly associated with lower birthrates. Another group of three questions concerned the teaching of contraceptive methods in schools (items 7–9). These responses were considered separately, and in each case the direction of the relationships is as expected, although the link does not seem to be especially close.

Abortion

Abortion is certainly an important issue for adolescent childbearing, although it is not clear whether the level of abortion would be expected to be negatively or positively associated with birthrates. On the one hand, each abortion eliminates a potential birth, but, on the other hand, societies with low fertility are likely to have achieved sufficient expertise in contraception to have a low level of unwanted pregnancy as well. The overall number of abortions was known with a fair degree of confidence for 22 countries; for three others—Hong Kong, Italy, and Singapore—estimates were available that were thought to be significantly below the real number (Tietze, 1983). Correlations were calculated both with and without the data from these countries; because their inclusion did not alter the results appreciably, it was decided to use the larger number of observations. Japan, however, was deleted from the calculation because it was unique in having one of the highest abortion rates combined with the very lowest teenage birthrates; thus it masked a strong positive relationship that is apparent among all the other countries.

Information on two other aspects of abortion was obtained from the country surveys. Neither the requirement of parental consent for abortions requested by young unmarried women nor the availability of abortions free of charge appears to be strongly associated with teenage childbearing.

Sex

Social attitudes about sex form a part of the background against which adolescents come to terms with their own sexuality, although such ideas are often communicated in informal and subtle ways. The country surveys once again provided an opportunity to address this topic. Direct questions were included on the minimum age for consensual intercourse (statutory rape law) and on the proportion of female students aged 15–16 who attend coeducational schools. Response to the former varied from age 14 in Austria to age 21 in Puerto Rico. Since Puerto Rico also has high teenage fertility, and the next highest age for consensual intercourse that was given was 18, Puerto Rico appeared as a distinct outlier; hence it was excluded from the correlation calculations. The coefficients, nevertheless, are positive. Thus, whereas a high minimum age for marriage without parental consent proved to be associated with low teenage birthrates, the opposite tends to be the case with respect to age of consent for sexual intercourse.

The last group of questions in the country surveys was designed to tap more general societal attitudes toward sex. The responses on media presentation of female nudity, nudity on public beaches, and sale of sexually explicit literature proved to be fairly highly intercorrelated in the expected way. An earlier question on media advertising of condoms, originally intended as a way of assessing contraceptive availability, was also considered ultimately to be more revealing of frankness concerning sexual matters. The responses to these four items were combined to form an index of openness about sex. No claim is made to have covered the subject systematically or precisely, but it seems possible nevertheless to interpret these data collectively as reflecting in some way an underlying social message. It was expected that societies that are relatively relaxed in their attitudes about sex would be able to deal realistically with adolescent sexuality. The rather high negative correlations with both dependent variables tend to bear out this notion.

Health

Several aspects of the overall health situation in the countries studied were of interest. Population per physician and per capita government expenditures on health care were included as general measures of access to health services, which might include reproductive health care or otherwise affect adolescent childbearing indirectly, but the results do not suggest any relationship. Maternal mortality, measured as the ratio of deaths to live births, was considered a more precise indicator of access to maternal and child health (MCH) services. For many countries, the data did not permit the separation of abortion-related deaths from maternal deaths, however; both, therefore, are in the numerator. Since only live births are included in the denominator, this distorts the ratio. In at least one case where the distinction could be made (Romania) a substantial majority of all the maternal deaths did stem from abortions. Abortion-related deaths occur mainly as a result of illegal abortion, and where this component is important, the measure may reflect lack of access to legal abortion and to contraceptive services rather than anything specifically to do with MCH care. In countries with low maternal mortality, this relationship may also reflect the relatively high rates experienced by teenage mothers. Hence the meaning of the positive coefficients shown in table 1.2 is somewhat uncertain.

Education

School attendance was hypothesized to relate to adolescent childbearing as an indicator of young people's investment in and sense of control over their own futures. It was hoped that measures of the proportion of females in school at ages 14–17 and ages 18–19 could be obtained, but data were found only for the 15–19-year-old group and were limited to 14 countries; the association with teenage birthrates is very weak. Data on secondary school attendance were more available but represented varying age groups, and the relationships are likewise weak. Per-capita government expenditure on education, although fairly highly correlated with the two dependent variables, is an even more imprecise substitute for the sort of educational measures desired, and there were only 18 countries for which those data were available. Thus, although all of the correlation coefficients related to education are in the expected direction, none of the measures available seems adequate to test this potentially important relationship very fully.

Social Integration

Adolescent childbearing is sometimes interpreted as symptomatic of a breakdown of the social order in general and of youthful alienation in particular. In so far as this is true, it could be expected to be associated with, although not necessarily caused by, a variety of other social ills. A number of such problems were considered. No comparable information was found on either juvenile delinquency or drug abuse. Both suicide among young people and divorce appear to be lower, if anything, where teenage fertility is higher. The mortality rate from liver cirrhosis, which was taken as an indicator of alcohol abuse, nevertheless is clearly and positively associated with birthrates for both younger and older teenagers.

A second and quite different aspect of social integration is population homogeneity. Minorities—whether of a racial, ethnic, religious, or linguistic character—could influence adolescent birthrates directly if they were large enough and their behavior departed significantly from that of the majority. The racial and ethnic contrasts within the United States are a case in point. In addition, countries composed of subgroups with different and possibly conflicting attitudes about youth, sex, and reproduction might find it more difficult to formulate and implement policies related to adolescent fertility at the national level. However, the attempt to construct an index of population homogeneity that could capture this concept was unsuccessful. Although statistics were available for at least a few countries on various characteristics, they were not found for many countries, and there was no common basis for defining or comparing subgroups (e.g., is protestantism one religion or many?). The only measure with any bearing at all on this topic that was known for at least half of the countries was the proportion of the population born outside the country. This variable was found unexpectedly to be moderately but negatively associated with the birthrates of both younger and older teenagers. Countries with high teenage fertility and low proportions of foreign born are Cuba, Puerto Rico, and Chile; countries with low teenage fertility and high proportions of foreign born are Singapore, Hong Kong, and Israel.

General Social Conditions

Several additional variables were included referring to conditions that focus less specifically on social problems. Population density was one.[5] The proportion of the population in large cities and the proportion of the labor force in agriculture represent other facets of urbanization. All three measures suggest consistently that population concentration and/or urbanization is negatively associated with adolescent childbearing. The correlation coefficients are particularly high for the proportion of the labor force engaged in agriculture. Although this factor is interpreted here mainly as an indicator of socioeconomic development, it may also specifically reflect the high fertility and early marriage traditionally associated with farming as a way of life.

Religiosity was measured on the basis of a survey conducted by the Center for Applied Research in the Apostolate in which samples of individuals in a number of countries were queried about the importance of God in their lives. The responses were coded on a scale of 1–10 and averaged for each country. This variable is very strongly correlated with the birthrates of both older and younger teenagers. Countries with the highest levels of religiosity have the highest birthrates. (The United States scores at the top—see Appendix 3.) It is unfortunate that this measure was available for only 13 of the countries included in the study.

Employment

Like school attendance, the employment situation of teenagers was thought to suggest the ease with which the transition to adulthood could be achieved and thus to reflect young people's assessments of their life prospects. Adequate statistics were hard to find. In addition, the definition of labor-force concepts, particularly those concerning unemployment, is not well standardized across countries, and the discrepancies are likely to be greatest for marginal groups like teenagers entering the labor force for the first time. For this reason, data on employment rates among young people could not be used. The sex-specific labor-force participation rates for 15–19-year-olds seemed somewhat less vulnerable to problems of comparability. However, their

---

5. Population density was converted to a logarithmic scale in order better to accommodate relative differences at the high and low ends of the distribution (Hong Kong and Singapore versus Australia and Canada).

association with the adolescent birthrates proved to be very weak, and only 18 countries were available for observation.

It was expected that teenage childbearing would be lower where job opportunities for women in general were more plentiful, in line with the well-documented negative association between fertility and women's employment. The correlations for the proportion of the labor force that was female turn out to be fairly strong in the case of the cumulative birthrate for 18–19-year-olds, but the direction of both coefficients is positive instead of negative. In the Netherlands and Spain teenage birthrates are low and there are relatively few women in the labor force; in Bulgaria, Hungary, and Romania the opposite is the case. Consistent with this result, the labor-force participation rate for women 35–44 years old is fairly strongly and positively related to the teenage birthrates. This variable was included because women in that age range would be the mothers of many current teenagers, and it might thus reflect lack of supervision in the home; hence a positive relationship was, in fact, anticipated in this case. Information on this subject, however, was found for fewer than half of the countries. Overall unemployment shows no particular association with younger or older teenage birthrates.[6]

General Economic Conditions

The final category of independent variables contains several measures of general economic well-being. It was thought that gross domestic product per capita (GDP) would be the most satisfactory indicator of relative economic development, but gross national product (GNP), which was very closely correlated with GDP for the countries where both measures were available, was ultimately selected because it provided substantially more observations. The expected negative relationship with teenage childbearing emerges quite clearly. However, the correlation coefficients are very low for the average annual growth in GNP. The two last variables are measures of income distribution. Although the proportion of total household income going to the highest 10 percent of households has no apparent relationship with teenage fertility, the cumulative birthrate for women under age 18 is clearly lower where the proportion of total household income going to the lowest 20 percent of households is highest, indicating a positive association between childbearing among very young women and the extent of poverty. It is regrettable that this item of information is missing for many countries, including all of the commmunist countries.

6. Puerto Rico was excluded from this calculation because it combined exceptionally high unemployment with very high teenage birthrates and thus gave a misleading impression of a closer relationship.

The results of the bivariate analysis are not easy to evaluate. Several of the substantive areas of most interest are very inadequately covered. Moreover, when a given correlation is low, it is usually impossible to tell whether this should be taken as indicative of the absence of a relationship or whether it may be due to shortcomings of the data. In a number of instances, the measures available are only rough approximations of the concept they were intended to represent and, despite the fact that numerous variables were excluded because the data obviously were not comparable from country to country, more subtle forms of noncomparability no doubt remain. In addition the variables derived from the responses to the country survey have to be regarded for the most part as subject to a considerable margin of error.

One further observation should be stressed with respect to missing data. In the course of data screening, many more items were tested and more relationships examined than appear in table 1.2. A principal conclusion from this entire experience is that whenever the information on a particular variable is incomplete, the countries for which it is available are unlikely to be a random selection of the set of developed countries as a whole. In other words, there is a tendency for the kinds of information collected to be associated with certain characteristics of a country—for example, level of development, geographic region, or type of economic system. Whereas such an association is not particularly surprising, it implies that special caution must be exercised in interpreting the findings for variables where there are more than a few countries missing. This is one of the main reasons why there was no attempt to study in depth the pregnancy rates for the small group of countries where the availability of abortion data made the calculation of these rates possible. The zero-order correlations between the 42 independent variables listed in table 1.2 and each of the eight dependent variables initially considered are shown for the countries having data on abortions by age in Appendix 6. Comparison of the coefficients for the cumulative fertility rates for women under age 18 and women 18–19 in Appendix 6 with those in table 1.2 indicates clearly that limitation to that particular small group of countries in many cases substantially changes the values and occasionally even the direction of the relationships with the independent variables.

MULTIVARIATE ANALYSIS

In spite of the problems encountered in the course of the bivariate analysis, there is evidence of a number of rather strong relationships. Because the independent variables that are most closely correlated with the adolescent birthrates are likely to be interrelated themselves in complex ways, it seemed desirable to gain some understanding of the structure of their effects on adolescent fertility in general and of the role of individual policy variables in particular. The possibilities for multivariate analysis were very limited, however, due to the small number of countries observed overall, and the additional complication of extensive missing data.[7] Hence the results must be taken as suggestive rather than conclusive, and they are presented here only in broad terms. Ordinary least squares regression procedures were used to identify and evaluate the principal determinants of the birthrates for the two age groups. A detailed description of the regression analysis and a table showing the results in quantitative form are provided in Appendix 7.

Independent variables having at least 19 observations (i.e., more than half the total number of 37 countries) and a correlation coefficient of 0.30 or higher with one or both of the teenage birthrates were considered. These relatively low thresholds are consistent with the exploratory nature of the exercise. Two variables meeting these criteria were excluded: (1) the proportion of females married at ages 15–19 was left out because of its special status as an intermediate variable and because of the additional possibility of a two-way flow of cause and effect between it and the dependent variable (see the discussion above of marriage); and (2) the abortion rate for women 15–44 was also omitted. The focus on birthrates rather than pregnancy rates meant that abortions to women below age 20 were not represented per se in the dependent variable; abortion, moreover, clearly has a direct negative effect on births in the sense that pregnancies that are aborted avert births that would otherwise almost certainly take place. However, the high, positive pair-wise correlations between the general abortion rate and the teenage birthrates suggest that the two phenomena may perhaps be viewed more profitably as codetermined by other conditions.

For women younger than 18 years old the most important determinants of the birthrate proved to be the proportion of the labor force employed in agriculture, liberal policies on maternity leaves and benefits, and the extent of poverty in the country. As observed above, each of these three factors is positively related to early childbearing. Once they are accounted for, open attitudes concerning sex tend to lower the birthrate, although this variable also dampens the impact of the proportion of the labor force employed in agriculture, with which it is inversely related. None of the other variables has any appreciable independent effect.

A high proportion of the labor force employed in agriculture and liberal policies on maternity leaves and benefits are likewise among the

---

7. Such procedures, moreover, depend heavily on statistical inference, which is inappropriate in the absence of a random sample.

most important forces associated with high birthrates for women aged 18–19. The third major determinant for these women is openness in the society about sex, which again is negatively correlated with the birthrate. Beyond these three variables, a national policy geared to raise the overall level of reproduction seems also to encourage childbearing among older teenagers.

These results suggest that fertility is likely to be higher throughout the teenage years in countries that are less developed socioeconomically (i.e., have a higher proportion of the labor force engaged in agriculture). In addition to this factor, which is generally considered to be outside the policy arena, several variables that are more or less open to policy manipulation appear to play a prominent role. These are openness about sex, equitable distribution of income, and policies on maternity leaves and benefits.

THE POSITION OF INDIVIDUAL COUNTRIES

Almost all of the developed countries conformed to the positive association between the birthrate of both younger and older teenagers and the proportion of the labor force employed in agriculture. Given the high level of development of the United States (2 percent of the labor force engaged in agriculture in 1980), the elevated fertility of American women younger than age 18 appears extremely anomalous; other highly developed countries (8 percent or fewer of those in the labor force engaged in agriculture) exhibit birthrates that are at the very most half the U.S. rate (i.e., Australia and Canada). Indeed, the U.S. rate is high enough to fall midway between those of the two countries studied that are the least developed (Bulgaria and Greece, both with 37 percent of the labor force engaged in agriculture). The position of the United States with respect to childbearing among women 18–19 years old is less extreme; although its birthrate is again the highest among the countries with 8 percent or fewer of those in the labor force engaged in agriculture, the rates of at least some such countries come closer to the U.S. level (e.g., Israel and the United Kingdom). Japan, which has a birthrate among women 18–19 years old that is by far the lowest of any country and has as much as 12 percent of its labor force employed in agriculture, is an outstanding case in the opposite direction.

There is a considerable spread of birthrates at each of the three designated levels of maternity leaves and benefits, but the overall positive relationship is quite obvious. The United States had to be omitted from this part of the calculation because there is no national policy. On the basis of a few comparisons of maternity-benefit policies in individual U.S. states with European countries, the United States appears to be less liberal (Kamerman et al., 1983); again the United

States would probably be in an anomalous position. The finding of a positive relationship of teenage birthrates with a generous maternity-benefit policy is puzzling. Since measures regarding maternity leaves and benefits are directed toward easing the burden of childbearing for working women, who are mainly adults, it seems unlikely they would have much direct impact on teenagers, especially those below age 18. This variable may be mediating the effects of public support in the general area of maternal and child care. It is highly positively correlated with the variable representing subsidization of abortion and, to a somewhat lesser extent, with such other variables in the present data set as proportion of government expenditure on income maintenance, family allowances, and paternal financial support, although neither of the latter appeared to be strongly related to teenage birthrates. It is notable that five of the seven countries with a high level of benefits have socialist governments (Bulgaria, Cuba, Hungary, Czechoslovakia, and East Germany), whereas several of those with low benefits are comparative newcomers in the developed group (Greece, Taiwan, Hong Kong, and Singapore), and may not have a tradition of government involvement in this area.

Examination of the relationships between teenage birthrates and openness about sex reveals that although all the countries found to be relatively open have low birthrates, the birthrates of countries classified as least open range from very low (Ireland and Singapore) to very high (Cuba and Puerto Rico). Thus open attitudes about sex seem to assure low teenage birthrates, but it is possible to achieve this result even when attitudes are conservative. The countries with low teenage birthrates that are nevertheless restrictive in sexual matters appear by and large to be those where teenage childbearing is kept in check by strong social sanctions against both early marriage and premarital sex (Hong Kong, Ireland, Japan, and Singapore). For women younger than 18, the U.S. birthrate is rather high, even given rather conservative American attitudes toward sex. For women 18 to 19 years old, however, the U.S. birthrate is well within the range of countries with similar attitudes. In a factor analysis, openness about sex was found to be positively linked with the proportion of female students taught about contraception in school; perhaps this can be thought of as part of an overall modern outlook on reproduction.

The proportion of total household income going to the lowest 20 percent of households is negatively associated with the cumulative birthrate of women under 18. Of the 19 countries for which this information is available, poor people appear to be at the greatest disadvantage in Canada, New Zealand, and the United States, all of which have large European immigrant populations. The U.S. birthrate is by far the highest of these three, but even those of the other two are approximately the same as the top rates exhibited by countries where the relative position of low income families is less extreme (Portugal and Yugoslavia).

The multivariate analysis suggested that the birthrate for older teenagers responds to government policy to influence overall fertility. The United States is one of a large number of countries taking a neutral position on fertility policy; some of these counties have much higher teenage birthrates than the United States, but the average of the group is clearly lower than that for the rather small selection of countries that seek to raise their level of reproduction (Bulgaria, Chile, East Germany, Greece, Israel, and France). Thus a part of the burden of such endeavors often seems to fall on women as young as 18–19 years old.

SUMMARY AND CONCLUSIONS

This statistical analysis has explored the determinants of adolescent fertility in developed countries around the year 1980. An effort was made to include the widest possible breadth of information with respect to both measures of fertility and national characteristics that might influence reproductive behavior among young people. There was particular interest in women below age 18 and in findings that could be useful for policy development.

A problem that arose early in the data collection process and persisted throughout the analysis was the incompleteness of the available data. The general dearth of information on abortions by age necessitated focusing on birthrates rather than pregnancy rates as had originally been intended. Many items of information concerning the independent variables that were known for most countries were lacking for a substantial minority, and some thought to be essential proved to be available for only a few countries. A number of the more prominent gaps in the range of national characteristics were filled by means of a country-level survey. Certain important topics, however—such as adolescent sexual activity, contraceptive use, and population heterogeneity—could not be covered at all. Despite these limitations, the data that were ultimately assembled cover a broad scope, both geographically and substantively.

The dependent variables considered were the cumulative birthrates for women under age 18 and for women aged 18–19. First, the pairwise correlations between these rates and each of 42 independent variables were examined. Fifteen independent variables having a reasonable number of observations and a strong enough association with adolescent fertility to warrant further study were selected. Several of the more interesting variables were dropped at this stage because of an insufficient number of observations. Among these the high negative pair-wise correlations of adolescent fertility with the extent of condom use among married women and the high positive correlation with religiosity deserve further exploration. The lack of appropriate measures of educational and employment opportunities resulted in the exclusion of these potentially important factors.

Regression analysis was employed to ascertain which of the selected subset of determinants were the more important ones for each age group. A number of tentative conclusions can be drawn from this effort. Relative level of socioeconomic modernization appears to be strongly linked with low fertility for both older and younger teenagers. Maternity leaves and benefits also are suggested as being of importance throughout the teenage years. Although this is a policy variable, the mechanism through which it might affect adolescent women is far from clear, and reduction of supports seems an unlikely route to choose to reduce their fertility. A third influential factor is openness about sex; although this might be considered as a determinant rather than a consequence of public policy decisions, there are probably many ways in which greater openness has been indirectly fostered by governments in various countries (e.g., through regulation of the media, appointment of commissions, and preparation of reports on related topics).

The one factor that seems to affect women under age 18 more than those aged 18–19 is the proportion of total family income that goes to the poorest 20 percent of families. This finding implies that very early childbearing may be tied to a general culture of poverty. On the other hand, women approaching age 20 are likely to be particularly affected by policies designed to raise the overall national level of fertility.

2
The Country
Case Studies

The findings from the 37-country study provided a number of important leads concerning the determinants of teenage childbearing—and, by extension, adolescent pregnancy—but the results were also inconclusive in many ways. Information about important aspects of teenage behavior, especially contraceptive use and sexual activity, were not available for most of the countries; and data on abortion, required for direct study of teenage pregnancy, were available for only about one-third of the countries. In addition some of the countries, although they technically met the criteria for level of development, were so different from the United States in their cultures or political and economic systems (e.g., Japan and Bulgaria) that it was questionable whether findings about them would be practically applicable in the United States.

For all these reasons it was decided to select a small group of countries to study in greater depth for comparison to the United States. The five countries chosen were Canada, England and Wales, France, the Netherlands, and Sweden. These countries were picked on the basis of three principal considerations: their levels of adolescent pregnancy were distinctly lower than that of the United States; they were generally similar to the United States in cultural heritage and stage of economic growth; and important data relevant to an evaluation of adolescent pregnancy were available.

More detailed information on births and abortions for women under age 20 could be collected than was available for most of the 37 countries, and a systematic effort was made to assemble quantitative data on marriage and cohabitation, sexual activity, and contraceptive practice.

21

It was considered crucial to pin down, insofar as possible, the part played by contraception in reducing pregnancy rates, as compared to limited exposure to the risk of pregnancy.

Material of a more descriptive nature was sought on a number of background topics. Both official policy and actual practice regarding access to contraceptive and abortion services were reviewed, and the systems for distributing these services were examined. Sex education was considered with respect to its content, its place in the school curriculum, and possible sources of information outside the educational system. Several aspects of teenage life were explored in order to gain some understanding of social and economic conditions that could affect motivation for early childbearing and the use or nonuse of contraception. These included the proportions of young people in school, the proportions employed and unemployed, the move away from the family home as well as government assistance programs relevant to young people in general and to young unmarried mothers in particular. Possible variation in the incidence of teenage pregnancy within each country was investigated. Relationships of changes in teenage pregnancy to program and policy innovations were also examined.

Teams of two project participants visited each of the five selected countries for one week during March and April 1984 and conducted interviews with government officials, statisticians, researchers, and service providers. These interviews provided opportunities not only to obtain the kinds of information mentioned above, but also to discuss attitudes and intangible factors that could rarely be documented in other ways.

The materials for the country reports thus cover a wide range, from hard facts drawn from national statistical sources to essentially subjective impressions. In general, more information is available for the United States than for other countries, and data have been included not only with a view to presenting as complete a picture as possible of the situation in that country, but also in order to compare specific tabulations given or observations made in the other country reports.

A comparative review of basic data for the six countries is useful. Table 2.1 reveals that the national populations vary by a factor of nearly 28 to 1. The United States is by far the largest country. France and England and Wales come next, each with roughly similar total numbers. The others, in descending order, are Canada, the Netherlands, and finally Sweden with only about eight million inhabitants.

The female population aged 15–19 differs not only in absolute numbers but also in its size relative to the population at large. Teenage women make up nearly 5 percent of the Canadian population but less than 3 percent of the Swedish population. The proportions for the

Table 2.1. *Total population and female population aged 15–19*

Country	Year	Total	Women aged 15–19	
			N	% of total
United States	1981	229,307,000	10,016,000	4.4
Canada	1980	23,936,300	1,153,600	4.8
England and Wales	1980	49,244,300	1,965,100	4.0
France	1982	54,085,000	2,093,408	3.9
Netherlands	1980	14,091,014	609,664	4.3
Sweden	1980	8,310,473	227,821	2.7

Source: United Nations, 1983, table 7.

other countries range between these extremes, typically about 4 percent.

Tables 2.2–2.8 present for the United States and each of the five other countries birthrates, abortion rates, and pregnancy rates, by single year of age and by selected age groups, for all the years for which data are available starting with 1971. Note that table 2.3 provides these data for the U.S. white population. The pregnancy rates shown in these tables have been calculated as the simple sum of the birthrates and abortion rates for women of a given age, tabulated by age at occurrence, and divided by the midyear estimate of the female population of that age. Figures 2.1–2.3 compare the birth, abortion, and pregnancy rates by single year of age for 1980. All the rates given for 14-year-olds include in the numerators events occurring to women younger than 14. Figures 2.4 and 2.5 display trends in the birthrates since 1971 for the age groups 15–17 and 18–19 years.[1]

The exceptional position of the United States is immediately apparent in figure 2.1. U.S. birthrates are higher than those of any of the other five countries at every year of age and by a considerable margin. The contrast is particularly striking for younger teenagers. The Netherlands has the lowest rates at every age. In 1980, Dutch women aged 19 were about as likely to bear a child as women aged 15 or 16 in the United States. The birthrates are also very low in Sweden, especially through age 17. Canada, England and Wales, and France compose an intermediate group. The Canadian birthrates are relatively high for women aged 14–16, but rise less steeply with age thereafter. The French rates are low at ages 17 and below but move up very sharply among older teenagers.

1. In France and Sweden births and abortions are normally tabulated by age achieved during the calendar year. The data shown in this chapter have been converted to age in completed years in order to match the data for other countries.

Table 2.2. *United States: Birthrates, abortion rates, and pregnancy rates per 1,000 women, by age and year*

	Age of woman								
	14	15	16	17*	18*	19	15–17*	18–19*	15–19
Birthrates									
1971	5.5	15.5	36.7	63.2	92.1	118.7	38.2	105.3	64.5
1972	5.8	16.2	38.3	63.6	88.0	105.9	39.0	96.9	61.7
1973	6.1	16.6	37.5	62.5	83.8	98.7	38.5	91.2	59.3
1974	6.0	16.1	36.3	59.6	81.3	95.9	37.3	88.7	57.5
1975	6.0	16.0	35.4	57.0	77.4	92.5	36.1	85.0	55.6
1976	5.7	15.0	34.0	53.5	73.2	87.6	34.1	80.5	52.8
1977	5.6	14.8	32.9	53.8	73.2	88.3	33.9	80.9	52.8
1978	5.3	14.0	31.0	51.0	72.5	86.8	32.2	79.8	51.5
1979	5.5	14.0	30.9	51.4	72.3	90.0	33.3	81.3	52.3
1980	5.5	14.4	30.9	51.5	73.4	91.4	32.6	82.6	53.3
1981	5.4	14.1	30.4	49.8	71.0	92.2	32.0	81.7	52.7
Abortion rates									
1973	5.6	11.1	20.1	25.4	29.6	28.3	18.7	28.9	22.8
1974	6.4	13.3	24.1	29.5	35.2	33.4	22.3	34.3	26.9
1975	7.2	14.5	26.0	31.8	42.6	41.2	24.1	41.9	31.0
1976	7.6	14.4	26.3	31.9	51.0	47.6	24.2	49.3	34.3
1977	7.6	15.9	28.0	34.7	56.2	52.1	26.2	54.1	37.5
1978	7.5	16.4	29.1	34.9	60.9	56.1	26.9	58.4	39.7
1979	8.3	17.6	31.1	37.4	64.0	59.9	28.8	61.9	42.4
1980	8.4	18.7	32.3	38.9	63.8	58.4	30.2	61.0	42.9
1981	8.6	19.1	32.3	37.8	63.4	60.3	30.1	61.8	43.3
Pregnancy rates									
1973	11.7	27.7	57.5	87.9	113.3	127.0	57.3	120.2	82.1
1974	12.4	29.4	60.4	89.1	116.6	129.4	59.6	123.0	84.4
1975	13.2	30.5	61.4	88.7	120.0	133.8	60.3	126.9	86.7
1976	13.3	29.4	60.3	85.4	124.2	135.2	58.3	129.8	87.1
1977	13.2	30.7	61.0	88.5	129.3	140.4	60.1	135.0	90.3
1978	12.8	30.5	60.1	86.0	133.5	142.9	59.2	138.3	91.2
1979	13.8	31.5	62.0	88.8	136.4	149.9	61.1	143.2	94.7
1980	13.9	33.1	63.2	90.4	137.2	149.8	62.8	143.6	96.2
1981	14.0	33.3	62.6	87.6	134.4	152.5	62.1	143.5	96.0

Sources: Births 1971–79 from G. Calot, unpublished data. Births 1980–81 from NCHS, *Monthly Vital Statistics Report*, vol. 31, no. 8, supplement, Nov. 20, 1982, table 2; and vol. 32, no. 9, supplement, Dec. 29, 1983, table 2. Abortions 1973–80 for age group 15–19 and 1976–80 for age groups 15–17 and 18–19 from S. Henshaw ed., *Abortion Services in the United States: Each State and Metropolitan Area 1979–80*, AGI, 1983, table 1. Abortions 1973–75 for age groups 15–17 and 18–19 estimated from S. Henshaw, unpublished data. Abortions 1981 for age groups 15–19, 15–17, and 18–19 from AGI, unpublished data. Abortions 1973–81 for single years of age estimated from Center for Disease Control, DHEW, *Abortion Surveillance: Annual Summaries 1975–1980* (Atlanta: 1977–82), table 6A. Female populations 1971–80 from *Current Population Reports*, Series P-25, no. 917, July 1982, table 2. Female population 1981 from *Current Population Reports*, Series P-25, no. 949, May 1984, table 2.

*Abortion rates and, therefore, pregnancy rates for 17-year-olds are apparently underreported and those for 18-year-olds overstated (see chapter 3). Thus pregnancy rates for 15–17-year-olds are probably slightly greater and those for 18–19-year-olds slightly smaller than the reported rates shown here.

Table 2.3. *United States: Birthrates, abortion rates, and pregnancy rates per 1,000 white women, by age and year*

	Age of woman								
	14	15	16	17	18	19	15–17	18–19	15–19
Birthrates									
1976	2.9	9.7	25.5	43.9	62.3	79.5	26.3	71.2	44.4
1977	2.7	9.6	24.7	43.8	62.3	78.3	26.1	70.5	44.1
1978	2.7	9.1	23.3	41.6	61.6	76.9	24.9	69.4	42.9
1979	2.7	8.9	22.9	41.8	61.8	79.9	24.7	71.0	43.7
1980	2.8	9.3	23.4	42.5	63.2	81.3	25.4	72.5	45.0
1981	2.7	9.3	23.1	41.0	61.3	82.4	25.1	71.9	44.7
Abortion rates									
1981	5.1	14.8	28.0	34.1	58.5	54.7	26.0	56.6	38.8
Pregnancy rates									
1981	7.8	24.1	51.1	75.1	119.7	137.1	51.1	128.5	83.4

Sources: Births from NCHS, *Monthly Vital Statistics Report,* vol. 27, no. 11, supplement; vol. 29, no. 1, supplement; vol. 30, no. 6, supplement (2); vol. 31, no. 8, supplement; vol. 32, no. 9, supplement, table 2. Abortions from AGI, unpublished data. Female population from Bureau of the Census, *Current Population Reports,* Series P-25, no. 917 and no. 949, table 2.

The high fertility of American teenagers is not a new phenomenon. Figure 2.4 demonstrates that the very large disparity between the United States and the other countries with respect to the birthrate for women 15–17 years old has existed at least since 1971. In all countries, including the United States, the trend over time has been downward, however. The decline in England and Wales and the Netherlands was particularly sharp in the early part of the decade, and their rates have dropped very little since 1977. In France, on the other hand, the downward turn did not occur until about 1974, and in Canada it came as late as 1976; but both rates then continued to decrease fairly regularly. The relative change was greatest in Sweden where the rate was 15 in 1971—higher than in France—but below five in 1981—nearly as low as in the Netherlands.

There was also a general reduction in the fertility of women 18–19 years old across the 11-year period (figure 2.5). In this case the excess in the U.S. rate, although not as large as that for younger teenagers, has increased somewhat over time. The U.S. rate declined sharply up to 1976 but has exhibited no clear trend since then. In the other countries the pattern is similar to that for the birthrates of younger women, with England and Wales and the Netherlands exhibiting a greater decline in the earlier years, the Canadian and French rates dropping more rapidly later on, and the Swedish rate moving consistently downward.

Table 2.4. *Canada: Birthrates, abortion rates,* and pregnancy rates per 1,000 women, by age and year*

						Age of woman			
	14	15	16	17	18	19	15–17	18–19	15–19
Birthrates									
1971	1.4	5.7	17.9	37.8	61.2	84.2	20.2	72.5	40.1
1972	1.4	5.8	18.5	37.4	59.0	76.9	20.5	67.8	38.7
1973	1.5	5.8	18.4	36.7	55.4	74.8	20.1	64.9	37.7
1974	1.4	5.8	18.1	34.9	51.3	69.4	19.5	60.4	35.6
1975	1.6	6.1	18.4	35.9	51.3	68.8	20.0	60.0	35.7
1976	1.6	5.6	17.2	33.1	49.3	65.7	18.5	57.5	33.7
1977	1.4	5.7	16.2	30.7	45.6	63.2	17.6	54.3	32.1
1978	1.5	5.3	15.2	27.8	42.3	58.2	16.2	50.2	29.7
1979	1.4	4.8	13.8	25.9	39.4	54.7	14.9	47.0	29.7
1980	1.4	5.0	13.4	25.7	38.5	53.6	14.9	46.2	27.6
1981	1.2	4.7	12.6	24.1	37.0	50.8	14.1	43.9	26.4
Abortion rates									
1980	3.1	7.3	15.3	19.9	24.6	25.2	14.3	24.9	18.6
1981	3.2	7.0	14.5	18.9	23.9	24.2	13.7	24.0	17.9
Pregnancy rates									
1980	4.4	12.3	28.7	45.7	63.1	78.9	29.2	71.1	46.1
1981	4.4	11.7	27.1	43.0	60.9	75.0	27.8	67.9	44.3

Sources: Births 1971–79 from G. Calot, unpublished data. Births 1980–81 from C. Tietze, unpublished data. Abortions 1980 from C. Tietze, unpublished data, and Tietze, 1983. Abortions 1981 from Statistics Canada, 1983a, Catalogue 82-211, assuming the same number of unreported abortions as given for 1980 in C. Tietze, 1983, op. cit. Female populations 1971–79 from G. Calot, unpublished data. Female populations 1980–81 from Statistics Canada, 1983b, Catalogue 91-519 Occasional, Nov. 1983 (population age 14 for 1980 estimated from population age 15 in 1981).

*Includes adjustment for abortions to Canadian women occurring in the United States and for nonhospital clinic abortions done in Quebec.

It is worth noting that the maximum difference in the birthrate between the United States and the other countries occurs at ages under 15. With more than 5 births per 1,000 women aged 14, the U.S. rate is around four times that of Canada, the only other country with as much as 1 birth per 1,000 women. Except for possible downward trends in the Netherlands and Sweden, where the rates have been consistently very low, there has been no clear change over time in fertility at this age.

In 1980, the relative positions of the countries with respect to the incidence of abortion was surprisingly close to the pattern observed for births (figure 2.2). The United States has by far the highest rates and the Netherlands by far the lowest at each age. The French rate moves up steeply as age increases,[2] whereas the Canadian rate is somewhat

2. As explained in chapter 6, the relatively low rates for France at very young ages could be due to greater underreporting at these ages.

Table 2.5. *England and Wales: Birthrates, abortion rates, and pregnancy rates per 1,000 women, by age and year*

	14	15	16	17	18	19	15–17	18–19	15–19
					Age of woman				
Birthrates									
1971	0.6	3.7	18.3	47.3	78.6	105.8	23.2	92.2	50.8
1972	0.6	3.8	19.2	47.3	73.9	98.0	23.1	85.9	48.2
1973	0.8	4.0	17.7	43.0	68.1	90.0	21.2	79.2	43.8
1974	0.8	3.7	15.7	40.9	62.8	84.1	19.8	73.3	40.3
1975	0.5	3.3	13.2	34.7	57.2	76.9	17.0	66.9	36.3
1976	0.5	3.2	12.0	30.0	49.6	69.8	14.9	59.5	32.3
1977	0.5	2.9	11.7	28.0	45.8	68.0	13.9	54.4	29.7
1978	0.5	3.1	11.4	27.6	46.1	64.0	13.9	55.0	29.7
1979	0.5	2.7	10.9	28.5	47.7	67.4	13.9	57.4	30.6
1980	0.5	2.5	10.7	27.6	47.9	67.5	13.5	57.6	30.7
1981	0.5	2.5	10.4	24.6	43.5	64.3	12.5	53.8	28.6
Abortion rates									
1971	1.9	5.1	10.8	13.4	15.8	15.6	9.8	15.7	12.1
1972	2.1	6.3	13.1	16.8	18.2	18.3	12.0	18.2	14.5
1973	2.2	6.6	15.1	17.5	19.8	18.8	13.0	19.3	15.4
1974	2.2	7.0	15.1	18.3	20.0	18.7	13.4	19.4	15.7
1975	2.4	7.5	15.2	18.2	18.8	17.8	13.6	18.3	15.4
1976	2.3	6.7	15.0	17.7	17.9	17.5	13.1	17.7	14.9
1977	2.3	7.0	14.7	17.8	18.5	17.2	13.0	17.8	14.9
1978	2.0	6.4	14.8	17.8	20.2	18.6	12.9	19.4	15.4
1979	2.0	6.7	15.3	19.2	21.2	21.2	13.6	21.2	16.5
1980	2.3	6.7	15.9	20.5	22.7	22.7	14.4	22.7	17.6
1981	2.3	7.4	15.9	18.9	20.9	21.3	14.1	21.1	16.8
Pregnancy rates									
1971	2.5	8.8	29.1	60.7	94.4	121.4	32.9	107.8	63.0
1972	2.7	10.1	32.3	64.1	92.1	116.3	35.0	104.2	62.6
1973	3.0	10.6	32.8	60.5	87.9	108.8	34.1	98.5	59.2
1974	3.0	10.7	30.8	59.2	82.8	102.8	33.2	92.7	56.0
1975	2.9	10.8	28.4	52.9	76.0	94.7	30.6	85.2	51.7
1976	2.8	9.9	27.0	47.7	67.5	87.3	28.0	77.2	47.2
1977	2.8	9.9	26.4	45.8	64.3	80.2	26.9	72.2	44.6
1978	2.5	9.5	26.2	45.4	66.3	82.6	26.8	74.4	45.1
1979	2.5	9.4	26.2	47.7	68.9	88.6	27.5	78.6	47.1
1980	2.8	9.2	26.6	48.1	70.6	90.2	27.9	80.3	48.3
1981	2.8	9.9	26.3	43.5	64.4	85.6	26.6	74.9	45.4

Sources: Births 1971–72 from OPCS, *1975 Birth Statistics: England and Wales,* Series FM1, no. 2, table 12.2. Births 1973–81 from OPCS, *1981 Birth Statistics: England and Wales,* Series FM1, no. 8, table 12.2. Abortions 1974–80 from C. Tietze, unpublished data. Abortion rates 1971–73, 1981 from OPCS, unpublished data. Female populations 1971–80 from G. Calot, unpublished data. Female population 1981 from OPCS, *Census 1981: Sex, Age and Marital Status: Great Britain,* table 2.

flatter. The rate for England and Wales also rises less after age 17 than might be anticipated. The chief difference between the pattern for births and that for abortions is found in Sweden, which has age-specific abortion rates as high as or higher than any of the other countries

Table 2.6. *France: Birthrates, abortion rates,* and pregnancy rates per 1,000 women, by age and year*

	Age of woman								
	14	15	16	17	18	19	15–17	18–19	15–19
Birthrates									
1971	0.4	2.6	9.8	26.9	56.6	95.1	13.0	75.9	38.3
1972	0.4	2.7	10.7	28.9	59.3	96.9	14.1	78.2	39.7
1973	0.4	2.6	10.5	29.1	59.2	95.3	14.0	77.2	39.3
1974	0.4	2.5	10.1	27.9	56.2	88.7	13.5	72.5	37.1
1975	0.3	2.4	9.3	24.8	51.4	82.0	12.2	66.7	33.9
1976	0.3	2.0	8.4	22.1	46.7	76.8	10.8	61.7	31.1
1977	0.3	2.0	7.7	20.9	45.2	75.0	10.2	60.1	30.1
1978	0.3	1.7	6.9	18.6	40.6	68.2	9.1	54.4	27.2
1979	0.3	1.6	6.3	16.7	37.3	64.6	8.1	50.9	25.2
1980	0.3	1.7	6.4	16.4	36.6	64.0	8.1	50.3	24.8
1981	0.3	1.6	5.8	15.2	33.6	58.9	7.6	46.2	22.9
Abortion rates									
1980	1.7	5.0	10.3	17.8	26.5	31.3	11.0	28.9	18.1
Pregnancy rates									
1980	2.0	6.7	16.7	34.2	63.1	95.4	19.1	79.2	43.0

Sources: Births, abortions, and female populations from G. Calot, INED, unpublished data; and Tietze, 1983.

*Includes adjustment for nonregistered abortions.

except the United States. The unexpected peaking of the U.S. rate at age 18 is probably due mainly to misstatement of age by women younger than 18 years old.

Abortion data going back to the early 1970s are available only for England and Wales and the United States. In the United States the teenage abortion rate climbed very substantially between 1973 and 1979–80, increasing by more than 60 percent for women aged 15–17 years old and more than doubling for women 18–19. In the most recent years the rates appear to have leveled off. There has been an increase in England and Wales as well, but it has been less dramatic than in the United States; the overall rise is about 40 percent. Most of the upward movement took place at the very beginning and at the very end of the decade. Sweden's abortion rates can be traced by single year of age (defined as completed years) only from 1975. Clearly a very dramatic decline has occurred, particularly among younger teenagers.[3] Except for a minute rise among women 18–19 years old, there has been little change in the abortion rates for the Netherlands since 1977, the period for which age-specific estimates covering all abortions performed on Dutch nationals can be made. No trend data are available for

3. The Swedish teenage abortion rate peaked in 1974–75 following a sharp rise. See chapter 8.

Table 2.7. *The Netherlands: Birthrates, abortion rates,* and pregnancy rates per 1,000 women, by age and year*

	\multicolumn{9}{c}{Age of woman}								
	14	15	16	17	18	19	15–17	18–19	15–19
Birthrates									
1971	.4	1.4	6.8	18.2	33.2	51.7	8.8	42.4	22.2
1972	.3	1.6	6.5	16.5	29.0	46.5	8.1	37.8	19.9
1973	.3	1.0	5.2	14.1	26.4	40.2	6.7	33.3	17.2
1974	.2	1.1	4.6	11.5	21.9	37.7	5.7	29.8	15.2
1975	.2	1.0	3.7	9.4	18.4	31.3	4.6	24.8	12.6
1976	.2	.8	3.2	8.0	16.1	29.2	4.0	22.6	11.3
1977	.2	.7	2.7	8.0	14.9	24.7	3.8	19.7	10.1
1978	.2	.7	2.8	7.2	14.1	22.5	3.6	18.3	9.4
1979	.1	.7	2.7	6.6	12.7	22.0	3.3	17.4	8.9
1980	.2	.7	2.4	7.1	13.3	22.5	3.4	17.9	9.2
1981	.2	.6	2.6	7.1	12.9	21.7	3.4	17.3	9.0
Abortion rates									
1977	.4	1.3	3.8	5.6	6.3	7.2	3.5	6.7	4.8
1978	.4	1.4	3.6	5.3	6.2	6.8	3.4	6.5	4.6
1979	.5	1.4	3.1	5.0	6.0	7.3	3.2	6.6	4.5
1980	.4	1.4	3.7	5.7	7.0	8.3	3.6	7.7	5.2
1981	.5	1.6	3.5	5.8	7.1	8.2	3.7	7.7	5.3
Pregnancy rates									
1977	.6	2.0	6.5	13.6	21.2	31.8	7.3	26.4	14.9
1978	.5	2.2	6.4	12.5	20.3	29.3	7.0	24.8	14.0
1979	.6	2.1	5.8	11.6	18.7	29.3	6.5	24.0	13.4
1980	.6	2.1	6.2	12.7	20.3	30.8	7.0	25.6	14.4
1981	.7	2.2	6.0	12.9	20.0	29.9	7.1	24.9	14.3

Sources: Births and female populations from G. Calot, INED, unpublished data. Abortions from E. Ketting, NISSO, unpublished data.

*Includes abortions to Netherlands residents only; and includes adjustment for abortions done in hospitals.

France; for Canada there may have been some decline between 1980 and 1981.

Having observed that the intercountry comparison of the abortion rates by single year of age is very like that of the birthrates, it is inevitable that the pregnancy rates must also follow this pattern (see figure 2.3). The U.S. rates are distinctively higher than the other five countries for each year of age, and those of the Netherlands are equally distinctively low. The relative positions of the intermediate countries differ somewhat by age. The French rates appear to be lower at age 16 and below and higher later, whereas the opposite is true in Canada.

In England and Wales and recently in Sweden, there has been a marked reduction in pregnancy rates over time. The drop amounts to 28 percent over 11 years in England and Wales and 40 percent over 7 years in Sweden. In Canada the pregnancy rate was 4 percent lower in

Table 2.8. *Sweden: Birthrates, abortion rates, and pregnancy rates per 1,000 women, by age and year*

	14	15	16	17	18	19	15–17	18–19	15–19
					Age of woman				
Birthrates									
1971	0.4	2.5	12.1	30.1	51.6	73.6	15.0	62.6	34.6
1972	0.1	2.4	12.1	29.2	49.8	71.6	14.5	60.9	33.4
1973	0.2	2.1	10.8	27.4	46.0	68.2	13.4	57.3	31.1
1974	0.1	1.7	9.6	25.2	47.8	73.3	12.3	60.6	31.7
1975	0.3	2.3	8.2	22.4	41.7	67.2	11.1	54.5	28.8
1976	0.3	1.4	6.6	19.3	36.3	59.4	9.1	47.9	25.0
1977	0.2	1.8	5.6	15.5	31.4	55.2	7.6	43.4	22.1
1978	0.3	1.1	4.7	12.9	28.4	49.2	6.1	38.9	19.2
1979	0.2	1.2	3.6	12.9	25.7	45.6	5.7	35.7	17.3
1980	0.3	0.9	3.7	11.1	23.5	43.1	5.1	33.3	15.7
1981	0.2	0.9	3.2	9.8	22.1	39.7	4.5	30.8	14.3
Abortion rates									
1975	5.4	16.1	29.2	33.3	32.9	31.3	26.2	32.1	28.6
1976	5.9	16.1	25.0	30.3	31.7	32.9	23.8	32.4	27.3
1977	5.7	14.1	22.4	28.7	29.8	30.0	21.7	29.9	25.0
1978	5.1	11.7	19.2	25.0	28.4	30.2	18.5	29.3	22.8
1979	3.9	10.9	17.9	22.6	27.4	31.6	16.9	29.5	21.8
1980	3.9	10.1	17.8	21.7	28.8	30.3	16.3	29.6	21.3
1981	3.6	8.0	16.7	21.4	26.2	30.0	15.3	28.1	20.1
Pregnancy rates									
1975	5.8	18.3	37.3	55.7	74.7	98.5	37.3	86.6	57.4
1976	6.2	17.5	31.6	49.5	68.0	92.3	33.0	80.2	52.3
1977	5.9	15.8	28.0	44.2	61.3	85.1	29.3	73.3	47.1
1978	5.4	12.8	23.8	37.9	56.9	79.4	24.6	68.3	42.0
1979	4.1	12.1	21.5	35.6	53.0	77.2	22.7	65.2	39.1
1980	4.2	11.0	21.5	32.8	52.3	73.5	21.4	62.8	37.1
1981	3.8	8.9	19.9	31.2	48.3	69.7	19.9	58.9	34.6

Sources: Births 1971–74 from G. Calot, INED, unpublished data. Births and abortions 1975–81 from C. Tietze, unpublished data. Female populations 1971–81 from G. Calot, INED, unpublished data.

1981 than in 1980. In the United States, however, the pregnancy rate rose by 17 percent between 1973 and 1981. There was essentially no change from 1977 to 1981 in the Netherlands.

The six countries on which this part of the study is focused thus represent a rather varied experience. The United States is at one extreme, with the highest rates of birth, abortion, and pregnancy among women below age 20. For births and pregnancies the contrast in 1980 is greatest at age 17 and below, but for abortion the relative difference between the United States and the other countries is similar across the various ages. Canada, France, and England and Wales are quite similar to one another, except that in 1980 Canada exhibited a flatter and France a steeper age curve for all three rates. Sweden is

Fig. 2.1. *Births per 1,000 women, by single year of age, 1980*

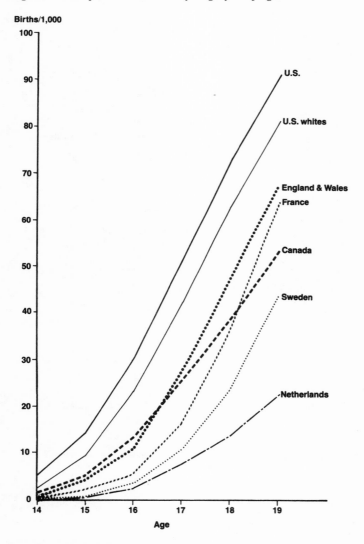

Source: Tables 2.2–2.8.

notable for its low birthrates, although in 1981 the abortion rate for women 15–19 years old was still higher than that of any country except the United States, despite a substantial recent decline. The Netherlands stands at the opposite extreme from the United States with extremely low rates of birth, abortion, and pregnancy among young women. The United States is the only one of the six countries in which

Fig. 2.2. *Abortions per 1,000 women, by single year of age, 1980*

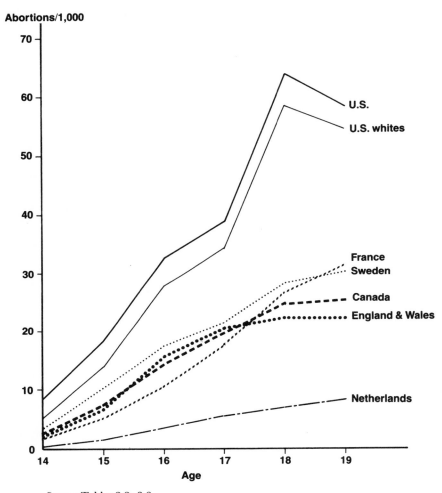

Source: Tables 2.2–2.8.
*Data for 1981.

the incidence of pregnancy has been increasing over time. This increase is due to the fact that the abortion rate rose more than the
birthrate declined. The principal characteristics shared by the six countries are a downward trend in the birthrates for all the ages concerned
and a tendency for the relative levels of the birthrates and abortion
rates to coincide.

It is well known that there is a large racial differential in adolescent

Fig. 2.3. *Pregnancies per 1,000 women, by single year of age, 1980*

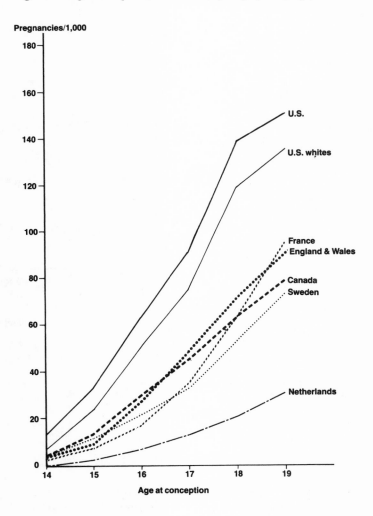

Pregnancies/1,000

U.S.

U.S. whites

France
England & Wales

Canada
Sweden

Netherlands

Age at conception

Source: Tables 2.2–2.8.
*Data for 1981.

pregnancy in the United States. The pregnancy rates of black teenagers are sufficiently higher than those of whites to influence the rates for the nation as a whole, even though blacks make up only about 12 percent of the total population. The questions thus arise whether the reproductive behavior of white American teenagers may actually be similar to teenagers in other countries, and whether the apparent contrast at the

Fig. 2.4. *Births per 1,000 women aged 15–17, 1971–81*

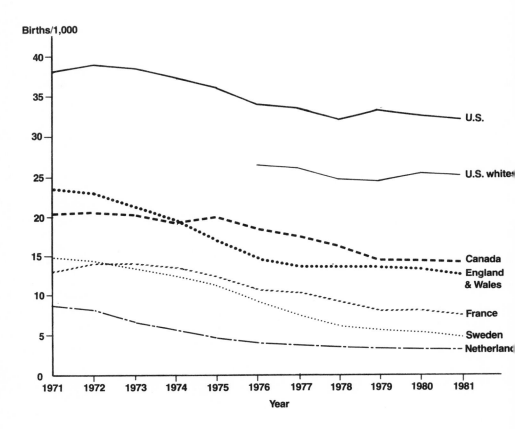

national level could be attributed to the presence in the United States of
a minority for which there is no counterpart elsewhere. For this reason
birth, abortion and pregnancy rates for U.S. whites are shown in table
2.3 and in figures 2.1–2.5. Restriction of the comparison to U.S. whites
reduces the differences between the United States and the other countries, but they remain considerable. At each single year of age the
birthrate for U.S. whites falls about half way between that of the U.S.
total and the next highest country (Canada for ages 14–16 and England
and Wales for ages 17–19). Moreover, for both younger and older
teenagers, the disparity in the birthrate between U.S. whites and other
countries increased somewhat from 1976 to 1981. The age-specific

Fig. 2.5. *Births per 1,000 women aged 18–19, 1971–81*

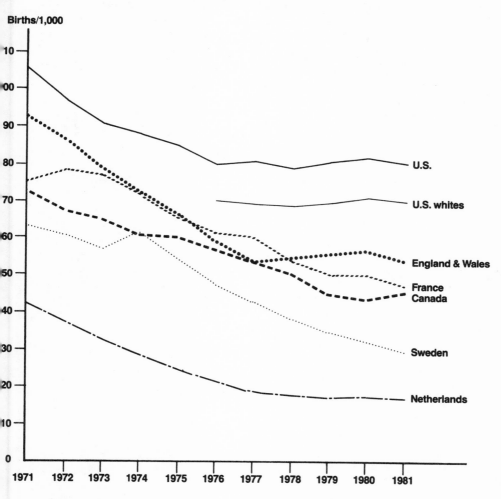

abortion rates for U.S. whites are much closer to those of the U.S. total than to those of other countries. Thus substantial differences remain in the pregnancy rates as well.

It might be argued that the U.S. white population contains minorities—Hispanics in particular—that are not present elsewhere that may have distinctive reproductive patterns. Examination of this point is hampered by the fact that there are relatively few statistics for Hispanics. It was found, however, that although, as a whole, Hispanic women aged 15–19 have higher fertility rates than non-Hispanic white women in this age group, their impact on the total white rate was marginal. In any case, the other countries studied also have minority-group populations, most of which have higher-than-average fertility. In sum, it appears that the principal explanation for the relatively high incidence of adolescent pregnancy in the United States must be sought in factors that influence the entire country.

3

The United States

During the past decade, adolescent pregnancy and child-bearing has come to be viewed as a serious and consequential problem by most Americans. This concern has increased despite the fact that teenage birthrates have been declining, as have those of adults, since the end of the 1950s. The decline was particularly dramatic during the 1970s, when public attention to the issue first became marked. In fact, the drop in adolescent fertility—about 42 percent between 1955 and 1982—is almost as great as that for all women of reproductive age (U.S. Bureau of the Census, 1984d, table 82; NCHS, 1984, table 3).

The reasons that adolescent pregnancy and parenthood have disquieted so many people, including people of very different social and political persuasions, are numerous and complex. First of all, it was during the late 1960s and 1970s that the sheer numbers of teenagers in the population—a result of the post-World War II baby boom—aroused interest in and controversy about virtually everything that teenagers thought and did.

Births to teenagers also became far more visible. Even though the teenage birthrate started to fall before 1960, the number of births to teenagers and the proportion of all births that occurred among adolescents continued to increase for 10–15 years after the total number of babies born in the United States began a precipitous decline (U.S. Bureau of the Census, 1984d, table 82; NCHS, 1984b, table 3). In addition, pregnant teenagers have become much more visible to their schoolmates, teachers, and the general community since, in 1972, it became illegal to expel a student from school because of pregnancy (Title IX, 1975, Educational Amendments of 1972).

Early marriages during the 1950s, perhaps half of them to pregnant brides, served to screen high levels of teenage sexual activity from the public view (O'Connell and Rogers, 1984). As fewer and fewer teenagers married during the 1960s and 1970s, and nonmarital birthrates began to soar, early sexual activity and premarital pregnancy became more apparent.

Surveys during the 1970s of sexual activity, contraception, and pregnancy among unmarried teenagers that demonstrated high and rising levels of sexual experience among adolescents of all races and socioeconomic groups received wide publicity. Once abortion was legalized nationwide in 1973, it became evident that teenagers were disproportionately having recourse to this means of terminating pregnancy, and teenage abortion rates rose steadily throughout the decade. Those who became mothers were more and more likely to remain unmarried, and to keep their children rather than give them up for adoption (Dryfoos and Scholl, 1981, table 31). Although the number of nonmarital births to teenagers has been falling since 1975, that decrease has resulted mainly from the declining number of teenagers in the population. Nonmarital birthrates among adolescents continue to grow. Although the increase is now less steep, half of all births to teenagers are nonmarital. The current rise is entirely among whites; nonmarital birthrates among black teenagers have recently been falling, though they are still much higher than those of whites (U.S. Bureau of the Census, 1984d, table 94; NCHS, 1984b, table 17). Teenage abortion rates appear now to be stabilizing (Henshaw et al., 1985), as are levels of sexual activity, at a point when just about half of all 15–19-year-old women report that they have had intercourse (Pratt et al., 1984, table 2).

Apprehension about adolescent childbearing has also increased with the publication of a large body of research documenting the adverse social, economic, and health consequences of early childbearing for the young parents and their children, as well as for the society as a whole. These include an increased likelihood of infant and maternal morbidity and mortality; of early truncation of schooling; of poverty and welfare dependency; of behavioral and cognitive problems among the children; of these children themselves becoming teen parents; of increasing probability of divorce and separation even when the pregnant teenager marries; and of having more future unwanted births (AGI, 1981 pp. 10–15; Makinson, 1985).

In short, apprehension about adolescent pregnancy and childbearing has mounted as the problem has become ever more visible and less confined to poor and minority populations, and as the adverse consequences have been clearly documented. Since more than 8 out of 10 teenage pregnancies are unintended, and 9 in 10 adolescents who fail to practice contraception are not already intentionally pregnant or seeking to conceive (AGI, 1981, figure 8), it would seem on the surface to be fairly easy to develop policies and design programs to prevent teenage pregnancies by helping adolescents to realize their own intentions. Frequent newspaper and magazine articles and television programs describe the problem and discuss ways to reduce the number of adolescent pregnancies and to ameliorate the adverse consequences of teenage births. However, there continues to be considerable uncertainty and disagreement about what can and should be done.

The detailed information that follows about adolescent sexuality, contraceptive use, and pregnancy in the United States and about some of the policies and programs that have been developed to deal with the problem relate to the total population of U.S. adolescents. As noted in chapter 2, although the pregnancy rates of black teenagers are considerably higher than those of whites, this disparity is not an important factor explaining the differences in pregnancy rates between adolescents in the United States and other developed countries.

PREGNANCIES

In 1981, 1 in 10 American women aged 15–19 had an abortion or a birth (table 2.2). Pregnancy rates rise steeply, from 14 per 1,000 among 14-year-olds to 153 out of every 1,000 19-year-olds (see table 2.2).[1] Pregnancy rates among adolescents rose steadily from 1973, when availability of data on abortion first allowed reliable estimates to be made, to 1980 (table 2.2). The slight decrease between 1980 and 1981 suggests that the rate may be stabilizing or beginning to decline. In fact, the pregnancy rate among 15–19-year-olds would have been lower than it was reported in 1981 if the distribution of women across those ages had been the same as it had been in the previous year. Between 1973 and 1980, however, 84 percent of the increase in pregnancy rates

1. The actual pregnancy rates are slightly understated since pregnancies are calculated here according to age at abortion or birth, not age at conception, which is younger, and since miscarriages are excluded. Abortion and pregnancy rates presented in this chapter are based on reported age-specific rates for 17- and 18-year-olds. Reported abortion rates for women aged 18 are generally higher than would be expected based on the rates through age 17 and higher than the rates reported among 19-year-olds (table 2.2). This may be because some unmarried 17-year-olds report their age as 18 (the age of majority in most states) to keep their parents from knowing of the abortion. Based on the assumption that 10 percent of abortions to 18-year-olds actually were obtained by women aged 17, in 1981, abortion rates were 44.2 per 1,000 17-year-olds, 57.1 per 1,000 18-year-olds, 32.3 per 1,000 15–17-year-olds, and 58.7 per 1,000 18–19-year-olds.

among 15–19-year-olds was due to actual rises in the rate of pregnancy rather than to changes in the age distribution of adolescents. The increases have been concentrated among 18–19-year-olds (table 2.2). Their pregnancy rates rose by 15 percent between 1973 and 1981. Increases in pregnancy rates among younger women during this time period were smaller.

The relatively high rates of adolescent pregnancy do not reflect a widespread desire among teenagers to start families at early ages. In 1981, 79 percent of all pregnancies to women aged 15–19 occurred outside of marriage—89 percent of pregnancies to 15–17-year-olds and 72 percent of those to 18–19-year-olds (NCHS, 1983, tables 2 and 15; Burnham, 1983; table 7, p. 18; Henshaw, 1984). Although 49 percent of pregnancies to women under age 20 that are conceived within marriage are intended, only 8 percent of those to unmarried adolescents are intended—or 16 percent overall (Burnham, 1983; Henshaw, 1984; NCHS, 1983; tables 2 and 15; Horn, 1985; O'Connell and Rogers, 1984; U.S. Bureau of the Census, 1984b). Thus, although 1 in 10 women aged 15–19 were pregnant in 1981, fewer than 1 in 50 intended to conceive.

PREGNANCY OUTCOMES

Between 1970 and 1981, the total fertility rate (TFR)[2] decreased by 27 percent, from 2.5 to 1.8 births per woman (NCHS, 1984b; table 4). The proportional drop was similar for women aged 20 and older and among adolescents. In 1981, adolescent fertility accounted for 15 percent of the TFR in the United States.

The decrease in the adolescent birthrate during the 1970s is a continuation of a long-term decline from a high of 97.3 per 1,000 in 1957, the peak of the post-World War II baby boom; but the decline is less steep than for adult women (Heuser, 1976; table 3A). Birthrates among adolescents have not declined because of a drop in pregnancy rates, but because increasing proportions of pregnant adolescents have had abortions rather than births (table 2.2). The percentage of adolescent pregnancies carried to term dropped from 72 percent in 1973 to 55 percent in 1979 and has remained stable since that time.

Abortion has been legally available throughout the United States since 1973 and, in a few large states, since 1970 (AGI, 1975). Although it is not known how many abortions occurred before 1973, because illegal abortions were not reported, the abortion rate for women aged 15–19

---

2. The total fertility rate represents the average estimated number of children a woman would have in her reproductive lifetime based on age-specific birthrates for the relevant periods.

in 1970 and 1971 has been estimated at about 20 per 1,000 (Forrest, 1984). The number of illegal abortions decreased substantially after 1973. One estimate is that it fell from 130,000 in 1972 to 17,000 in 1974 (Cates and Rochat, 1976). Presumably, very few abortions are now performed by a nonphysician or self-induced (Henshaw et al., 1984). Abortion reporting is quite complete.

Abortion rates rose quickly after national legalization in 1973, but the rate of increase has slowed since 1979 (table 2.2). Between 1979 and 1981, there were only slight changes in the rates of any single-year age-group. Abortions obtained by women under age 20 accounted for 29 percent of all abortions in the U.S. in 1981 (Henshaw et al., 1985).

The percentage distributions in 1981 of outcomes of pregnancies to adolescents (excluding miscarriages) are shown in table 3.1. Forty-five percent ended in abortion. Ninety-four percent of all abortions followed nonmarital pregnancies (Burnham, 1983, table 7). An estimated 54 percent of nonmarital conceptions to women under age 20 were terminated by abortion in 1981 compared to 13 percent of marital pregnancies (Burnham, 1983, table 7; Henshaw et al., 1985; NCHS, 1983, tables 2 and 15; O'Connell and Rogers, 1984, table 1). Younger pregnant women were more likely to obtain abortions than older women. Six in 10 pregnancies to those under age 15 ended in abortion compared to 4 in 10 among those aged 18–19.

More than half of adolescent pregnancies result in births, but fewer than 3 in 10 end in marital births. About one-third of these are conceived out-of-wedlock, but the women marry before the birth. Only 18 percent of teen pregnancies are maritally conceived and carried to term—fewer than 1 in 10 pregnancies to women aged 15–17, but almost a quarter of those to 18–19-year-olds.

Half of all adolescent births occurred outside of marriage in 1981.

Table 3.1. *United States: Percentage distribution of pregnancy outcomes, by age of woman, 1981*

Age	Pregnancies	Abortions	Births Nonmarital	Legitimized nonmarital conceptions	Postmarital conceptions
≤14	100	61	35	4	0
15–17	100	48	33	10	9
18–19	100	43	24	9	24
15–19	100	45	27	10	18

Sources: Henshaw, 1984; NCHS, 1983, tables 2 and 15; O'Connell and Rogers, 1984, table 1; U.S. Bureau of the Census, 1984b, table E.

This is a higher proportion than among older women. Although adolescents accounted for 15 percent of all births in 1981, 39 percent of all nonmarital births were to teens (NCHS, 1983, tables 2 and 15). The percentage of adolescent births occurring outside of marriage was only 32 percent in 1971 (NCHS, 1975, tables 1–32). This increase over the decade is a result of increased proportions of unmarried adolescents who had intercourse and of increased reluctance to marry in order to legitimate a birth. The percentage of pregnant adolescents marrying fell from 48 percent in 1965–69 to 29 percent in 1980–81 among 15–17-year-olds, and from 61 to 34 percent among 18–19-year-olds (O'Connell and Rogers, 1984).

Birthrates among married adolescents are very high, as shown in table 3.2. Five percent of all women aged 15–19 gave birth in 1981—35 percent of married teenagers and 3 percent of those who were unmarried. Marital birthrates are higher among the younger adolescents in part because so many are pregnant when they get married. Only 46 percent of marital births to those aged 15–17 were conceived after marriage, compared to 72 percent of those to 18–19-year-olds and 65 percent of marital births to all 15–19-year-olds. As table 3.2 shows, birthrates among unmarried women are much lower than among those who are married, but they are nonetheless quite high.

Most marital and nonmarital births to women under age 20 in the United States are not planned. Data for women aged 15–24 surveyed in 1982 show that 75 percent of their first births that occurred before age 20 (roughly between 1972 and 1982) were unintended. For women remaining unmarried at the time of their first birth, 84 percent reported the birth was unintended; 76 percent of those who married before the birth and 44 percent of those who conceived after marriage

Table 3.2. *United States: Births per 1,000 women, by marital status at birth and conception, 1981*

Age	Total	Married	Unmarried
Marital status at birth			
15–17	32.0	446.7	20.8
18–19	81.7	326.8	39.6
15–19	52.7	351.0	28.0
Marital status at conception			
15–17	32.0	204.7	27.4
18–19	81.7	233.8	55.5
15–19	52.7	228.0	38.2

Sources: NCHS, 1983, tables 2 and 15; O'Connell and Rogers, 1984, table 1; U.S. Bureau of the Census, 1984a, table 2; 1984b, table E; 1982c, table 1.

Table 3.3. *United States: Pregnancy, birth, and abortion among women aged 15–19, by race, 1981*

Measure	Total	White	Black
Pregnancy rate*	96	83	163
% pregnancies ended as abortions	45	47	41
Abortion rate*	43	39	66
% pregnancies ended as births	55	54	59
Birthrate*	53	45	97
% births conceived nonmaritally	67	57	92
Rate of nonmaritally conceived births†	38	28	93
% births nonmarital	49	35	86
Nonmarital birthrate†	28	17	87
% nonmaritally conceived births that are legitimated	27	39	7
Rate of maritally conceived births†	228	232	212
Marital birthrate‡	351	351	374

Sources: Burnham, 1983, table 1; Henshaw et al., 1985; NCHS, 1983, tables 2 and 15; O'Connell and Rogers, 1984, table 1; U.S. Bureau of the Census, 1982c, table 1, and 1984a, table 2.
*Per 1,000 women aged 15–19.
†Per 1,000 unmarried women aged 15–19.
‡Per 1,000 married women aged 15–19.

also reported unintended births. Thus a total of 61 percent of those married at the time of birth said they had not intended to become pregnant (Horn, 1985).

Survey data show higher birthrates (U.S. Bureau of the Census, 1982a, 1983c) and greater use of abortion (Henshaw and Martire, 1982) among lower income women than among those of higher income, indicating that pregnancy rates are probably higher among poor adolescents as well. Although race is sometimes used as a proxy when data by socioeconomic status are not available, it is not clear to what extent differences in adolescent pregnancy between the two racial groups are due to income or to other factors.[3]

Table 3.3 shows that, although the pregnancy rate among black teenage women is almost twice that of whites, the pregnancy rate for all adolescents is only slightly higher than that of whites because most of the U.S. population is white. Whites account for 83 percent of women aged 15–19 and for 72 percent of their pregnancies. Whites are only slightly less likely than blacks to carry their pregnancies to term, but they are considerably less likely to have births that are conceived out-

3. In 1981, 41 percent of black and 14 percent of white women aged 15–21 lived in households with incomes below the federally defined poverty level.

side of marriage. As a result, although the pregnancy rate of whites was 86 percent of the overall rate in 1981, their rate of nonmaritally conceived births was only 73 percent of the overall rate and 30 percent of the black rate.

White adolescents are twice as likely as blacks to be married—8 vs. 4 percent, respectively, of those aged 15–19 in 1981 (U.S. Bureau of the Census, 1982c, table 1)—and if they have a nonmaritally conceived birth, they are much more likely than blacks to marry before the birth. Thus, if white adolescents have a baby, they are much less likely than blacks to conceive or bear the child outside of marriage. Whites account for half of all nonmarital births and 9 in 10 of all marital births to U.S. women aged 15–19 (NCHS, 1983, tables 2 and 15). As a result, black-white differences have little effect on marital birthrates but strongly affect nonmarital rates.

PROXIMATE DETERMINANTS OF PREGNANCY

Marriage and Cohabitation

As of 1980, the percentage of women aged 15–19 who were married rose steeply with age from 1 percent of 15-year-olds to 20 percent of 19-year-olds (table 3.4). Another 2 percent of 15–19-year-olds were not married but were living with a man. The percentage cohabiting also rises steeply with age. A smaller proportion of adolescent men are married than women. Among 15–19-year-old men in 1981, only 2 percent were married (U.S. Bureau of the Census, 1982a, table 1).

Increasing postponement of marriage has affected adolescent pregnancy rates, as fewer women plan to marry and start a family while in

Table 3.4. *United States: Percentage distribution of women, by marital and cohabitation status and age, 1980*

Age	Total	Unmarried		Married
		Not cohabiting	Cohabiting	
15	100.0	98.8	0.2	1.0
16	100.0	97.0	0.6	2.4
17	100.0	94.4	0.6	5.0
18	100.0	87.0	2.6	10.4
19	100.0	76.3	4.0	19.7
15–19	100.0	90.4	1.7	8.0
15–17	(100.0)	(96.2)	(0.5)	(2.8)
18–19	(100.0)	(81.5)	(3.3)	(15.2)
20–24	100.0	53.3	5.3	41.4

Source: Westoff, 1984.

their teens. The proportion of 18–19-year-olds that had never married increased between 1971 and 1981 from 77 percent to 85 percent, and of 20–24-year-olds, from 37 percent to 52 percent (U.S. Bureau of the Census, 1972a, table 1). The percentage of adolescent women married and living with their spouses has correspondingly decreased since the early 1970s, especially among 18–19-year-olds (figure 3.1).

Fig. 3.1. *United States: Percentage of 15–19-year-old women married and living with their husbands, by age, 1968–82*

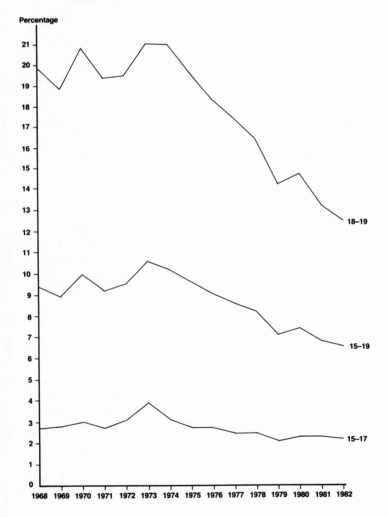

Source: U.S. Bureau of the Census, 1969–71, 1972a; 1973, 1974a; 1975–81, 1982a; 1983a, table 1; 1974b, 1983b, table 2.

The proportion of unmarried couples living together increased in the United States during the 1970s. Among never-married women aged 18–19, for example, the percentage living with a man rose from 0.2 percent in 1970 to 2.5 percent in 1980 (Sweet and Bumpass, 1984). The rise in cohabitation did not compensate for the drop in the proportion married, however. The total percentage of women aged 18–19 who were currently married or cohabiting in 1980 was 18.5, less than the 22.5 percent who were currently married in 1970 (U.S. Bureau of the Census, 1972a, table 1).

Many teenage marriages are precipitated by a premarital pregnancy. Among first marriages of adolescents that occurred between 1975 and 1979, 23 percent of the brides were pregnant—33 percent of brides aged 17 and younger and 18 percent of those aged 18–19. Another 10 percent were not pregnant at the time of the wedding but already had borne at least one child before they married (U.S. Bureau of the Census, 1984c, table 8). The proportion of 18–19-year-old brides who were pregnant at marriage grew from 11 percent in 1950–54 to 18 percent in 1960–64, and has remained at that level since then. There have been continual increases in the percentage of brides under age 18 who were pregnant at marriage, from 14 percent in 1950–54 to 21 percent in 1960–64 to 33 percent in 1975–79.

SEXUAL ACTIVITY

Although the proportions of adolescents who married decreased during the 1970s, the fraction of unmarried adolescents who had ever had intercourse rose sharply, resulting in an increase in the overall proportion of all adolescents who had had sexual relations. About 1 in 10 women aged 32–44 in 1982, who turned 20 between 1958 and 1970, reported that they had first had intercourse before age 16, and one-third said they had done so before age 18. About 1 in 5 of those aged 22–26, who turned age 20 between 1976 and 1980, had had intercourse before age 16, and nearly half had had coitus before age 18 (Campbell, 1984). The first national survey of sexual activity, contraceptive use and pregnancy among married and unmarried adolescent women was conducted in 1971; the most recent was in 1982. According to surveys in 1971, 1976, and 1979, the percentage of never-married women aged 15–19 who had had intercourse increased by half, while the percentage of all women aged 15–19 rose by one-third (table 3.5). Between 1979 and 1982, the percentage of never-married women who had had intercourse decreased among those aged 17 and younger and increased slightly among 19-year-olds, as seen in table 3.5 and in figure 3.2.[4] It is clear that the proportion of adolescents who had

4. Since the 1979 and 1982 surveys differed in methodology from those conducted in 1971 and 1976, there is some question as to whether the proportions of sexually experi-

Table 3.5. *United States: Percentage of all women and never-married women who ever had intercourse, by age*

Age	All marital statuses				Never-married women			
	1982	1979	1976	1971	1982	1979	1976	1971
15	19	22	19	15	19	21	18	14
16	31	36	28	24	29	35	25	21
17	44	49	45	32	41	46	41	27
18	58	59	54	47	53	53	45	37
19	72	71	68	62	65	63	55	47
15–17*	32	36	31	23	30	34	28	20
18–19*	65	65	61	55	59	58	50	41
15–19*	46	48	43	36	41	42	35	28

Sources: 1982: Pratt and Hendershot, 1984, tables 1 and 3; U.S. Bureau of the Census, 1983a, table 1, 1983b, table 2; Westoff, 1984. 1979: Dryfoos and Bourque-Scholl, 1981, table 5; U.S. Bureau of the Census, 1980, table 1, and 1982b, table 2. 1976: Zelnik and Kantner, 1977, table 1; U.S. Bureau of the Census, 1977, table 1, and 1982b, table 2. 1971: Zelnik and Kantner, 1977, table 1; U.S. Bureau of the Census, 1972a, table 1, 1972b, and 1982b, table 2.

*Percentages by single year of age applied to numbers in the total U.S. population, according to distribution by marital status.

had intercourse increased during the 1970s, but apparently it has stabilized since 1979 for 18–19-year-olds and has declined among younger teenagers to levels only slightly higher than in 1976. (Almost all of this decline occurred among blacks.)

In 1982, slightly fewer than half of women aged 15–19 had had intercourse. At age 15, the youngest age surveyed, 19 percent had already experienced coitus, increasing by more than 10 percentage points with each year of age to 72 percent of all 19-year-olds. In 1971, half of all women had had intercourse by age 18.7. The median age of first intercourse dropped to 18.1 in 1976, to 17.6 in 1979, and was 17.9 years in 1982.

By 1982, 84 percent of married women aged 15–19 had had intercourse before marriage (Pratt and Hendershot, 1984); 83 percent of women of all ages who had had coitus had never been married, and women who had delayed intercourse until after marriage accounted for only 3 percent of all those with any sexual experience.

enced estimated from the 1979 survey (which covered only metropolitan-area women) are too high or the estimates from the 1982 survey (which had higher nonresponse rates, especially among unmarried teens) are too low. Adjustments for what may be underestimation in 1982 of the proportion of never-married black women who had ever had intercourse to the 1979 levels would increase the percentage of all never-married women aged 15–19 who were sexually experienced only from 41 to 42 percent and the percentage of all women from 46 to 47 percent.

Fig. 3.2. *United States: Percentage of women who have ever had intercourse, by age*

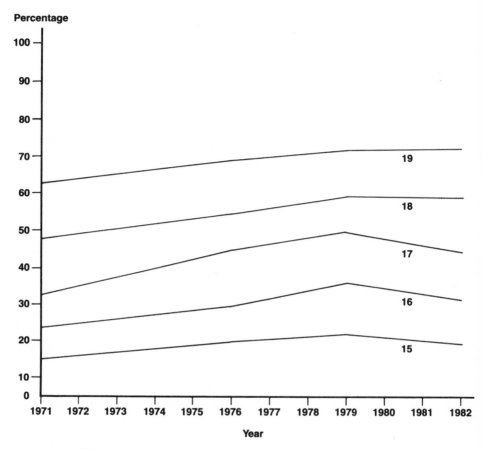

Source: Table 3.5.

Among never-married women aged 15–19 surveyed in 1976 and 1979, 52–58 percent of those who had ever had intercourse had had coitus during the previous four weeks. In 1982, 83 percent of never-married women who had ever had intercourse had done so in the previous three months (table 3.6). Estimates of the percentage of all teenagers, and of all those who were never married, who had intercourse during a recent time period are also shown in table 3.6. Four in 10 women aged 15–19 in 1982 reported that they had had intercourse in the previous 3 months, and (based on 1976 and 1979 survey estimates) about 3 in 10 had done so during the previous four weeks. Of

Table 3.6. *United States: Percentages of women who have had intercourse recently, by age, time period, sexual experience, and marital status*

Year	Age	Time period	Sexually experienced never-married	All women Total	All women Never-married
1976	15–19	Last 4 weeks	52	27	18
1979*	15–19	Last 4 weeks	58	30	24
1982	15–19	Last 3 months	83	39	34
	15–17	Last 3 months	82	27	25
	18–19	Last 3 months	83	56	49

Sources: 1976: Calculated from table 3.5 (Zelnik and Kantner, 1977, table 6). 1979: Zelnik, 1983. 1982: Pratt and Hendershot, 1984, table 3.
*Metropolitan-area women only.

this latter group, 48 percent had had sex 1–2 times during the month— 18 percent of 15–17-year-olds and 35 percent of 18–19-year-olds, compared with 29 percent who had had sexual relations 6 or more times (Zelnik and Kantner, 1977, table 6, p. 60). As of 1982, 20 percent of single 15–19-year-olds who had had intercourse in the previous three months said that they had done so 1 or fewer times a month; 29 percent said that their frequency was 2–3 times: 25 percent said 4 times; and 26 percent said more than 4 times (Mosher, 1985).

About half of unmarried adolescent women who have had intercourse report they have had more than one sexual partner. Some 8–11 percent, probably those who have had intercourse over the longest period of time, have already had 6 or more partners (Zelnik and Kantner; 1977, Zelnik, 1983).

Most adolescent women have a close relationship with their first sexual partner. Among sexually experienced metropolitan-area women aged 15–19 surveyed in 1979, 9 percent reported they were engaged to their first sexual partner and 55 percent said they had been dating only one person (Zelnik and Shah, 1983, table 3). Adolescent women beginning intercourse at early ages are more likely than those beginning at older ages not to have an ongoing relationship with their first partner.

There are few data available on sexual activity among male adolescents. In 1979, about 57 percent of metropolitan-area men aged 15–19 in 1979 had ever had intercourse—a figure higher than the 46 percent of women of the same age (Dryfoos and Bourque-Scholl, 1981, tables 1 and 2). The median age at which young men begin intercourse is about half a year younger than for women. Adolescent men are much less likely than women to have been engaged or to have been going steady with their first sexual partner (Zelnik and Shah, 1983, table 3).

CONTRACEPTIVE USE

Only about half of never-married adolescent women use a contraceptive method the first time they have intercourse (table 3.7). Among never-married users in 1982, almost half had a partner who used the condom and about a quarter practiced withdrawal. Fewer than 1 woman in 10 go to a clinic or a doctor in advance of first having intercourse to get oral contraceptives.

The proportion of metropolitan never-married women who used some contraceptive method increased between 1976 and 1979, but it did not change between 1979 and 1982. The increased use between 1976 and 1979 came from increased use of male methods—condom and withdrawal—from 59 percent of users in 1976 to 74–76 percent in 1979 and 1982. The use of oral contraceptives at first intercourse has declined since 1976.

Older adolescents are more likely to practice contraception at first intercourse and are slightly more apt than younger teens to use oral contraceptives rather than the condom or withdrawal. Thus 53 percent of never-married 18–19-year-old women interviewed in 1982 had used a method at first coitus compared to 40 percent of 15–17-year-olds; 18 percent of the older users employed the pill compared to 15 percent of the younger users (Pratt et al., 1984).

Although 73 percent of sexually experienced unmarried metropolitan adolescents in 1979 had used a contraceptive at some time, only

Table 3.7. *United States: Percentage distribution of never-married metropolitan-area women aged 15–19 who ever had intercourse, and of those who used a contraceptive method at first intercourse, by method used at first intercourse*

Method	Total			Users		
	1982	1979	1976	1982	1979	1976
Any method	50	51	39	100	100	100
Pill	8	9	10	16	18	26
IUD	0	*	*	0	1	1
Diaphragm	*	*	0	*	1	0
Condom	23	19	15	47	38	40
Withdrawal	15	18	8	29	36	19
Rhythm	2	2	2	4	3	5
Other	2	1	4	4	3	9
None	50	49	61	0	0	0
Total	100	100	100	100	100	100

Sources: 1982: 1982 National Survey of Family Growth, Cycle III, unpublished tabulations. 1979 and 1976: Dryfoos and Bourque-Scholl, 1981, table 8.
*<0.05 percent.

34 percent had employed a method each time they had intercourse (Zelnik and Kantner, 1980, table 7). Forty-five percent of women aged 15–19 in 1979 who were premaritally sexually active and who did not practice contraception at first intercourse started doing so subsequently. Seventy percent of never-married sexually active metropolitan women interviewed in 1979 reported that they had used a contraceptive method the last time they had intercourse, an increase of 19 percentage points since the first time they had intercourse (table 3.7). Most of the increase in use between first and most recént intercourse came in adoption of the pill, a 22-point increase. The percentage using some method at last intercourse rose from 64 percent to 70 percent between 1976 and 1979, due primarily to increased use of male methods (Dryfoos and Bourque-Scholl, 1981, tables 8 and 9). Sixty-nine percent of never-married women aged 15–19 in 1982 who had had intercourse within the previous three months and were not pregnant, postpartum, or seeking pregnancy had practiced contraception during the previous month. Sixty-two percent of these women had used the pill (Bachrach, 1984, tables 3 and 9).

Patterns of current use among all sexually experienced adolescent women are shown in table 3.8. Although 49 percent of those who had ever had intercourse were not using a method, 22 percent were not exposed to the risk of unintended pregnancy because they were not recently in a sexual relationship or they were pregnant or trying to become pregnant.

Among those exposed to the risk of unintended pregnancy, 30

Table 3.8. *United States: Percentage distribution of women aged 15– 19 who have ever had intercourse, and of those exposed to risk of unintended pregnancy,* by current contraceptive method used, 1982*

Method	Have ever had intercourse	Exposed to risk
Pill	33	46
IUD	1	1
Diaphragm	3	4
Condom	11	15
Rhythm	1	1
Other	2	3
None	49†	30
Total	100	100

Sources: Pratt et al., 1984, tables 2 and 7; Bachrach, 1984, table 3.

*Excludes those who are contraceptively sterile and those who have ever had sex but not in the last three months or are pregnant or trying to get pregnant.

†22 percent were exposed to the risk of unintended pregnancy and 27 percent were not exposed.

percent of 15–19-year-olds—compared to just 13 percent of women aged 20–24—were not practicing contraception, putting the teenagers at considerably higher risk of becoming pregnant. Forty-six percent of 15–19-year-old women exposed to the risk of pregnancy in 1982 were using the pill, three times the proportion dependent on the condom, the next most popular method.

The reasons many adolescent women do not always practice contraception include their ignorance about their pregnancy risk and their attitudes and lack of knowledge about the methods they could use, as well as problems in access to the medical care system. Fifty-one percent of unmarried women aged 15–19 in 1976 who had not practiced contraception at last intercourse, even though they didn't want to get pregnant, thought they could not become pregnant for various reasons (e.g., it was the wrong time of the month or they had sexual relations too seldom). Of the 49 percent who thought they could get pregnant, the most common reason for failing to employ a method (given by four out of five nonusers who realized they could get pregnant) was that they hadn't expected to have intercourse (Zelnik and Kantner, 1979, table 3).

In a 1982 survey of women exposed to the risk of unintended pregnancy who were currently using no contraceptive the most common reason cited for nonuse (by 44 percent) was concern about side effects (Forrest and Henshaw, 1983, table 6). There has been a great deal of publicity about the pill since studies in the mid-1970s indicated the possibility of harmful side effects (Jones et al., 1980). This kind of publicity has been reinforced by statements from some feminists that the pill and the IUD are harmful to women and have been pushed upon them by male scientists and doctors who do not have women's interests at heart. Rising concern with fitness and natural foods has also made some women wary about putting what appear to be unnatural chemicals or devices in their bodies. A 1985 Gallup survey found that 76 percent of women over 18 think the pill entails "substantial risk" to health; 58 percent of those stating an opinion said use for women under 35 carried more health risk than did childbirth. Women not only greatly overestimate the health risk of pill use but also underestimate its effectiveness. Among those responding, 36 percent thought the pill is less than 90 percent effective (Gallup Org., 1985).

The pill is neverthless, by far, the most popular reversible method of contraception available, and approval of it has risen steadily since the late 1970s (Forrest and Henshaw, 1983). Approval may continue to increase as more recent information on the health benefits of the pill are disseminated and new low-dosage formulations become more widely used. Among adolescents at least, the concern about side effects seems to be focused more strongly on the minor effects related to nausea and weight gain than on fear of the more serious risks that may occur to older women and smokers (Kisker et al., 1985).

CONTRACEPTIVE SERVICES

Contraception is widely available within the United States, but it is not always accessible to adolescents. Since 1968 the federal government has helped to fund family planning clinics. Publicly subsidized clinics were established primarily to serve poor adult women, who still represent about three-quarters of the total caseload (Torres, 1985). The law requires, however, that clients be served without regard to marital status or age; and, since 1978, in complying with that law federally funded clinics have provided services for adolescents (Kenney et al., 1982). Parental notification or consent has never been mandated by the legislation establishing the program, although parental involvement is encouraged. A 1982 attempt to require notification through administrative regulation was widely publicized, bitterly fought, and finally declared invalid by federal courts (AGI, 1984; Donovan, 1983; Kenney et al., 1982). The 2,500 federally funded family planning agencies operate 5,200 clinic sites throughout the United States. They are run by local and state health departments, local affiliates of the Planned Parenthood Association of America, hospitals, and other agencies, such as neighborhood health centers (Torres and Forrest, 1985).

In 1981, 30 percent of all adolescent women who were at risk of unintended pregnancy at some time during the year made a medical visit to a family planning clinic (Torres and Forrest, 1983b). In 1982, 77 percent of women aged 15–19 who had ever had intercourse had received medical services or counseling about contraception during the previous three years; 49 percent of those who had ever made a family planning visit (38 percent of all who had had intercourse) said their most recent source of care was a clinic. At the most recent clinic visit, about half obtained medical birth control services (Pratt and Hendershot, 1984). Nonprescription as well as prescribed contraceptive methods are available from family planning clinics.

Thirty-three percent of all female clinic patients in 1981 were adolescents. Since 1969, 18 percent of patients have been aged 18–19, while the proportion aged 17 or younger rose from 9 percent in 1972 to 15 percent in 1979 and remained at that level through 1981 (Torres and Forrest, 1983b).

Three contraceptive methods must be obtained from or prescribed by a physician or nurse clinician—the pill, the IUD, and the diaphragm. In 1981, 79 percent of adolescent clinic patients obtained the pill, 2 percent the IUD, and 4 percent were fitted for diaphragms (AGI, 1983, table 7). The IUD is generally considered unsuitable for most adolescents due to concern about increased risk of pelvic inflammatory disease and subsequent infertility among adolescents who are likely to have more than one sexual partner (Planned Parenthood, 1984). In 1980, about 1 in every 100 U.S. women aged 15–19 who had ever had sex was hospitalized with pelvic inflammatory disease (Mascola et al., 1983, table 2; U.S. Bureau of the Census, 1984a).

The 1982 national survey found that 17 percent of women aged 15–19 who had ever obtained birth control services or counseling had done so before they first had intercourse (Pratt and Hendershot, 1984). Twenty-seven percent of adolescent women who ever used a prescription method were virgins when they got the method—24 percent of those who first obtained their method from a clinic and 32 percent of those who went to private doctors (Zelnik et al., 1984). Eighty-eight percent of teenage clinic patients have already had intercourse before they first come to a clinic for contraceptive services (Kisker, 1984a). Sexually active teenagers wait an average of 13–14 months after starting intercourse to come to a clinic (Kisker, 1984b; Zabin and Clark, 1981). The mean delay between first intercourse and first use of a prescription method is 11 months for clinic clients in metropolitan areas and 13 months for patients of private physicians (Zelnik et al., 1984a, table 4).

This long delay is of concern to those trying to provide services. Forty-five percent of all premarital pregnancies to teenagers occur to those who have been sexually active for less than six months, and 36 percent occur within the first three months after first having intercourse (Koenig and Zelnik, 1982). The reason given most often among new teenage clinic clients as the most important for making their first clinic visit is that they are afraid they might be pregnant (Zabin and Clark, 1981, table 9). The most important specific reason for delaying coming to a clinic is fear that their families will find out (Zabin and Clark, 1981, table 10). A 1979–80 survey found that 20 percent of family planning agencies require parental consent or notification for patients aged 15 and under and 10 percent require it for women aged 16 and 17, even though they are not required to do so by the federal government (Torres et al., 1980). Although state laws vary, persons aged 18 and older are generally considered to be adults. Almost half of family planning agencies engage in outreach activities directed at teenagers and half have programs to provide parents of adolescents with instruction and counseling, as well as programs to encourage adolescent clients to involve their parents in their contraceptive decision (Torres, 1984). A 1979–80 patient survey found that 43 percent of new patients under age 18 said their parents knew of the clinic visit; 48 percent of these said that their parents had suggested the visit (Torres et al., 1980).

Another factor contributing to delay in coming to a clinic, cited by 25 percent of new patients, is fear of being examined (Zabin and Clark, 1981, table 10). Pelvic examinations are required before prescription of the pill, for insertion of the IUD, or diaphragm fitting and, in federally funded clinics, they are often even required before nonprescription methods are supplied.

In 1983, the average charge for an initial contraceptive visit and a three-month supply of pills was $50, but 91 percent of clinics have sliding-fee scales depending on the patient's income, and 35 percent serve teenagers without charge (Torres, 1984). In 1981, at least 32 percent of adolescent clinic clients received free services; for another 9 percent, the costs were covered by Medicaid. For those who did pay, the average fee was $11 (Chamie et al., 1982).

PRIVATE PHYSICIANS AND PHARMACIES

Physicians

Almost as many adolescents at risk of unintended pregnancy make visits to private physicians for family planning each year as go to clinics. In 1981 the figures were 27 percent and 30 percent respectively (Torres and Forrest, 1983a). In 1982, 45 percent of 15–19-year-old women who had ever made a visit for contraceptive service or counseling had been to a physician for their most recent visit. At that visit, 62 percent received birth control services (Pratt and Hendershot,1984).

Thirty-five percent of general and family practitioners (GFPs) and obstetrician-gynecologists (ob/gyns) surveyed in 1983 would not provide contraception to minors without parental consent—41 percent of GFPs and 20 percent of ob/gyns. Fourteen percent (almost all of the GFPs) do not provide contraceptives to any minor, and 21 percent provide them only with parental consent (Orr and Forrest, 1985).

Whereas in family planning clinics all contraceptive methods must be offered, the medical profession is not unanimously in favor of providing all methods to adolescents. Thirteen percent of GFPs, 4 percent of ob/gyns, and 10 percent of pediatricians who will prescribe contraceptives for adolescent women will not prescribe the pill, and some who do prescribe it are reluctant to do so for young women who have intercourse infrequently. In addition, 39 percent of doctors will not prescribe the diaphragm, and 77 percent will not insert the IUD in adolescents. Only 11 percent provide all three methods (Orr, 1984a).

GFPs and ob/gyns charge an average of $42 for an initial visit; 56 percent of those who provide contraceptive services accept Medicaid reimbursement, and 17 percent reduce their fees for poor patients (Orr and Forrest, 1985). Given the fees and fee policies of many physicians, it is not surprising that 65 percent of adolescent clinic patients say they go to a clinic rather than a private physician because a doctor is too expensive (Chamie et al., 1982).

A large proportion of adolescents in the United States are not accustomed to making physician visits on their own. In fact, 23 percent of adolescent patients choose a clinic because they do not know a doctor to visit (Chamie et al., 1982). In 1980, 72 percent of all women and men aged 15–24 in the United States made at least one visit to a physician (White, 1984). Except for poor unmarried mothers or daughters in poor female-headed families, public coverage of medical expenses is not available. Most adolescents must pay for physician services themselves or involve their parents in paying or filing for reimbursement from private medical insurance.

Pharmacies

It costs about $107 per year to purchase the pill in pharmacies. Like other contraceptives, it can be obtained for less through family planning clinics. The annual cost in pharmacies is $95 for diaphragms; $50 for spermicides; $30 for condoms (Torres and Forrest, 1983a). In 1981, 62 percent of pharmacies reported displaying condoms on the aisles or counters within easy access; 83 percent displayed contraceptive foam in this manner. Eleven percent reported they had age restrictions on the sale of contraceptives (usually 17 years), and 5 percent discouraged teens from purchasing them (Chamie et al., 1982).

ABORTION SERVICES

Availability

Abortions are performed in 2,900 service locations. Services are heavily concentrated in the larger metropolitan areas. In 1982, 28 percent of all women lived in counties with no abortion providers, and 44 percent lived where there was no facility reporting 400 or more abortions a year. Only 42 percent of ob/gyns and just 3 percent of either GFPs or general surgeons will perform abortions (Orr and Forrest, 1985). In 1982, 82 percent of all abortions were provided on an ambulatory basis in nonhospital facilities, mainly clinics. Most hospital procedures are also done on an outpatient basis (Henshaw et al., 1984). Fewer than 6 percent of all abortions in 1982 involved an overnight stay in a hospital (Henshaw et al., 1984, pp. 121–124).

The federal government prohibits use of Medicaid funds for abortions except where the woman's life is endangered. In 1985, 14 states and the District of Columbia used their own funds to pay for abortions for poor women on welfare (Donovan, 1985). For many teenagers the cost of a clinic abortion, averaging about $200, can be prohibitive. Hospital abortions cost two-to-four times as much, and charges are higher for abortions at longer gestations (Henshaw et al., 1984). Although only 9 percent of all women who obtained abortions in 1981 did so more than 12 weeks from their last menstrual period (Henshaw et al., 1985, table 1), 23 percent of abortions obtained by girls under age 15, and 15 percent of those obtained by women aged 15–19, occurred in the second trimester when abortions are more expensive and more risky (Grimes, 1984, figure 3).

In 1979–80, 44 percent of all abortion providers required parental consent for girls aged 15 and under; 33 percent required it for 16-year-olds; and 30 percent for patients aged 17. Clinics were less likely than hospitals to require consent. Consent requirements were not only promulgated by institutions, but by physicians themselves. Fifty-three percent of physicians who perform abortions require parental consent for some or all minors (Orr and Forrest, 1985). Fifty-five percent of unmarried minors obtaining abortions reported that their parents already knew; 24 percent of them said their parents had suggested the abortion (Torres et al., 1980).

SEX EDUCATION

Schools

National polls conducted since 1965 have shown wide approval of sex education in public schools, ranging from 7 in 10 in 1965 and 1969 to 8 in 10 since the mid 1970s. Schools vary widely in terms of the amount, form, and type of sex education provided. The most frequent goal of sex education programs is to increase students' knowledge of reproduction in order to inform sexual decision making. The reduction of sexual activity or pregnancy among teenagers is an explicit goal in a minority of programs (Sonenstein and Pittman, 1984; Kirby, 1984). Although no state prohibits it, only Maryland and New Jersey and the District of Columbia require sex education to be included in school curricula. (New Jersey mandates "family life education" and leaves to local community boards what topics will be included.) Thirty-one states and the District of Columbia have guidelines about sex education in schools, but what is taught is generally determined by the nation's 16,000 local school districts (Kenney and Orr, 1983), covering 21,000 secondary schools (NCES, 1982, tables 8 and 52).

In 1982, 80 percent of school districts covering secondary schools in cities with populations over 100,000 offered some sex education (Sonenstein and Pittman, 1984). A 1978 survey of public high schools found that 36 percent offered a separate course on sex education or family life. About three-fourths of the sex education programs include information on the likelihood of pregnancy, contraception, and abortion, usually introduced around ages 14–15 (Orr, 1982). About three-fourths of adolescents have some sex education before leaving school (Zelnik and Kim, 1982), and about 4 in 10 have a separate sex education course (Kenney and Orr, 1983). More than half of adolescents receive sex education in school that includes contraceptive information by the time they graduate from high school (Zelnik and Kim, 1982).

One of the problems in expanding sex education programs is the lack of qualified teachers (Cooper, 1982) even though 86 percent of teachers surveyed in 1984 felt sex education should be included in public high schools and 75 percent favored including it in grades 4–8 (Gallup, 1984b; 1985a). Only 30 percent of colleges for teacher education offer courses designed to prepare teachers of sex education (Thompson, 1983). Most teachers of high school sex education have credentials in physical education, home economics, science, or social studies (Orr, 1982).

Media

Some adolescents talk with their parents about sex, and even more obtain some sex education in school; but all are exposed to sexual messages from television, the movies, newspapers, and magazines. A review of the few studies of television programs that have been done (Orr, 1984b) showed an increase in explicit and implicit sexual behavior on television during the 1970s. Most frequently, sexual intercourse is implied. References to extramarital sex are much more common than references to sex between married couples, and programs seldom portray sexual relationships as "warm, loving, or stable" (NIMH, 1982).

In addition, radio and television commercials and print advertising often have clear sexual overtones aimed at selling products ranging from designer jeans to automobiles. Although sexual references are frequent on television, the emphasis is on titillation. Portrayals of male-female relationships depict these as highly romanticized or exploitive. There is almost no realistic information about sex and no mention of use of contraceptives (although abortion often evokes tearful decisions among characters on soap operas). A wide variety of personal care products, including vaginal douches, sanitary napkins, and tampons, are advertised on television, but advertising of nonprescription contraceptives is banned by most television stations. (Advertising of any prescription drug or device, which includes the pill, IUD, and diaphragm, is prohibited by the federal government.)

Television and radio news and talk programs do cover topics related to sexuality with increasing frequency, often in the context of adolescent pregnancy. They usually present factual information, sometimes including reference to private physicians or Planned Parenthood as sources of care, and provide exposure to the differing viewpoints of experts or of the audience. Newspapers and magazines have also dealt with topics related to sexuality over the past few years in news and feature articles as well as in advice columns. Such columns are found in almost every paper and woman's magazine. They usually deal with general questions about relationships or health and answer questions related to sex along with other topics. Seldom are such columns devoted exclusively to sexual matters.

Magazines that are popular among adolescent girls provide some interesting insights into the types of messages about sex to which American adolescents are exposed. These magazines reveal a series of double messages about sexuality and female assertiveness. Teenagers are offered advice about making intelligent decisions about sexual involvement. A recurrent theme is that they must be in control of their sexuality. In the same magazines, dozens of advertisements feature women in seductive, often passive circumstances and poses, intimating that they must attract men at any cost.

Parents

In spite of the fact that by age 15, one out of every five American girls has had intercourse, most parents do not talk to teenage children about sex or about birth control. Among 15 surveys of the first or most important source of information about sex for young people (many of which included college students in their early twenties), it was found that, at best, parents play only a minor role as sources of sexual information for their children (Fox, 1983). In only one study was "the family" listed as the major source of sex education, and then by fewer than half the teenage respondents. More commonly cited were friends, reading, media, and schools. In a 1979–80 national study of family planning clinic clients who were obtaining pills, IUDs, or diaphragms (AGI, 1982), 65 percent of those aged 17 and younger said they had ever talked with their parents about birth control. In addition, recent research indicates that there is a good deal of misunderstanding about what parents think they have communicated to their children about sex-related issues and what teenagers think they have heard from their parents (Newcomer and Udry, 1985).

ATTITUDES ABOUT SEX AND CONTRACEPTION

Sexual activity among adolescents is viewed by many Americans as the problem that must be contended with in order to reduce teenage pregnancies. In 1981, a federal program to coordinate and develop services to adolescent mothers was altered to add as a main focus the prevention of sexual activity among unmarried teenagers. This legislation seeks to encourage pregnant teens to carry to term and to give up the babies for adoption. Although support for provision of contraceptive services by the federal government to sexually active adolescents is widespread, there have been demands that such services be stopped because they foster sexual activity among unmarried adolescents (Ford and Schwartz, 1979; Schwartz and Ford, 1982; Helms, 1984).

National survey data, however, suggest that the majority of people see premarital sexual relations as acceptable, and that approval has increased during the 1970s. The Gallup Poll shows a doubling of acceptance of premarital sex among Americans between 1969 and 1985. In 1969, only 24 percent of U.S. adults with an opinion on the matter thought that it was not wrong "for a man and a woman to have sex relations before marriage." By 1973, that fraction had increased to 47 percent, and by 1985, to 57 percent. (Notably, Catholics were more likely to find premarital sex not wrong [64 percent] than Protestants [49 percent], probably because of the growing influence of morally strict fundamentalists among the Protestant groupings [Gallup, 1985b, p. 28].)

While most Americans accept premarital sexual relations, sexual activity among young teenagers is often viewed as a problem, even among teenagers themselves. In a survey of students aged 12–18 in one large city, 86 percent of girls and 81 percent of boys who had already had sex felt that the best age for beginning sexual activity was older than they were when they started (Zabin et al., 1984).

RELIGION

Religion is a powerful force in American life. As noted in chapter 1, and shown in Appendix 2, Americans score higher on an index of religiosity than any other developed country for which there are data. And, as table 1.2 demonstrated, there is a very high correlation between religiosity and teenage fertility—the higher the index, the higher the birthrate of both younger and older teenagers. A Gallup survey conducted in the mid-1970s found that religious beliefs were more important to Americans than to the people of any other country except for India (Gallup, 1985c, pp. 9–10). Although separation of church and state is written into the U.S. Constitution, the influence of religion has not declined recently in America as it has in many other countries—including those that have established churches, such as Sweden and England. What is more, a large and growing number of Americans share religious convictions that are fundamentalist in nature. For example, 38 percent of Americans in 1985 said they believed that every word of the Bible represented divine revelation and was to be taken literally (Gallup, 1985c). The influence of fundamentalist pastors and of organizations such as the Moral Majority has grown rapidly since the late 1970s. Many of these have been among the most outspoken critics of teenage sexual activity and of nonmarital sexual relations in general.

Surveys of Americans aged 13–18 show that 95 percent believe in God, and 8 in 10 say religion is important in their lives. Although only one-fourth of teenagers have a high degree of confidence in organized religion—a proportion much lower than the 64 percent of adults, the percentage belonging to and attending church is similar to those aged 18 and older (Gallup, 1984a, p. 62ff). Yet the gaps that teenagers perceive between religious teachings and the behavior they observe in the world around them undoubtedly contribute to the tension and ambivalence with which teenagers view sexuality.

ECONOMIC OPPORTUNITY

Ninety-one percent of young women and 96 percent of young men aged 15–17 live with one or both parents. By age 18–19, this proportion is reduced to 70 and 84 percent, respectively. Eighteen-year-olds are able to vote, and at age 18 men must register for military service (although service itself is voluntary). This is also the age when most Americans graduate from high school and go on either to higher education or to a job. By age 20–24, just 31 percent of women and 48 percent of men are living with their parents (U.S. Bureau of the Census, 1983a).

Poor adolescents are more likely to become pregnant and to have babies. Some people believe that lack of economic opportunity is a key reason many adolescents have babies, because they see little reason to postpone childbearing until education is completed and they are established in a career. There are wide discrepancies in income in the United States. In 1980, the median family income was $21,000, but 19 percent of families had annual incomes below $10,000, compared to 7 percent with incomes over $50,000 (U.S. Bureau of the Census, 1982d, table 16).

As shown in table 3.9, one-third of adolescents aged 16–17 are working, usually at a part-time job, whereas half of those aged 18–19 are employed. Another 10–16 percent in both age groups do not have jobs but are looking for work. About one-fourth of teenagers in the labor force are unemployed, more men than women, and more younger than older adolescents. Unemployment is highest among black teenagers, who are most likely to be poor. Federal job training programs that provide training and jobs for some adolescents tend to serve

Table 3.9. *United States: Percentage of young men and women employed and looking for work, by age and sex, 1982*

Sex and age	Total	Employed	Looking for work
Female			
16–17	41	31	10
18–19	61	48	13
20–24	70	61	9
Male			
16–17	45	33	12
18–19	68	52	16
20–24	85	71	14

Source: U.S. Bureau of the Census, 1983f, table 21.

a small proportion of those wanting to work, and they have been cut drastically in recent years due to federal budget decisions.

Unemployment insurance is available only to those who have already worked for a specified period of time in a covered position. Thus adolescents who have not yet had a job do not receive unemployment payments. If they are laid off from a covered job, benefits are low, limited to a certain number of weeks and linked to their previous wage. In 1981, unemployment benefits averaged $107 per week (U.S. Bureau of the Census, 1983d, table 648).

A birth to a young adolescent decreases her chances of finishing school, but problems with school often occur prior to the pregnancy. Almost all adolescents under 18 are in school, however, as shown in table 3.10. After high school about half of 18–19-year-olds remain in school, usually full-time in college or other post-high school education.

HELP FOR PREGNANT ADOLESCENTS

Eligibility requirements for welfare, which provides money for food, housing, other expenses, and, through welfare, eligibility for Medicaid, vary from state to state, and sometimes from county to county. The major national welfare program is Aid to Families with Dependent Children (AFDC). In most states to be eligible a woman has to be unmarried and have at least one child or be a daughter in such a family. Some states, however, also cover families with an unemployed father and, for Medicaid at least, pregnant women who would be eligible after giving birth. (Federal legislation that became effective in October 1984 extends Medicaid coverage nationally to poor married mothers and expectant women.) To meet the income criteria to qualify for welfare and, therefore, for Medicaid, in 1982 women had to have a monthly income

Table 3.10. *United States: Percentage of young men and women enrolled in school, by age and sex, 1982*

| Age | Total | Sex | |
		Female	Male
14–15	99	98	99
16–17	91	90	91
18–19	48	47	49
20–21	34	33	35

Source: U.S. Bureau of the Census, 1983d, table 219.

below a limit that ranged from $141 to $613 for a family of four, which is 18–79 percent of the federally defined poverty level of $775 per month (AGI, 1983, pp. 185–86).

Adolescent mothers who are not married usually do not receive financial support from the child's father. Among all mothers aged 18–24 in 1981 not living with the child's father, 15 percent received child support payments compared to 39 percent of older mothers living apart from the child's father. Mothers of all ages who never married are one-sixth as likely to receive child support as women who have been married. The mean income from child support for those 18–24-year-old mothers receiving it was $1,008 in 1981 (U.S. Bureau of the Census, 1985).

There are a number of special services to provide adolescents with prenatal care and help in schooling and employment. They tend, however, to be concentrated in urban areas and to serve extremely disadvantaged teenagers. These services are generally provided by public school systems, health departments, local governments, and voluntary agencies, and they are almost always subsidized by the local, state, or federal government. A 1979–80 survey (Wallace et al., 1982) found that 80 percent of cities of 100,000 or more population had some sort of special program for pregnant adolescents; many of these services were not designed specifically for teenagers, however. Such programs often include medical care, special education classes, counseling or referral for job training or placement, and day care. Services are seldom provided by a single organization or at one site, making it difficult for many to move through the numerous systems to get care.

A small federal program in recent years has funded a number of demonstration projects around the country to identify new and possibly more effective ways to help pregnant teenagers and to delay future pregnancies. It also seeks to encourage adoption, but now that abortion is legally available, only about 4 percent of unmarried adolescents take that option (Zelnik and Kantner, 1977).

DISCUSSION

Many of the changes that occurred in the United States in the 1970s were continuations of trends begun much earlier, but the greater availability of survey statistics has made people more aware of the trends. Adolescents growing up in the United States in the late 1970s and early 1980s have been subject to many conflicting messages. Sexual messages are pervasive in the media to which children are exposed. They usually extol sexual attractiveness as a good in itself, and very few deal with sex in terms of personal relationships or discuss the risks inherent in sex or ways to avoid sexually transmitted disease or unintended pregnancy. While the majority of people support sex education in public schools and the provision of contraception to adolescents, vocal minorities see these not simply as inadvisable, but as evils that should be eradicated, as should nonmarital sexual activity, especially among adolescents.

Some studies of adolescents and reports from professionals who work with them suggest that, in this environment, although teenagers feel pressures to engage in sexual relations, it is often difficult for them to acknowledge that they are or want to be sexually active and to take responsibility for avoiding pregnancy or sexually transmitted diseases. Whereas for the girls at least, it is acceptable to be "swept away" by passion or "love" and let intercourse just happen, it is not acceptable to plan for or anticipate sex. Until a relationship is an established one, adolescents often feel they are not worthy of respect if they plan for sex.

Such attitudes, of course, hinder contraceptive use because contraceptives must be obtained in advance and be on hand before sex begins. Difficulties in negotiating one's way through the medical system, often for the first time alone, and coming up with the money to buy contraceptives make it even more difficult to get over the personal barriers to becoming a consistent contraceptor. It is often those with the fewest current skills and future options who, when they become pregnant unintentionally, go on to have babies. Lack of employment opportunities is often cited as a key reason why adolescent birthrates are so high.

In today's environment adolescence can be an especially difficult time. If teenagers are not sexually active by their late teens, they are viewed as odd and out of step by their peers. If they have a contraceptive on hand before a steady relationship is established, they may be considered promiscuous by revealing that they expected to have intercourse. If they don't use a method, they are called irresponsible. Many adolescents cannot talk with their parents about sex and contraception, and if they try to get a method on their own, they may be afraid that their parents will find out; they may have difficulty finding a provider or scheduling an appointment and covering their absence from home or school; or they may have trouble getting enough money to pay for contraceptive help. If they get pregnant and decide to have an abortion, they cannot remain unaware of the newspaper articles about organized opposition to abortion or statements by President Reagan that abortion is equivalent to murdering a baby; they may have to pass through pickets or demonstrators to get into the abortion facility. If there is no clinic near their home, they are apt to have difficulty finding a doctor or hospital willing to perform an abortion. If they have a baby, they will find that medical care is expensive and that it is not easy to get on welfare or to obtain publicly funded services. If they do succeed, welfare allows for a minimally sufficient lifestyle, and they will have a hard time making ends meet.

On the other hand, half of teenage girls do not began sexual activity until they are about 18 years old. Whereas they may not use a contraceptive the very first time they have intercourse, most do so eventually. Even though many teenagers do not practice contraception consistently, most women exit from their teen years without ever having been pregnant. Most physicians will serve even unmarried minors in confidence as will most clinics. Teenagers can obtain counseling, physical examinations, and contraceptives free or at low cost from clinics around the country. While there is not unanimous approval for teenagers to be sexually active, most people agree that if they are, they are acting responsibly when they practice contraception. If an adolescent does become unintentionally pregnant, legal, safe abortion services are available, usually on an outpatient basis. If a teenager who is unintentionally pregnant has a baby and, as most do, decides to keep it, her family usually rallies around to help to the extent it can. In most large cities, some types of programs are available to provide her with some help to get through the pregnancy safely and to continue her education or get a job.

American society as a whole is concerned about the levels of adolescent pregnancy and childbearing in the United States. There are arguments going on about who or what is to blame for teenage pregnancy. There are also more healthy attempts to decrease the difficulties adolescents face in dealing with their sexuality and with pregnancy if it occurs and to increase the support and guidance available to teenagers. The country is groping for ways to decrease levels of adolescent pregnancy and childbearing. While this goes on, however, teenagers are exposed to numerous messages, which are often contradictory and ambiguous. The net result is that teenagers in the United States are more likely to become pregnant than adolescents in the other countries examined in the following chapters.

4
Canada

anada is two nations culturally: Quebec, which is predominantly French, and the other provinces, where English is the dominant language and the culture is similar to that of the United States. Almost half of non-French Canadians trace their ancestry to England or Scotland (Statistics Canada 1981a, table 4.19, p. 137), while about 30 percent of U.S. residents who reported foreign ancestry named England or Scotland (U.S. Bureau of the Census, 1982e, table 45, p. 37).[1] The United States has about three times the proportion of residents reporting German ancestry as does English Canada. Both countries have a large number of residents of Irish background and small numbers from many other European countries. An important ethnic difference is that the United States has large proportions of people who are black and Hispanic—12 percent and 6 percent, respectively (U.S. Bureau of the Census, 1982e, table 36, p. 32). In Canada, racial minority groups make up a much smaller proportion. American Indians and Eskimos constituted less than 2 percent of the Canadian population in 1971; 1.3 percent were Asians; and only 0.3 percent were black or West Indian (Statistics Canada, 1981a, table 4.19, p. 137). In 1976, only 0.2 percent reported their "mother tongue" to be Spanish (Statistics Canada, 1981a, table 4.16, p. 136).

1. The U.S. figure is not exactly comparable to the Canadian figure because U.S. respondents were permitted to name more than one country of ancestry and 17 percent reported no ancestry other than "American."

66

Quebec, with 26 percent of Canada's population (Statistics Canada, 1983b), has retained a distinctive culture and politics, owing in part to Canada's decentralized federal system of government and Quebec's determination, reflected in provincial and national policy, to maintain its French culture and identity. Fertility patterns in Quebec have been different from those of the other provinces, and teenage pregnancy is much lower. Therefore, in addition to overall Canada-U.S. comparisons, the analysis below will consider provincial differences within Canada, especially the difference between Quebec and the rest of the country.

ADOLESCENT PREGNANCY

Fertility

The recent fertility history of Canada closely parallels that of the United States. Both countries experienced baby booms after World War II, which peaked at about the same time. In both countries, fertility reached its highest postwar level in 1957 (Statistics Canada, 1978; and NCHS, 1984b, table 1, pp. 1–7). The total fertility rate in Canada in 1981 was 1.7 children per woman (Statistics Canada, 1983c, table 5, p. 9), slightly lower than that in the United States (1.8). Nevertheless, the fertility rate of Canadian teenagers (26.4 births per 1,000 women aged 15–19 in 1981) is only half that of U.S. teenagers (52.7) (figure 4.1).

The U.S.-Canadian difference is large for both the younger and older teenagers, although it is slightly greater for the younger ones. For ages 15–17, the Canadian fertility rate is 56 percent lower than the U.S. rate (tables 2.2 and 2.4). Among those aged 18–19, the difference is 46 percent.

Abortion

The U.S.-Canadian difference with respect to legal abortion rates is slightly greater than the difference in birthrates. The adolescent abortion rate in Canada in 1981 was an estimated 17.9 per 1,000, 59 percent lower than the U.S. rate; the fertility rate was 50 percent lower. Unlike fertility, abortion shows a slightly greater difference for women aged 18–19 than for those aged 15–17.[2]

2. The abortion rates shown in table 2.4 and figures 2.2 and 4.1 were adjusted to include an estimated 4,000 abortions obtained in the United States by Canadian residents and 5,500 abortions provided in nonhospital facilities in Quebec and therefore excluded from Statistics Canada reports. These estimates were made by Christopher Tietze (1983, p. 21) and added to both the 1980 and 1981 abortion statistics. It was assumed that the age distribution of the women who obtained abortions outside the country was the same as

Hormonal postcoital contraception (both DES and the oral contraceptive Ovral) are known and used in Canada; in fact, Canadians pioneered the use of Ovral for this purpose. Judging from the fact that DES was described in publicly funded guides to birth control methods and that Ovral achieved acceptance in Canada before it did in the United States, it appears likely that postcoital contraception has been used more in Canada than in the United States, where neither DES nor Ovral has been approved by the Food and Drug Administration for postcoital contraception. Therefore use of the morning-after pill may account for a small part of the U.S.-Canadian difference in recorded adolescent pregnancy rates. Menstrual extraction may be available in some locations in Canada as well as in the United States, but its use is not believed to be widespread.

Canadian teenagers terminate 41 percent of their pregnancies by abortion (disregarding spontaneous fetal loss) compared to 45 percent among U.S. teenagers (table 3.1).[3] Abortion services appear to be less accessible to many Canadian women than they are to American women. A major obstacle in Canada is the requirement that abortions be performed only in hospitals and be approved by a therapeutic abortion committee consisting of at least three physicians. The committee must certify that the continuation of the pregnancy would be likely to endanger the life or health of the pregnant woman. A woman must be referred for an abortion by a general practitioner, and the abortion must be performed by a physician who is not on the abortion committee. Thus five physicians are involved in every abortion. Except in Quebec, where the requirements are not enforced, abortions are available only in the 25 percent of public general hospitals with committees willing to approve abortions (Statistics Canada, 1983a, table 6, p. 50, and table 69, p. 123). In many of these hospitals the need for committee approval causes a delay of several weeks, during which time the woman is not certain that she will be permitted to have the abortion. A second

that for the abortions reported by Statistics Canada. For the nonhospital abortions in Quebec, it was assumed that the age distribution was the same as for those performed in hospitals. The teenage abortion rate may be slightly overestimated if teenagers were underrepresented among the women traveling to the United States for abortion services, but it may be underestimated if, as was suggested by an official Canadian commission, some hospital abortions were omitted from the official statistics (Minister of Supply and Services, 1977). Whereas some illegal (mostly self-induced) abortions occur in Canada, as in the United States, the number is probably small. It is unlikely that any inaccuracies in the assumptions would have a major effect on the estimated abortion rates or on the conclusions drawn from them in this book.

3. These figures are based on the age at which the birth or abortion occurred; based on age at which conception occurred, the proportion is significantly lower in both Canada and the United States.

Fig. 4.1. *United States and Canada: Births, abortions, and pregnancies per 1,000 women aged 15–19, 1981*

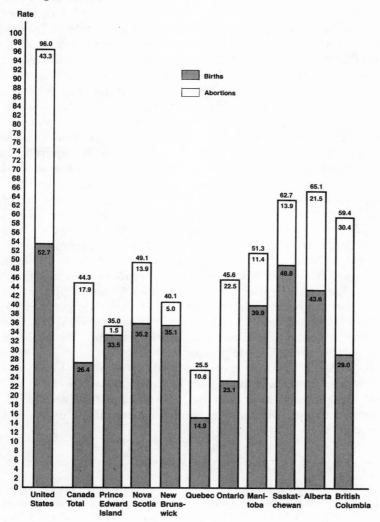

Source: See sources in table 4.4.

obstacle is the practice of having abortion patients spend one or more nights in the hospital. In 1981, 36 percent of abortions involved at least one night of hospitalization. In the United States in 1982, only 6 percent of abortions involved hospitalization, and not all of these required an overnight stay (Henshaw et al., 1984).

On the other hand, in most large Canadian cities there are hospitals with expedited committee procedures where large numbers of abortions are performed efficiently. In principle, the service is free under Canada's provincial health plans; but in practice, outside of Quebec Province, it appears that the majority of women must pay part of the physicians' charges. This is because many obstetrician/gynecologists either have opted out of the health plan or bill patients on top of the health plan. The charges are usually modest compared to those for abortions in the United States. In most provinces, the law permits teenagers aged 16 and over to obtain abortions without parental consent, although many if not most hospitals require parental involvement. For girls under age 16, parental consent is usually required.

The availability of abortion services in hospitals with expedited procedures varies by province. Services are most available in Quebec, Ontario, and British Columbia. In these provinces, 42–51 percent of teenage pregnancies that do not end in miscarriage are terminated by abortion. Services exist but are less accessible in the Prairie Provinces and Nova Scotia; in these provinces, 22–33 percent of teenage pregnancies end in abortion. Services are difficult or impossible to obtain in Prince Edward Island, New Brunswick, and Newfoundland; and these provinces appear to have very low abortion ratios.[4] Thus it appears that the percentage of pregnancies terminated by abortion is affected by the availability of abortion services. In the provinces with the most available services, the percentages are similar to those in the United States. Most of the population lives in these provinces.

When estimated abortion rates and birthrates are combined into pregnancy rates, the Canadian rate is 44.3 per 1,000 women aged 15–19, which is 55 percent lower than the U.S. rate of 96.0 (tables 2.2 and 2.4). The percentage difference is about the same for younger and older teenagers.

TRENDS IN ADOLESCENT PREGNANCY

Both total and teenage fertility fell rapidly in Canada between 1971 and 1981, by 22 percent and 34 percent, respectively. The adolescent birthrate was 40.1 births per 1,000 women aged 15–19 in 1971, 33.7 in 1976, and 26.4 in 1981. In the United States, the adolescent birthrate fell by about the same proportion as the Canadian rate between 1971 and 1976 (16–18 percent) but remained steady between 1976 and 1981 (table 2.2).

4. The number of adolescent births is unavailable for Newfoundland, so the ratio cannot be calculated. The abortion figures for all the Maritime Provinces may be understated since residents of these areas may obtain unreported abortions in Quebec or in the United States.

Legal abortion rates among teenagers increased in both Canada and the United States over the decade 1971–81. The Canadian abortion law was liberalized in 1969, and the number of abortions increased rapidly in subsequent years. According to Statistics Canada, the abortion rate peaked in 1979 for women under age 18 and in 1980 for women aged 18–19 (Statistics Canada, 1984, table 7, p. 47). In the United States, the adolescent abortion rate has generally followed the same pattern, but the signs of recent peaking of the rates are less clear (table 2.2).

The trends in pregnancy rates, however, are different for the two countries. The adolescent pregnancy rate in Canada fell by at least 15 percent between 1971 and 1981. (The drop is even greater if a substantial number of Canadian teenagers obtained unreported or out-of-country abortions in 1971.) In the United States the pregnancy rate *increased* by an estimated 14 percent over the same period (table 2.2 and chapter 3).

REGIONAL VARIATION IN ADOLESCENT PREGNANCY

In Canada, as in the United States, there are wide regional variations in adolescent fertility, abortion, and pregnancy rates (see figure 4.1). Quebec has by far the lowest adolescent fertility rate, 14.9 per 1,000 teenage women, which is 35 percent lower than that of the next lowest province, Ontario, and 44 percent lower than that of all Canada. The adolescent abortion rate in Quebec is very low, 10.6, in spite of the fact that Quebec is the only province where nonhospital abortions are permitted.[5] The only provinces with lower abortion rates are the Maritimes (except Nova Scotia), where abortion services are virtually unavailable.

At the other end of the spectrum are the Prairie Provinces, with birthrates approaching those of all U.S. teenagers and comparable to those of U.S. whites. However, the abortion rates (and the pregnancy rates) in the Prairie Provinces are much lower than those in the United States. The relatively low abortion rates and the agricultural character of the Prairie provinces might suggest a pattern of intentional early marriage and childbearing. However, this is apparently not the case, since women from these provinces have relatively high nonmarital fertility.[6] Nineteen percent of all births in Saskatchewan and 18 percent in Manitoba were to unmarried women in 1981 (Statistics Canada,

5. The Quebec abortion rate of 10.6 includes an estimate of the number of nonhospital abortions. It is possible that the number of such abortions has been underestimated but probably not by enough to affect the conclusions.

6. Data on the marital status of teenagers giving birth were not published by province.

1983c, table 7, p. 11). Thirty-five percent of nonmarital births in Canada occurred to teenagers in 1981 (Statistics Canada, 1983c, table 8, p. 12). Therefore it can be inferred that a large proportion of the teenage fertility in Saskatchewan and Manitoba is nonmarital and, probably, unplanned. It is interesting that Saskatchewan, which is considered the Bible Belt of Canada, has the highest teenage birthrate, just as the Bible Belt states in the United States have the highest adolescent birthrates. Ontario and British Columbia have relatively low birthrates, as well as relatively high abortion rates. The Maritime Provinces, by contrast, have birthrates above the national average but, as noted above, have low abortion rates.

MARRIAGE AND COHABITATION

Marital status is associated with fertility for a number of reasons. Married teenagers often desire pregnancy and childbirth, and many marry after becoming pregnant. Only 4 percent of Canadian women aged 15–19 are legally married (Statistics Canada, 1983b, table 6, p. 95, and Norland, 1983, table 1, p. 3), a figure which is one-half the U.S. proportion. When marital status is taken into account, the U.S.-Canadian fertility differential is reduced. Among unmarried Canadians aged 15–19, the birthrate is 16.4. For all unmarried U.S. teenagers it is 28; for whites it is 17 (table 3.3). Thus when Canadians are compared to U.S. whites, there is little difference in the nonmarital birthrate. Unmarried Canadians, however, have fewer abortions and their overall pregnancy rate is lower.

Among married teenagers the fertility rate is 286 per 1,000 in Canada and 351 in the United States (table 3.3). The relatively high marital fertility rate among teenagers in the United States does not mean that a large part of U.S. adolescent fertility is desired. As was noted in chapter 3, only 4 in 10 first births to married teenagers and one-fourth of all births to adolescents were planned. It is possible that the proportion planned is even lower in Canada, since the proportion of teenage births that occur within marriage is lower (40 percent) there than in the United States; however, any difference in desired childbearing would account for only a small part of the Canada–U.S. differential in adolescent fertility.

Cohabitation is more common in Canada than in the United States. Six percent of Canadian women aged 18–19 were reported in the census to be in common-law unions in 1981; an unknown additional percentage who reported themselves to be roommates were also cohabiting (Norland, 1983, table 1, p. 3). In the United States, only 3 percent of the same age group were cohabiting in 1980 (table 3.4). It is not clear whether a high rate of cohabitation would tend to increase pregnancy because of the greater exposure to coitus or whether it would decrease pregnancy because of the greater consistency and effectiveness with which established couples use contraceptives.

SEXUAL ACTIVITY

The only published, nationally representative data on sexual activity among Canadian teenagers come from a survey commissioned by the Committee on the Operation of the Abortion Law. It was conducted by the Gallup organization in 1976 and included a questionnaire distributed to 15–17-year-olds as well as to older women and men. Questionnaires were completed by 3,574 adults and 554 teenagers of both sexes aged 15–17. The results are shown in table 4.1.

The Canadian survey asked respondents, "On an average, how often do you have sex (sexual intercourse)?" The answer categories were: "never," "a few times each year," "once a month," "once in a while," "two or three times a week," and "more than three times a week." Table 4.1 shows the percentage of Canadian women giving any answer other than "never"; the U.S. figures show the proportion who have ever had intercourse. On the basis of this comparison, for all age groups shown, the proportion of women who have had sexual relations is substantially higher in the United States than in Canada. At age 15, the Canadian proportion is 56 percent below the U.S. proportion, compared to 48 percent lower at age 16–17, and 17–25 percent lower for the age group 18–23. The U.S. figures are adjusted to include married as well as unmarried women, with the assumption that all ever-married women have had sexual intercourse. For the United States, the minimum estimate assumes that 55 percent of unmarried women aged 18–23 have had intercourse; this estimate is based on Zelnik and Kantner's

Table 4.1. *Percentage of Canadian women who report that they "have intercourse" and of U.S. women who report that they have ever had intercourse; by age, 1976*

Age	Canada	U.S.
15	8	19
16–17	19	36
18–23	60	72–80*

Sources: Canada: Minister of Supply and Services, 1977, table 14.1. U.S. 15–19: Dryfoos and Bourque-Scholl, 1981, table 3.8. U.S. 20–23: Tanfer and Horn, 1984, and marital status from G. Masnick and M. J. Bane, *The Nation's Families: 1960–1990* (Boston: Auburn House, Joint Center for Urban Studies of M.I.T. and Harvard University, 1980), table 2.4.
*72 is minimum estimate; 80 is maximum estimate.

report that 55 percent of all 19-year-olds were sexually active in 1976. The maximum estimate utilizes data from a 1983 survey that found that 79.6 percent of never-married women aged 20–24 had ever had intercourse (Tanfer and Horn, 1984).

The relatively low rate of sexual activity among Canadian teenagers may be due in part to underreporting. The Canadian researchers assumed that all women under age 18 who had ever had intercourse would give a response other than "never" to their question. This assumption is not necessarily valid; a sexually experienced girl who had not had intercourse in several months and who did not intend to have intercourse in the near future could logically have selected the response "never" rather than "a few times a year." Although the proportion of such respondents is likely to have been low, there is no way to estimate it.

The Canadian survey found that, as in the United States, young men report higher rates of sexual intercourse than young woman. Thirty percent of the males aged 15, 42 percent of those 16–17, and 73 percent of those 18–23 reported having had intercourse (Minister of Supply and Services, 1977, table 14.1, p. 335).

Other surveys of sexual activity have been conducted among special populations of Canadians, usually high school or university students. Of three studies of Canadian high school students, one found a proportion of young women sexually experienced that was higher than the Kantner and Zelnik figures for U.S. teenagers of about the same age (Hundleby, as reported in Herold, 1984); one found a proportion similar to that among U.S. teenagers (Stennett et al., as reported in Herold, 1984); and one found a lower proportion (Herold, 1984, p. 19). A fourth study yielded much higher rates of sexual activity, but this study suffered from a very low response rate (41 percent) because of parental consent procedures (Meikle et al., 1981). According to Herold, seven studies of unmarried Canadian university students were conducted between 1975 and 1982 (Herold, 1984, p. 13). The proportions of female students sexually active ranged from 45 to 66 percent, averaging 56 percent. Four U.S. studies between 1974 and 1980 found proportions sexually active ranging from 57 to 64 percent and averaging 61 percent (De Lamater and MacCorquadle, 1979; Robinson and Jedlicka, 1982; and Rees and Zimmerman, 1974). The actual U.S.-Canadian difference would be somewhat greater than that suggested by this comparison because Canadian students enter the universities one year later than do American students and are, therefore, one year older on average. In addition, when married teenagers are counted among the sexually active, the difference would increase because about 8 percent more U.S. than Canadian 18–19-year-old women are married (15.2 percent vs. 14.1 percent) (Statistics Canada, 1983b, table 5).

Considering only the report of the Committee on the Operation of the Abortion Law, known as the Badgley Report (Minister of Supply and Services, 1977), the lower sexual activity rate of the younger Canadian teenagers would explain the difference in pregnancy rates in this age group. However, the Badgley Report probably underestimated sexual activity because of the wording of the question. Also, the studies of high school students cited above show fewer differences between Canada and the United States than were found in the Badgley Report. Therefore it is not possible to draw a definite conclusion about whether sexual activity differences account for the Canadian-U.S. differences in pregnancy rates among teenagers aged 15–17.

Among women aged 18–23, the Badgley Report suggests a level of sexual activity that is only about one-fifth lower than in the United States. Studies of college and university students suggest a similar degree of difference. This difference explains only a part of the 53 percent difference in pregnancy rates. Thus among older teenagers there remains a significant difference in teenage pregnancy rates that is not explained by differences in the proportion who have had sexual relations.

Because the adolescent fertility and pregnancy rates of Quebec are especially low, the levels of sexual activity in this province are of particular interest. Unfortunately, the Badgley Report did not present sexual activity rates for teenagers by province. However, research on this topic has been conducted in Quebec. One study surveyed students in a university and a technical school in Quebec, as well as several universities and technical schools in other provinces, using the same questionnaire (Hobart, 1980). The survey was first conducted in 1968 and repeated in the same institutions (plus one additional university and two additional technical schools in English- speaking provinces) in 1977. The respondents were unmarried men and women aged 18–25. Among the female students in Quebec in 1977, 65 percent had had intercourse, compared with 63 percent in the English-speaking provinces. In 1968, the percentage that had experienced coitus was lower in Quebec than in the other provinces, 30 percent vs. 44 percent. Thus it appears that the proportion of unmarried females who have had sexual relations has increased in Canada, as well as in the United States, and more rapidly in Quebec than in other parts of Canada.

Three other studies conducted in Montreal, Quebec, reported rates of sexual activity roughly similar to those found in other Canadian provinces (Crépault and Gemme, 1981; Herold, 1984). In addition, a study of university students in Ontario showed no difference between French-speaking and English-speaking students in the proportion that had experienced coitus (Pool and Pool, 1978). These results suggest that in the late 1970s, the level of sexual activity among adolescents was not markedly lower in Quebec than in other provinces and that other factors, specifically, contraceptive use and/or patterns of sexual activity, must account for Quebec's low fertility and pregnancy rate.

CONTRACEPTIVE PRACTICE

While lower levels of sexual activity may account for some of the difference in adolescent pregnancy between the United States and Canada, a major part of the difference may be attributed to better contraceptive practice by Canadian teenagers. Studies suggest that Canadian teenagers are more likely than U.S. teenagers to be using a method currently, to use a contraceptive at first intercourse, and to be using oral contraceptives.

The most complete Canadian data come from the Canadian Fertility Survey of 1984, which interviewed a national random sample of 5,315 women aged 18–49, of whom 316 were aged 18–19. This survey found that 50 percent of 18–19-year-old women were "currently using" a contraceptive method (table 4.2). This compares with only 37 percent of American women in the same age group interviewed in the 1982 U.S. National Survey of Family Growth. Because 65 percent of 18–19-year-old U.S. women in 1982 said that they had had intercourse, and it

Table 4.2. *Canada, 1984, and United States, 1982: Percentage distribution of contraceptive use for women aged 18–19 of all marital statuses*

	Canada (N=316)	U.S. (N=949)
Contraceptive use		
Pregnant, postpartum, or seeking pregnancy	3.2	7.9
Noncontraceptively sterile	0.0	0.4
Other nonusers	46.8	55.0
Using a method	50.0	36.7
	100.0	100.0
Contraceptive method		
Female sterilization	0.6	0.0
Male sterilization	0.0	0.5
Pill	84.2	64.0
IUD	1.3	1.4
Diaphragm	0.0	7.1
Condom	8.9	18.9
Foam	0.0	0.6
Rhythm	1.9	2.4
Withdrawal	3.2	2.7
Other	0.0	2.4
	100.0	100.0

Sources: Canada: special tabulation of the Canadian Fertility Survey provided by T. R. Balakrishnan, The University of Western Ontario; U.S.: special tabulation of the National Survey of Family Growth, Cycle III, produced by AGI.

is likely that some sexually active Canadian teenagers were not practicing contraception, these results suggest that the Canadian-U.S. difference in sexual activity rates is small or nonexistent among older
teenagers.

The opinion survey sponsored by the Committee on the Operation
of the Abortion Law obtained data on contraceptive use by younger
teenagers. Respondents were asked, "What birth control or contraceptive method are you or your partner now using?" The percentages
using no method are shown in table 4.3. Also shown in table 4.3 are the
results of a U.S. study that asked unmarried teenagers what method
they used at last intercourse and whether they had ever used a method.
The proportion who had never used a method was higher than the
Canadian proportion who were currently using no method. Similar
Canadian-U.S. differences are apparent in data on contraceptive use at
first intercourse.

A study in Ontario in the mid-1970s found that "slightly more than
one-third of the high school males and females did not use any method
at first intercourse" (Herold, 1984, p. 89). A study in Saskatchewan,
which has a relatively high pregnancy rate, reported that 62 percent of
a sample of 15–19-year-old men and women used no method at first
intercourse (Weston, 1980, p. 42). U.S. data show 61 percent of 15–19-
year-old never-married metropolitan women used no method at first
intercourse, according to a 1976 study; in a 1979 study, the figure was
49 percent (table 3.7). Canadian studies of college students found that
22 percent (Herold, 1984, p. 89), 26 percent, and 30 percent (Barrett,
1980) of young women used no method at first intercourse; two U.S.
studies found that 55 percent of college students used no method
(Chilman, 1980, p. 157). Together these studies suggest that the Canadians are more consistent users of contraceptives.

Table 4.3. *Canada: Percentage of sexually active women who used no
contraceptive; United States: Percentage of never-married sexually active women who
used no method at last intercourse and who have never used a method; by age, 1976*

| | | U.S. | |
| | Canada | % who didn't use at last | % who never |
Age	% not using	intercourse	used a method
15	34	46	38
16–17	17	41	30
18–19	—	30	18
18–23	15	—	—

Sources: Canada: Minister of Supply and Services, 1977, table 14.4. U.S.: Zelnik and
Kantner, 1977, table 9.

Among teenagers practicing contraception, a higher proportion of Canadians than Americans use the pill, the most effective reversible method. Table 4.2 shows that, according to the national fertility surveys, 84 percent of Canadian contraceptive users employed the pill—significantly more than the 64 percent of American users. American teenagers were more likely than Canadians to use the condom and diaphragm, methods with higher use-failure rates.

The Badgley Report also contained data on contraceptive use in 1976. Of the female respondents using contraceptives, the proportion employing the pill was 55 percent among the Canadian respondents aged 15–17 and 76 percent among those aged 18–23. The 1976 Zelnik and Kantner study found only 37 percent of U.S. 15–17-year-old unmarried users reporting that they had employed the pill at last intercourse; 62 percent of those aged 18–19 did so (Zelnik and Kantner, 1977, table 12.) Of married users aged 15–24, 63 percent employed contraceptives in 1976 (Ford, 1978, table 1, p. 285). Data are also available from the Canada Health Survey, conducted in 1978–79. This survey found that 17.3 percent of all Canadian women aged 15–19 were using birth control pills (Statistics Canada, 1981b, table 99, p. 183). In the United States in 1982, it was estimated that 15 percent of 15–19-year-old women were using oral contraceptives (calculated from tables 3.5 and 3.8). Because more American than Canadian teenagers have had intercourse, these results suggest that the proportion of sexually experienced teenagers using oral contraceptives is higher in Canada.

Other published data, as well as information obtained in the course of the country visit, suggest that Canadians adopted the pill more rapidly than did U.S. women in the late 1960s and early 1970s. Canadians have overwhelmingly favorable attitudes toward pill use, the principal exceptions being some feminists and academics who are concerned about perceived adverse health effects. The pill is almost universally considered the method of choice for teenagers both by teenagers themselves and by the physicians who provide contraceptive services. It may be relevant that most Canadian women obtain pill prescriptions from general practitioners rather than from specialists, who might be more concerned about the possibility of harmful effects of the pill on some women. However, as in the United States, a pelvic examination, blood pressure, and other tests are ordinarily required before the pill is prescribed.

Contraceptive practice in Quebec is of special interest due to the province's low adolescent pregnancy rate in the face of sexual activity rates that appear to be similar to those of English-speaking Canada. The only data on contraceptive use by teenagers come from studies in individual high schools (Dupras and Levy, 1981). In eight different studies, the proportion of students who said they had used a contraceptive method at first intercourse ranged from three in ten to two in three. The proportion tended to increase over the period covered by the surveys, 1970–76.

For some time, couples in Quebec have demonstrated a high determination to limit their fertility. In 1971, the fertility rate in Quebec was a low 57.8 per 1,000 women of reproductive age (Statistics Canada, 1978), even at a time when 40 percent of married couples in the province were relying on the relatively ineffective methods of periodic abstinence and withdrawal (Henripin and Marcil-Gratton, 1981). The evident high motivation and ability of married women to prevent accidental pregnancy may carry over within the same culture to unmarried women and teenagers.

FAMILY PLANNING SERVICES

Although the Canadian primary medical care system, like that of the United States, is based on the individual private practitioner, universal medical insurance makes medical care more accessible to Canadian than to U.S. teenagers. In the Canadian system, there is no charge for physician services. The only charge for family planning services is the cost of birth control pills or other supplies, which must be purchased in pharmacies. A cycle of pills cost about $US 6 in 1984, which was about one-fourth to one-third less than in the United States. (In some Canadian family planning clinics, teenagers are given their first three cycles of pills without charge.) There is no charge to women on welfare. Unlike the situation in the United States, many young teenagers are said to be accustomed to making appointments with and visits to their physicians without parental assistance. Thus it apparently requires less special initiative for a teenager to seek contraceptive care from a private physician in Canada than it does in the United States.

However, there are still barriers to obtaining services from private physicians, particularly for young teenagers. A study of physicians in Manitoba in the early 1970s found that 47 percent would not prescribe oral contraceptives to an unmarried girl aged 17 without parental consent (Latif and Boldt, 1977), and 17 percent would not do so even with parental consent. A later national survey of family practitioners and obstetrician/gynecologists conducted around 1980 found that 43 percent of physicians were reluctant or unwilling to provide birth control services to single minors without parental consent, and 3 percent would not always do so even with parental consent (Boldt et al., 1982). A similar U.S. study found that only 20 percent of obstetrician/gynecologists and 41 percent of general and family practitioners were unwilling to serve unmarried minors without parental consent (Orr and Forrest, 1985). Even if a young women is assured of a favorable attitude on the part of her physician, she may be embarrassed to reveal her sexual activity or may fear that the physician will tell her parents. Problems of embarrassment and confidentiality appear to be a concern of Canadian teenagers in the same way that they are of young people in the United States (Herold and Goodwin, 1979).

For these reasons, there is a clear need for clinics to provide family planning services, particularly to teenagers. Before 1970, however, clinic services were provided only by a handful of underfunded voluntary agencies in different parts of the country. Until 1969, the dissemination of birth control information and the sale of contraceptives was a criminal offense in Canada, and although contraceptives had been available in drugstores and were prescribed by doctors, the federal government could play no role in support of family planning. The Quebec provincial government was among the first to enter the field of family planning when it provided funds for Le Centre de Planification Familiale in 1967. Also in 1967, Ontario's minister of health announced legislation to encourage that province's 43 local health boards to open family planning clinics. Several municipalities established clinics before 1970, notably Montreal, which operated nine clinics in 1967.

In 1969, the sale of contraceptives was legalized, and in the same year the abortion law was liberalized. Beginning in 1970, the federal government played an important role in encouraging the development of family planning services. The Family Planning Division began in 1972 to provide funds to the provinces and to voluntary agencies, especially the Planned Parenthood Federation of Canada, then called the Family Planning Federation of Canada, to establish services. Among the other recipients of federal funds were the Service de Regulation des Naissances, which provides instruction in the sympto-thermal method of periodic abstinence, and the Province of Quebec (LeClair and Johnson, 1973).

Stimulated by federal financing, family planning clinic services expanded greatly during the 1970s. It was federal policy to provide financing for experimentation and service development, not for ongoing support, and in 1979 federal financing was eliminated with the expectation that the provinces would take responsibility for continuing the services. The cutbacks were apparently stimulated by economic conditions rather than by political forces hostile to family planning. However, family planning subsidies were cut more than most other government programs. Many of the provinces did not make up for the federal cuts, and the clinic system has been shrinking in some of them.

The most developed clinic systems exist in Quebec, Ontario, and British Columbia. Quebec has an extensive network of local community health centers (CLSCs), which have added separate family planning services to their other primary health services (Gourgues, 1980). It is the only province with publicly operated clinics that provide general medical care; about 10 percent of the population receives its medical care from the clinics. There is never a charge to the patient for services provided by a CLSC. Most, but not all, of the CLSCs have separate family planning clinics. Some are now providing abortion services. Ontario has a system of public health units that provide certain preventive services, much like county health departments in the United States. Most of these units also provide family planning services, and the system is considered the model program for Canada. British Columbia has a network of 17 Planned Parenthood clinics whose development was stimulated by federal grants and whose support has been taken over by the provincial government. Recently, however, all provincial funding has been cut off, and the future of many of the clinics is in peril.

Except for New Brunswick, the Prairie and Maritime Provinces rely mainly on a few voluntary agencies for family planning services. These provinces did not replace the funding lost due to the federal cutbacks, and clinic services are unavailable to most residents, many of whom live in small towns and rural areas. New Brunswick has created a network of family planning clinics in health units and hospitals.

The main role of the clinics in most areas is to serve teenagers and transients who have no private physician. In Ontario in 1980, 54 percent of patients served were under age 20, and one-third of the teenagers were under age 17 (Ontario Ministry of Health, 1981). Many of the clinics have outreach programs and special clinic sessions for teenagers. Most clinics provide confidential medical services to young teenagers without parental involvement, although some require parental consent. Interpretations of the law vary; some physicians believe that it requires parental consent. Referrals by school nurses are encouraged by the provincial health department. Family planning services are also available in university health clinics.

The Canadian family planning clinic system overall appears to be less developed than that of the United States. Even in Ontario, which is said to have Canada's most extensive system, there were about 7 medical clinic visits by teenagers per 100 females aged 15–19 in the population in 1980 (Ontario Ministry of Health, 1981), while in the United States there were about 27 visits per 100 teenagers. In addition, there were 4 clinic visits by Ontario teenagers for counseling and referral per 100 adolescents in the population. Patient visits to Ontario clinics grew by about 50 percent between 1980 and 1983, suggesting that there was a high level of unmet need for services during the 1970s. All clinic visits are covered by national health insurance. It is notable that even without an extensive clinic system, a higher proportion of Canadian than of

American teenagers are using oral contraceptives. This reflects the high accessibility of private-physician services in Canada and/or a high degree of motivation to prevent pregnancy on the part of the Canadian adolescents.

SEX EDUCATION

The education system in Canada is much like that in the United States—highly decentralized, with a great deal of authority exercised by school boards and individual schools. The provinces set general guidelines for curricula, which may or may not be followed. A large proportion of students attend Catholic schools.

In 1964, a survey of 55 urban school systems in Canada revealed that none of the provincial departments of education had made provision for sex education or family life education as a separate subject. To the extent that these subjects were taught, it was on the initiative of the school board or the individual teacher. None of the 55 systems surveyed taught sex education as a subject, although one was preparing a program for introduction on a trial basis in a few schools. Thirty-five of the systems said that aspects of sex education were included in other subjects such as health, science, social studies, and home economics. However, contraception was rarely mentioned as one of the topics covered (Deiseach, 1977).

By the time a more complete survey of school districts was made in 1975–76, the situation had changed markedly. At that time, 32 percent of school boards responding to the survey said they had some provision for teaching family life education. Responses varied widely by province. Ontario had the highest proportion, 45 percent. Percentages were also high in Prince Edward Island, British Columbia, and Newfoundland. The proportions in the Prairie Provinces and Quebec were low. Of the systems where family life education was offered, it was treated as a separate subject in 26 percent and as part of other subjects in 40 percent; both approaches were used in 43 percent. Relatively few teachers had had special training. Seventy-nine percent of the family life education teachers responding to the survey said that birth control methods were covered for grades 9–13, but most of these teachers were from Ontario, the province with the most developed sex education programs (Deiseach, 1977). A similar survey of sex education instructors in the United States in 1978 found that 78 percent include contraceptive methods in their courses (Orr, 1982, table 3, p. 310). In 1976, the provincial departments of education still did not require sex education programs. They had taken official notice of the subject, however, and some local programs had been approved. It appeared that several had taken the first steps toward establishing official guidelines (Deiseach, 1977).

In Quebec, starting around 1970, the education department attempted to adopt official guidelines for a sex education program, but as of 1984 it had still not implemented them. As a temporary measure, the Ministry of Social Affairs, with the agreement of the Ministry of Education, established a program whereby school nurses and social workers would offer instruction in the schools "to provide young people of senior high school age with the basic information regarding contraception and sex" (Gourgues, 1975). The program was instituted in 1973 and by 1976–77 reached 64,464 students (Gourgues, 1980), about half of the number who would have been leaving or graduating from secondary school in that year. The focus of the program was on students in their last year of school who did not intend to go to college; the assumption was that these were the students most likely to have problems of large families and poverty in the future.

A replication of the survey of Canadian school systems has just been conducted by the Planned Parenthood Federation of Canada. The results show that 50 percent of the school districts offered a family life education program or activity in 1984. Eighty-seven percent of the urban school districts offered such a program or activity (Nolte, 1984). A national survey of 978 school nurses in 1980 asked whether there was a family life education program in their schools. According to the responses of the nurses, 69 percent of the schools had such a program, 26 percent did not. (In 5 percent of the schools, the nurses did not know if their schools had programs or not.) Ontario had the highest proportion of schools with programs, and the Prairie Provinces the lowest (Chatterton, 1982, table 9, p. 19).

The Canadian sex education programs appear to have been at a level of development similar to those in the United States in the mid-1970s. The 1976 Canadian survey found that 59 percent of school districts in the largest urban areas had family life education programs; in the United States, a 1971 study of large school districts around the country found that approximately 55 percent offered a sex education program, and a 1982 study of almost 200 districts in large U.S. cities found that about three-fourths offered some sex education (Kenney and Orr, 1983). A 1979 survey of a random sample of teenagers in Saskatchewan found that 36 percent of the young women had had instruction on birth control in school (Weston, 1980, p. 20). This compares with 49 percent of U.S. teenagers surveyed in 1976. Saskatchewan, however, is below the Canadian national average in the extensiveness of its sex education programs. The adequacy of teacher training for family life education is a matter of concern to Canadians. In a recent survey of family life education teachers, only 53 percent of respondents said they had taken courses to prepare them for teaching that subject (Nolte, 1984).

Proportionately more Canadian than U.S. students attend Catholic schools, in which they are reportedly less likely to teach methods of contraception other than periodic abstinence. There are few sex education programs organized by churches or other groups outside of the schools.

Public opinion about sex education is about the same in Canada and the United States. A 1984 Gallup survey in Canada found that 83 percent of the public believed that sex education should be taught in schools. In a 1982 Research Center survey in the United States, an almost identical 82 percent said they were in favor of sex education in the schools.

The mass media in English-speaking Canada are generally similar to those in the United States in their presentation of information about contraception and sexuality. The advertising of contraceptives other than the pill and IUD is permitted, but it is regulated by the Food and Drug Directorate (Royal Commission on the Status of Women in Canada, 1974).

CANADIAN SOCIETY

Canada's society is similar economically to that of the United States. Both countries are highly industrialized. Canada is only slightly less affluent than the United States; the per capita income was $8,684 in 1979, as compared to $9,869 in the United States. In spite of its great size, Canada is highly urbanized, with 76 percent of the population residing in urban areas (Statistics Canada, 1981a, table 4.11); in the United States, 74 percent of the population lived in metropolitan counties in 1980. Four percent of the gross domestic product is derived from agriculture, compared to 3 percent in the United States (U.S. Bureau of the Census, 1982e). The proportion of the population living on farms was 4.5 percent in Canada (Statistics Canada, 1981a, table 4.11, p. 134) and 3.8 percent in the United States (U.S. Bureau of the Census, 1982e, table 1134, p. 649).

In both countries women have moved into the labor force in large numbers. Women constituted 40 percent of the labor force in 1980 in Canada and 42 percent in the United States. Among women aged 15–19, 52 percent of Canadians and 53 percent of U.S. residents were in the labor force (U.S. Bureau of Census, 1982e, table 1534, p. 872).

Teenage unemployment increased in Canada during the 1970s, as it did in the United States. The unemployment rate of women aged 15–19 was 12.5 per 1,000 in 1970, after which it fell until 1974, then rose sharply to a peak of 17.2 in 1978, fell slightly to 15.3 in 1980, then rose again to 18.9 in 1982 (Statistics Canada, 1983d, p. 256). Among Canadians of both sexes, 84 percent of those aged 14–17 were enrolled in school in 1980–81. Also in that school year, twelfth-grade enrollment for both sexes was 75 percent of the level that second-grade enrollment had been 10 years earlier, suggesting that about three-fourths of teenagers complete the Canadian equivalent of high school in the United States (Statistics Canada, 1983e, table 28, p. 125).

Thus Canadian economic and social trends parallel those in the United States. Canadians themselves tend to look to the United States to help them foresee what trends are likely to occur in their own country. However, Canadians perceive themselves as less likely to go to extremes than their American counterparts, whether in regard to the sexual revolution, foreign policy, or the latest fashions.

Canada has had a higher rate of immigration than the United States. In 1971, 15 percent of the Canadian population was foreign-born (Statistics Canada, 1981a, table 4.21) as compared to 5 percent of the U.S. population (U.S. Bureau of the Census, 1982e). Although the U.S. statistics may omit some illegal aliens, the proportion foreign-born is clearly higher in Canada. Because of restrictions on immigration, recent immigrants to Canada tend to be middle class and are reported to have average or above-average incomes compared to native-born Canadians. Few data on the adolescent fertility of the immigrant groups are available, so it is impossible to assess their effect on the national adolescent fertility rate. It is thought by some observers that the immigrant groups impose traditional cultural norms of abstinence on their teenagers, thereby tending to reduce adolescent pregnancy. Others, however, believe that the immigrant families are undergoing a process of cultural change and generational conflict, causing a breakdown of norms and high teenage pregnancy.

Social support programs appear to be more generous in Canada than in the United States. An unmarried teenage mother who lives with her parents and has one child can expect to receive monthly payments of about $US 385 if her parents' income is below a certain level. Welfare payments are available to low-income couples, while in the United States it is difficult for a mother to obtain public assistance if her husband is living at home. The health insurance system pays for almost all medical costs.

Paternal financial responsibility for children born out of wedlock is about the same in Canada and the United States. In both countries, an unmarried mother may obtain a court order for financial support if she proves paternity, but few do so because of the cost of the necessary court procedures and the difficulty of enforcing the court order.

English Canada displays the same range of attitudes about sexuality as that in the United States. Some Canadian people react to teenage sexuality by advocating programs to encourage contraceptive use, while others attempt to maintain and restore traditional moral standards by opposing sex education and family planning programs. The latter is the strategy supported by fundamentalist religious groups, which are influential in some areas. There is a strong right-to-life movement, stimulated in part by U.S. influences, particularly in the Prairie and Maritime Provinces. These forces have succeeded in keeping abortion services restricted to only one-fourth of the general public hospitals (Statistics Canada, 1984). On the other hand, there is a possibility, difficult to document, that Canadians as a whole have a more tolerant attitude toward sexuality. Canadians say that there is a fair degree of acceptance of out-of-wedlock childbearing, and statistics show that 60 percent of teenage mothers are unmarried at the time of the birth. For U.S. teenagers, the proportion is 50 percent; and it is only 35 percent among U.S. whites. This suggests that unwed pregnant U.S. teenagers, especially white teenagers, are under greater pressure than Canadians to marry to legitimize the birth. (It could be argued that more public financial support is available to single teenage mothers in Canada than in the United States. However, the U.S. system provides a disincentive to marry because medical and financial support are rarely available to married teenagers, whereas low-income Canadian married couples are eligible for welfare.) As noted above, more Canadian than U.S. teenagers are cohabiting. A 1977 Gallup survey reported that 60 percent of Canadians felt that having sexual relations with someone other than the marriage partner was always wrong, while 72 percent of Americans indicated such feelings in a National Opinion Research Center survey the same year (Canadian Institute of Public Opinion, 1977).

In Quebec, in contrast to the United States, forces favoring sexual and reproductive freedom have maintained political ascendancy since the late 1960s. In reaction against many years—probably centuries—of domination by conservative religious and political elements, a strong progressive and feminist movement has affected prevailing public attitudes in what is described by some as a revolution. Some of the more striking manifestations of the new orientation are public financing of nonhospital abortions (which are illegal under the federal abortion law), early support of family planning clinics and sex education, and the existence of a Department of Sexology at the University of Quebec in Montreal. A quotation from a paper by Denis Lazure, Quebec's minister of social affairs, further illustrates attitudes toward sexuality in that province:

> This is the international Year of the Child; not too long ago, our
> government passed legislation recognizing children as full-fledged

citizens; now we are attending a seminar on children and sexual development. All these factors are the stuff of dreams—dreams of a world without taboos, where every child can develop fully from a sexual point of view.

Indeed, for too long now the subject of children's sexual development has been merely endured; worse still, until very recently, sexual development of adolescents was viewed as merely a necessary evil.

Every child has a fundamental right to sexual development, in the same way that he has a fundamental right to life, to proper food, and to education. Acceptance of the child's right to sexual development is the acceptance of that development for its own sake, not merely acceptance of its more satisfying manifestations or its more disturbing consequences (Lazure, 1980, p. 16).

Attitudes toward fertility control play a central role in the new liberated spirit of Quebec. The province historically had an extremely high fertility rate, and large families are associated with ecclesiastical control of the society. Fertility control is seen as part of a revolt against the church and the burden on women of large families. The importance given to fertility control may be seen in the recent fertility rate of Quebec, which in 1982 was the lowest in Canada and lower than that of any U.S. state (Statistics Canada, 1984b, table 5; NCHS, 1984b, table 6, p. 19). Nevertheless, attitudes are still sharply divided at both the policy and individual level. Quebec's Ministry of Education still had not approved sex education guidelines as of mid-1984 after almost 15 years of study. The distribution of public opinion about sexual matters in Quebec is roughly similar to that in other provinces. A study of university and technical school students across Canada in 1977 found that 84 percent of French-speaking (mainly Quebec) and 80 percent of English-speaking Canadians approved of premarital intercourse for females if they are in love. Nine percent of French-speaking and 19 percent of English-speaking Canadians disapproved even if the woman is engaged. A previous study that asked the same questions in 1968 revealed much more conservative attitudes, particularly among the French-speaking group (Hobart, 1980). These studies support the commonly held view that Quebec moved rapidly from being more conservative than other provinces to being similar to or slightly more liberal with regard to sexual matters.

In English-speaking Canada, the media strongly reflect the influence of the United States. The majority of the most popular programming is created in the United States. Newspapers carry some of the same advice columns as in the United States, including Dear Abby and Ann Landers. One sign of a slightly more liberal attitude was the late-night broadcasting of blue movies in Toronto a few years ago. Nevertheless, contraceptives are not advertised on television, and policies in the print media are similar to those in the United States.

French Canada, however, supports its own indigenous television and film industry, and the social changes in Quebec have evidently been reflected in the media. The abruptness of the change in the sexual behavior of teenagers in the mid-1970s attracted a great deal of media attention. Observers note that because of the visibility and seeming irreversibility of the change, everyone was faced with the reality of the need for contraceptives, which was extensively discussed in the media. One member of the Department of Sexology of the University of Quebec said he appeared on television about twice a year during this period, as did other sexologists. The attitude expressed was that contraceptive use should become an integral part of a young person's sexuality; the importance of responsibility was stressed. The use of contraception was also portrayed on soap operas. One popular series featuring a family with four adolescents regularly discussed contraception. The net effect of the media attention was to encourage acceptance (though not necessarily approval) of the change and promote a sense of the importance of responsibility in sexuality, that is, use of contraceptives. Teenagers reportedly became hypersensitive to the need for practicing contraception if they were sexually active. During the 1970s, condoms were more and more often openly displayed in drugstores rather than kept behind the counter.

National population policy in Canada appears to have had little effect on teenage pregnancy and fertility. Although some concern about limiting world population growth was voiced at the time the family planning clinic program was initiated, controlling population was never official policy. In fact, more concern has been expressed, particularly in Quebec, about fertility levels that are below replacement. One apparently pronatalist national policy is in effect, a family allowance that provides a monthly payment for each child in a family. This allowance was reportedly introduced as a device to redistribute funds to poor provinces and families rather than to encourage childbearing. Quebec, being more pronatalist than other provinces, augments the federal family allowance.

In Canada, as well as the United States, fertility appears to be substantially higher among women of low education and, presumably, low socioeconomic status than among more educated women (Statistics Canada, 1983f, table 5). (Exact comparisons with the United States are difficult because of problems with obtaining comparable measures of socioeconomic status in association with fertility data.) One possible explanation of the fertility and pregnancy differences between the countries might be a difference in the class structure. Canadian experts suggested that Canada is a more uniformly middle-class country, lacking the large low-income group that has very high teenage fertility in the United States. The available economic data, however, do not bear out this impression. In Canada, according to World Bank statistics, 3.8 percent of total household incomes goes to the poorest 20 percent of households, while in the United States the figure is 4.5 percent (Appendix 3). If these figures accurately reflect the class structure, differences in social stratification do not explain the differences in teenage pregnancy rates. It is still possible, however, that the United States has a different or more widespread culture of poverty.

One further difference between Canada and the United States is the intangible one of national character. Canadians appear to be more law-abiding and to have more respect for authority than Americans. The difference is immediately apparent to the U.S. visitor who is struck by the lack of graffiti and litter in the streets, even in a large metropolitan area such as Toronto with almost three million inhabitants. In spite of its large immigrant population of many nationalities, Toronto is considered to be one of the best planned and functioning cities in North America. The homicide rate in Canada is lower than in the United States: 2.5 per 100,000 population in 1978, compared to 9.4 in the United States (U.S. Bureau of the Census, 1982e, table 297, p. 179). The difference is reflected in the youth culture: Canadian teenagers are reported to have better relations with their teachers and there is less vandalism and violence in the schools. Teachers are said to be more respected, and education is highly valued. Canada spent 8.1 percent of its gross national product on public education in 1979, compared to 6.3 percent spent in the United States in 1977 (U.S. Bureau of the Census, 1982e, p. 863). One might hypothesize that teenagers with a positive identification with authority would follow adult norms of responsibility in sexual behavior and use of contraceptives. Conversely, where teenagers are hostile or ambivalent toward authority and where premarital intercourse is viewed as an act of rebellion, adult norms regarding contraceptive use would be ignored.

DISCUSSION

Canada's teenagers experience pregnancy and childbearing at lower rates than do U.S. teenagers. Among younger teenagers, at least some of the difference may be attributable to lower rates of sexual activity. Among those aged 18–19, however, real differences remain when sexual activity is taken into account. The large black and Hispanic populations in the United States represent high-fertility cultures that account for some of the difference, but the Canadian rates remain lower when the comparison is limited to the white U.S. population. A small part of the difference may be attributable to a higher rate of marriage and desired fertility in the United States but cannot explain the large difference in abortion rates.

The data suggest that the contraceptive behavior of Canadian teen-agers contributes to their lower pregnancy rates. One factor is greater use of the pill. In part this may be due to less ambivalent acceptance of the pill as a safe, effective method for teenagers. Older Canadian women also used the pill at a higher rate than did U.S. women in the 1970s (Henripin and Marcil-Gratton, 1981). Another factor is simply that a higher proportion of those who are sexually active use contraceptives.

A basic question is why this is so. An important aspect of the Canadian contraceptive service delivery system that is advantageous to teenagers is the national health insurance system, which makes medical contraceptive services available from physicians at no charge except for the cost of supplies. The accessibility of private physicians may be part of the explanation of the high level of pill use. In the United States, not only must most teenagers pay for a private physician visit, but in many areas most contraceptive services are provided by obstetrician/gynecologists, and teenagers must surmount the additional barriers faced when trying to obtain services from a specialist. In Canada, most contraceptive services are provided by general practitioners. The Canadian system offers younger teenagers less of an advantage because of the reluctance of many doctors to serve minors. This may account for the fact that pregnancy rates of younger teenagers are not much lower in Canada than in the United States, when the proportion sexually active is taken into account, whereas for older teenagers the pregnancy rate is considerably lower when sexual activity is considered.

The relatively low Canadian teenage pregnancy rate cannot be attributed to the family planning clinic system, which is much less extensive and serves relatively fewer patients than the system in the United States. Similarly, sex education in the schools cannot explain the difference, except perhaps in Quebec, which has a program specifically directed at pregnancy prevention. Further evidence that family planning programs and sex education do not explain the fertility differential is the fact that the difference was present in 1971, before the clinic programs reached a high level of development.

This is not to say that the programs have had no effect. Ontario and British Columbia, two of the three provinces with the most extensive clinic programs, had the highest percentage declines in teenage pregnancy between 1971 and 1981 (table 4.4). Ontario was also the province where the largest proportion of school districts had family life education programs in 1976. Quebec, the other province to develop extensive clinic services, apparently experienced an increase in pregnancy

Table 4.4. *Teenage pregnancy rates* in the United States, Canada, and provinces, 1971, 1981; and percent change 1971–81*

| | U.S. Total | Canada | | | | | | | | | |
		Total	Prince Edward Island	Nova Scotia	New Brunswick	Quebec	Ontario	Manitoba	Saskatchewan	Alberta	British Columbia
1971	84.1	51.1	50.2	64.4	57.5	22.4	63.4	62.4	57.4	70.2	78.7
1981	96.0	44.3	35.0	49.1	40.1	25.5	45.6	51.3	62.7	65.1	59.4
Percent change	+14	–14	–30	–24	–30	+14	–28	–18	+9	–7	–25

Sources: Births: Canada, see table 2.4 (C. Tietze, unpublished data); Provinces, for 1981, Statistics Canada, 1983c; Statistics Canada, *Vital Statistics*, vol. 1. Births 1971: Catalogue 84-204, and for 1971, Statistics Canada, 1983c, Catalogue 84-204, Ottawa, 1984. Abortions: Numbers for 1981, Statistics Canada, 1983a, Catalogue 82-211. Estimate for Quebec was increased by 5,500 unreported abortions (all ages) and figures for all provinces were increased by their proportional share of 4,000 abortions occurring in the United States (C. Tietze, op. cit). Numbers for 1971, Statistics Canada, *Therapeutic Abortions 1972*, Catalogue 82-211, 1973, table A-5, and increased by 3,849 abortions occurring in New York City (ibid., table A-6, p. 13) and 2,460 occurring in upstate New York (New York State Department of Health, *Report of Selected Characteristics on Induced Abortions Recorded in New York State, January–December, 1971*, Albany, 1972, table 6). Abortions were distributed to provinces according to Statistics Canada, 1972, op. cit., table A-5. It is assumed that 35 percent of abortions were obtained by women aged 15–19, based on the national figure for 1972 (Statistics Canada, 1972, op. cit., table B-1, p. 19). Population: 1981, Statistics Canada, 1983b, Catalogue 91-519; 1971, Statistics Canada, *Revised Annual Estimates of Population, by Marital Status, Age and Sex for Canada and the Provinces 1971–1976*, Catalogue 91-519, Ottawa, 1979.

Note: Births by age of mother are not available for Newfoundland.

*Births plus abortions per 1,000 women aged 15–19.

rates. However, the number of abortions in 1971 is probably underestimated, and Quebec evidently experienced a rapid rise in sexual activity rates (Hobart, 1980). The Prairie Provinces, by contrast, were below the national average in both their fertility decline and their development of sex education and family planning programs. Within Ontario, a statistical study using health districts as the unit of analysis found that adolescent pregnancy rates declined most between 1975 and 1979 in the districts with the best family planning and sex education programs (Orton and Rosenblatt, 1981).

The Quebec experience shows the potential impact of public and media attention to the issue of adolescent sexual behavior. Quebec experienced only a small increase in pregnancy rates during a period of dramatic increase in teenage sexual activity, apparently due in part to intense media coverage of the rapid change in teenage sexual patterns. This coverage was said to have made teenagers aware of the availability of contraception and the importance of taking responsibility for preventing pregnancy.

Other, less tangible factors may have contributed to effective contraceptive use by Canadian teenagers. Among these are more accepting attitudes toward sexuality, conservatism (which may include an aversion to risk taking), and respect for authority. It should be remembered that a number of other factors that could affect the pregnancy rate could not be taken into account because of the absence of data. These include the use of postcoital contraceptives, the frequency of intercourse, and the length of sexual relationships. It would be particularly helpful to know the proportions of Canadian and U.S. teenagers who have multiple partners and very short-term relationships, since contraception is likely to be practiced most effectively among couples who are in stable, long-term relationships.

5
England and Wales

Talk to the average knowledgeable Britisher about teenage pregnancy and one might think he is in the United States: increasingly bleak employment prospects among young people are driving up illegitimacy rates among teens who have nothing else to look forward to; Britain's version of the U.S. Moral Majority, the Responsible Society, is having more and more success with its attacks on sex education, provision of contraception to young teenage girls, and sexual permissiveness in the media; a socially and fiscally conservative administration is cutting back on health and social welfare programs, with some of the deepest cuts in preventive services like family planning; Catholic-dominated right-to-life groups are trying to restrict severely Britain's liberal abortion law; teenagers delay coming to family planning clinics or physicians for effective contraception because of embarrassment or fears that their parents will find out; the media titillate young people about sex, while refusing to allow advertisement of contraceptives; school sex education programs are uneven, inadequate, too late, often teach nothing specific about contraception, and school-based programs never provide contraceptives to young people.

But something must be different. The pregnancy rate of English teenagers is only 48 percent of that of comparable Americans; the abortion rate is 40 percent, the birthrate is 55 percent. In addition, teenage pregnancy rates are lower in England today than they were a decade earlier, whereas in the United States, they are higher. Yet the proportion of English teenagers who have had intercourse is about the same as that of Americans. There are two possible explanations for

93

these pregnancy differences: either the English teenagers are having sexual relations less often than the Americans, or they are better contraceptors. Although some of the people interviewed suggested that the former may be part of the answer, the data presented below clearly indicate that English teenagers who have had intercourse are far more likely than Americans to have used contraceptives at first intercourse and to be using contraceptives currently.

Although this chapter focuses on teenage pregnancy in England and Wales, some of the data presented below refer also to Great Britain (England, Wales, and Scotland) and to the United Kingdom (England, Wales, Scotland, and Northern Ireland). Because the population of England and Wales constitutes 91 percent and 88 percent of the populations of Great Britain and the United Kingdom, respectively, the conclusions would not differ had all estimates been restricted to England and Wales.

TRENDS IN REPRODUCTIVE BEHAVIOR: FERTILITY

Fertility rates in England and Wales have declined considerably among women in all age groups since the late 1960s, particularly during the early 1970s (figure 5.1). As a result, there has been a decrease in the total fertility rate (TFR) from 2.5 children per woman in the late 1960s to 1.7 children a decade later. As in the United States, a leveling off of fertility rates occurred in the late 1970s, followed by a modest increase, with the TFR hovering at about 1.8 or 1.9 children per woman in the early 1980s. The teenage birthrate, which comprises about 8 percent of the TFR, has followed a similar pattern over time: a decline of about 40 percent during the 1970s, with a leveling off at about 30 births per 1,000 women aged 15–19 since 1977.

The data presented in chapter 2 (table 2.5) indicate that the drop in fertility—about 44 percent—occurred to approximately the same extent among younger and older teenagers. Almost all of the decline had occurred by 1977. Since 1977, the fertility rate has risen and subsequently declined, so that the rates among women under age 20 in 1981 were only slightly lower than those in 1977.

Because neither census nor vital registration data in Britain include information on ethnic origin, few demographic estimates are broken down by race or ethnic group. Analyses of recent survey data indicate that about 4.5 percent of the resident population of Great Britain consists of "colored" persons, the majority of whom are of New Commonwealth and Pakistani (NCWP) origin from the Caribbean, Africa, and the Indian subcontinent (OPCS, 1982). There appear to be large fertility differences at all ages among the NCWP subgroups as well as between these women and women born in the United Kingdom. For

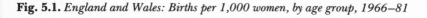

Fig. 5.1. *England and Wales: Births per 1,000 women, by age group, 1966–81*

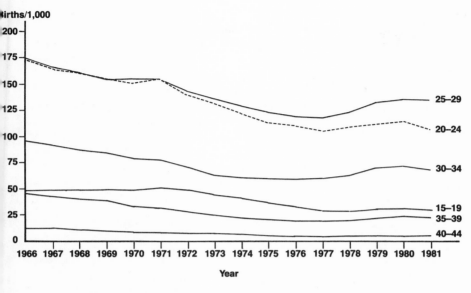

Sources: United Nations, *Demographic Yearbook,* various years; E. Lawrence, ed., *Annual Abstract of Statistics,* 1984 Edition, Central Statistics Office (London: HMSO, 1984).

example, in 1971, women born in the United Kingdom had a total fertility rate of 2.3 children per woman in contrast to 5.4 for women born in India, Pakistan, and Bangladesh, and 3.4 for women born in the West Indies (OPCS, 1978). The differences are especially large for teenagers: In 1981 in England and Wales, the birthrate for 15-19-year-old women born in the United Kingdom was 27 per 1,000 in contrast to rates of 341, 68, 107, and 64 for women born in Bangladesh, India, Pakistan, and the Caribbean, respectively (OPCS, 1984a).

Fertility differences by social class are also substantial. For example, a follow-up study of a group of women born in 1946 showed that women who had had a birth in their teens were more likely to have had parents who were manual workers and to have been less educated than women who had either had a birth in their early twenties or had not yet borne a child at the time of the survey (Kiernan, 1980). In general, the length of time between marriage and first birth is directly related to socioeconomic status (Central Statistical Office, 1984).

ABORTION

Whereas the teenage birthrate in England and Wales declined through most of the 1970s, the abortion rate rose considerably following the

Fig. 5.2. *England and Wales: Abortions per 1,000 women, by age group, 1969–81*

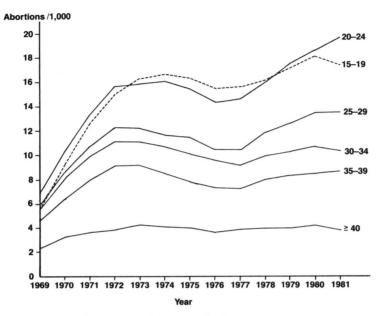

Source: Tietze, 1983, table 5, pp. 46–47.
Note: Rates for 15–19-year-olds include abortions for women under age 15.

1967 Abortion Act. As seen in table 2.5, the abortion rate increased by
39 percent for 15–19-year-olds from 1971 to 1981. Almost all of the
increase occurred before 1973 and after 1978. The most recent rate of
17 abortions per 1,000 15–19-year-olds in 1981 is about 60 percent as
high as the teenage birthrate.

The proportionate increase in the abortion rate over the past decade
for teenagers and for women in their twenties is somewhat higher than
that for older groups (figure 5.2). In addition, teenagers and women in
their early twenties have had higher abortion rates than women in all
other age groups. As discussed in a later section of this chapter, teenagers also differ from older women with respect to the length of
gestation at which abortions take place and the type of abortion procedure used.

PREGNANCY

In spite of a rising abortion rate among teenagers, the teenage pregnancy rate in England and Wales (defined here as the sum of the
birthrate and the abortion rate) declined by about 25 percent between
1972 and 1976 and has remained fairly constant since 1976 at between

Table 5.1. *England and Wales: Number of teenage nonmarital conceptions per 1,000 women, by age,* 1970–81*

Year	Nonmarital conception rate†					Abortion rate for unmarried women				
	<16	16	17	18	19	<16	16	17	18	19
1970	7.9	46.2	69.9	80.0	78.6	2.5	9.2	11.7	14.6	15.7
1971	8.7	50.7	70.9	78.8	77.6	3.2	13.2	15.7	18.6	20.2
1972	9.2	50.3	71.1	76.0	75.1	3.8	15.3	19.4	21.7	24.0
1973	9.1	49.8	67.2	72.8	68.9	4.1	16.6	19.4	22.3	23.4
1974	8.6	44.7	62.5	67.1	66.6	4.2	16.7	19.8	21.6	23.8
1975	8.2	40.9	56.9	60.7	59.8	4.3	16.4	19.0	20.1	21.9
1976	7.9	38.6	52.7	54.8	54.8	4.2	16.2	18.5	19.2	20.5
1977	7.6	38.0	52.6	56.5	54.9	4.1	16.2	18.6	19.8	19.8
1978	7.6	39.1	54.6	61.4	60.3	3.9	16.5	19.5	21.7	21.5
1979	7.6	39.3	57.2	65.3	67.0	4.2	17.3	21.4	23.6	24.9
1980	7.2	36.4	54.1	63.3	65.5	3.9	16.4	20.6	23.3	24.4
1981	7.2	36.4	51.1	58.8	60.3	4.1	16.2	20.1	22.0	22.2

Year	Out-of-wedlock live birthrate					Legitimation rate for premaritally conceived live births				
	<16	16	17	18	19	<16	16	17	18	19
1970	3.7	15.2	19.0	21.4	21.7	1.7	21.8	39.0	44.0	41.2
1971	3.8	15.3	19.3	20.6	21.1	1.6	22.2	35.8	39.6	36.2
1972	3.8	15.1	18.6	19.3	20.1	1.6	19.9	33.1	35.0	31.1
1973	3.7	14.8	18.4	19.6	19.2	1.3	18.4	29.4	30.9	26.2
1974	3.4	13.5	17.4	19.2	19.1	1.0	14.5	25.3	26.3	23.7
1975	3.1	12.8	16.9	18.0	18.1	0.8	11.7	20.9	22.7	19.7
1976	2.9	12.6	16.2	16.7	17.1	0.8	9.8	18.0	18.9	17.1
1977	2.9	12.7	17.1	18.0	18.2	0.7	9.2	16.9	18.7	17.0
1978	3.0	13.7	18.0	20.2	20.4	0.7	8.9	17.1	19.5	18.4
1979	2.9	14.0	19.4	21.7	22.5	0.5	7.9	16.4	19.9	19.6
1980	2.8	14.1	20.0	22.6	23.0	0.4	5.8	13.5	17.4	18.1
1981	2.7	14.9	19.4	22.7	23.7	0.4	5.4	11.6	14.1	14.5

Source: OPCS, 1984b.

*According to estimated age at conception.

†The nonmarital conception rate is equal to the sum of the abortion rate for unmarried women, the out-of-wedlock birthrate, and the legitimation rate for premaritally conceived births; it excludes spontaneous fetal loss.

45 and 48 pregnancies per 1,000 15–19-year-olds (table 2.5). Thus the decline in teenage birthrates has more than offset the rise in abortion rates for each age between 15 and 19. The reduction in the teenage pregnancy rate over the decade is particularly large for older teens.

Table 5.1 shows nonmarital pregnancy rates for the period 1970–1981, by ages at conception from under age 16 to age 19. For each age, the nonmarital conception rate declined over the decade, particularly between 1972 and 1976. There also appears to be a decrease in the rate during the most recent two years, primarily among older teens.

In contrast to the large increase in the abortion rate among unmarried teenagers over the decade, especially for 16- and 17-year-olds, there has been a large decrease in the rate at which conceptions occurring outside marriage have been legitimated. This rate is only about one-third to one-fourth as high in 1981 as it was in 1970.

A decline in the out-of-wedlock birthrate for teenagers between 1971 and 1977 was followed by an increase after 1977. In the 1980s, teenagers accounted for about one-third of all out-of-wedlock births. During the 1970s and early 1980s the proportion of out-of-wedlock births registered by both parents increased, suggesting a rise in cohabitation or at least an increase in shared parental responsibility. Fifty percent of teenage out-of-wedlock births in 1982 were jointly registered, a figure that is not substantially below the 59 percent of all out-of-wedlock births registered by both parents in 1982 (OPCS, 1984b).

Figure 5.3 categorizes all conceptions of 15–17 and 18–19-year-olds for the period between 1970 and 1981 according to pregnancy outcome. There is a substantial rise in the proportion of conceptions that terminate in abortion from the early 1970s to the early 1980s, particularly for 15–17-year-olds. Forty percent of pregnancies among those aged 15–17, compared to 24 percent of those among 18–19-year-olds, terminate in abortion. On the other hand, there has been a large decrease in the percentage of conceptions that occur outside marriage and are subsequently legitimated. The proportion of conceptions that occur within marriage has also decreased, while the proportion that terminate in out-of-wedlock births has increased for both age groups. Because 16 is the legal minimum age for marriage in Britain, the proportion of pregnancies that are legitimated or occur after marriage is higher for older teens: about half of conceptions for 18–19-year-olds terminate as births within marriage compared with about a quarter for 15–17-year-olds.

Comparisons of pregnancy outcomes between England and Wales and the United States indicate rather similar distributions of pregnancies ending in abortion, marital births and out-of-wedlock births. For example, in 1981, almost half of births to 15–19-year-olds occurred out of wedlock in both countries. However, the chance of an out-of-wedlock pregnancy being legitimated was considerably higher in England and Wales—36 percent of nonmaritally conceived births to 15–19-year-olds were legitimated in England and Wales in 1981 (OPCS, 1984a) compared with 27 percent in the United States (table 3.3). Three-fourths of all conceptions of teenagers in England and Wales occurred outside marriage in 1981, a fraction only slightly lower than in the United States. Although no data for England are available on the extent to which teenage pregnancies are wanted or unwanted, data on

Fig. 5.3. *England and Wales: Percentage distribution of conceptions, by type of outcome, age group at conception, and year of conception, 1970–81*

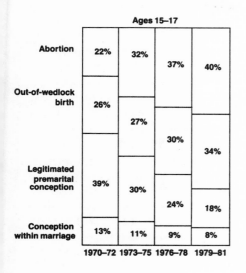
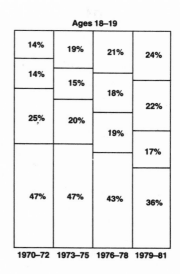

Source: OPCS, 1984b.

nonmarital conceptions suggest that the pattern is similar to that in the United States, where an estimated 84 percent of teenage pregnancies are unintended (chapter 3). Data on abortion and pregnancy are not available by race or ethnic group. However, a recent study of young teenage women seeking advice about contraception and abortion in south London (Skinner, 1984) found that West Indian (primarily Jamaican) teenagers appear to have higher abortion and pregnancy rates than other young women in that area.

PROXIMATE DETERMINANTS OF TEENAGE PREGNANCY: MARRIAGE AND COHABITATION

Relatively few teenage pregnancies occur within marriage, particularly among the young adolescents (table 5.1 and figure 5.3). Moreover, the proportion of pregnancies experienced by all teenagers within marriage and, especially, the proportion of births occurring within marriage has declined considerably over the past decade. The declining prevalence of marriage among teenagers has undoubtedly contributed to the decrease in marital births and the concomitant increase in the proportion of conceptions that terminate as out-of-wedlock births.

The percentage of teenagers who have ever been married has decreased over the decade from a high in 1971 of 10.8 percent of young women and 2.8 percent of young men to only 1.1 percent of 15–19-year-old males and 4.5 percent of 15–19-year-old females in 1981. The changes over the past decade imply more than a 50 percent reduction in first-marriage rates for teenagers.

The decline in marriage rates has not been compensated for by a substantial increase in cohabitation, as in Sweden. Although cohabitation has become more prevalent in recent years, only 4 percent of 18–19-year-old British women were cohabiting in 1979 (and 12 percent were married). This value is lower than that found in other countries of Western Europe, particularly in Scandinavia (Brown and Kiernan, 1981). For example in 1980, 16 percent of 18–19-year-old women were cohabiting in Sweden (Brown and Kiernan, 1981).

The proportion of teenagers cohabiting in Britain is slightly higher than in the United States, where 3 percent of 18–19-year-olds were reported cohabiting in 1980 (table 3.4). However, the percentage of married teenagers is considerably lower than it is in the United States. The net effect is that the proportion of teenagers married or cohabiting is much greater in the United States than in Britain.

The fact that American teenagers are more likely to be married than their English counterparts is partly responsible for the lower teenage pregnancy rate in England and Wales. However, the higher percentage of married 15–19-year-olds in the United States (8.0 percent vs. 4.5 percent in England and Wales) accounts for only about one-sixth of the difference in pregnancy rates between the two countries. Hypothetical pregnancy rates calculated under a variety of assumptions indicate that the reported teenage pregnancy rate in England and Wales of 59 conceptions per 1,000 15–19-year-olds would rise to 68 if the level of teenage marriage in England and Wales were the same as that in the United States. This rate of 68 compares to an estimated rate of 118 in the United States.[1] However, 80 percent of the difference in the conception rates can be accounted for by the fact that the nonmarital conception rate among American teenagers is twice that of English teens. In other words, if English teenagers had the same nonmarital pregnancy rates as their American counterparts, the overall teenage pregnancy rate in England and Wales would be 109, a value only 8 percent lower than that reported in the United States.

1. These pregnancy rates differ from other estimates presented in this book and this chapter because they refer to age at conception rather than age at outcome.

AGE AT FIRST INTERCOURSE

In England, Wales, and Scotland, it is a criminal offense for a man to have intercourse with a girl under age 16. The girl under age 16 who has intercourse, however, cannot be prosecuted. In spite of the legal constraints on age at intercourse, sexual activity occurs prior to age 16.

Data on sexual activity of British teenagers are available from two national surveys that took place in the mid-1970s. The first survey involved interviews with about 1,500 young men and women aged 16–19 in England and Wales during 1974–75 (Farrell, 1978). The second survey, fielded in 1976, was based on a sample of 6,589 single and ever-married women aged 16–49 in Great Britain; the sample included 860 teenagers (Dunnell, 1979).

In the mid-1970s, 11–15 percent of teenage women and 27–34 percent of teenage men had had intercourse prior to age 16 (table 5.2). This percentage increased to about 50 percent of young men and 30 percent of young women by age 17, and to about 70 and 50 percent by age 18. Fifty-seven percent of all 16–19-year-old men and 48 percent of comparable women reported that they had experienced intercourse (Farrell, 1978). Data from the 1976 survey (table 5.3) indicate a rate of sexual experience among 16–19-year-old women—44 percent—that is very similar to that estimated in the 1974–75 survey, i.e., 48 percent (Farrell, 1978; Dunnell, 1979).

A comparison of the experience of 16–17-year-old single women with that of 18–19-year-olds (table 5.3) indicates that the older teens are about twice as likely to have had sexual intercourse: 29 percent of 16–17-year-olds and 56 percent of 18–19-year-old single women had ever had intercourse. Between 60 and 70 percent of sexually experienced teens reported that they were having a sexual relationship at the time of interview. Thus 11 percent of unmarried 16–17-year-olds and 40 percent of 18–19-year-olds were exposed to the risk of pregnancy.

Although the first detailed study of sexual activity among teenagers in Britain was carried out in 1964 (Schofield, 1965), evidence from earlier fertility surveys suggests that the age at first sexual intercourse has been declining for the past 30 years or so (Bury, 1984a). A comparison of estimates from Schofield's 1964 study with those from Farrell's 1974–75 survey suggests a large increase in sexual activity over the decade. For example, among 16–19-year-olds in 1964, 23 percent of the men and 12 percent of the women had had sexual intercourse; a decade later, 57 percent of the men and 48 percent of the women had had intercourse (Schofield, 1965; Farrell, 1978).

The values shown in tables 5.2 and 5.3 agree closely with corresponding estimates of teenage sexual activity in the United States.

Table 5.2. *England and Wales: Percentage of men and women who had had sexual intercourse, by age, 1974–75*

	Men: Age at interview					Women: Age at interview				
Age at intercourse	16 (N=181)	17 (N=211)	18 (N=186)	19 (N=198)	16–19 (N=776)	16 (N=170)	17 (N=189)	18 (N=216)	19 (N=190)	16–19 (N=765)
16	27					13				
17	33	49				14	32			
18	33	51	64			15	27	49		
19	34	59	71	75		11	28	48	63	
Percent having had intercourse	33	51	68	76	57	23	41	55	71	48

Source: Adapted from Farrell, 1978, p. 23. Responses for "refusals" (to answer the question) have been distributed in the same manner as the remaining responses.

Table 5.3. *Great Britain: Percentage distribution of women, by sexual activity status and age, 1976*

| | Age at interview | | | |
| | Single women | | Single women | All women |
Sexual activity status	16–17 (N=448)	18–19 (N=332)	16–19 (N=780)	16–19 (N=860)
Ever had intercourse	29	56	40	44
Currently sexually active	(18)	(40)	(27)	—
Sexually active in past, but not currently	(11)	(16)	(13)	—
Never had intercourse	71	44	60	54
Total	100	100	100	100

Source: Adapted from Dunnell, 1979, pp. 5, 52. Responses for "refusals" (to answer the question) have been distributed in the same manner as the remaining responses.

Forty-one percent of single 16–19-year-old women in 1976 had experienced intercourse in the United States (Zelnik, 1976), in comparison with 40 percent of single 16–19-year-old women in Great Britain in the same year. Surveys in both countries indicate that half of the young women had had intercourse by age 18. Comparisons by single years of age (see chapter 9) suggest, however, that English teenagers may initiate intercourse at slightly older ages than their American peers, and have higher rates of sexual activity throughout the remaining teenage years. Because of lack of data in Great Britain, it is not possible to compare the regularity or frequency of sexual intercourse of British and American teenagers.

CONTRACEPTIVE USE

Most contraceptives are provided through family planning clinics or general practitioners (GPs). Under the National Health Service, birth control advice and most contraceptive supplies are provided free by both sources. Because the contraceptive service statistics collected by the central government are not complete with regard to the provision of contraceptive services by GPs and because these data are not tabulated separately by age group, all of the data on contraceptive use presented below are derived from sample surveys. The surveys indicate a large increase in use of contraceptives, especially of the pill, since 1970. For example, results from the 1970 and 1975 national surveys of family planning services indicate that the proportion of 16–19-year-old women who have ever used the pill increased from only 8 percent to 37 percent over the five-year period (Bone, 1978).

The most recent detailed data on contraceptive use among teenagers are provided by the 1976 Family Formation Survey (Dunnell, 1979). Estimates of ever-use and current use of contraceptive methods are shown in tables 5.4 and 5.5. The data indicate that over 90 percent of sexually experienced unmarried teenagers have practiced contraception at some time—even the 16-year-olds. About 65 percent of sexually experienced 16–19-year-olds have ever used the pill. Forty-one percent have used the condom, whereas very few have used the IUD or other methods, such as the diaphragm and spermicides.[2] The estimates in table 5.5 suggest that almost all currently sexually active women are using some method of contraception and that the pill is by far the most popular method, even among the younger adolescents. Pill use is somewhat higher and condom use somewhat lower among the older teenagers. A comparison of these estimates with those for sexually active, fecund, single women in their twenties indicates that the older women, almost all of whom are practicing contraception, are more apt to be using the pill than are the teenagers and are substantially less likely to be using the condom. Use of the diaphragm or IUD by teenagers is virtually nonexistent. There has been a recent increase in requests for the morning-after pill among teenagers in Britain, following an extensive publicity campaign in 1982 (Bury, 1984a). National estimates of contraceptive use among teenagers in Britain are not available more recently than the 1976 Family Formation Survey.

Clearly, there are large differences in methods used at different stages of teenagers' sexual lives. Although more than 90 percent of sexually experienced female British teenagers said they were currently using contraceptives (table 5.5), only 57 percent (and 53 percent of males) reported having used birth control at their first sexual encounter (table 5.6) (Farrell, 1978). The condom was the method most likely to be used at first intercourse. The data for females especially indicate a large proportion switching from the condom as the first method to the pill as the most recent method.

The estimates in table 5.7 show that 33 percent of male and 40 percent of female sexually experienced 16–19-year-olds have practiced contraception consistently. Over half of all teenagers have used a birth control method at some stage but not during all sexual encounters.

2. Data from the 1974–75 survey in England and Wales (Farrell, 1978) are consistent with those from the 1976 survey in terms of estimates of ever-use of any contraceptive method. However, the earlier study reports much higher proportions ever having used withdrawal and the condom and a lower proportion ever having used the pill. Some of these differences may be due to the fact that the Farrell study precedes the 1976 Family Formation Survey by almost two years, a period during which there was a substantial increase in pill use among teenagers. Some of the discrepancies also may be due to differences in questionnaire design, reporting and sampling errors.

Table 5.4. *Great Britain: Percentage of sexually experienced single women aged 16–19 who ever used a contraceptive method, 1976*

| | Ever used | | | | |
| | Age at interview | | | | |
Method	16 (N=48)	17 (N=70)	18 (N=96)	19 (N=77)	16–19 (N=297)
Withdrawal	21	11	22	19	18
Condom	40	47	34	45	41
Pill	50	53	71	80	65
IUD	0	0	0	1	0
Other	19	1	5	1	6
Any method*	88	91	94	95	91
No method	12	9	6	5	9

Source: Adapted from Dunnell, 1979, pp. 52 and 55.
*The percentage of women who used any method is less than the sum of method-specific use because of multiple use of methods.

Nevertheless, the consistency of use reported here is much higher than that reported in Schofield's study of British teenagers carried out in the early 1960s: of girls who had experienced sexual intercourse, only 20 percent consistently used birth control, and 61 percent never did (Schofield, 1965).

There are no estimates for Great Britain of the interval between first

Table 5.5. *Great Britain: Percentage of single women aged 16–19 currently exposed to the risk of pregnancy* who are currently using a contraceptive method, 1976*

| | Age at interview | | |
	16–17 (N=73)	18–19 (N=125)	16–19 (N=198)
Withdrawal	7	6	6
Condom	27	14	19
Pill	56	75	68
IUD	0	0	0
Other	3	1	2
Currently using†	91	92	91
Not using	9	8	9

Source: Adapted from Dunnell, 1979, pp. 53 and 55.
*Excludes teenagers not in a current sexual relationship and those who are infecund, pregnant, or trying to conceive.
†Percentage currently using a method is less than the sum of method-specific use because of multiple use of methods.

Table 5.6. *England and Wales: Percentage of sexually experienced 16–19-year-old men and women, by first method and most recent methods of contraception used, 1974–75*

Method	Men (N=433)			Women (N=357)		
	At first sexual experience	First method	Most recent method	At first sexual experience	First method	Most recent method
Condom	37	54	44	36	51	28
Withdrawal	9	27	13	10	23	10
Pill	4	6	28	8	17	53
Rhythm	2	3	2	1	2	2
Chemicals	1	1	1	1	2	1
Cap	*	*	*	*	*	*
IUD	*	*	1	*	*	*
Other	*	1	1	1	3	2
Any method	53	90	90	57	94	94

Source: Farrell, 1978, p. 28.
Note: Some used more than one method, e.g., condom with chemicals, at one time.
*<0.5 percent.

intercourse and first use of contraception. Based on a reinterview of his 1960s' sample, Schofield reports that teenagers became consistent users about five years after first intercourse (Schofield, 1973). Recent evidence from scattered clinics suggests that at least in some parts of Britain a higher proportion of teenagers are now attending clinics before first intercourse. For example, at a birth control clinic for young people in Edinburgh, 24 percent of new teenage clients in 1983 attended before they ever had intercourse, compared to 13 percent in 1973. These data also indicate that teenagers are visiting clinics at a younger age. For example, there were no patients under age 16 at the Edinburgh youth clinic in 1973, but 10 percent of teenage patients in 1980 were under 16 (Bury, 1984b).

In summary, estimates for Britain (table 5.5) and for England and Wales (table 5.6) derived from two surveys in the mid-1970s suggest that the vast majority of sexually experienced teenagers are using contraceptives; about 90 percent are using either the pill or the condom. Although these estimates imply an exceedingly high level of contraceptive use, the estimates are consistent with those from a recent survey (1982) in Scotland in which all of the single women in a "current" sexual relationship reported contraceptive use at last intercourse (Bone, 1984).

Overall these data imply more frequent use of contraceptives by British than American teenagers. Whereas 91 percent of never-married sexually experienced 16–19-year-old females in Britain in 1976

Table 5.7. *England and Wales: Percentage distribution of consistency of contraceptive use by men and women aged 16–19, 1974–75*

Use status	Men	Women
Always used	33	40
Sometimes used	57	54
Never used	10	6
Total	100	100

Source: Adapted from Farrell, 1978, pp. 31 and 27.

had ever used a birth control method (table 5.5), 75 percent of never-married sexually experienced 16–19-year-old females in the United States in 1976 had done so (Zelnik and Kantner, 1977, p. 62). Among contraceptive users, a higher proportion of teenagers had used the pill; American adolescents, particularly 18–19-year-olds, were more apt to have used the IUD and less effective methods such as douching, foams, jellies, and creams. Use of the condom was about the same in Britain and the United States.

Contraceptive use at first intercourse is considerably higher in Britain than in the United States. Whereas 57 percent of women aged 16–19 in 1974–75 had used a method at first intercourse in England and Wales (table 5.6), 39 percent of never-married 15–19-year-old women in the United States in 1976 had done so (Zelnik and Kantner, 1978, p. 136). Nevertheless, among women who did use a birth control method the first time, American teenagers were more likely to have used the pill and less likely to have used the condom than English teenagers (Zelnik and Kantner, 1977, table 9; 1980, table 7). As of the mid 1970s, the proportions of sexually experienced teenage women who always used a method are greater in England and Wales than in the United States: 30 percent in the United States (Zelnik and Kantner, 1977, table 9) and 40 percent in England and Wales (table 5.7).

CONTRACEPTIVE SERVICES

Background

Britain's first birth control clinic was set up in London in 1921, five years after the first U.S. clinic was founded in New York by Margaret Sanger. The National Birth Control Council, the predecessor of the the current Family Planning Association (FPA), was organized in 1930. In 1967, the government empowered local health authorities to provide birth control to unmarried as well as married women on social as well as health grounds and to use voluntary organizations like the FPA as their agents. It was not until 1968, however, that the FPA reversed its own policy against serving unmarried women, and it was 1970 before the association required that its clinics provide such services. Because most FPA clinics would not serve unmarried minors, the Brook Advisory Centers were established in 1964 to provide free birth control advice and supplies to young and single people.

On April 1, 1974, the National Health Service (NHS) was reorganized to make contraceptive advice and supplies available free of charge (the FPA clinics had charged a fee) to all persons, whatever their age or marital status, at all NHS family planning clinics, hospital clinics, and FPA clinics. Contraceptives are virtually the only drugs available without a prescription charge. Practically all Britons are enrolled in the NHS.

General practitioners entered the NHS family planning service in 1975 on reaching agreement with the Department of Health and Social Services (DHSS) on an item-of-service payment (in 1984 about $10 per patient per year). Whereas clinic programs and policies are largely determined by the local health authorities, the GPs are responsible directly to the national government. FPA clinics were turned over to the NHS. A home-visitor service, largely inherited from the FPA, is also provided by the NHS to reach patients who have problems coming to the clinic. The FPA continues to run 22 clinics for demonstration purposes, but its activities are now largely confined to information and education.

Clinic Services

There are several clinics in each health district. Patients have a choice of going to a clinic or to their own or another GP, 95 percent of whom provide family planning services. Forty-two percent of family planning services in 1980 were provided through clinics and the remainder by general practitioners. The number of patients served in the clinics grew by less than 3 percent between 1975 and 1982. However, the number of teenage patients grew by 19 percent over the same period; the number of 16–17-year-olds grew by 46 percent; and the number under age 16 about doubled. The DHSS recommended as early as 1974, and reiterated the policy in 1980, that "it may be helpful to make separate less formal arrangements for young people" when developing family planning services, and that "staff should be experienced in dealing with young people and their problems" (Bury, 1984a). In addition to the 19 Brook Advisory Centers—11 in London and 8 outside of London—however, there are only 80 young people's advisory centers identified among the 1,750 NHS family planning clinics. These special youth clinics vary in quality and comprehensiveness of service (Bury, 1984a).

The great majority of clinics, especially those in rural areas, have no special youth services, according to the officials interviewed for this book.

Of those programs aimed specifically at youth, the Brook Advisory Centers—which are funded by the government, fees, and private contributions—are the most important. They provide advice and practical help with contraception, abortion, pregnancy testing, VD, sexual, and emotional problems. More than 10 percent of all teen clinic patients are seen in the Brook centers.

Girls under Age 16

Although the age of consent for sexual intercourse is 16, the law provides that contraceptives must be made available without charge to persons of all ages—including those under 16. A government memorandum issued in 1974 made clear that, although it would be "prudent to seek the [under 16-year-old] patient's consent to tell the parents," it was not unlawful to prescribe contraception for her without informing her parents. In 1980, the DHSS revised its memorandum to doctors and urged that they "always seek to persuade the child to involve the parent or guardian" and that "it would be most unusual to provide advice about contraception without parental consent." In the final analysis, however, it is still up to the doctor's clinical judgment as to whether or not to prescribe contraception without telling the parents.

A widely publicized court case was brought by Victoria Gillick, the mother of five daughters under 16, seeking to prohibit doctors from prescribing contraceptives to girls under 16 without the parents' consent. The courts initially upheld the practice of leaving the question up to the physician; that decision was subsequently reversed on appeal but was appealed again by the government to the law panel of the House of Lords, Britain's highest court. The Lords reversed the ruling of the appeals court and found that girls under 16 have the legal capacity to consent for contraceptive services providing that they have "sufficient understanding and intelligence to know what they involve." They held that parental rights over a child exist for the benefit of the child, not the parent, and that a physician providing contraceptives to a girl under 16 without parental consent would not make himself or herself liable to criminal prosecution, if the doctor's treatment was based on a good-faith clinical judgment of what is best for the young patient's health. Although the British Medical Association and nearly all other professional groups opposed this proposed British variant of the U.S. "squeal rule," many doctors appear to be much more cautious than they used to be about providing contraceptive services to girls under 16 on a confidential basis; and many young teenagers are apparently reluctant to seek advice from their family doctors for fear of being turned away, getting in trouble with the law or having their parents notified.

A 1981 poll of readers of one of the country's most popular woman's magazines found that 8 in 10 parents of teenagers approve of providing contraceptives to girls under 16, but only one quarter approve of doing so without the parents' knowledge (Chester, 1981). In fact, as in the United States, most young teenagers apparently do inform their parents of their visit to a birth control clinic or are brought there by their parents (Bury, 1984a).

Younger teenagers in 1975 appeared about as likely to attend a clinic as to see a general practitioner for family planning services; older teenagers, like adult women, were somewhat more likely to go to their GP (Bone, 1978). One observer suggests that younger teenagers are more likely than those who are older to go to a clinic rather than to their family doctor "because they feel that they are more likely to get a sympathetic and confidential hearing" (Bury, 1984a).

Knowledge and Methods

Studies conducted in 1975 found that 98 percent of all teenage women and 90 percent of teenage men had heard of family planning clinics and knew what they were for, and most knew of a service nearby (Farrell, 1978, and Bone, 1978). Nearly half of sexually experienced teenage women in 1975 had gone to a GP for contraception—overwhelmingly, their family GP—and over one-fifth had been to a family planning clinic. However, more than half of those who were sexually experienced said they would prefer to go to a clinic than to a doctor—mainly because the clinics employed specialists who knew more about birth control and, secondarily, because they thought there was less likelihood that their parents would be informed than if they went to a GP.

There are no data for England and Wales as a whole on contraceptive methods obtained by teenagers, and there are no data on methods prescribed by private physicians to any of their patients. The investigators were told that GPs almost always prescribe the pill for teenagers. GPs are not allowed to offer condoms free of charge, and many send a young woman to a clinic if she wants to purchase condoms, to have a diaphragm fitted, or to have an IUD inserted. The clinicians interviewed indicated that although British doctors are less hesitant to prescribe IUDs for teenagers than are doctors in the United States because the prevalence of pelvic inflammatory disease among teenagers in Britain is only about one-fourth the rate in the United States (Mascola et al., 1983, and Adler, 1980), most teenagers request and most doctors prescribe the pill. In the Brook centers, more than 90 percent of teenage patients were given pill prescriptions in 1982 (Brook, 1983).

Several of the people interviewed said they believed British youth were more apt to continue pill use than young women in the United States, due to the fact that triphasic and biphasic pills, which give better cycle control and have fewer unpleasant side effects, have been available in Britain for several years. (Biphasics and triphasics have only fairly recently become available in the United States.) In Great Britain only pills with 50 micrograms of estrogen or less are sold, whereas in the United States higher-dose pills, with greater risk of complications, are taken by some 12 percent of women who use the pill (Ory et al., 1983).

Postcoital contraceptive pills were licensed and marketed in the United Kingdom in 1984.[3] Morning-after pills, as well as IUDs inserted within five days of unprotected intercourse, are advertised widely by the FPA, the Brook centers, and the Pregnancy Advisory Service (a charitable, nonprofit organization), and had been available from these and some other clinics for several years before licensing of a commercial product. Many physicians and family planning clinics, however, are not yet familiar with postcoital methods and do not prescribe them. The situation in England contrasts with that in the United States where doctors are reluctant to prescribe postcoital contraceptives—except in rape cases—because no product has been approved for this purpose by the Food and Drug Administration (Johnson, 1984).

Males

Few men go to birth control clinics for contraception. Even fewer go to GPs, who do not provide free condoms. Only 1.4 percent of family planning clinic patients are men; and only 0.7 percent of teenage patients are males. Despite special efforts to attract young men to its services, the Brook clinics report only 2 percent of its new patients and 1 percent of its total patients in 1982 were males (Brook, 1983). Very few men come for condoms, although the law has required that condoms be available free from clinics since 1975. It is estimated that only 7 percent of condoms used in the United Kingdom during 1981 were supplied free of charge from the NHS. A number of clinics require that men wanting condoms register as patients, have a medical consultation and obtain a written prescription, so that the clinic, as one clinic director said, will not "become a mecca for youngsters (probably on motorcy-

3. These consist of two tablets containing 50 mcg of ethinyl estradiol and 0.5 mg of norgestrel (marketed as Eugynon in the United Kingdom and Ovral in the United States) taken within 72 hours after unprotected intercourse, and another two tablets taken 12 hours later.

cles), who would come along just for a dare to prove manhood by collecting condoms." The great bulk of condoms—about 120 million annually—are purchased commercially from pharmacies, barbers, vending machines (mainly in pubs), and, most recently, supermarkets (Chambers, 1984).

ABORTION SERVICES

Since the Abortion Act of 1967 took effect in Great Britain in 1968, abortions up to point of viability (presumed to be 28 weeks' gestation) have been provided free to eligible women through the National Health Service. To qualify, two physicians must agree that continuation of the pregnancy would involve risk to the life of the pregnant woman, or injury to her physical or mental health or to that of her children greater than if the pregnancy were terminated, or that there is a substantial risk that the child would be born with severe physical or mental handicaps. The woman's "actual or reasonably foreseeable future environment" is to be taken into account when determining health risks, so that abortions may be and are performed for social reasons, although the physician's own biases may influence this determination.

A husband may not veto his wife's decision to have an abortion. Girls under age 16 generally require written consent of their parents or, if they are institutionalized, of their social worker. However, in 1984, at the time of this study, if the teenager did not want her parents informed, the doctor could perform the procedure in confidence provided that he or she was satisfied that the minor was sufficiently mature to provide informed consent and that the doctor believed the abortion was in the girl's best interests. Abortions may not be performed in doctors' private offices; they must be performed in hospitals or in registered clinics. Physicians may refuse to perform abortions. Eleven attempts have been made in Parliament to restrict the operation of the 1967 act, but none has succeeded thus far.

In 1981, 27 percent of all abortions to resident women in England and Wales were obtained by teenagers. Only 48 percent of abortions are performed without charge through the NHS (Central Statistical Office, 1984). Two-thirds of abortions obtained by girls under 16 are performed without charge through the NHS, but these make up only 46 percent of abortions for 16–19-year-olds—about the same proportion as for women in their twenties. Younger teenagers and women aged 45 and older are most likely to get a free NHS abortion. Fifty-two percent of abortions are performed in private hospitals and clinics (where the fee for a first-trimester abortion averaged something under $200 in 1984). The private sector includes both for-profit and charitable institutions.

The latter sometimes subsidize abortions for women who have difficulty paying.

Why so many women pay for abortions in the private sector rather
than obtain a free abortion from the NHS is partially answered by a study
done in Camden, a borough of London. The investigators found that
although most women would prefer to have an abortion through the
NHS, mainly because of lower cost, most went to private institutions for
"reasons which centered on the speed of referral in the non-NHS services or the delays involved in the NHS; anticipation of hostility or poor
treatment through their own or friends' experiences of NHS abortions;
or because their doctors were perceived as being against abortion."
Indeed, the study did find that delays were much longer in the NHS. In
the Camden area both NHS and private sources were readily available.
In other parts of the country this is not the case. For example, there are
30 health districts where 25 percent or fewer abortions were done
through the NHS. When NHS abortions are less available, teenagers and
poor women, for whom cost is a particularly important factor, are
especially hard hit (Clarke et al., 1983).

Teenagers are more likely than older women to delay obtaining an
abortion until later periods of gestation, as seen in table 5.8. The same
pattern of later abortions to teenagers is noted in the United States.
However, a higher proportion of abortions (91 percent) are performed
in the first trimester in the United States than in England and Wales
(Henshaw et al., 1985). It is notable that whereas the proportion obtaining early abortions has been declining in England and Wales and the
proportion obtaining abortions at 17 weeks or later has been increasing, in the United States the opposite trend has been occurring. The
major reasons believed responsible for this difference are the higher
proportion of nonresidents who come to England because they cannot
get late abortions in their own countries and the greater utilization of

Table 5.8. *England and Wales: Percentage distribution of women obtaining
abortions, by weeks of gestation since last menstrual period, 1981*

Weeks of gestation	Age				
	<16	16–19	20–29	>30	All women
<12	70	75	82	88	82
13–19	25	22	16	11	16
≥20	5	3	2	1	2
Total	100	100	100	100	100

Source: OPCS, 1983a, p. 12.

instillation procedures, which must be performed at later periods of gestation than dilation and evacuation (Tietze, 1983). However, the proportion of residents who obtain late abortions is also somewhat higher in England and Wales than in the United States.

Only 26 percent of abortions were performed on an outpatient basis in England and Wales in 1981, compared to 93 percent of all abortions performed in the United States (OPCS, 1983a; AGI, unpublished data). Outpatient abortions are allowed only if the patient is less than three months pregnant, if she lives within 2 hours of the facility where the procedure is to be performed, and if the doctor agrees to make a home visit. Data are not available as to whether teenagers are more or less likely than older women to obtain an abortion on an outpatient basis.

At present, counseling about contraception is provided for almost all women who appear for abortions, and most women leave the abortion facility planning to use an effective method. In the Camden study, for example, two-thirds of the abortion patients planned to use the pill or IUD and only 4 percent said they would use no method. But most observers agree that the counseling is often superficial and that there is seldom follow-up with abortion patients to see if they are using contraceptives effectively.

SEX AND CONTRACEPTIVE EDUCATION

Most education services in the United Kingdom are not subject to detailed central control. There have been a number of general statements from governmental agencies favoring sex and family life education, the most recent from the Department of Education and Science in 1981 stating that "moral education, health education (including sex education) and preparation for parenthood and family life are essential constituents of the school curriculum" (Health Education Council, 1983). Even more than most other subjects, the government leaves this one for the Local Education Authorities (LEAs) to work out; and the LEAs tend to leave the matter to the individual school head teacher, offering, at most, guidelines or encouragement. The law since 1982 requires schools that do offer sex education to inform parents of "the manner and context" in which such instruction is provided (Reid, 1982).

Recent data on provision of sex education are unavailable, but data from a decade ago show that at least 90 percent of 16-year-olds had received sex education in the schools (FPA, 1982b). (Most British teenagers do not continue in school past the permitted school-leaving age of 16.) However, the only subject taught in all the sex education programs is physiology; "emotional and personal relationships" is taught to 67 percent of the young people; 65 percent learn about venereal diseases;

only 55 percent are taught anything about contraception (FPA, 1982b). Farrell's study, which found a similar proportion taught about contraception, showed that only half of these got information about specific methods, and only 37 percent were taught anything about abortion (Farrell, 1978). In the United States, Zelnik and Kim (1982) found that in 1976, 73 percent of 15–19-year-old girls had had some sex education in school, and 55 percent had had some instruction about modern methods of contraception. Thus it would appear that sex education was much more prevalent in the mid-1970s in Britain than in the United States in 1976, but that the proportion getting instruction on contraception did not differ greatly.

Farrell found that the mean age at getting any kind of sex education was about 13, with reproduction first taught at about age 10, sexual intercourse at ages 11–12, and contraception at about age 14. Sonenstein and Pitman (1984) found that reproduction was first taught to American girls in 1982 at about ages 10–11; intercourse at ages 12–13; and contraception at ages 14–15. Thus, in the mid-1970s, British teenagers were getting instruction in these subjects at about the same ages as American teenagers were in 1982. It should be noted, however, that because the figures for the United States are from the 1980s and for Britain from the 1970s, and because both the quantity and quality of sex education in Britain appear to have improved since the mid-1970s, the current gap between the two countries may be greater than these figures suggest.

Certainly there was improvement in England during the preceding decade. For example, the percentage of boys who reported getting any kind of sex education increased from 47 percent in 1962 to 87 percent in 1975 (Schofield, 1965, and Farrell, 1978). Farrell notes that the percentage of teenagers who said that they had had any sex education in primary school was only 9 percent; but 16 percent of 16-year-olds, compared to 9 percent of those aged 19, said that they had received such instruction—suggesting a rapid improvement in a short period. The author adds that there had been some increase since 1972 in the percentage of adolescents who said they learned about the various sex education topics. A survey conducted for the magazine *Woman's Own* in 1981 also suggests improvement in sex education (Chester, 1981).

Although students in a sex education course may be taken on a field trip to a birth control clinic, there are no known school-related programs through which contraceptive advice and supplies are provided as there are in Sweden and as have been tried experimentally in some schools in the United States (Dryfoos, 1985). School nurses sometimes informally refer students to a local birth control clinic, but the majority of sex education programs, even those that discuss contraception, do not give addresses of the local family planning clinic. Because most teenagers leave school at 16, and those under 16 cannot legally consent to sexual intercourse, most schools are apparently reluctant to get involved in the provision of contraceptives for young people in the under-16 age group.

There has been widely publicized criticism of expanded sex education in the public schools by the Responsible Society, Britain's secular and very low-key version of the American Moral Majority. It claims that sex education has increased promiscuity, illegitimacy, and abortion among teenagers; but studies in England, as in the United States, show no relationship between sex education and sexual activity (Reid, 1982). The Responsible Society has also been carrying on a campaign to allow parents to withdraw their children from sex education classes. Various surveys show that parents are overwhelmingly in favor of sex education in the schools and that they do not want to withdraw their children from such classes; indeed, a majority believe that it should be required. More than 9 in 10 favor teaching about contraception in the public schools; 7 in 10 approve of teaching about abortion and sexuality; only about a quarter approve of teaching about sexual techniques (Farrell, 1978; FPIS, 1983b; Chester, 1981). In the United States, as in Britain, most people favor sex education, including contraceptive education, in the schools; but the proportions approving are not as high in the United States where 8 in 10 favor teaching sex education in the schools and 7 in 10 approve of teaching about contraception.

ADVERTISING AND THE MEDIA

In most ways the British media are far more open about sex than the media in the United States. Nudity, at least female nudity, is seen fairly commonly on television, especially on one of the commercially run stations, which is more open about sex than the government-operated BBC. Restrictions on television advertising are more stringent than those imposed on programming, but some television commercials for various products nevertheless feature nude and seminude subjects. However, brand-name advertising of contraceptives or pregnancy-testing services on television and radio is generally prohibited. Public service announcements about family planning in general, which do not talk about specific methods, may be broadcast. However, when the FPA produced a 30-second televison spot encouraging teenage boys to use birth control when they have sexual relations, it was rejected on the ground that it might appear to condone promiscuity. (The script was finally revised and broadcast—after 9:00 P.M. so as not to cause offense.)

Condoms and spermicides are advertised in some newspapers and magazines, but many will not carry them; ads for pregnancy testing services are strictly controlled by the government. Ads for abortion services are only rarely accepted by newspapers, and restrictions on such ads are imposed by the authorities. Posters advertising the Pregnancy Advisory Service, which provides abortion services privately on a nonprofit basis, are displayed in the underground, buses, and elsewhere (as are those for Lifeline, the antiabortion advisory group), but the wording and character of such ads is carefully controlled. (The word *abortion*, for example, may not be displayed in large letters.) Extremely provocative ads for X-rated movies are often accepted by the transportation advertising agencies, while rather innocent ones from agencies that provide abortion counseling and services are rejected (Hayman, 1977).

Features on family planning are quite common, often of high quality, and they are generally written by women journalists for women readers in the women's section of the newspaper or in women's or teen magazines (Goodchild, 1984). Stories on complications of contraceptives, particularly the pill, receive wide and often sensational publicity, as in the United States.

Regularly featured in virtually all newspapers and magazines are the so-called agony columns—actually quite extensive advice and information services—which knowledgeably tackle readers' problems about a variety of personal problems, many of them sexual in nature. Columnists regard themselves as agents for information services (like the FPA, the Brook centers, or the Health Education Council). One "Agony Auntie" interviewed (Marjorie Proops of the *Daily Mirror*) said she receives 500–1,000 letters a week from readers aged 9–97. A large proportion of her letters are from teenagers, and 90 percent of them are about sex and contraception. All the letters are answered personally and thoughtfully, with material enclosed from the various agencies that might be helpful.

Phone-in programs on local radio in which experts on sexual and relationship difficulties give frank advice to people with problems are now commonplace in Britain. Organizations like the FPA and the Brook centers often provide expert help. Sex education programs for schools, as well as general audiences, are carried as part of continuing education programs on radio and television.

There have been recent attempts through mass-media health-education campaigns to encourage sexually active teenagers to practice contraception. Because of concerns about promoting promiscuity, the wording of the messages has been made less explicit (Bury 1984a). Farrell (1978) concluded in her study that such campaigns increase teenagers' awareness of contraceptive services and, perhaps even more important, serve to make their use more acceptable. She points out that with most young people leaving school at 16, the media remain among the few channels through which to provide sex education to most teenagers.

PARENT-CHILD COMMUNICATION AND ATTITUDES ABOUT SEX AND CONTRACEPTION

Farrell's data show that more than 6 out of 10 16–19-year-olds say it is easy for them to talk to their mothers about things that are important to them. However, a much smaller proportion had ever talked to a parent about reproduction, sex, and birth control. A little under half of the young people who had talked about intercourse with a parent expressed satisfaction with the discussion.

Dunnell's 1976 survey showed that 60 percent of British women aged 16–49 approved of sex before marriage, ranging from 33 percent of women 45–49 to 70 percent of those aged 16–19. However, one-fourth of those approving expressed qualifications, such as "only if going steady" or "if marriage planned." In the United States a slightly smaller proportion of women expressed approval in a 1978 survey—54 percent (Singh, 1980, table 3). In the United States, as in Britain, approval was negatively related to age.

Farrell's 1974–75 study indicates that fewer than one-fifth of parents of teenagers definitely approve of premarital sex, while one-third clearly disapprove. The attitudes of the teenagers were quite different. Half definitely approve, and only 1 in 10 clearly disapprove. The 1981 *Women's Own* survey found that only one-tenth of women of all ages who responded thought premarital sex unacceptable; another one-tenth "reluctantly" found it acceptable; and just one-fifth thought it "perfectly" acceptable. Most approved if there was a stable or caring relationship, and most disagreed with the statement that premarital sex usually has more bad than good consequences (Chester, 1981). Despite this apparent liberalism, a little over half the women agreed that sexual permissiveness had gone too far, and three-fourths agreed that teenagers today are under too much pressure to have sex.

One interesting datum from the 1975 Farrell survey: asked about the recommended course of action for an unmarried pregnant teenage girl, two-fifths of young people, but only one-fourth of their parents thought she should have an abortion; half of young people and their parents preferred that she have an out-of-wedlock birth.

SEXUALLY TRANSMITTED DISEASES

Comparable rates of gonorrhea and hospitalized pelvic inflammatory disease (PID) are available for teenagers in England and Wales and the United States for 1977 (Adler, 1980). These show a rate of hospitalized PID of almost 100 per 100,000 for 15–19-year-old females in England

and Wales, compared to a rate of more than 400 in the United States (Mascola et al., 1983, p. 26ff). Reported gonorrhea rates in 1977 were 525 for 16–19-year-old females in England and Wales (Adler, 1980), compared to more than 1,400 per 100,000 for 15–19-year-olds in the United States (Mascola et al., 1983, p. 27ff). Although rates are undoubtedly underreported in both countries, it appears that gonorrhea and PID rates among teenagers are considerably higher in the United States than in England and Wales. PID rates could be lower in England and Wales because of higher prevalence of pill use—which protects against PID caused by gonorrhea (Ory et al., 1983, pp. 44–45). The higher reported prevalence of gonorrhea in the United States further suggests that U.S. teenagers start sex earlier than their English counterparts and that they may have more partners—both factors that have been generally found to have a negative impact on consistent and effective contraceptive use.

EDUCATION

Educational standards below the university level are established by the national government. Detailed control is exercised by local education authorities, which delegate much of the responsibility for such matters as curricula, teacher hiring, and textbook choice to the head teachers of individual schools. There are three stages of education: primary, which is compulsory and takes the child from nursery school to age 11 or 12; secondary, which is compulsory up to age 16 and is optional for another two years; and higher education.

Unlike the United States, where more than 9 in 10 young people are still in school at age 16 (Grant and Eiden, 1982), fewer than one-third of English 16-year-olds are full-time students, and only a little over half are in school even part-time (table 5.9). Girls are more likely to remain in school than boys, and boys are more likely than girls both to be employed and to be unemployed. One-third of girls and one-fourth of boys get further education after leaving school (Central Statistical Office, 1984). The difference between Britain and the United States in length of schooling is very large for all teenagers, not just 16-year-olds, although 16 is the age at which the break with school in Britain is most likely to occur. Sixty-seven percent of all 16–19-year-olds are still in school in the United States (U.S. Census Bureau, 1979b), compared to just 43 percent of British 16–19-year-olds (OPCS, 1983b).

EMPLOYMENT

Two-thirds of 16–19-year-old women and three-fourths of comparably aged men are in the labor force, compared to 7 in 10 women and 9 in 10 men aged 20–24. Being in the labor force does not necessarily mean

Table 5.9. *England and Wales: Percentage distribution of 16-year-olds in school, employed, and unemployed, 1981–82*

School/employment status	Total (N=839)	Men (N=431)	Women (N=408)
In School			
Full-time	30.5	28.8	32.3
Work-study program	16.2	12.5	20.1
Employed			
Studying part-time	7.3	10.8	3.6
No study	22.2	23.8	20.7
Unemployed			
Not in training program	14.1	14.6	13.5
Youth Opportunities Program*	9.6	9.5	9.7
Total	100	100	100

Source: Central Statistical Office, 1984, p. 46.
*A public training program for unemployed youth.

having a job. About 3 in 10 16–17-year-olds who are in the labor force are out of work, a much higher percentage than of older workers (opcs, 1983b). Virtually the same proportion of young people are unemployed in the United States, and the differential between teenage and older workers is also similar (U.S. Census Bureau, 1982e).

Although a much larger proportion of British than of American teenagers are out of school and looking for work, there are many more government assistance programs in Great Britain, including the Youth Opportunities Program, unlimited unemployment insurance, welfare, and housing assistance. Welfare programs in the United States tend to be restricted to special categories, such as unwed mothers, the old, and people with specified handicaps like blindness.

Not only is unemployment higher among younger than older workers, but the increase in unemployment since the early 1970s has been much steeper for teenage workers than others. The proportion of 16–17-year-old men in the labor force who were unemployed rose from 5 to 25 percent between 1973 and 1981; for 18–19-year-olds, it rose from 5 to 20 percent. Smaller proportional increases occurred among older workers (figure 5.4). In the United States, the increases were not so great for any age group, and the proportional differences in the increases between younger and older workers were also not so large (U.S. Census Bureau, 1982e).

SERVICES AND BENEFITS FOR TEENAGE MOTHERS

In the United Kingdom, under national health insurance, all pregnant women are entitled to prenatal care, delivery and postnatal care, and

Fig. 5.4. *Great Britain: Percentage of men aged 16–44 in the labor force who are unemployed, 1973–81*

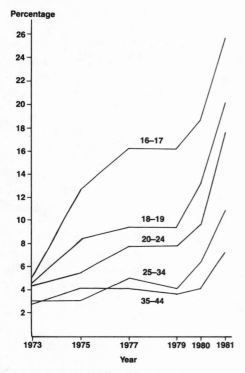

Source: OPCS, 1983b, table 4.2, p. 91.

pediatric care for their babies. In the United States, where there is no national health insurance, in general, only the very poor—those eligible for Medicaid—are entitled to federal assistance for maternity and child care.

There are no nationally mandated health services or welfare benefits for teenage mothers in the United Kingdom, but there are special benefits for single mothers. Mothers under age 16, however, are not eligible for most welfare benefits in their own right and are, therefore, largely dependent on their parents for help. Teenage mothers over age 16 are eligible to receive a wide array of services and benefits. A child benefit is paid to all families with children. Of special importance to teenage mothers is the special supplemental benefit provided for first children of single mothers.

The Supplementary Benefit, which is a means-tested program, constitutes the major support for single-mother families. One-parent families constitute just 18 percent of those who receive these benefits;

however, they cover 45 percent of single-mother families. Receipt of supplementary benefits qualifies beneficiaries for exemptions from National Health Service charges; qualifies children for school meals, free milk, and vitamins; and may exempt them from day care charges. Day care services vary widely with local borough authorities. Single mothers get preference for day care. But even in the best boroughs there is a long waiting list. Another benefit, the family income supplement, is a modest income supplement used largely by single-parent female-headed families where the mother is working part-time.

CONCLUSIONS

The pregnancy rate of British teenagers is much lower than that of their American counterparts, but it is higher than in most of the other countries described in this book. Donald Reid of the U.K. Health Education Council finds that "the main reason for the current high level of teenage pregnancies . . . lies in the paradoxical combination of increased sexual activity with lingering puritan attitudes. It is never going to be easy (nor popular with parents) to promote the idea that virgins of either sex should always carry contraceptives 'just in case'. Yet, our present understanding of teenage attitudes suggests that encouraging the 'anticipation of sexuality' is exactly what we should be doing" (Reid, 1982).

The availability of special welfare benefits for unmarried mothers in the United States does not help to explain the difference in nonmarital birthrates between the United States and England and Wales, since England and Wales also has special benefits for unwed mothers, and these are much more inclusive than those available in the United States.

Although some observers believe sexual activity levels are lower among British than U.S. teenagers, the data indicate little or no difference in the proportion of all teenagers who have ever had intercourse. Most of the differences in pregnancy rates, however, appear to be attributable to better contraceptive use by Britons. Those differences reflect less the type of contraceptives used than earlier and more prevalent use among English as compared to U.S. teenagers. The following are some of the factors that may account, at least in part, for better contraceptive use among English than among American teenagers.

1. Contraceptives are free and widely available from doctors and family planning clinics. Indeed, contraceptives are the only drugs available to all persons without a prescription charge through the NHS. Ninety-eight percent of teenagers know of a source, generally a local source, where they can get medical contraception, know that it is free,

and that it will be offered to them in confidence. Those under 16 may not be so sure that their parents will not be told against their will, but there are nearly 100 special youth clinics, and, in most of these, teenagers are assured that services are confidential.

2. Although there are constituencies that oppose contraception and sex education—as well as abortion—they are not as well organized, as well financed, or as powerful as they are in the United States.

3. Although the provision of sex education is very uneven, it appears that more British than U.S. teenagers get some instruction.

4. As in the United States, brand-name advertising of contraceptives is prohibited on television. Television programming, however, is far more frank than in America and has more sex education documentaries, which can be quite explicit. Ads in print media appear more often and in more general publications than in the United States. The Agony Aunties and consumer advice services play a more significant role in advising teenagers than do U.S. advice columnists.

5. Although there have been some widely publicized campaigns to stop or sharply restrict school sex education and provision of contraception to young teenagers, the government has attempted to oppose such initiatives, in the courts when necessary. In the United States, in contrast, it was necessary to take the government to court to prevent it from initiating restrictions on provision of contraceptives to teens.

6. In general, all governmental agencies and the people who work for them seem genuinely concerned about the problem of teenage pregnancy, accept the fact that teenagers do have sex, and, therefore, seek to help them to the extent possible to get adequate means of protection and to provide the option of free abortion if they do get pregnant.

7. The availability of free abortions, free pregnancy testing, and postcoital contraception shows that the government stands behind efforts to prevent unwanted childbearing among young people. The U.S. government has stopped paying for abortions (although some states still do), and the current administration would like to make all abortions illegal. Postcoital contraceptives are not legally available in the United States (though they are used widely in rape centers). The availability of free pregnancy testing services and postcoital contraception is one way to bring young people into clinics for contraception soon after they begin sexual activity so that they can be counseled to become continuing contraceptive users.

8. The early school-leaving age and entrance into the world of work may affect teenagers' exposure to the risk of pregnancy (through reduced leisure time and contact with peers) and their maturity about contraceptive use.

9. Nonmedical methods of contraception—especially condoms—

are not only available from birth control clinics, but are widely available in pharmacies, barbershops, vending machines, and supermarkets, and they are available by mail order through newspaper and other ads.

10. English teens may initiate coitus somewhat later and, comparative gonorrhea rates suggest, may have fewer sexual partners than their American counterparts. Both factors could help explain why contraceptive prevalence is higher among teenagers in England and Wales than in the United States, since consistent and effective contraceptive use is generally positively related to age and to the level of commitment to a sexual relationship.

Whatever the shortcomings of Great Britain when compared to other countries that have had some success in reducing teenage pregnancy, it does seem far ahead of the United States when it comes to government acceptance of teenage sexuality and determination to provide the means to prevent unwanted teenage pregnancy and unwanted teenage births.

6
France

I n France, the complex issues involving early childbearing, adolescent sexual activity, sex education, and fertility control services for young, unmarried persons appear to be almost inextricably related to a subtle ideological tug-of-war that is taking place on a much broader front. On one side are the feminists, who have successfully championed the causes of contraception and abortion and the rights of adolescents to fertility control and sex education. This movement is spearheaded by Yvette Roudy, minister of the Rights of Women, and the French Family Planning Association (Mouvement Français pour le Planning Familial) is firmly in this camp. On the other side are the more traditional proponents of the family, with a fundamentally pronatalist outlook, whose leader is Georgina Dufoix, the minister of Social Affairs and National Solidarity. Although, among the traditional group, adults are very much the center of attention, the young enter the picture both as children in their families of origin and as potential parents. Thus there is a certain institutionalized ambivalence of attitudes.

The present situation is the outcome of a long history. The transition to low fertility started toward the end of the eighteenth century in France, about 100 years earlier than in other European countries. Concern about slow population growth, both absolutely and relative to Germany and Britain, subsequently became a major preoccupation. During the depression years of the 1930s, when the birthrate was very low, pronatalist forces were especially vocal. The manufacture, importation, and sale of contraceptives remained illegal until 1967. Neither exhortation nor laws had much effect on personal behavior, however;

the average French family had between two and three children in the
first two decades after World War II, and the practice of fertility control
was almost universal. The means available were, however, generally
limited to withdrawal, rhythm, abstinence, and illegal abortion.

Thus, when contraception was legalized and modern methods were
introduced in the late 1960s and early 1970s, the change for French
women was very dramatic. In effect, control of reproduction simultaneously "came out of the closet" and became easy. The investigators
were told that the rapid spread of modern contraception was directly
connected with the fact that 60 percent of gynecologists in France are
women. Older women often expressed bitterness about their own
struggle to avoid unwanted births. They asserted with feeling that
women, including adolescents, have a right to obtain contraceptives
and abortions. They were apt to be envious of the younger generation
but also sometimes gave the opinion that young people are spoiled
today.

For all of its militancy and rhetoric, the French feminist movement
does not appear to be against men. It is mainly a practically oriented
effort to gain economic independence and reproductive freedom. It
was constantly repeated that men have recently begun to take more
interest in their children and more responsibility for contraception.
French men are said to be "macho," in that they don't like to use the
condom, but they are not necessarily in favor of large families.

It is important to keep in mind that there are large differences within
the country, particularly between Paris and the provinces. This per-
tains both to people's attitudes and to the impact of national policies.
Even more than the capital cities of most other countries, Paris is the
focus of power, prestige, and new ideas and thus is to some extent a
world apart. Although the Mitterand government has initiated some
movement toward decentralization, the administration of the country
has up to now emanated almost exclusively from Paris. For practical
reasons, the investigators' visit to France was confined to Paris and its
immediate environs; an effort was made to achieve a country-wide
perspective, but there was no way of ascertaining the extent to which
this was successful.

REPRODUCTIVE BEHAVIOR

French adolescents around 1980 had a pattern of fertility that was
intermediate among the group of six countries studied and that was
substantially lower than that of the United States. The birthrates of
women under age 18 were nearly as low as those of comparable young
women in the Netherlands and Sweden, but they rose steeply at ages 18
and 19 to levels more comparable with Canada and the United King-

dom (figure 2.1). The decline in teenage fertility that characterized the preceding decade emerged as a clear trend somewhat later in France than in the other countries (except Canada)—about 1975 for women less than 18 years old and 1974 for women aged 18–19 (figures 2.4 and 2.5).

The French birth statistics are tabulated by age achieved during the calendar year with the result that the women in each age group are on the average half a year younger than those in the same age category in the other countries where age is defined in terms of completed years. For purposes of the comparisons in chapter 2, the French data have been adjusted to match the other countries. However the more refined data presented in this chapter are taken directly from the original sources and refer to age achieved during the calendar year.

Fertility of women aged 20 and older fell by over 30 percent from 1972 to 1975, then levelled out, and recovered to some extent at the beginning of the 1980s (table 6.1). Thus the trends for teenagers were different from those for older women in both parts of the period. From 1972 to 1981 the overall decline in teenage fertility was 76 percent, and it dropped from 6 percent to 4 percent of total fertility.

Childbearing among married teenagers followed a trend similar to that for adults, declining in the early 1970s and then levelling out after 1975 (table 6.1). In contrast, the pattern for the nonmarital rate follows a very shallow U-shape. As verified below, the continuing decline in the rate for all teenagers during the late 1970s and early 1980s must then be due to a shift in the marital-status distribution of the underlying

Table 6.1. *France: Total fertility rate and number of births per 1,000 women, by marital status,* age,† and year*

Year	TFR	TFR for women ≥20	Births per 1,000 women for ages <20		
			All	Marital	Nonmarital
1972	2,429	2,282	29	485	7
1973	2,323	2,176	29	457	7
1974	2,125	1,987	28	411	7
1975	1,927	1,801	25	374	7
1976	1,837	1,722	23	366	6
1977	1,876	1,765	22	391	6
1978	1,841	1,742	20	383	6
1979	1,875	1,783	18	378	6
1980	1,967	1,877	18	388	7
1981	1,964	1,880	17	383	7

Source: Les Collections d'INSEE, 1981 (94D), table 19.

*Rates per 1,000 women of the relevant marital status.

†Age defined as that reached during the calendar year, rather than age at outcome. The rates, therefore, differ from those in table 2.6.

population; there was a decrease in the proportions that were married and had high birthrates, along with a corresponding increase in the proportions of unmarried women, who were comparatively less likely to bear children.

The proportion of marital births conceived before marriage (defined as those occurring within six months of the date of marriage) was rising up to about 1975, when it started to decline (Conseil Economique et Social, 1979, p. 829).[1] The relative importance of forced marriage precipitated by an unanticipated pregnancy, as opposed to planned marriages where the pregnancy happened to precede the wedding, is not known. The peak in the single-year marital birthrates for 1980 at ages 16 and 17 suggests that among young adolescents, at least, the former must often have been the case (table 6.2). The nonmarital birthrate, on the other hand, rises with each year of age, and the proportion of all births occurring outside of marriage declines from 81 percent at age 15 to 23 percent at age 20.

The relative importance of nonmarital births has been increasing in France in recent years. In 1975, 8 percent of all births took place outside of marriage; by 1981 the proportion was 13 percent (INED, 1983, table 4). However, the circumstances under which nonmarital births occur have also changed over time. Whereas they used to be the result primarily of accidental pregnancies outside marriage, they now often occur in stable unions and, therefore, may be more likely to be intended. The increased stability of the unions is suggested by the fact that, in 1962, only 23 percent of the fathers claimed paternity, but in 1980, 50 percent of the fathers did so (INED, 1983, p. 669).

Because of the difference in the way age is defined, it is difficult to make precise comparisons of refined measures between France and the other countries in this study. However, the 1981 French nonmarital rate of 7 births per 1,000 women less than 20 years old represents an appreciably lower level than the U.S. rate of 28 for women aged 15–19, even allowing for the fact that the French women are on the average six months younger (table 3.2). The proportion of all births occurring to French women 15–19 years old that were out of wedlock was also lower (42 percent, Collections d'INSEE 1981, table 18) than in the United States (49 percent, table 3.3), despite the age difference, which would tend to have an offsetting effect.

Reference was made in chapter 2 to the difficulty of estimating the numbers of abortions by age for France and the consequent lack of detailed information on pregnancies. There is estimated to be about one unregistered abortion in France for every two that are registered

1. The proportion of brides who were pregnant at marriage fell from 26.3 percent in 1972 to 17.2 percent in 1979 (INED, 1981, p. 736).

Table 6.2. *France: Births per 1,000 women,* by age, marital status, and percentage of births occurring outside of marriage, 1980*

| Age | Births per 1,000 | | | % of births out-of-wedlock |
	Marital	Nonmarital	Married and unmarried	
<15	0	†	†	100
15	229	1	1	81
16	309	2	4	63
17	315	6	11	51
18	240	10	24	40
19	240	19	51	31
20	223	24	77	23

Sources: Les Collections d'INSEE [D94], table 18; Les Collections d'INSEE [D90], October 1982, table 2.

*Rates per 1,000 women of the relevant marital status; age defined as that reached during the calendar year.

†<0.05.

(INED, 1983, p. 676). The overall incidence of abortion and especially the age distribution of the women involved are thus uncertain.[2] The principal reason for nonregistration appears to be that the registration regulations are not strictly enforced for private clinics. Expert opinion suggested that women under age 18 are probably overrepresented among unregistered abortions but that there is no real reason to believe the age distributions are otherwise dissimilar. All of the persons consulted by the investigators agreed that although the rules may occasionally be bent, probably there are not many abortions in France that are performed by an unauthorized person or in an unaccredited place.

There is little suggestion of overreporting of abortions at age 18 in the French data, as there is in the United States. Although the investigators were told of instances where an underage French girl would try to obtain an abortion armed with her older sister's identity card, the procedure for checking age may be secure enough in France so that misstatement of age is uncommon.

2. In addition to unregistered abortions performed in France, some abortions take place outside of the country, mainly in the United Kingdom. Based on the number of abortions performed on French residents that were reported in England and Wales for 1982, it appears that, after taking underregistration into account, these would have the effect of further increasing the abortion rate for women below age 20 by about 4 percent. The data presented in this study have been adjusted for underregistration of abortion on the premise that the age distribution of unregistered abortions is the same as that of registered abortions. They have not been adjusted for abortions taking place outside the country. Thus they can be assumed to be underestimates, especially those for women under age 18.

The proportion of registered abortions obtained by women younger than 18 was 4 percent, and by women under age 20, 13 percent. In contrast, in the United States, 28 percent of all abortions were obtained by women below 20 years of age (chapter 3). Adjustment for the difference in definition of age and for underregistration of abortions obtained by French women under age 18 would reduce the difference, but it nevertheless seems likely that the proportion of all abortions obtained by young women is lower in France than in the United States.

MARRIAGE AND COHABITATION

Since marriage implies regular sexual activity, the extent to which young people marry has an important bearing on their exposure to the risk of pregnancy. This question is well documented in the French statistics, and there is a certain amount of information also on cohabitation. Relatively little is known directly about sexual activity or about contraceptive use among young people. One recent survey asked questions concerning the initiation of sex of a representative sample of adults. A number of others conducted since the late 1970s have yielded data on sexual activity and contraceptive use for particular segments of the population, e.g., students, clinic clients, or adolescents at specified ages.

Marriages involving teenagers are not common in France, although women are more apt to marry before age 20 than are men (4.6 percent vs. 0.4 percent in 1980). In 1980, a minute percentage of women aged 16 (0.4 percent) and 17 (1.8 percent) were married, but at age 19 the proportion was 14.6 percent (Collections d'INSEE [D90] 1982). In the United States, 20 percent of women are married at age 19 (Westoff, 1984). Thus a lower likelihood of being married could be one factor contributing to the lower fertility of young French women.

The average age at marriage, which had been declining for both sexes following World War II, began to rise quite steeply around 1974 (INED, 1983, p. 686). This decrease in earlier marriages was accompanied by an increase in the proportion of young people who cohabited informally. Except for men below age 20, among whom cohabitation remained insignificant, the proportions in informal unions at all ages grew approximately threefold between 1975 and 1981 (from 0.5 percent to 1.2 percent among women aged 15–19 and from 3.0 percent to 8.2 percent among those 20–24. For men aged 20–24 the increase was from 1.9 percent to 6.5 percent). A 1978 survey found that 5.6 percent of 18–19-year-olds of both sexes were currently cohabiting; another 6.1 percent were still single but had cohabited at some time in the past; and 1.4 percent had married after having previously cohabited (Gokalp, 1981, Tables 52 and 53). This development tended to offset the decrease in exposure to the risk of pregnancy resulting from delay in marriage.

Cohabitation was beginning to become more common around this time in a number of countries, including the United States. Two percent of all U.S. women aged 15–19 were cohabiting in 1980 (table 3.4), a marginally greater proportion than reported for France in 1981. In addition, the proportion married is significantly higher in the United States; 8 percent of American 15–19-year-olds were married in 1980 compared to 5 percent of French teenagers. Thus overall exposure to the risk of pregnancy as a result of participation in a sexual union appears to be lower in France than in the United States and may account for some of the difference in the pregnancy rates between the two countries.

SEXUAL ACTIVITY

In March of 1984, the magazine *Le Nouvel Observateur* published figures on age at first intercourse based on a survey taken the previous month. The sample consisted of 1,000 persons aged 18 and older selected to represent the adult population of the country. The age group 18–24 represents persons who would have been approximately 14–20 in 1980. (It is important to keep in mind that the numbers of respondents in this age group may be as few as 100 for each sex.) Their median age at initiation can be roughly calculated as 18.1 for women and 16.8 for men.[3] About 4 percent of responding women had had intercourse before reaching age 15, 28 percent before reaching age 17, and 70 percent before reaching age 19. (Among the men, the comparable percentages are 9, 53, and 89). Recent surveys in the United States yield a nearly identical median age at initiation for women, very close to 18 years (chapter 3). The estimated median age for men, 17, is slightly younger than that for the United States (chapter 3). However, the U.S. data suggest that the curve of initiation of sexual activity is somewhat different from that in France: more U.S. teenage women appear to have had intercourse at the youngest ages than in France, but fewer by age 19.

In the French survey, a high proportion of older persons failed to answer the initiation question, but comparison of the responses for ages 18–24 with those that were obtained for ages 35–49 suggests a decline over a period of around 20 years in the median age at first

3. Nonrespondents—11 percent of women and 14 percent of men—are not included in the calculations. The actual median age for women could be lower than 18.1 since some additional women aged 18 at the time of the survey might have their first sexual experience before attaining age 19, but the maximum effect would be very small.

intercourse of about 1.5–2.0 years for each sex. The figures from this survey for the older ages accord reasonably well with comparable data for 1972 presented by Pierre Simon (Henri Leridon, personal communication, 1984). The experience of rising sexual activity among teenagers is common to all the countries in the study.

A series of three surveys of postsecondary-level students carried out in 1977, 1979, and 1982 also shows a regular rise over time in the proportion sexually active for both sexes combined, from 74 percent at the first to 81 percent at the second and 84 percent at the third survey (*L'Etudiant,* 1979 and 1982). In the report of the 1982 survey, the comment is made that the difference between men and women in the average age at initiation of sex had declined since 1977, implying that the age at inititation was dropping faster for women than for men. These samples cover students in universities and in other advanced training programs; the ages represented are approximately 18–24 and the sample includes persons of all marital statuses. Similar surveys of students in academic high schools, aged about 15–18, indicate that 41 percent were sexually active in 1978 and 44 percent in 1980. (*L'Etudiant,* 1979 and 1980).

Comments were often made to the investigators that regular sexual activity usually does not begin until some time after the initial experience. Many young people apparently have their first sexual contact during the summer vacation, when a prolonged relationship is not possible. In a survey of 15–18-year-olds conducted in 1981 for *Parents* magazine (1982), more than one-third of the sexually experienced respondents said that they had had their first intercourse during July or August. However, there is no way to assess what the quantitative implications might be in terms of coital frequency.

CONTRACEPTIVE USE

In the five student surveys, respondents who had ever had intercourse were also asked whether they "used a means of contraception regularly." The results for women are shown in table 6.3. The question was apparently asked of all respondents, whether or not they were sexually active, and it was intended to refer to their personal use of a method. In at least some of the surveys, it was asked of both sexes. Although the reported level of use among young men was low (where mentioned, less than 10 percent), the overall proportion of young women who were using a method would understate correspondingly the proportion of couples having some protection, since it is unusual for both partners to be using a method simultaneously. Taking these qualifications into account, the data on the whole suggest very extensive use of contraceptives among French students at both levels of education. (The apparent

Table 6.3. *France: Contraceptive use among female students, 1977–82*

Type of institution and year	Percentage using any method		Percentage of users				
	All students	Ever had intercourse*	Pill	IUD	Other	Total	N
Postsecondary							
1977	47	73	86	4	10	100	4,475‡
1979	58	80	86	5	10	100	2,950‡
1982†	66	—	85	5	10	100	958
Academic high school							
1978	18	72	85	2	13	100	5,110‡
1980	20	58	88	1	11	100	2,105

Sources: 1982: *L'Etudiant*, 1982; 1980: *Les Dossiers de l'Etudiant*, 1980; 1979 and 1977: *L'Etudiant*, 1979; 1978: *Les Dossiers de l'Etudiant*, 1978, pp. 19–24.
*Assuming that all those practicing contraception had had intercourse.
†The proportion of females ever having had intercourse is not given.
‡These totals also include the boys surveyed; proportions female not available.

decline in use among sexually active female students in academic high schools from 1978 to 1980 is, however, somewhat puzzling. One explanation could be a concomitant rise in the use of the condom and withdrawal.)

The distribution of methods that is shown in Table 6.3 is biased by the probable omission of male methods. Presumably male use refers mainly to the condom and withdrawal. Withdrawal is used by a much higher proportion of married couples in France than elsewhere in northwestern Europe (Berent, 1982, Table 6 and p. 17), and it is certainly "available" to teenagers. Among the methods covered, the pill is by far the most popular; it is used by about 6 out of 7 female contraceptors at both levels of education. The IUD is a little more common among older than among younger students.

The Mouvement Français pour le Planning Familial (MFPF) also conducted a survey in 1981 covering various aspects of contraceptive information and use (MFPF, 1983). The sample was composed of two parts—1,108 female clients of MFPF centers, and 2,025 women interviewed elsewhere. The latter were intended to be generally representative of the population at large, including women not currently sexually active, although it is not at all clear how well that intention was achieved. Thirty-one percent of the first group and 12 percent of the second group were 15–19 years old. The results by age are reported for the two groups together. Three-fourths of the young women said that they or their partners were currently using a method, a fraction that is undoubtedly higher than would otherwise be the case because more than half of them were clinic patients. Among users, the distribution by method shows that 80 percent were using the pill, 2 percent the IUD, 6 percent the condom or diaphragm, 11 percent withdrawal or rhythm, and 1 percent sterilization. Thus the pattern is very similar to that found in the student surveys.

It is difficult to compare these fragmentary figures with data for the United States. The 1976 and 1979 surveys of never-married U.S. women aged 15–19 indicate that about two-thirds of those who had ever had intercourse used some method the last time they had had coitus (chapter 3). In 1982, the fraction currently using a method was nearly the same for nonpregnant sexually experienced women of all marital statuses in that age group (table 3.8). This proportion is lower than that in any of the French student surveys except the most recent one at the secondary school level. About half of U.S. contraceptors were relying on the pill and only a tiny fraction on the IUD. Thus French youth appear to be more apt to practice contraception, to employ modern medical methods, and to use contraceptives more effectively than their American counterparts.

CONTRACEPTIVE AND ABORTION SERVICES

Contraception

The history of the French family planning movement is closely connected to the changing legal status of contraception in that country. Until 1967, birth control was forbidden in France. The pill began to be smuggled into France as early as 1956, but it was available only to a few selected women with the right contacts abroad. In that same year, the association Maternité Heureuse—later to become the influential Mouvement Français pour le Planning Familial—was founded. Its main activities were education and the establishment of a system whereby French women could obtain diaphragms that were mailed to them (after a fitting in France) from England through cooperative links with the British Family Planning Association.

In 1961, the MFPF opened a limited number of family planning clinics. These operated illegally but were never prosecuted; in 1967, a parliamentary commission headed by Lucien Neuwirth recommended revocation of the restrictive law of 1920 and the legalization of contraceptive import and manufacture. The proposal contained a number of regulations to control the practice of contraceptive care. Among these was the provision that family planning clinics were not actually allowed to provide contraceptive supplies. The only approved source of supplies was a pharmacy. Minors could obtain contraceptives from pharmacies only if they had a doctor's prescription and written consent from their parents or guardians.

A statute incorporating these recommendations was signed into law in December 1967 by President Charles de Gaulle and Prime Minister Georges Pompidou. However, no practical steps were taken to make contraceptive services more widely available; and unless women lived in an area of the country served by an MFPF clinic, or where private doctors were willing to prescribe a birth control method (unlikely at that time), methods were still hard to obtain. The medical profession dragged its feet in providing contraceptive services, and many pharmacists refused to stock the pill, so that even women with a legitimate prescription were not automatically assured of a regular supply.

In 1974, again at the instigation of Deputy Neuwirth, a new law was approved by parliament. The major thrust of this legislation was to revoke the clause of the 1967 law preventing family planning clinics from providing supplies on their premises. In addition, clinics were instructed to provide clients below age 18 with free and confidential birth control services. The law also provided that all government MCH centers (*centres de protection maternelle et infantile*) should offer prenuptial and postnatal family planning services, infertility and genetic counseling, general family planning services, and family education programs. For adults, the cost of any contraceptive supplies provided, as well as of any necessary lab tests or other services, was to be reimbursed through the social security system.

Throughout the entire period leading up to 1974, according to journalist Isabelle Maury, vigorous opposition to family planning came from many different sources, the most influential of which were the Catholic church, political leaders, and the mass media (Maury, 1981–82). Some of the arguments made against birth control remained couched in purely demographic terms. Other opponents feared the spread of sexual permissiveness. Among the most militant campaigners on behalf of family planning were a handful of pioneer doctors, many of them women, feminists, and left-of-center politicians. The medical profession as a whole was gradually won over to the cause of contraception largely as a way of minimizing abortion, which was also the subject of debate at this time.

Reflecting the broad divisions in French society, even after passage of the 1974 law, service availability remains uneven. In 1984, there were an estimated 750–800 family planning centers in France, 30 of them run by the MFPF. Some clinics are in hospitals, many are in MCH centers, and the remainder are operated under a variety of auspices. Two *départements* have no clinic at all, and 15 have only one. There are also about 90 official family planning information centers. These are operated mainly by the MFPF, but others are run under the auspices of the French Marriage Guidance Council, a lay organization called Couple et Famille (which is said to represent the views of liberal Catholics), and a Christian group called CLERC (Comité de Liaison des Equipes de Recherche) that favors natural family planning methods.

The most recent government initiative in the area of family planning was taken in 1981 by the newly appointed minister for women's rights and the status of women, Yvette Roudy, a member of the then newly elected Mitterand government. She launched what must surely be one of the most ambitious public education campaigns ever undertaken in peacetime. Starting on 17 November, and continuing through December of that year, the mass media, primarily television and the radio, were used to relay to the whole of France a single message: contraception and contraceptive information is the right of all citizens. Prime-time hours on television were used for spot announcements (made by the well-known French movie director Agnes Varda), and leaflets containing the addresses and telephone numbers of all the family planning outlets in each département were distributed to town halls, post offices, libraries, and other public places. Posters were exhibited on trains, subways, and buses, and billboards were displayed in major cities. This publicity campaign was mentioned often by the persons interviewed by the research team, and it was invariably described as a highly significant landmark in the development of French political involvement in and commitment to family planning.

There is no easy way to evaluate how accessible to adolescents family planning services really are. Although the centers are said to be located in places that are geographically accessible, many are apparently open for only a few hours a day or have irregular schedules that are not widely publicized. In an attempt to overcome this possible barrier to young people, the MFPF has, since 1976, introduced a program know as "Mercredis Libres" or "Mercredis Jeunes." It derives its name from the fact that French public schools are all closed on Wednesday afternoons, and the program is aimed at attracting young people into the clinics on those afternoons, without prior appointment. A series of activities are planned, and the teenager is free to participate or not. These include large and more intimate discussion groups and private counseling appointments. The MFPF has estimated that about 135,000 adolescents visited their clinics during 1980 (Chrétien, 1981). Some other sponsoring agencies have adopted the "Mercredi Libre" idea, but many have not.

The main messages disseminated through government-subsidized brochures are that minors are entitled to family planning services and associated lab tests free of cost from all clinics and that their visits will be held in the strictest confidence. From age 18 on, young people covered by the social security system can claim a 70 percent reimbursement on all contraceptive services and supplies. However, students between the ages of 18 and 20 are attached to the social security system through their parents, who would thus be aware of the services obtained. Various other government agencies produce brochures containing lists of family planning centers, announcing the "Mercredis Libres" and informing young people of their rights.[4]

Is this message getting across? The informal view of the Roudy campaign is that it served to put family planning on the map and, briefly, in the public eye. However, most observers maintain that more sustained and long-term measures are needed to continue to reach each new group of teenagers coming into their sexually active years. Two recent studies suggest that the average teenage patient load at family planning centers is disproportionately middle-class or upper-class, well educated or, at least, planning to pursue higher education (Longourdeau, 1978; and Réquillart, 1983). Furthermore, the investigators were told that many centers do not publicize their services sufficiently and that some even fail to comply with the government directive to provide free services to all people 18 and younger. There is also no way of knowing what proportion of sexually active teenagers receive contraceptive assistance from private doctors (who would have to be paid). At least one observer believes that the Roudy campaign did not reach those most in need, i.e., the poorer, less educated teenagers living outside of the large French cities.

The provision for confidentiality of services for young people is considered to be very important, although it may not always be carried out in practice. Few young women come to the centers with a parent, and most say they do not want their sexual activity known at home. As seems to be the case in the United States, the researchers were told that parents actually accept their daughters' use of contraceptives more easily than the sexual activity it implies.

The pill is the method most commonly approved for use by teenagers. A review of a number of articles appearing in professional medical magazines, and dealing with contraceptive services for young as well as older women, shows that all reject the IUD as a suitable method for adolescents.[5] Barrier methods are grudgingly acknowledged as useful in certain circumstances. Full approval is reserved for the pill, characterized as "a practical method not requiring premedita-

4. See *J'aime, je m'informe* (Jeunesse et Sports); *La Contraception , un droit fondamental* (Ministère des droits de la femme); *La Contraception— un enfant, si je veux, quand je veux* (MFPF); and *En France, 1000 centres d'information* (Droits de la femme et Ministère de la Santé).

5. See P. Arvis, G. Priou, E. Fraisse, and J.-Y. Grall, "La contraception chez l'adolescente," *La Pratique Médicale*, 7:57, 1983; M. Buhler, "La contraception féminine en 1983: pour une contraception personnalisée," *Tempo Médicale*, 126:15, 1983; D. Serfaty, "Face à la contraception," *Impact Médicin*, 1983; and "Une contraception chez la Jeune Fille," *Impact Médicin*, Oct. 9, 1982.

tion or vaginal manipulation," and as a "first-choice method" for adolescents. One article in this series states quite simply that very few private doctors have much experience with adolescent contraceptive patients because they see them so rarely.

The diaphragm is apparently sought only infrequently by young French women, and it is associated in the public mind with a minority of feminist women with strong ecological leanings (or with young Americans). In addition, few doctors apparently know how to fit the diaphragm. Although the condom may well be used at first intercourse, it is disliked by both young men and young women and, moreover, it is generally thought of primarily as a means to prevent sexually transmitted disease. In fact, the predilection for the pill is so strong, particularly among young women gynecologists in their 30s, that they express considerable impatience with any complaints on the part of the newer generation of users. The need for careful supervision of the pill was mentioned repeatedly, and pride was expressed that the quality of this service is now very high in France. One doctor said that she did not routinely do a complete physical exam at the time the pill was first prescribed but always did it within the first few months of pill use.

Both the morning-after pill and postcoital insertion of the IUD were listed among the services available in the centers visited. How well known they are, how accessible they are overall, and how often they are utilized remains in question.

Almost all of the clinic clientele is female. Whenever the question of male participation in contraceptive decision making arose, there were exclamations of annoyance and disgust. Men have no legal responsibility for the children they may father, although the investigators were told that they can claim paternity without the mother of the child ever knowing they have done so. If the mother sues for financial support, she must grant the father the right to visit the child. However, there was general agreement that this situation is changing and that young men are showing more concern than they did formerly.

Abortion

The provision of abortion services is very strictly regulated in France. The three major pieces of legislation authorizing first-trimester abortions were passed in 1975, 1979, and 1982. After each statute was written into law, a flurry of highly detailed administrative regulations was circulated to the appropriate public and private officials responsible for putting the law into practice. The 1975 law, containing the major provisions of the legislation, remains little changed. Abortion is legal on demand (*"sur la demande de la femme"*) for women in distress (*"en situation de détresse"*) on account of an unwanted pregnancy. Abortion may be performed only until the tenth week of gestation (that is, 12 weeks since the last menstrual period), and unmarried minors must obtain the consent of one parent or legal guardian.

A rather elaborate authorization procedure has been devised. A woman seeking an abortion must present herself at a doctor's office, clinic, or hospital department. The consulting doctor is required to counsel her and to provide her with an information packet (*dossier-guide*) whose contents are strictly regulated. A week of "reflection" is then required before the second medical consultation takes place. If the doctor is opposed to abortion, he is required to refer her to another source for her second consultation. During the week of reflection the woman is also required to take part in a private interview or counseling session with a social worker, midwife, or marriage guidance counselor from an accredited agency to discuss her situation and her options. No earlier than 48 hours following this interview, she must again submit a written request for an abortion. If these steps have been followed, the consulting doctor is then required to arrange for the termination of her pregnancy or to perform it. Despite these seemingly complex requirements, the procedure itself was never cited as an obstacle to the acquisition of an abortion except possibly because of the time delay involved.

At the initial consultation, the doctor is required to warn the woman that there are certain health risks associated with abortion, principally the possible compromise of further pregnancy and childbearing. The information packet must contain a full list of social services available to a woman who might decide to continue her pregnancy and an up-to-date list of agencies and facilities that will assist her if she wishes to terminate the pregnancy. The law very specifically requires that the counseling session with an accredited social work or health agency be conducted with the woman alone, who should be allowed to discuss her decision free from any outside influence. In other words, the mother, mate, husband, or any other relation of the women is not permitted to be present at that interview.

Abortions must be performed in an accredited hospital or other facility. When the abortion law was reenacted in 1979, a ministerial decree required abortion services to be established in all regional hospitals and in all general hospital centers. However, the availability of services remains very uneven, since local hospital authorities exercise a great deal of discretion in how far they will go to meet the official requirement. A ministry of health circular dated October 1982 documented the inadequacy of services in many regions (Journal Officiel de la République Française, 1983, pp. 159–66). It also presented a profile of service activity (table 6.4). Public hospital services fall into two basic categories: three-fourths are integrated into ob/gyn or surgical departments; the remainder are facilities that have been set up quite sepa-

Table 6.4. *France: Percentage distribution of abortion providers, by type of service and number of reported abortions performed, 1982*

Type of provider	Providers	Reported abortions
Public sector	48.0	65.0
Integrated*	(36.0)	(30.5)
Separate†	(12.0)	(34.5)
Private sector	52.0	35.0
Total	100.0	100.0

Sources: "Douzième rapport sur la Situation Démographique de la France," *Population,* Numéro 4–5, Juillet–Octobre 1983, p. 673; Circular DGS/2A, No. 12, October 12, 1982, from the minister of Social Affairs, Solidarity, and Health.
*The hospital abortion service is an integral part of the ob/gyn or surgery department.
†The service is a separate facility within the hospital not linked to either the ob/gyn or the surgery department.

rately from any existing service. Private-sector facilities constitute the third major type of provider. Because there are probably differentials in the nonreporting of abortions according to type of provider, the distribution of abortions performed that is shown in the table may be misleading; it suggests, however, that the separate services in public hospitals (only 12 percent of all abortion providers) are meeting a disproportionately large part of the demand (almost 35 percent of all abortions performed).

The same ministerial circular also criticized the quality of abortion services. It claimed that many hospital abortion services were not well publicized, and it required all hospitals offering the service to post information about the availability of abortion at the entrance, where all other services are announced. A number of specific suggestions were made concerning ways in which abortion services could be made more helpful.

No information is available about the quality of the services provided in the private sector. However, private facilities that perform abortions are forbidden from permitting more than 25 percent of all surgical and obstetrical procedures in any given year to be pregnancy terminations. This provision was meant to prevent the emergence of abortion "mills."

The law is also very specific in its requirement that all women undergoing abortions should receive contraceptive counseling and services. A circular from the ministry of public health, dated June 1980, establishes the mechanisms through which these contraceptive services may be provided. In the accredited public hospitals where abortions are performed, all women must receive a postabortion counseling session from a physician or midwife. The circular notes that in one-half of all such hospital centers, there already exists a family planning center operating under contract with the regional health authority. The circular suggests that if these centers are found to be inadequate in providing postabortion contraceptive services, their contract can be revoked. If no such center exists, individual or group counseling sessions must be held for all abortion patients.

At the end of 1982, the social security system assumed the responsibility for reimbursing women for 80 percent of the cost of their abortions (the same proportion that is reimbursed for all other hospital procedures). The cost in 1984 was about 1,000 French francs ($125.00). There has been criticism that, whereas in the case of most other procedures women need pay only the 20 percent of their bill that they are responsible for, in the case of abortions, they are being required initially to pay the entire cost of the abortion and then submit a request for the 80 percent reimbursement.

The restriction of abortions to 10 weeks' gestation and the requirement of parental permission clearly present obstacles to abortion for young women. The gestation requirement is apparently meticulously respected. Until 1979, enforcement of the parental permission requirement was rather flexible. Some services did not require proof of age; others permitted an adult family member other than the parent to sign a minor's consent form. In 1980, the minister of Health and Social Security, Jacques Barrot, put pressure on the hospitals to tighten up their eligibility procedures, and the regulations are now generally followed. As a result of this more stringent application of the law, family planning professionals believe, adolescents, especially the very young, could be forced to seek illegal abortion alternatives because it is precisely these young women who are least likely to be able to talk to their parents and least likely to recognize at an early date that they are pregnant. In addition, current medical procedures usually involve a stay of at least two nights in the hospital, partly because a large majority of the doctors use general anesthesia. These factors must add to the apprehension and inconvenience experienced by young clients.

The MFPF prepared a report on requests for abortions it received between June 1982 and May 1983 from women who were unable to obtain them legally (MFPF, 1983). The MFPF is in effect the court of last resort for those who fail to get approval for a legal abortion in France. Of 1,626 applicants who were French nationals, 27 percent were less than 18 years old. In addition, 274 requests came from foreigners, 7 percent of whom were under age 18. The proportion of requests made by minors had risen appreciably since 1978, due, presumably, to the stricter enforcement of regulations concerning parental consent. For 9 out of 10 of the young applicants, the immediate reason for not being able to obtain a legal abortion was having passed the limit of 10 weeks' gestation. It was noted that these young women came disproportionately from disadvantaged families.

The vast majority of women applying to MFPF for abortions *"hors de la loi"* were assisted to obtain them by being sent to England, through a collaborative agreement—with the British Pregnancy Advisory Service—that has been in existence since 1973. Although illegal in principle, the system operates openly and is very efficiently organized. Payment is sometimes a problem, but one tenth of the abortions are provided free of charge. As mentioned above, 3,825 abortions were obtained in 1982 in Britain by French residents, of whom one-third were women under age 20.

Adolescent pregnancy is not seen as a social problem in France. One reason may be that it does not happen very often, especially at the younger ages. The issue is addressed mainly in terms of individuals in need of help. The positive possibilities of motherhood are by no means excluded from consideration. It was mentioned earlier that the information packet given to every woman who applies for an abortion must include a list of all the resources available to help her should she change her mind and decide to have the baby. Catholic organizations are active in urging young women to continue their pregnancies. During the interviews, the researchers were told that awareness of the assistance for lone parents is a factor in delayed application for abortion; the allocation is 3,000 francs per month (about $375.00) until the child is three years old. The likelihood that a young woman will continue her pregnancy is in fact much higher if she comes from a poor family. Pregnant students are allowed to stay in school, although for practical and emotional reasons they rarely do so.

Until now, residential care for unmarried pregnant women who have to leave home has been provided through maternity homes (*maisons maternelles*). Once the baby is born, if residential care is still needed, the mother and child have to move to a maternity residence (*hôtel maternel*), where they can stay until the child is three years old. In order to avoid the added burden of shifting from one place to another and the abandonment of babies, which this system apparently encouraged, the two types of institution are being combined in maternal centers (*centres maternels*). Altogether there are about 100 institutions providing this type of service in France, with room for approximately 2,700 women. Increasingly, the clientele in these institutions come from very difficult home situations. The emphasis in these centers is on the teaching of basic skills for daily life and the development of a sense of family. The researchers were given the impression that instruction about contraception is not high on the list of priorities.

Under Simone Veil, Mme. Roudy's predecessor, an interagency

council was established with the responsibility of overseeing and advising on activities in the area of sexual information, birth control, and family education. The council is financed by several ministries including Health, Family Affairs, and the Rights of Women. In 1982–83 they conducted a working group on sexuality, maternity, and adolescence. The report of this working group stresses the predicament of adolescence, the quest for emotional fulfillment, and the role of sex in the larger context of personal relationships (CSISRNEF, 1983). Contraception and abortion are considered acceptable and necessary, but a narrow focus on birth prevention is thought to evade the main point, which is the underlying need for closeness and love. Forming a family addresses this need and is also a means of self-expression. It is recognized that the young people who opt for childbearing are likely to be those who have few opportunities of other kinds, and they need a great deal of help along the way. A strong plea is made that both the individuals involved and society at large could gain a great deal from the creation of a supportive environment.

SEX EDUCATION

Since 1973, the intention to provide sex education to all adolescents in France has been clearly inscribed public policy (Circulaire Fontanet, ref. in Maury, 1981–82, p. 13). This resolve was strengthened in 1981 at the time of Mme. Roudy's drive to promote public awareness of family planning and contraception, when sex education was designated to include not only the physiology of reproduction, but also fertility regulation and "the means to make the choices of attitudes and convictions that are necessarily a part of an aware social life" (Savary, 1981). Even in 1984, however, the reality was apparently very far from reaching this goal. Five to 10 years earlier, much less was being done. Other sources of information, including parents, medical and family planning services, and the media, have helped in varying degrees to fill the gap, but the coverage, nevertheless, appears far from adequate.

The educational system in France is highly centralized, and the curriculum is set by the Ministry of Education. Local authorities, however, have considerable latitude about how the prescribed curriculum is implemented and about the training and hiring of teachers. If not themselves opposed to the concept of sex education, they are apparently often intimidated by the fear of parental reactions. Sex education used to be viewed as an incitement to sex, and this attitude is still prevalent in some circles. All schools are now coeducational, although this was not the case as recently as the late 1970s.

Sex education was formerly limited to the explanation of human reproduction in natural science courses for students aged about 13.

Reproduction is now part of the curriculum for the fifth class (age 12), and contraception is discussed in the third class (age 14). However, students who go into the nonacademic educational stream may not have this exposure. The new policy is to discuss sexuality in any course, whenever and wherever the subject comes up; but considering how often the comment was made that neither teachers, nor students, nor parents are at ease with the topic, it seems unlikely that this policy will take hold very soon. As in the other countries studied, there has up to now been almost nothing about sexuality in the teachers' training program.

More than one of the experts visited mentioned that when sex was discussed at all, the presentation was too theoretical. At the same time, the opinion was repeatedly expressed that young people are not interested in facts but are preoccupied rather with love and relationships. It was difficult to evaluate the extent to which this represented a convenient rationale for avoiding the central issues, but, significantly, the researchers were told that the powerful national union of family associations (UNAF) favors education (affective aspects), while it opposes information (facts).

In their reply to the country survey that was conducted as a part of the 37–country study (chapter 1), the MFPF estimated that between two-thirds and nine-tenths of French women are now taught about contraceptive methods in school before they reach age 18, although there are no statistical data to confirm this fact. Recent U.S. surveys indicate that somewhere over half of American female students have had a sex education course in school that includes information on modern contraceptives (see chapter 3).

Apart from the regular teaching program, sex education can be sponsored by the schools in a number of ways. Outside organizations may be invited to make presentations in class or after school. One group active in this area is Couple et Famille, a national network of voluntary associations providing sex education and counseling at the community level; it has prepared some good materials to accompany its presentations. Another is the French Students Union (MNEF), which provides supplementary health insurance for students and has an active health program. The school nurse may be a source of information and may refer students to a family planning center. Every school has a social worker who is available for counseling and who supervises special activities. Concern about drug abuse has led the Ministry of Education to promote the establishment of health clubs, in or outside the schools, where young people can discuss and receive counseling in all kinds of problems, including those related to sex. In general, there has been more stress recently on sex education as a part of overall health education.

The feeling is very strong that the primary responsibility for sex education rests with the parents. Although the schools are justified in taking on sex education in view of the occurrence of pregnancy among the students, there is regret that yet another of the parents' duties has passed outside the family. Even if the parents of today are incapable of doing the job, people hope that the new generation, whose attitudes are more relaxed, may do better in their turn.

The family planning service network itself has played a significant role in helping to educate young people, more or less as a by-product of its medical function. The fact that a majority of gynecologists are women not only means that the news about modern contraception and abortion spread quickly in the adult population, but also that a young woman can probably find a sympathetic source of information in the medical profession more easily than might otherwise be the case. The Mercredis-Jeunes sessions run by MFPF, MNEF, and other agencies are attended by many adolescents who come simply to talk and learn, rather than for a medical consultation.

The family planning publicity campaign conducted by Mme. Roudy in 1981 made extensive use of television and radio. Apart from this, there has been very little on these media to provide the public with information on sex and contraception until very recently. Certain women's magazines have carried responsible and informative articles. The research team was told by a writer for *Marie-Claire* that the articles the magazine has published on contraception have been more popular then those on any other topic. However, *Prima,* the women's magazine with the widest circulation, is conservative and has not thus far carried anything on contraception. Much of what has appeared in the popular press has been more sensational than objective reporting; an article in *Elle* attempted to exploit the notion that women were abandoning the pill, although doctors responded with denials of this. Magazines for youth have generally been very slow to take up contraception. An exception is *OK*, a splashy, popular teenagers' magazine that has for several years carried a question-and-answer column on sexuality between its readers and Dr. David Elia, a leader of the family planning movement. As in the United States, sex is romanticized in the media, and the presentation of male and female roles is highly stereotyped (CSISRNEF, 1983, p. 25). Direct advertisement of any type of contraceptive is forbidden, as is that of any pharmaceutical product.

Some of the surveys cited earlier in the discussion of contraceptive use also included questions on contraceptive information. Only half of the postsecondary students surveyed in 1982 thought they had been well informed about contraceptive methods. The source mentioned most commonly was books and magazines (34 percent) followed by parents (16 percent), a friend (14 percent), a doctor (13 percent), and a teacher (11 percent) (*L'Etudiant,* 1982). The MFPF sample was asked about both their actual source of contraceptive information and the source they would have preferred. Among women younger than 20 years old, friends were at the top of the actual list, while parents were by far the most desired source; school came second in both rankings (MFPF, 1983, p. 12).

THE TRANSITION TO ADULT ROLES

As in other developed societies, the period of time required for French youth to shift from the dependent status of childhood to that of social and economic independence has lengthened in recent years. School attendance has been prolonged, and difficult economic conditions have made it harder and harder to find and keep regular work. Thus young people now tend to move between periods of employment, periods of further training, and periods of unemployment (Gokalp, 1982, p. 201). For most men this stage includes fulfillment of their military service obligations as well. As discussed above, marriage has been declining and cohabitation has been increasing. Each of these behaviors in turn influences the decision to leave the parental home and establish an independent residence. Whereas, formerly, the majority of young people had finished school, found a job, or entered an apprenticeship, and become at least partly financially independent by age 18 (Gokalp, 1982, p. 201), the transitional period now often extends into the mid-20s.

In 1959, the school-leaving age was raised from 14 to 16 years (effective for those born after 1953). In addition, there has been a pronounced tendency for more young people to stay in school beyond this age. The long-term trend toward extended schooling accelerated rapidly in the late 1970s, probably a consequence of the economic recession (Gokalp, 1982, p. 201). As shown in table 6.5, by 1981, 75 percent of men aged 17, and 40 percent of those aged 19, were in school; for females the proportions were appreciably higher—84 percent at age 17, and 48 percent at age 19. These proportions seem to be roughly comparable to those found in the United States, although fewer French students continue their education beyond the secondary level (chapter 3).

Most of those who were not in school had joined the labor force. By age 19, almost half of all men were in the labor force. At ages 18 and below women were less likely than men to seek work, but by age 19 nearly as many women as men were in the labor force (table 6.5). Substantial proportions of young people were unemployed, however. Women appear to fare considerably worse than men: 28 percent of women aged 18–24 in the labor force were unemployed compared to 15 percent of men. The difficulty of getting a first job increased dramat-

Table 6.5. *France: Percentage distribution of men and women, by employment and school attendance, according to sex and age, 1981*

Sex and age	In labor force			In school	Other not in labor force†	Total
	Employed	Unemployed	Total			
Men						
15–17	6.8	2.5	9.3	89.6	1.1	100.0
15			0.6	99.0	0.4	100.0
16			3.8	95.5	0.7	100.0
17			23.2	74.7	2.1	100.0
18–24	52.5	9.1	61.6	27.4	10.9	100.0
18			39.3	58.2	2.5	100.0
19			47.4	40.3	12.2	100.0
20–24			68.8	18.8	12.4	100.0
Women						
15–17	1.6	3.6	5.2	93.3	1.5	100.0
15			0.1	99.2	0.7	100.0
16			1.7	97.1	1.1	100.0
17			13.0	84.3	2.6	100.0
18–24	41.8	16.2	58.0	29.0	13.0	100.0
18			25.7	70.2	4.1	100.0
19			44.4	48.0	7.6	100.0
20–24			66.9	17.4	15.7	100.0

Source: Employment Survey of March, 1981, Collections d'INSEE [D87], tables PT01 and DEM02.

*Age defined as that reached during the calendar year.
†Excluding people in the armed forces.

ically during the 1970s. The proportion of young people who still did not have work nine months after leaving school tripled from 11 percent in 1973 to 33 percent in 1979, and those with the least education were most affected (Gokalp, 1982, p. 202). Labor force participation among teenagers appears to be considerably more widespread in the United States, though much of it is probably part-time (chapter 3). Fewer U.S. women in the labor force are reported to be unemployed, however, while the proportions are roughly similar in the two countries for men. Military service removes substantial proportions of young French men from both school and the labor market starting at age 19 and continuing into the early 20s. The proportions of women not in school and not in the labor force starts to climb around age 20 when marriage and family responsibilities begin to intervene.

A 1978 survey of persons aged 18–25 showed that the median age for leaving home and establishing an independent residence is about 20 years for women and about 22 years for men (Gokalp, 1982, p. 204). Thus the pattern seems to be quite similar to that in the United States (chapter 3). The reasons most commonly given by both sexes in France for leaving the parental household are to live closer to work or studies

(30 percent) or marriage (31 percent); cohabitation accounts for an additional 10 percent; and a simple desire for independence is cited by 18 percent. For obvious reasons, unemployment is likely to keep young people at home and dependent upon their families, although this is less true of women than men because, for the former, the alternative is more apt to be a couple relationship, which can also provide some support.

In the course of the investigators' visit to France, it became evident that the attitudes of young people reflect the uncertainty of prevailing conditions. There is pessimism about the prospects of getting work. One response is an increasing focus on education as a means of obtaining employment. Another is to retreat into talk of happiness, which makes communication with adults difficult. In the 1980 survey of secondary school students and the 1979 survey of postsecondary students, a general feeling of malaise was documented; two out of three respondents felt that the human race was going through a period of regression rather than progress (*L'Etudiant,* 1979 and 1980).

POPULATION SUBGROUPS

The population of France is diverse in several respects. There are sizable differences in socioeconomic status. And there is a fairly large immigrant population; many immigrants come from non-European cultures. These characteristics are not independent of one another.

Reference has already been made at a number of points to the contrast between one part of the country and another. In rural areas, people are apt to be more conservative, and health and social services are often less available. New ideas tend to emanate from Paris, which is the nerve center of virtually all organizations. Perhaps most significant for the purposes of this study is the more than threefold variation among the 95 départements in the incidence of registered abortions (by place of residence) (INED, 1983, pp. 674–75). In general, abortion rates are low in the northern and western parts of the country, due presumably to inadequate services.

The problems associated with low socioeconomic status were brought up repeatedly during the interviews. Certainly France does not seem to have progressed as far in the direction of achieving an egalitarian society as the Netherlands and Sweden, although it would appear to be well ahead of the United States.[6] Informed observers

6. One indicator of socioeconomic disparities is the proportion of total household income going to the lowest 20 percent of households, a variable used in the 37–country study (chapter 1); calculated for a year in the late 1970s, this is 8.1 for the Netherlands, 7.3 for the United Kingdom, 7.1 for Sweden, 5.3 for France, 4.5 for the United States, and 3.8 for Canada.

believe that young people growing up in poor families start sexual relations earlier and use of contraceptives later than others. It is also believed that upper-class families are the only ones who talk to their children openly and easily about sex. A 1980 study of young MFPF clients tends to bear out these assertions (Réquillart, 1983). It certainly seems clear that the young women who carry their pregnancies to term come largely from underprivileged backgrounds.

In 1976, about 7 percent of the resident population of metropolitan France consisted of foreigners (INED, 1982, p. 773). Foreigners accounted for 11 percent of births in that year, and the proportion crept up to 12 percent by 1981 (INED, 1983, p. 668). These figures underestimate the presence of the foreign-born in the country, however, since many foreigners have acquired French nationality over the years (approximately 30,000 per year from 1975 to 1981 (INED, 1983, p. 681). The dominant nationalities among the foreign population are, in order of numbers, Portuguese, Algerian, Spanish, Italian, Moroccan, and Tunisian. A small but racially and culturally very distinctive group comes from the Caribbean. By and large these people merge into the lower levels of urban society. Young people growing up in immigrant families often have to leave school and cannot get work. Although many come from areas where there is a very strong family tradition, their children may experience acute cultural conflict during adolescence.

SUMMARY AND CONCLUSIONS

It is not particularly clear why there should be less adolescent pregnancy in France than in the United States. Is it even true that the pregnancy rates are lower for French teenagers?

There is no reason to doubt the birth statistics for either country, and the birthrates can be assumed to be essentially accurate as given. When it comes to abortion, however, the French statistics are open to serious question. Both the total number and the age distribution of unregistered abortions are hardly more than guesstimates. It is virtually certain that the abortion rates as calculated for women less than 20 years old in 1980 are too low. But they would have to be enormously higher to result in pregnancy rates equal to those in the United States: for instance, the rate of 18 for age 17 would have to be quadrupled and the rate of 31 for age 19 would have to be nearly tripled. There does not seem to be any indication that underestimation of this order has occurred.

There is no such thing as an easy and confidential abortion for a young woman in France. Most abortions involve staying in the hospital, and women under age 18 must have parental permission. Also, during the period to which these data apply, abortion was not reimbursed under health insurance. These inhibiting conditions make it unlikely that a very large proportion of abortions is unaccounted for, and altogether the difference between France and the United States in the incidence of adolescent pregnancy must be accepted as largely a real one.

It should, then, be possible to explain this difference in terms of the proximate determinants of pregnancy. Either there must be less sexual activity among French teenagers, or they must be making better use of contraception. However, largely due to the absence of a solid basis for comparison, the conclusions that emerge remain rather uncertain.

Based on a single French survey with a small sample, the median age at the initiation of sex seems to be very much the same in the two countries; the proportions sexually experienced are relatively low at the younger ages in France, but then rise more steeply than in the United States. This pattern fits with the greater differential in the pregnancy rates observed at the younger ages. No evidence was found bearing on the frequency of sexual contact in France once the first experience has occurred, except for that implied in the data on marriage and cohabitation. Fewer French women than U.S. women marry before they reach age 20, and it appears that cohabitation at early ages may also be less prevalent. Thus on the basis of exposure through participation in a sexual union, lower pregnancy rates would indeed be expected in France, and, in particular, fewer intended pregnancies would be expected than in the United States. But since marriage is also a way of legitimating an unintended pregnancy, its role is at best ambiguous.

The statistical evidence is weakest on the crucial issue of contraceptive use. The data from several French surveys of special groups are nevertheless reasonably consistent with one another. They do suggest that the practice of contraception is better among French than among U.S. teenagers. The overall level of contraceptive use appears to be somewhat higher and there is more reliance on the most effective methods. Partly due to the logic of the situation and partly due to absence of statistics making any sort of case to the contrary, it is tempting to conclude that this is a significant part of the explanation for the difference in the pregnancy rates.

Looking beyond the proximate determinants of pregnancy at institutional arrangements, the supply side of the contraceptive picture can be considered. Signs of effective contraceptive practice could be expected to be backed up with evidence of ready access to contraception. In France as in the United States, however, the delivery of services has fallen well short of the ideal, certainly in the period before 1980. To be sure, free and confidential services for teenagers are mandated by law, and there are now outlets fairly well spread throughout the country. Some of them clearly do a superb job, but only a small fraction have made a special effort to meet the needs of teenagers. The family planning centers are supposed to report regularly on their activity for evaluation purposes, but this system is not yet functioning properly. In line with the survey results mentioned above, the doctors say that most young clients do take the pill; and the follow-up of pill patients is apparently very thorough. Information about where and how to find services is widely available, although it is not distributed to adolescents in any systematic way. The role of private doctors is completely unknown. The response to requests for contraceptive advice from unmarried teenagers probably would be very mixed, ranging from condemnation and refusal on the part of more than a few physicians to truly sympathetic treatment.

Similarly, in neither country around 1980 was the exposure of the teenaged population to sex education during their school careers even close to universal. Considerable progress has nevertheless been made since then in both countries. Although France has had all along the advantage of a national policy clearly stating the need for sex education in the school curriculum, the effect of this support must inevitably have been undermined by the tolerance of very widespread failure to respond. In both France and the United States, there is a strong current of feeling that sex education should be handled at home, even though in reality such education typically does not take place.

In terms of the wider social setting, France has some advantages over the United States. It is a smaller country with a highly centralized administration and network of communication. Although the population contains certain sizable minorities that are ethnically very distinct, it does not have the racial problems of the United States. The differences between rich and poor are greater than in some other European countries, but there is no underclass in the sense that it exists in the United States. All of these factors probably influence adolescent reproductive behavior indirectly through such mechanisms as attitudes toward authority, willingness to conform, and sense of belonging.

Young people in France face real difficulties in making the transition from childhood to adulthood. Employment opportunities are few and job security is very uncertain. Many stay in school hoping to be able to start from a better position, but this prolongs the years of financial dependence. Whatever their feelings of frustration or alienation, however, few seem tempted to express themselves by having children.

The French situation is particularly interesting in view of the ambiguous social message that is conveyed concerning childbearing. Young women are evidently tuned in, by and large, to the wave length that tells them about their rights to contraception and abortion. There is also some awareness that they will not be left entirely to their own devices should they intentionally or unintentionally have a child. But more general arguments favoring family life and parenthood apparently do not make much of an impression, at least as applied to this stage in their careers. Young people get an ambiguous message in the United States as well, and this is sometimes cited as one of the underlying reasons for high rates of pregnancy. Perhaps the essential difference is that in France the alternative to birth control that is presented is less likely to be that sex is bad and more likely to focus on the virtues of procreation.

7

The Netherlands

SOCIAL BACKGROUND

D uring the past 20 years, there has been an enormous change in the Netherlands with respect to attitudes and behavior concerning reproduction, birth control, and sexuality. Fertility has declined sharply, modern methods of contraception have been widely accepted, and, at the same time, Dutch society has become exceptionally open about matters related to sex. Yet traditional ways persist in certain closely associated aspects of life. The attention of women remains largely focused on the domestic scene, and relatively few go out of the home to work.

Following World War II, the Netherlands had the highest fertility of any country in Northern and Western Europe except for Ireland. The completed family size of Dutch women born in the early part of the twentieth century averaged almost three children, when it was closer to two in most other countries of the region. The birthrate began to fall rapidly in 1965; by 1980, fertility was well below the number required for generational replacement.

Although less efficient methods of contraception had been in common use for some time, the practice of family planning was publicly legitimated only with the advent of the modern methods. Family doctors, who provide the front line of medical care in the Netherlands, accepted the responsibility for prescribing the pill in 1964, and since 1971 its prescription and purchase have been covered by public health insurance. Use of the pill rose dramatically in the 1960s and early 1970s to a level higher than that of any other country. The IUD was introduced in this period also. Since the 1970s, contraceptive sterilization has become very popular among women who wish to terminate childbearing. The condom also continues to be widely used. As one of the people who was interviewed remarked, the use of contraception has become "as ingrained as not going through a red light."

In countries where voluntary control of childbearing has led to the possibility of population stability, or even a decline, public concern is often expressed about the low level of fertility. In the Netherlands, however, the government views progression toward a stationary population with equanimity. The principal demographic problems are seen as population density and the changing age distribution.

One factor in the very rapid spread of modern contraception appears to be the role of the media. In 1972, a television program that had been prepared to educate doctors on contraception was seen by the general public as well. Popular information programs began to appear. Books explaining the various methods of contraception were widely distributed. Mass circulation magazines took up the topic, although, as in other countries, sensational topics, such as scares about the pill, have sometimes been exploited at the expense of more objective reporting.

With this development came a remarkable increase in the presentation of materials related to the general topic of sex. A 1977 Television series entitled *"Open en Bloot"* (roughly translated as "Naked and Frank") made an extraordinary impact on the public consciousness. Even though large parts of Dutch society remained traditional in outlook, the system of allocating air time to groups representing different points of view made it possible for a program of this sort to be shown and to be seen by anyone. Discussion of sex on television and radio and in the popular press has become commonplace. Such discussions range from the biological facts to the emotional side of sexual relationships, homosexuality, and sexual problems. Young people have been exposed to these influences along with their elders. One might say the entire society has concurrently experienced a course in sex education.

The Dutch perceive their society as composed of a number of divisions based essentially on religious affiliation. Formerly most education, social life, and political activity took place within the confines of these groups, which are referred to as "pillars." The changes that have occurred over the last 20 years have been accompanied by a rapid process of secularization. In a recent survey, as many as 44 percent of all persons aged 15 and older reported that they had no religion. At the same time there has been considerable liberalization of opinion within the major religious groups. Trends in attitudes concerning sex were monitored in comparable surveys of adults aged 21–64 taken in 1968 and 1981. Over half disagreed with the statement "Sex is natural—even outside marriage" in 1968, but only 24 percent disagreed in 1981 (*Sex in Nederland,* 1983, table 4.8). Among Calvinists, the most conservative group, the percentage dropped from 71 percent to 45 percent. The percentages for Dutch Catholics are 63 percent and 27 percent.

Thus many sexual taboos have been broken down. Sexual expression has come to be regarded as not only a good thing, but something to which every member of a society is entitled. Contraception, which used to be thought of in terms of family planning, is now associated also with sexual liberation. Because of a very deep-seated respect for individuals, there is tolerance of the personal life of others and freedom of choice within broadly prescribed limits. In this context, the investigators were told that, on the whole, parents accept the sexual activity of their teenage children, without encouraging it.

It is possible that this transition has come about so rapidly that women's occupational aspirations have not had time to catch up. Although many more married women are taking paid jobs outside the home in recent years than they used to, female labor participation rates are low compared to other countries, and much of their work is part-time. In the course of the country visit, reference was repeatedly made to the continued dominance of the model of the woman in her home. Family life is very active, and women do not seem to feel the need for economic independence. Nevertheless, there was general agreement that the winds of change are in the air. The Dutch tradition of democracy has meant that women have been very free since the seventeenth century, and women's organizations have been active since the late 1960s.

The economy of the Netherlands has experienced a serious recession during this last decade. Unemployment is typically mentioned as the most serious problem facing the nation. There is also a very strong feeling, reinforced by tax policy, that a family should be able to get along on the earnings of one worker, which cannot fail to constitute a deterrent to the employment of married women. At the same time, the level of welfare support is high, and assistance is available to provide a decent standard of living for virtually everyone. Hence, few women find it necessary to take unfulfilling jobs for reasons of direct need.

In sum, Dutch society seems to contain many contradictions without open conflict. Its pragmatic and nonconfrontational way of resolving problems has allowed a striking and fundamental departure in the area of sex and reproductive behavior to occur with a minimum of fuss. Individual rights and a family orientation are maintained in a political climate that is on the whole very liberal. An appreciation of the setting provides a start toward understanding the unique position of the Netherlands with respect to adolescent pregnancy.

ADOLESCENT PREGNANCY

The comparative data presented in chapter 2 demonstrate clearly that the Netherlands is characterized by a far lower level of adolescent pregnancy than any of the other countries in this study. Sweden has the next-to-lowest rates, but in 1980, among women aged 15–19, the relative difference between the Netherlands and Sweden was just as great as that between Sweden and the United States. (The absolute difference between the Netherlands and Sweden was, however, much smaller than that between Sweden and the United States.) Moreover, the abortion rate was very much lower in the Netherlands than in Sweden (36 percent compared to 58 percent). Thus it is hardly surprising that the mention of teenage pregnancy in the Netherlands does not elicit many expressions of alarm.

As in the other countries, the recent trend in teenage births has been downward, although there has been little change since about 1977. In general, adult fertility has declined as well. The fertility of women in their early to mid-20s declined continuously between 1973 and 1982, but the relative drop for women aged 20–24 was less than that for those aged 15–19 (Central Bureau of Statistics, Dec. 1983, table II). The fertility rates for women between the ages of 28 and 35 actually started to rise around 1975, while those for adjacent age groups plateaued. The drop in the fertility of very young women can be seen in one sense as part of an overall shift in childbearing from the early years to the middle years of the reproductive age span. By 1982, teenagers ac-

Table 7.1. *The Netherlands: Number of births per 1,000 women under age 20, by age and marital status; and percentage of births occurring outside of marriage; 1975–81*

Year and age	Birthrate		% of births outside marriage to women <20
	Marital	Nonmarital	
<20			
1975	227.0	2.0	15.4
1976	217.6	2.1	17.9
1977	211.4	2.1	20.1
1978	220.3	2.2	22.3
1979	235.8	2.2	23.6
1980	263.9	2.4	25.4
1981	284.7	2.4	25.7
1980:			
14	0.0	0.2	100.0
15	221.2	0.5	72.6
16	368.5	1.1	43.4
17	434.5	1.4	23.0
18	309.0	3.6	26.3
19	219.4	4.6	18.9
15–17	407.1	1.0	31.9
18–19	244.2	4.1	21.7
15–19	263.9	2.2	23.8

Source: Central Bureau of Statistics, unpublished tables.

counted for less than 3 percent of the total fertility rate (Central Bureau of Statistics, Dec. 1983, table II, p. 15), compared to about 15 percent in the United States during the early 1980s.

There has traditionally been a minimum of nonmarital fertility in the Netherlands, compared to other countries in the region. The nonmarital fertility rate, which had been between 3 and 4 per 1,000 unmarried women of all ages in the 1950s, crept up to over 5 in the 1960s (Central Bureau of Statistics, Nov. 1983, figure 3). It then dropped abruptly in the early 1970s, a period when abortion was becoming more accessible. Around 1974, the nonmarital fertility rate began to rise again, reaching 6.5 per 1,000 in 1981 (Central Bureau of Statistics, Nov. 1982, p. 8). This development coincided with increased cohabitation and postponement of marriage among young people, trends that could signify the beginning of a change in the implications of out-of-wedlock childbearing.

Both marital and nonmarital fertility among teenagers have been rising since about 1977 (table 7.1). Such a rise is not inconsistent with a decline in the overall rate during a period when there was a decrease in the proportion of the underlying population base that was married. The proportion of all births that take place outside of marriage has also been rising. In 1981, the U.S. marital fertility rate for women aged 15–19 was only 24 percent higher than the Dutch rate, whereas the nonmarital rate was more than ten times as high, and the proportion of all births that occurred outside of marriage was twice as high (tables 3.1 and 3.2).

Like the United States, the Dutch marital rate peaks at age 17, suggesting that in both countries very early marriage is apt to follow a pregnancy. In the Netherlands, the proportion of teenage brides who gave birth within seven months, which had been 36 percent in 1971, dropped to a low of 14 percent around 1977 and then began to rise again (Central Bureau of Statistics, Nov. 1982, table II). On the other hand, the proportion of marital births to teenagers that occurred within seven months of marriage declined substantially, from 41 percent in 1975 to 29 percent in 1980 (Leliveld and Ketting, 1984, p. 46). The proportion of U.S. brides giving birth within seven months of marriage was 23 percent for the 1975–79 period; and it had been rising steadily since the 1950s (Chapter 3); in 1981, 36 percent of marital births to U.S. teenagers occurred within seven months of marriage (table 3.1).

While the birthrates remained more or less constant after 1977, the abortion rates for Dutch teenagers rose perceptibly in 1980 and were nearly the same in 1981. Both the level and the trend of the abortion rate for women 15–19 years old have been quite similar to those for all women of reproductive age, dropping from over 6 per 1,000 in 1971 to around 5 toward the end of the decade and then turning upward again (Ketting and Schnabel, 1980, table 2; Ketting 1983, p. 23; Stimezo, 1983). In fact, 1980 was a peak year for abortion overall, due quite likely to a round of negative publicity about the pill (Ketting, personal communication).[1] In general, however, the rates are so low that there is not much scope for significant downward movement. Even in 1980, the abortion rate for 19-year-old Dutch women was no greater than the rate for 14-year-olds in the United States.[2] Reported abortions in the Netherlands include menstrual extractions, which are available in a few facilities and are only done following a positive pregnancy test.

In recent years, 1 woman out of 6 obtaining an abortion has been under age 20 (Ketting and Leliveld, 1983, p. 31), compared to almost 2 in 3 in the United States (chapter 3). Among Dutch adolescents who obtained abortions in the early 1980s, 4 percent were married, 81 percent were single and still living with their parents, 11 percent lived on their own, and 5 percent were cohabiting (Stimezo Nederland, unpublished data). Six percent of U.S. women aged less than 20 who had abortions were married (chapter 3).

The combination of a slackened decline in the birthrates and only minor change in the abortion rates since 1977 has resulted in fairly stable pregnancy rates in the Netherlands during this period.

THE PROXIMATE DETERMINANTS OF PREGNANCY

The level of pregnancy in a given population is, in an immediate sense, the result of the level of sexual activity and the extent to which contraceptives are used by those who are sexually active. Indirect information on sexual activity can be obtained from statistics on marriage and cohabitation, since participation in a sexual union implies regular sexual activity. Marriage statistics for the Netherlands are compiled from the continuous population register, whereas those on cohabitation have been obtained from such surveys as the 1982 Netherlands Fertility Survey.

There was a considerable decline between 1971 and 1972 in the proportions married (from 4.9 percent to 2.2 percent for 15–19-year-old women; and from 0.7 percent to 0.2 percent for comparably aged

---

1. The same phenomenon probably accounts for a barely noticeable rise in the birthrates in 1980.

2. To estimate age-specific abortion rates we assumed that the age distribution of women having abortions in hospitals (about 18 percent of all abortions to Dutch residents in 1980) was the same as that for free-standing clinics; this procedure is not thought to reduce the accuracy of the results appreciably.

men) (Central Bureau of Statistics, unpublished tabulations). More women are married at each individual year of age than men, but even among women, the proportions exposed to childbearing in this traditional sense are inconsequential up to, and in recent years including, age 18. The proportions of teenagers that are married have also been dropping in the United States, but they remain much higher than in the Netherlands (table 3.4 and figure 3.1).

On the other hand, the proportions of women living in informal unions with men have been increasing rapidly in the Netherlands, at least until very recently. Whereas only a little over 5 percent of women interviewed in the 1982 fertility survey who were born between 1950 and 1954 had cohabited by the time they reached age 20, about 9 percent of women born between 1955 and 1959 had done so. The rise in cohabitation was not enough to compensate entirely for the drop in marriage, however; overall, fewer women in the younger than the older cohort had experienced either one or both types of union before they were 20 years old (Central Bureau of Statistics, April–May, 1983, figures 1–3). Moreover, the youngest women in the survey, who were born between 1960 and 1964 and were only aged 18–22 when interviewed, appeared to be less likely to cohabit as well as to marry while still in their teens. At the time of the survey, 9.1 percent of this cohort were living with a man to whom they were not married, and 13.2 percent were currently married, making a total of 22.3 percent in a stable sexual union. Although teenage cohabitation appears to be more common in the Netherlands than in the United States, the overall proportions in a sexual union in the Netherlands are lower (table 3.4).

Direct data on sexual activity and on contraceptive use usually come from special surveys; two recent surveys cover Dutch youth. In 1979–80 the Central Bureau of Statistics conducted a study of the living conditions of young people. The 1981 *Sex in Nederland* survey, which was commissioned by the popular magazine *Nieuwe Revu*, also included a youth sample. Neither of these surveys is ideal for the purposes of this study. The 1981 youth sample was very small, comprising 527 16–20-year-olds of both sexes, and representative of the unmarried population. The 1979–80 survey covered 2,480 individuals of both sexes and all marital statuses between the ages of 17 and 24, yielding a total of 970 17–19-year-olds; the somewhat larger sample size is offset by the facts that there is less material on the topics of most interest and the format of the questions makes it harder to compare the results with those for other countries. Each of the surveys may suffer also from design problems of a less evident nature. Data from both are presented here in order to evaluate the consistency of the picture that they present for the Netherlands before attempting ultimately to make comparisons between the Netherlands and the United States.

The respondents in the 1981 survey were asked whether they had ever had sexual intercourse, and if so at what age this had first taken place. The question referred explicitly to complete sexual intercourse. The results are shown in table 7.2. About one-third of women aged 16–17 were sexually experienced as were almost two-thirds of those aged 18–20.[3] However, the data on age at first intercourse indicate that only 22 percent of the older group had had intercourse before reaching age 17, compared to 28 percent of the younger teenagers. Hence there must either have been a marked trend toward earlier initiation of sex in the very recent past, and/or there is substantial sampling error in the data due to small numbers. Only one out of five 16–17-year-old men and fewer than half of those aged 18–20 said that they had ever had intercourse.

Two surveys, fielded in 1968 and 1974, covered the same age range. As long as reasonable comparability of the age distributions by sex is assumed, the proportions who have had sexual relations can be used to infer trends over time. On the basis of these results, Ketting has observed that there was a continuous and substantial rise in the proportions of women ever having had sexual intercourse during the 13-year period (Ketting, 1983, p. 23). This trend is common to all the countries in the study.

The respondents to the 1981 survey who had had sexual relations were queried about how well they knew the person with whom they first had intercourse. A large majority of the women, but only a little over half of the men, who had ever had intercourse said that their first partner was someone whom they knew very well in the sense that they were going steady or were actually engaged (table 7.2). Very few of either sex had had intercourse the first time with someone they hardly knew at all.

Several additional items pertinent to this investigation were included in the 1981 questionnaire. About one-third of sexually experienced men, and three-fourths of sexually experienced women, reported that they had had only one partner. Well over half of both sexes had had intercourse more than 10 times since the first experience. For almost half, the most recent occasion was within a week of the interview; for 94 percent of the young men and 86 percent of the young women, it was within the previous six months (*Sex in Nederland,* unpublished tabulations).

The 1979–80 survey took a somewhat different approach. The respondents were asked whether they had had intercourse during the previous six months and if so, how often. The results are shown in

---

3. One researcher who has worked with these data commented that the female sample may have been biased toward low sexual activity.

Table 7.2. *The Netherlands: Percentage distribution of men and women aged 16–20, by experience of sexual intercourse, age at which intercourse first occurred, and relationship with partner, 1981*

	Men			Women		
	16–17 (N=127)	18–20 (N=135)	Total (N=262)	16–17 (N=132)	18–20 (N=128)	Total (N=260)
Never had intercourse	81.1	51.2	66.0	65.6	38.4	52.3
Had intercourse	18.9	48.8	34.0	34.4	61.6	47.7
Total	100.0	100.0	100.0	100.0	100.0	100.0
Age at first intercourse						
13	2.3	2.4	2.4	0.0	1.7	0.8
14	2.3	3.1	2.7	3.8	1.7	2.9
15	5.4	4.0	4.7	11.5	5.1	8.5
16	5.5	9.4	7.5	13.0	13.7	13.5
17	3.2	15.8	9.5	6.0	14.6	10.2
18		11.0	5.5		21.3	10.2
≥19		3.1	1.6		3.4	1.6
Knew partner						
Very well (engaged)	7.9	28.9	18.6	29.9	49.3	39.4
Not so well	8.6	17.0	12.8	3.0	7.4	5.2
Hardly at all	2.3	2.9	2.6	1.5	4.9	3.2

Source: Sex in Nederland, 1981 survey youth sample, unpublished tabulations.
Note: Percentages are of those responding.

tables 7.3 and 7.4. Nonrespondents have been excluded from both the numerators and the denominators of the proportions. Consistency checks against later questions on contraceptive use suggest that most nonrespondents actually had had intercourse, so these figures are to some degree underestimates. The proportions indicated as having had sexual relations within six months are quite consistent with those from the 1981 survey: 47 percent of unmarried men and 52 percent of unmarried women aged 18–20, compared to 49 percent of men and 53 percent of women in the 1981 survey. The frequency of sexual contact varies predictably with age and marital status and is, on the whole, lower for teenage men than for teenage women (table 7.4). Just under half of sexually experienced unmarried women aged 18–19 had had intercourse frequently during the six-month period prior to interview.

How do these data compare with the United States? The most recent U.S. surveys suggest that close to half of all unmarried women are sexually experienced by the time they turn 18, although as recently as 1976, the figure was around 43 percent (table 3.5). This proportion is quite similar to those found for women in the 1981 Dutch survey. However, the proportion of unmarried U.S. men who had ever had intercourse at this point in their lives is substantially higher, suggesting that, contrary to the Dutch pattern, in the United States, men start to

Table 7.3. *The Netherlands: Percentage who had intercourse during the past six months, by sex, marital status, and age, 1979–80*

Sex and marital status	Age									
	17		18		19		18–19		20–24	
	N*	%	N*	%	N*	%	N*	%	N*	%
Males										
Had intercourse										
Not married	157	20	145	38	134	50	279	44	552	60
All	158	20	147	39	135	50	282	44	669	69
Women										
Had intercourse										
Not married	108	31	144	43	113	53	257	47	353	68
All	108	31	145	43	127	58	272	50	691	84

Source: Central Bureau of Statistics Youth Survey, unpublished tabulations.

*Numbers and percentages are for those responding to the question. Nonresponses ranged from 18 percent of 18–19-year-old women to 7 percent of those aged 20–24; and from 16 percent of 20–24-year-old men to 14 percent of those 18–19.

have sexual relations earlier than women (chapter 3). The proportion of both men and women who were engaged to or going steady with their first partner appears to be somewhat lower in the United States (chapter 3).

In 1982, 56 percent of all U.S. women aged 18–19, and 49 percent of never married women, had had intercourse within the three months prior to interview (table 3.6); in 1979–80, 50 percent of all Dutch women in this age group, and 47 percent of those who were not married, had had intercourse within the previous six months. The comparison lacks precision in various respects but points again toward general similarity of the behavior of young women in the two countries. It should be kept in mind, however, that female sexual activity may be underestimated in both of the Dutch surveys.

As to frequency of sexual activity, although direct comparisons are impossible, it is notable that 36 percent of Dutch women aged 18–19 in 1979–80 said they had had sexual relations frequently. In 1979, 40 percent of U.S. women of comparable age who had had intercourse at all in the previous four weeks said that they had done so six or more times (Johns Hopkins University, 1979).

Both the 1981 and the 1979–80 surveys included questions on contraceptive practice. In the 1981 survey, respondents were asked whether they had used any method the first and the most recent time that they had intercourse, and, if so, what method had been used in each case. Although the numbers underlying the results in table 7.5 are very small, it seems clear that a very large majority of sexually active

THE NETHERLANDS   163

Table 7.4. *The Netherlands: Percentage distribution of sexually experienced young men and women, by sex, marital status, and age, according to frequency of intercourse, 1979–80*

Sex, marital status, and frequency of intercourse	Age				
	17	18	19	18–19	20–24
Men					
Not married	(N=31)	(N=55)	(N=67)	(N=122)	(N=314)
Only once	19	9	6	7	2
A few times	39	38	37	38	29
Periodically	13	22	16	19	13
Frequently	29	31	40	36	56
Total	100	100	100	100	100
All	(N=32)	(N=57)	(N=68)	(N=125)	(N=401)
Only once	19	9	6	7	2
A few times	38	37	37	37	20
Periodically	13	21	16	18	9
Frequently	31	33	41	38	70
Total	100	100	100	100	100
Women					
Not married	(N=33)	(N=62)	(N=60)	(N=122)	(N=239)
Only once	15	13	5	9	3
A few times	30	27	27	27	19
Periodically	9	11	22	16	13
Frequently	45	48	47	48	65
Total	100	100	100	100	100
All	(N=33)	(N=63)	(N=74)	(N=137)	(N=577)
Only once	15	13	4	8	1
A few times	30	27	22	24	8
Periodically	9	11	18	15	6
Frequently	45	49	57	53	85
Total	100	100	100	100	100

Source: Central Bureau of Statistics Youth Survey, unpublished tabulations.

adolescents in the Netherlands practice contraception. More than three-quarters of female respondents reported that they used a method the first time they had intercourse and close to nine-tenths reported use on the most recent occasion. There appears to be little change with age, but women were somewhat more prone to say they had used a method than men, possibly because men had partners who were younger or because they were not aware that their partners were taking the pill.

The results from the Central Bureau of Statistics youth survey, which are shown in table 7.6, support the impression of widespread contraceptive use, although the level is somewhat lower, especially for women. In this case, the question related to use during the previous six months, and once again the sample sizes are small. At ages 18–19, three women out of four reported having used a method. There is a positive association between age and use between the ages of 17 and 19, es-

Table 7.5. *The Netherlands: Percentage distribution of sexually experienced young men and women who practiced contraception, and percentage distribution of users, by type of method used, according to sex and age, 1981*

Time of intercourse and contraceptive method	Age					
	Men			Women		
	16–17*	18–20	16–20	16–17	18–20	16–20
First intercourse	(N=24)	(N=69)	(N=93)	(N=46)	(N=79)	(N=125)
Used a method	57	81	75	76	78	78
Method	(N=12)	(N=50)	(N=62)	(N=35)	(N=58)	(N=93)
Pill	—	48	44	41	70	59
Condom	—	50	54	56	26	37
Other	—	2	2	3	4	3
Total	—	100	100	100	100	100
Most recent intercourse	(N=24)	(N=69)	(N=93)	(N=46)	(N=79)	(N=125)
Used a method	83	77	79	89	88	88
Method	(N=19)	(N=51)	(N=70)	(N=40)	(N=66)	(N=106)
Pill	—	74	74	83	70	78
Condom	—	22	22	15	28	20
Other	—	4	4	2	2	2
Total	—	100	100	100	100	100

Source: Sex in Nederland, survey youth sample, unpublished tabulations.
*Data on method of contraception practiced unavailable.

pecially among the young men. Women who were pregnant, or wished to become pregnant, at the time of interview were coded as nonusers, even though they might well have practiced contraception earlier in the six-month period, which would tend to reduce the proportions of young women shown as using a contraceptive. This bias is probably small for the age range considered here but would nevertheless tend to increase with age.

The two surveys yield similar pictures of the distribution of methods employed by young people (tables 7.5 and 7.7). Although the condom appears to be relied on often at the first sexual experience and among the youngest users, the pill is overwhelmingly the method of choice as time goes on. Men tend to report more use of the condom than women, possibly because young men are more likely than young women to report use of this male method. It may also reflect more casual relationships with different partners as well as the likelihood that their partners are younger. The IUD begins to attract a following only as women marry and move into their 20s. Very little use of other methods is reported.[4]

4. The 1979–80 survey specifically mentioned rhythm and withdrawal in addition to the methods distinguished in the table.

Table 7.6. *The Netherlands: Of the young men and women who had intercourse in the previous six months, the percentage who ever practiced contraception during that period, by sex, marital status, and age, 1979–80*

| | Age | | | | | | | | | |
| | 17 | | 18 | | 19 | | 18–19 | | 20–24 | |
	N	%	N	%	N	%	N	%	N	%
Men										
Not married	46	48	75	65	73	86	148	76	385	83
All	47	49	77	65	74	85	151	75	530	81
Women										
Not married	63	56	88	74	85	78	173	76	285	87
All	63	56	89	74	99	76	188	75	617	77

Source: Central Bureau of Statistics Youth Survey, unpublished tabulations.

Table 7.7. *The Netherlands: Percentage distribution of contraceptive users, by sex, age, and method used, 1979–80*

| Sex and method | Age | | | | |
	17	18	19	18–19	20–24
Men					
Not married	(N=22)	(N=49)	(N=63)	(N=112)	(N=321)
Pill*	45	71	68	70	80
IUD	0	0	2	1	3
Condom*	55	22	25	24	14
Other	0	6	5	5	2
All	(N=23)	(N=50)	(N=63)	(N=113)	(N=429)
Pill*	48	72	68	70	82
IUD	0	0	2	1	4
Condom*	52	22	25	24	12
Other	0	6	5	5	1
Total	100	100	100	100	100
Women					
Not married	(N=35)	(N=65)	(N=66)	(N=131)	(N=251)
Pill*	86	83	83	83	84
IUD	3	2	5	4	6
Condom*	11	8	11	9	6
Other	0	8	2	5	3
All	(N=35)	(N=66)	(N=75)	(N=141)	(N=478)
Pill*	86	82	83	82	82
IUD	3	2	5	4	6
Condom*	11	9	11	10	7
Other	0	8	1	4	5
Total	100	100	100	100	100

Source: Central Bureau of Statistics Youth Survey, unpublished tabulations.
*A small minority of pill and condom users mentioned using other methods also.

Other studies have shed some further light on contraceptive use among young women. Ketting has shown that among all women 15–19 years old, the proportion using the pill rose from about 20 percent in 1976 and 1977, to around 25 percent between 1978 and 1980, and then to 30 percent in 1981 (Ketting, 1983, table 2). This rise reflects increased sexual activity as well as greater reliance on the pill among the sexually active. The Netherlands Fertility Study indicated that in 1982, 85 percent of contraceptive users aged 18–19 were using the pill and 13 percent the condom (Central Bureau of Statistics, Jan. 1983, table 5.11).

The extent of use and the use of effective methods, both documented here, undoubtedly contribute to the low level of adolescent pregnancy in the Netherlands. The contrast with the United States is quite striking. In 1979, only half of unmarried U.S. metropolitan women aged 15–19 who had ever had intercourse reported that they used a method at their first experience (table 3.7) and two-thirds at their most recent experience (chapter 3). In 1982, half of all U.S. teenage women who had ever had intercourse reported that they were currently using a method (table 3.8). The lower level of use in the United States is partly due to the relatively large fraction of nonusers who were already pregnant or wished to become pregnant—9 percent of all women 15–19 years old (Forrest and Henshaw, 1983, table 2). Even if these women were excluded from the U.S. data, however, the proportions would not approach the levels observed for the Netherlands (88 percent in 1981, 75 percent in 1979–80). As in the Netherlands, the pill and the condom were the most popular methods among U.S. teenagers, but other less reliable methods, especially withdrawal, account for a much greater proportion of all contraceptive use in the United States (tables 3.7 and 3.8). A third factor could also be operating, namely, less effective use of a given method, although there are no statistics to substantiate this.

Finally, the Netherlands is one of the few countries where the morning-after pill has been used extensively. The two-dose procedure starting within 72 hours of unprotected intercourse is now preferred. Something less than 2 percent of women aged 15–19 have recourse to this treatment annually, representing close to four times the incidence of abortion (Ketting, 1983 p. 23). It is difficult to assess the effect on the pregnancy rate because there is no way of knowing the proportion of cases in which a conception actually occurred. Ketting observes that if one assumes a pregnancy would have ensued one-third of the time, the morning-after pill is having an impact equal to that of abortion. In that case, the pregnancy rate for women 15–19 years old would currently be in the neighborhood of 20 per 1,000, still well below that of the other countries in this study. In addition to the morning-after pill, there is some use of the IUD as a postcoital contraceptive (i.e., insertion within 72 hours after intercourse).

CONTRACEPTIVE AND ABORTION SERVICES

Evert Ketting, using a phrase coined by American demographers in 1970, suggests that no other country has come as close to exemplifying the "perfect contraceptive population" as the Netherlands (Ketting and Schnabel, 1980, p. 393). If this is so, the achievement is remarkable for its suddenness. Contraceptives were not readily available in the Netherlands until the 1960s, and the first birth control clinics were started in the latter part of that decade. Following the introduction of the pill in 1964, however, the use of modern contraception was extremely rapid. The 1982 National Fertility Study showed that by that year 39 percent of all women aged 18 to 37 were currently using the pill and only 24 percent were neither pregnant nor infecund and not using any method at all; the corresponding figures for married women are 34 percent and 12 percent, respectively (Central Bureau of Statistics, Jan. 1983, table 5.11).

An appreciation of the role of the general practitioner or family doctor (*huisarts*) in the organization of the Dutch health care system is one key to understanding how this came about. The Dutch family doctor is the central figure in the provision of primary health care in the Netherlands, a respected person, often a family friend, and the medium through whom access to secondary health care is obtained. The Dutch Society of Family Doctors took an early interest in the issue of contraception. The initial evaluation of experience with the pill was carried out by three general practitioners, based on their own patients. The results were reported in 1969 and 1970. In 1972, the society undertook a major project to inform all general practitioners about contraception. Small group discussions were held all over the country, covering such issues as contraception for young people and abortion as well as basic teaching about methods. The pill could be prescribed directly by the family doctor, whereas patients had to be referred to specialists for other highly effective methods such as the IUD and sterilization, resulting in a strong disposition toward use of the pill (Ketting, 1983, p. 19).

Another outstanding feature of the system is the provision for insurance coverage of medical expenses. About 70 percent of the population comes under the national health insurance scheme (the Sickness Fund) to which all persons with incomes up to a certain level belong. People with higher incomes are covered by private insurance.

The financial rules governing the insurance arrangements are determined by the Sickness Fund Council. In 1971, the decision was made to include the pill under insurance coverage, adding greatly to its accessibility. The diaphragm and the IUD are also covered; sterilization, although not specifically included, is paid for in practice. General practitioners are reimbursed annually, according to the number of Sickness Fund patients for whom they care.

Overall, about 90 percent of people who want contraceptive care—mainly the pill—presently go to their family doctor. It had been assumed that general practitioners would eventually obviate the need for alternative contraceptive services completely, but there have proven to be certain groups for whom this approach is not entirely satisfactory. One such group is young people. Although many adolescents do turn to their family doctors for contraceptive care, some do not do so for various reasons. Confidentiality is important to some young people who fear that their parents may find out if they go to the family physician. Apparently there is some justification for this concern. If privacy is requested, the doctor is required to comply, but teenagers do not always realize that they have the right to make such a request. They also fear a moralistic response to their request for care, and there still are family doctors in the Netherlands who take less than a positive view of providing young, unmarried women with contraceptives. Finally, many teenagers no longer live at home and, thus, do not have easy access to their family doctors. An adolescent is likely to look upon her doctor as related to her family rather than to her personally, and often a new relationship is not established until contraceptives have been used for some time. Only 5 percent of family doctors are female, although the proportion is higher among those recently entering the field.

The second major source of contraceptive services in the Netherlands is a network of family planning clinics run by the Rutgers Stichting. This organization is an offshoot of the Dutch Society for Sexual Reform (NVSH), a group that originated after World War II to lobby for the liberalization of sexual and ethical standards in the Netherlands. At the height of its influence, in the early 1960s, the group had up to 300,000 members and ran counseling bureaus in most small towns and all large cities. As general practitioners began to become involved in family planning, the need for the service component of the NVSH declined, and there was conflict between those who were interested primarily in the advocacy of sexual liberation and those who wanted to focus on clinic activities. In 1969, the remaining clinics split away and were renamed Rutgers "houses" in memory of an early Dutch birth control pioneer. Since that date, the Rutgers Stichting has carved out for itself an important niche as a provider of reproductive health services and sex counseling, particularly for young people.

Throughout the Netherlands, 70 percent of patients in the approximately 40 Rutgers Stichting clinics are under the age of 25, and 25 percent are under the age of 18. About 70 percent of the agencies' contraceptive service budget is provided under a grant from the Ministry of Social Services, enabling it to offer reduced fees to teenagers. Patients under 18 are charged 12.5 guilders (just over $US 4.00) a visit; those 18 and over, 27 guilders ($US 9.00). If a teenager is able to prove that she is at high risk of an unplanned pregnancy, and cannot afford any fee, the agency provides the adolescent with free services.

The government, the investigators were told, recognizes the special role played by the Rutgers Stichting in making services available to the hard-to-reach—particularly single women, the very young, and members of recently arrived immigrant groups—and has thus far not cut back on its support. The Rutgers Stichting has a reputation for offering nonmoralistic, confidential, client-centered services, characteristics that must certainly appeal to women who are ambivalent about sexual activity, who lack contraceptive knowledge or confidence, or who do not want their families to know that they are seeking birth control services. The atmosphere in the clinics visited was informal, the settings were comfortable, clean but not forbidding or institutional, and the manner of the staff working in them appeared relaxed and cheerful. Psychosexual counseling services are available at the larger centers, although they are used infrequently by teenagers.

Another important element in the Rutgers Stichting program is the training of general practitioners about contraception. The out-patient birth control clinic at the Academic Hospital of Leiden University has also remained active as a part of the teaching program there. But the researchers were told that the typical medical school graduate may not have had any training about contraception, and many general practitioners are insufficiently experienced to provide methods other than the pill. There is a serious oversupply of doctors at present in the Netherlands, and the Rutgers Stichting has no problem staffing its medical services. The clinic in Amsterdam employs mainly female doctors, although no effort has been made to follow suit in other parts of the country.

The director of the Rutgers Stichting estimates that it meets about 5 percent of the overall need for family planning services. He said that most of its young clientele comes for contraceptive help after having become involved in a regular sexual relationship. Very often the immediate reason for the visit is to get a pregnancy test. Perhaps because the Rutgers Stichting serves largely the most vulnerable segment of the population, only a small minority report that they used any method the first time they had intercourse.[5] The director speculated that perhaps

5. Another informant mentioned that this pattern tends to repeat itself with each new partner.

the goal of preparing young people before the need for contraception arises may simply be unrealistic. A common pattern for young girls is to remain clinic clients for three to five visits, or about two years, and then to move on to their general practitioner, as it becomes more acceptable to their parents or relatives that they use contraceptives, or, as a part of growing up, they learn to make their own choices.

Rutgers Stichting is the principal but not the only provider of clinic services in the Netherlands. The MR70 clinic in Amsterdam is an important, independent center for family planning. It receives no government funding, and patients must pay for the services they receive, although the fees are lower for young people. Roughly 12 percent of its clientele is below age 20, and it also sees many women from immigrant families. The atmosphere and attitudes of staff are similar to those in the Rutgers Stichting centers.

Reference has been made to a number of reasons why the pill is a particularly popular method in the Netherlands. In addition, there is a strong conviction that it is the optimal birth control method for teenagers. Medical and lay representatives of the family planning movement are aware of the findings about the method's health risks, as documented in long-term epidemiological studies. However, they emphasize that the major problems are concentrated among older women, particularly among those who smoke. They claim that young people are ideal candidates for the pill because the young do not like coitus-related methods, because the pill is easy to use, and because it has a high success rate and low health risks for young people. A pelvic exam, often feared by teenagers, is not considered an absolute prerequisite to prescription of the pill. After weighing the pros and cons, the conclusion has apparently been reached that the inconveniences or even possible long-term consequences of pill use are far outweighed by the adverse effects of early childbearing.

This affirmation of pill use, which is echoed in the preference of the young themselves for this method, seems to arise naturally out of a number of social attitudes about which there is a broad general consensus: early sexual activity is here to stay; it may not be such a bad thing; sex may even be a good thing if not engaged in recklessly and unthinkingly; the individual can and should be responsible for his or her actions; society has a stake in the consequences of individual behavior; and the individual should assess his or her behavior in terms of its impact on the wider social group.

The need for a choice of methods is recognized nevertheless. Condoms, which require no medical intervention, are popular and easily available from a variety of outlets. Diaphragms are not very acceptable to the young. The sponge was not yet available at the time of the investigators' visit in 1984. Recently there has been increasing demand for the IUD and, although pelvic inflammatory disease occurs in as many as 15 percent of IUD patients, it is felt that this should not be a major problem in a society where the disease can be recognized very early and treatment is highly accessible. The injectable contraceptive, Depo-provera, is sometimes offered.

The respondents in the youth sample of the 1981 *Sex in Nederland* survey were asked to evaluate some of the more common methods. Almost 90 percent of 16–20-year-olds said that the pill was both morally acceptable and effective.[6] The condom was rated equally high on moral grounds but less than two-thirds thought it was effective. The IUD was considered somewhat less morally acceptable, though also effective enough. Quite a few had never heard of the diaphragm, rhythm, or withdrawal. Most of those who had heard of these methods thought they were morally acceptable, but rhythm and withdrawal, in particular, were viewed as quite ineffective. The proportions of women reporting favorable opinions about the various methods in the United States rank them more or less the same except that the IUD is viewed with less favor there (Forrest and Henshaw, 1983, p. 55).

Until recently abortion was theoretically illegal in the Netherlands, but it has in fact been easy to obtain since the early 1970s. In 1980–82, an average of 19,400 abortions were performed annually on Dutch women (Stimezo, 1983). More than 80 percent of these occurred in clinics, most of which are operated by a voluntary nonprofit group called Stimezo (the National Abortion Federation of the Netherlands).[7] The remainder were performed in hospitals. Stimezo charges 340 guilders (about $US 115.00) for a first-trimester abortion, whereas they are performed free in hospitals under the national health insurance system. Women who cannot pay for an abortion tend to be referred to hospitals, although in cases of special need, social security will often cover the clinic costs. Very few abortions take place in hospitals in the primarily Catholic southern part of the country; the most abortions, by far, are performed in the secular areas of the north.

There are 14 Stimezo-affiliated clinics in the country and six non-member clinics. Most of them perform abortions only up to the twelfth week following conception. Three clinics specialize in later abortions. The ultimate limit is 22 weeks, although a very few later abortions are obtained in England each year by Dutch women. The Stimezo service is considered to be excellent, and the investigators were told that there is little need for postabortion counseling because it is not a traumatic

6. The word used in the original Dutch (*veilig*, meaning "safe") could refer either to health risks or to the risk of pregnancy.

7. An additional 29,000 procedures were performed in Stimezo clinics on nonresident women, mostly from West Germany, Belgium, Luxembourg, Italy, and Spain.

event for women there. Contraceptive advice is always included in the service; nevertheless, repeat abortions do occur.

Parental consent is required for an abortion, in principle up to age 20, but in practice only up to age 16. In the absence of parental permission, an abortion can be performed if three doctors agree that it is necessary or with the authorization of the Federation of Institutions for Unmarried Mothers (FIOM). Young women who are undecided about having an abortion are also referred to the FIOM. This organization originated, as its name suggests, to provide assistance for unmarried women who are pregnant or have children. Counseling and help in obtaining health, education, housing, daycare, and employment services are provided. The need for such services has dwindled, however, and more of the organization's efforts are now devoted to abortion counseling. Young women who are pregnant are given very straightforward advice about the realities of childbirth and motherhood. The final decision is always up to the woman, not her parents or partner. The investigators were told that the few women who continue their pregnancies are likely to be from emotionally or economically deprived backgrounds. Often there is a history of drug or alcohol abuse and of running away from home. Observers believe that some such young women want to have babies because a baby represents something in the world that is theirs to love and be loved by.

Public assistance is available regardless of parental status; hence there is no economic motivation to have a child. The father of the child is not required to contribute to its support unless the mother sues for payment. On the other hand, men can only obtain paternal rights through marriage or adoption. While young men are said to be less concerned about contraception than young women, there were many suggestions that in the Netherlands they have a significantly greater sense of responsibility than their counterparts elsewhere about not getting their partners pregnant.

SEX EDUCATION

Sex education has been incorporated into the school curriculum in the Netherlands only to a very limited extent. The task of providing the necessary information falls essentially on private organizations. The media have contributed enormously to knowledge and awareness of sexual matters among people of all ages. But there is a general consensus that much ignorance remains, and that there is a need for improvement.

Discussion of sex in the formal school program has usually been limited to the biological facts about reproduction. However, it is now official policy to proceed to integrate a broader version of sex education into the curriculum. An interdepartmental committee established to study ways of improving contraceptive behavior among young people and other groups in need of special attention has recommended to the government that the instruction cover the social and psychological aspects of sex, as well as the more technical aspects. Sex education is being incorporated into a new health education course.

One serious obstacle to developing a more adequate program has been the lack of teacher preparation; there is very little sex education in the teacher-training courses. Understandably, many experienced teachers are reluctant to take on this sensitive subject, and the excuse is proffered that the students already know whatever they need to know. Some excellent materials have been developed for both teachers and students, but they are not being widely used. Parents are another potential problem, and parents' reactions to the new course will be observed with care. In general, conservative religious groups in the Netherlands have been more likely to express opposition to sex education than to fertility control services, which are seen as a medical matter. Even among the most thoughtful proponents of sex education there is some doubt as to whether sex education should be compulsory and some feeling that the school may not be the best environment for the discussion of this topic at ages around puberty.

In the absence of a full school curriculum, the government has funded the Rutgers Stichting, the major private family planning association, to provide educational services. This seems to offer a convenient way of fulfilling what is perceived as an important obligation without becoming unduly embroiled in a politically controversial subject. The Rutgers Stichting has six educational teams working throughout the country. Group sessions are given at the association's own centers, and visits are made to classrooms upon invitation from the schools. All of the personnel working in the program are women. Although schools in the Netherlands are now universally coeducational, the students may be separated by sex for these presentations. Rutgers Stichting has developed a range of accompanying teaching materials. The content originally stressed the biomedical fundamentals of contraception. Recently more emphasis has been given to sexuality and relationships, but a move back toward the earlier approach is now being considered because the need for basic facts is felt to be so great. The Rutgers Stichting is made acutely aware of this need through the very large number of phone calls it receives requesting specific information, often of the most elementary nature.

The Rutgers Stichting parent organization, the Netherlands Union for Sexual Reform, also has an ongoing public education program. It is a political activist group and receives no government funding. Sex education in the schools has been one of its prime goals.

The impact of mass communication as a means of disseminating basic information and lowering the barriers to open discussion has been very profound. The role of radio and television is particularly interesting. A complicated arrangement exists to assure that differing points of view will be represented within the limits of the air time available. Private broadcasting organizations, which usually represent particular constituencies, are licensed to produce programs. They are supported partly by the government with the proceeds from the sale of licenses for television and radio receiving sets and partly by fees from their own membership. Other groups may also qualify for an allotment of time. Programming is essentially up to the organization or group. Once on the air, however, the group has potential access to nearly every home in the country. Thus television and radio have been instrumental in forming a base of information about sexuality among other matters common to the whole country.

The "Open en Bloot" series; which had such a dramatic effect, was presented by the Socialist television organization but was viewed by a much broader audience. The popularity of the program speaks for the demand for such types of programs and has stimulated continued efforts to provide programming on this general subject. At the time of the team visit, the Socialists were broadcasting a very frank Sunday-morning radio series about intimate topics, while the overall Netherlands Broadcasting Station sponsored a television program about puberty; and a weekly phone-in radio program hosted by a teenage girl, with backup from a panel of experts, reached a wide audience.

Similar types of information have been disseminated through the press. Mass magazines have carried many different kinds of articles. A question-and-answer column directed towards adolescents, which appeared in a monthly parents' magazine starting in 1971, very quickly became devoted almost exclusively to questions about sex (Wafelbakker, 1984). Whatever the means of communication, however, popular sources of information put a high premium on novelty. Television, radio, and magazines cannot be depended upon to cover the same areas year after year in order to meet the basic needs of each new crop of adolescents.

It might be added that the possibilities for capitalizing on the commercial aspects of sex have not been ignored. Shops selling sexually explicit literature flourish even in small towns and villages where they clearly depend on local trade. News items on negative findings about the pill have sometimes been played up out of proportion.

The 1981 *Sex in Nederland* survey included a number of questions on what people actually knew about reproduction and contraception. The vast majority of both young men and women felt that they had been adequately informed on sexual matters. Interestingly, the proportions are slightly lower among those aged 18–20 (79 percent of men and 80 percent of women) than among those aged 16–17 (85 percent and 83 percent, respectively); this small difference may reflect increasing education over time or simply greater awareness of the complexities of the topic as age increases. Sixty-one percent of the men and 70 percent of the women said the topic of sex came up in conversation at home at least from time to time. In contrast, fewer than 20 percent of the adults (aged 21–64) interviewed in the same survey thought that their parents had been frank and open about sex with them; within the adult group, the proportion is strongly inversely related to age, suggesting the extent of change over time. Roughly half of the young respondents who reported that sex was ever discussed at home said that the subject was touched off by television, newspapers, movies, or books; the most common reason given for the topic not coming up was that the parents were inhibited about discussing sex with their children.

Knowledge of how conception occurs and how to avoid pregnancy is virtually universal even among those aged less than 18. The main sources of information on the facts of reproduction are parents and school, according to the *Sex in Nederland* survey; and they are of approximately equal importance (mentioned by more than 40 percent of teenagers). If only one parent was mentioned by respondents to the survey, it was almost always the mother. The proportions who learn about contraception in school are much lower (20 percent of young men and 28 percent of young women); and fewer than 15 percent of young people said they were told about contraception by their parents; young men are particularly unlikely to learn about contraception from either source. Friends, the media, and personal experience were mentioned very seldom by survey respondents; the largest group of respondents, especially the young men, referred to other sources of information on contraception, possibly the Rutgers Stichting centers. Although familiarity with contraceptive methods is quite general, only about half of the women aged 18–20 and one-third of the men in that age group knew the time at which conception is most likely to occur. U.S. surveys show knowledge among young women of the time of greatest risk within the menstrual cycle to be roughly the same (Zelnik and Kantner, 1977, table 4).

THE TRANSITION TO ADULTHOOD

The potential pitfalls associated with the completion of education, departure from the parental home, and initiation of full-time employment are cushioned in various ways in the Netherlands. Yet the transition process is often not easy, and young people do not necessarily have any more reason to take an optimistic view of their prospects as adults than their peers in other countries.

School is compulsory to age 16, covering six years of primary school and at least four years of secondary school. About 70 percent of primary school students and 60 percent of secondary school students attend private schools, mostly sectarian institutions (Central Bureau of Statistics, 1982, table 7.2, p. 103). Over one-third of students at both levels are in Catholic schools. The majority of Calvinists also attend separate schools. Both public and private schools are free for the 10 years of compulsory education, after which modest fees are charged on a sliding scale according to the parents' income. Peripheral expenses associated with attendance at private schools (e.g., school trips) may not be insignificant, even in the earlier grades. In the third year of secondary school (when students are 14–15 years old), a selection process begins that distinguishes increasingly between academic and practical training, but transfers between the two tracks are possible at several stages (Netherlands Information Service, 1983, pp. 15–16).

Virtually all young people of both sexes remain in school through age 15 (table 7.8). Thereafter the proportion of full-time students drops off fairly gradually for young men and more steeply for young women. From ages 15 to 17 it is possible to attend school part-time and take a job as well. The rise in part-time school attendance at these ages partly compensates for the decline in full-time schooling but, again, much more so for young men than for young women. Thus by age 19, 7 out of 10 women, but only half the men, have left the educational system. Overall, 70 percent of men and 63 percent of women aged 15–19 are enrolled full-time. In the United States, the proportions of men enrolled in school are roughly the same as those in the Netherlands, but there is very little difference by sex, so that the proportions of young

Table 7.8. *The Netherlands: Percentage of population attending school, by sex and age, 1980*

| | Men | | | Women | | |
| | In school | | | In school | | |
Age	Full-time	Part-time	Not in school	Full-time	Part-time	Not in school
15	98.8	0.5	0.7	98.4	0.5	1.1
16	90.1	7.0	2.9	87.8	7.8	4.3
17	70.1	13.4	16.5	66.1	9.0	24.9
18	51.6	14.4	33.9	41.0	7.1	51.9
19	38.2	11.2	50.6	24.0	6.2	69.8
15–19	69.8	9.3	20.8	63.4	6.1	30.4

Source: Central Bureau of Statistics, *Statistical Yearbook of the Netherlands, 1982*, table 27.

American women in school are appreciably higher by the later teen years than in the Netherlands (table 3.10).

Unemployment is very high in the Netherlands, and the problem is especially acute for young people. About a quarter of the population aged 15–19 years old was in the labor force in 1980, accounting for the vast majority of those not in school. The proportion was a little higher for women (28 percent) than for men (26 percent) (Central Bureau of Statistics, Jan. 1983, table 1.1.3). However, on average, 17 percent of teenage men and 24 percent of teenage women who did not intend to be self-employed were registered as unemployed during the year (Central Bureau of Statistics, Dec. 1981, table 1.5.3). Both the proportions in the labor force and the proportions unemployed are considerably higher than the corresponding figures for the United States in 1982 (table 3.9). Moreover, in the United States, both proportions were somewhat lower for women than for men. There is a widespread impression in the Netherlands that many young people stay in school only because the prospects for getting a job have been so poor. Insofar as employment prospects have tended to improve recently, it is the young people just leaving school who are most likely to be hired, and there is a possibility that several age groups may end up with substantial numbers of individuals who never find work at all.

The figures given above suggest that the new generation of women does think more in terms of employment than previous generations, though girls still tend to leave school earlier than boys. Many women work until their first child but then find it difficult to get back into the labor force. Indeed, until well into the 1970s, marriage, pregnancy, and childbirth were common grounds for the dismissal of female employees (van de Kaa, 1975, p. 484). Not working may appear entirely normal to a young woman, and the notion of a girl's devoting herself to filling her hope chest still has some currency. The fact that the shift toward greater female labor force participation began to gather strength just as the nation moved into a period of economic recession undoubtedly slowed the pace of change. This fact, coupled with the pervasive belief that one income should be sufficient to support a family, could make women's ambition to work seem unrealistic or self-centered. All in all, the desire for a career could apparently account only minimally for the effective practice of contraception to postpone childbearing among teenage girls.

At the same time, adolescents in the Netherlands receive considerable support from the state. After age 16, any young person who is not in school is entitled to housing separate from his or her parents at public expense. The number of young people living independently, which had been rising, is now beginning to decline again, probably as a reflection of the difficult economic situation. Those unemployed receive social security, and if they stay at home, they are likely to have money left over to spend as they want. This situation may in turn diminish motivation to work. Thus, while young people facing adulthood seem to have little reason to fear desperate poverty, there may also not be much to stimulate long-term planning or investment in the future.

POPULATION SUBGROUPS

With a total population of just over 14 million people, concentrated in a small land area, the Netherlands is to all appearances a homogeneous and tightly integrated nation. Yet it comprises three major and several minor religious groups, and in the period since World War II, there have been several waves of immigration resulting in small but not insignificant minority populations. There is also some differentiation within the country by socioeconomic status and geographic location.

As noted earlier, the separation between the different religious groups has been so profound that they are visualized as self-contained "pillars." The Catholics compose the largest group, with approximately 40 percent of the population (Netherlands Information Service, 1983, p. 12). The Dutch Catholic Church has become well known for the independent and forward-looking attitudes of its leadership, including its announcement in the late 1960s that the pill was an acceptable means of birth control. Most Catholic doctors apparently behave like other physicians regarding such issues as prescription of contraceptives to minors. Over 20 percent of the population belongs to the Dutch Reformed Church. The conservative Calvinists represent about 10 percent of the population; the heritage of their antirisk mentality permeates Dutch society and is said to have favored cautious and responsible behavior with respect to early childbearing. Groups representing a number of other beliefs also have some influence, ranging from the humanists to religious fundamentalists. The proportion of people who claim to have no religious affiliation varies considerably according to how the question is asked, but it is a large and growing element. The influence of religion on all aspects of life, traditionally very strong, has diminished rapidly, along with all the other changes that have taken place in the last two decades.

Aliens represent less than 4 percent of the Dutch population (U.S. Bureau of the Census, 1983p, table 6c), but this figure is somewhat misleading about the impact of foreigners because many immigrants from the former colonies have Dutch nationality. Moreover, due to their age distribution, the foreign component in the school population is much higher than in the population at large. The first large group of immigrants came from Indonesia at the time of independence. During the period of rapid economic growth in the 1960s and early 1970s, there was an influx of workers from Southern Europe and the Mediterranean countries, including substantial numbers of Turks and Moroccans. In 1975, around the time of the independence of Suriname, there was yet another surge of immigration from that country, and the Surinamese, who are primarily black, now constitute the largest minority. Economic recession has tended to stimulate resentment of the immigrants, but there is not considered to be any serious race problem.

With the exception of the Indonesians, who are now essentially integrated into Dutch society, immigrants tend to have views on family life and reproduction that are very different from those of the native Dutch. The need for special services for these groups is widely recognized. Minority women run a particularly high risk of unwanted pregnancy, and the Rutgers Stichting organization considers them a primary target group, along with youth, but has found them hard to reach. Nevertheless, adaptation to the prevailing mode of reproductive behavior is thought to be proceeding at a reasonably rapid pace.

POLICY MAKING AND IMPLEMENTATION

Because the Netherlands is a self-consciously pluralistic society, the formulation of policy at the national level could be problematic. Special conventions, mostly of an informal nature, have been developed to accommodate different points of view and achieve a coherent and workable result. During the brief visit of the research team, it was not possible to investigate this process in any depth, although it has obviously been instrumental in shaping the current setting of adolescent pregnancy.

Until the mid-1960s, the political and social scene was dominated by a coalition between the Calvinist and Roman Catholic pillars. Their conservative, religious outlook prevailed partly because of the effective isolation of the various pillars from one another. As this isolation declined, and all kinds of information circulated more and more freely, secular and moderate forces came to the fore.[8] The Christian Democratic Party, representing the Calvinists and Roman Catholics, is in power again at this writing, but the climate of opinion remains permissive and progressive. With the exception of a few extreme fundamentalist groups, all points of view have tended to converge, and pillarization as such has greatly diminished.

Nevertheless, strategies of accommodation continue to play a prominent role in the ongoing process. Government seeks to impose as little as possible: the best policy is thought to be the least policy. Another trend is to hand over to private organizations activities that are consid-

8. This phenomenon and its relationship to population politics are examined in van de Kaa, 1983.

ered important but too controversial for direct involvement. Subsidization of the Rutgers Stichting sex and contraceptive education program and contraceptive services to minors are cases in point. Such cooperation between the public and private sectors is stressed in many ways. For example, the Rutgers Stichting and other private groups provided input for the report of the Interdepartmental Committee for the Improvement of Contraceptive Behavior.

A third option followed is allowing accepted practice to deviate from the legal status. An outstanding example of this kind of solution is the situation regarding abortion, which also illustrates the complexities of the policy-making process in other respects. According to a law dating from the nineteenth century, most abortions were illegal. Starting around 1970, however, abortion began to be accepted as a medical procedure and ultimately became very readily available. Its practice was governed by a set of more or less formal regulations. But attempts to address the legal question directly were frustrated for a long time by the unwillingness of the conservative political forces to give way on this particular issue. In 1981, a new law was finally passed, which represented a difficult compromise; and it has resulted in a somewhat more restrictive situation than the ad hoc policy that prevailed before legalization.[9] However, the new law was not implemented during a lengthy period while the Ministries of Health and Justice worked out administrative details. It finally went into effect on November 1, 1984, but there is confidence that any ensuing problems, such as reduced access to abortion for young people, can again be resolved through de facto modification, and actual changes in practice will be minimal.

This kind of maneuvering takes place not only on the national political scene, but in other settings as well. A crucial stage in the development of contraceptive services was the debate within the medical profession in the late 1960s concerning the physician's role and responsibilities. As soon as that issue was resolved, the specific question of providing contraceptives to young, unmarried people arose. At this writing, both the exclusion of the pill from health insurance coverage and the possibility of including reimbursement for the costs of clinic abortions are being debated in the Sickness Fund Council. However, once a consensus is reached on a given topic, the country is so small and communications are so direct that it is usually understood and accepted even by those who may not agree with it. Visible protest, such as that of the Catholic priest Pater Koopmans against abortion, is viewed as eccentric.

9. The current law places some minor restrictions on clinic abortions after the thirteenth week of pregnancy and requires a five-day waiting period between application for an abortion and the operation.

8

Sweden

T he contrast between Sweden and the United States in the reproductive behavior of teenagers is striking. In 1980, the teenage birthrate in Sweden was only 29 percent, and the abortion rate only 50 percent of the teenage rate in the United States. Swedish adolescents were experiencing a rate of pregnancy that was only 38 percent of that of American teenagers. What lies behind these relatively low rates for Swedish women?

TRENDS IN REPRODUCTIVE BEHAVIOR: FERTILITY

Fertility has been declining overall in Sweden, as in most other developed countries. In 1983, the TFR stood at 1.6 births per woman, a level that had been fairly constant since 1976. Teenage fertility, on the other hand, continued to decline at a rapid rate, from 35 per 1,000 women aged 15–19 in 1971, to 25 in 1976, to 14 by 1981 (Statistics Sweden, 1984; and table 2.8). Since the mid-1970s, teenage fertility dropped from 5.3 percent to only 2.5 percent of the TFR. (In the United States in 1980, teenage fertility made up 14 percent of the TFR [Appendix 1]).

The changes in the fertility of 15–17-year-olds are even more dramatic. In 1971, their fertility rate was 15, but by 1981 this had dropped to 4 per 1,000. By the mid-1980s, the fertility of these younger teenagers will probably approach zero, and what remains will be concentrated entirely among 17-year-olds.

181

ABORTION

One possible explanation for the extremely low fertility rates among Swedish teenage women could be a high abortion rate rather than a low pregnancy rate. In 1979, 63 percent of pregnancies experienced by 15–17-year-olds, and 37 percent of those experienced by those aged 18–19, were terminated by abortion (Tietze, 1983, table 7, p. 51). Thus it is obvious that the teenage birthrate would be significantly higher without recourse to abortion. Nevertheless, the evidence indicates quite clearly that the abortion rate among teenage women has declined dramatically since 1975, from 28.6 per 1,000 women aged 15–19 to 20.1 by 1981 (table 2.8). This sharp decline followed a continuous rise from the mid-1960s. What is more, the younger the age, the greater the decline in the abortion rate between 1975 and 1982. The decline for those aged 15 and 16 was on the order of 50 percent, while among 19-year-olds it was only 1 percent. Among adults, the abortion rate has generally stabilized (Familje planering och abort, 1983, p. 31). The sharp contrast between the trend in the teenage abortion rate and that for adults is depicted in figure 8.1, where the age-specific rates since 1975 are expressed as a percentage of the 1975 level for each age group. Adult women typically experienced a rise in their rate of abortion followed by a decline back toward the 1975 level, while the trend for teenagers is continuously and dramatically downward.

It is noteworthy that the teenage abortion rates in 1975 were nearly the same in Sweden (28.6 per 1,000 women) as in the United States (31.0) but diverged dramatically in the ensuing six years (tables 2.2 and 2.8). By 1981 the Swedish rate had *fallen* by 30 percent, while in the United States it had *risen* by 43 percent. This drop in the Swedish rate is eloquent testimony to the potential effectiveness of public policy.

PREGNANCY

The decline in the abortion rate among Swedish teenagers since 1975, and a continuing decline in the teenage birthrate can only imply a decline in the rate at which teenagers become pregnant. The pregnancy rates between 1973 and 1981 are shown by single years of age for all women in figure 8.2.[1] The decline since 1975 shows up prominently for teenagers, especially those aged 17–19, as well as for young adult women up to age 25. Among women at older ages, there is some evidence of a gentle rise in the pregnancy rate, probably due to the postponement of childbearing to older ages.

---

1. The data are in a somewhat different form from the pregnancy rates given in table 2.8, which are adjusted for slight differences in definitions of age.

Fig. 8.1. *Sweden: Frequency of abortions by age, 1976–82, as a percent of the frequency in 1975*

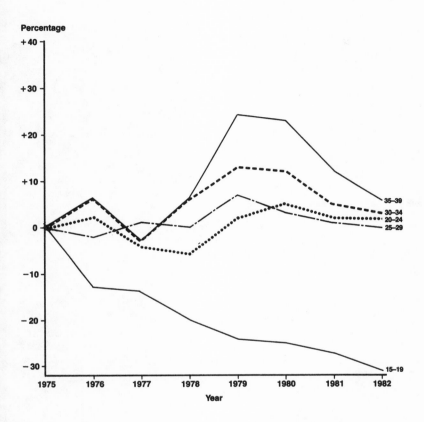

Source: Familje planering och abort, 1983, fig. 8.5b, p. 124.

The contrast with the United States, where the pregnancy rate at the end of the decade was 14 percent higher than in 1971, is particularly striking. In 1981, the teenage pregnancy rate in Sweden was only one-third of the rate in the United States (tables 2.2 and 2.8).

Changes in the Swedish pregnancy rate could result either from changes in sexual activity or from changes in contraceptive practice. A reduction in the amount of exposure to the risk of pregnancy might be inferred if young women have recently postponed marriage or if there is any evidence that the age at which sexual intercourse begins has increased in recent years.

Fig. 8.2. *Sweden: Pregnancies per 1,000 women, by five-year age groups, 1973–82*

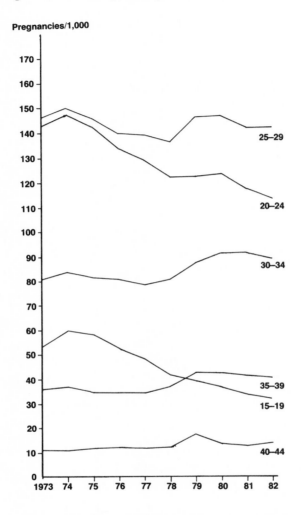

Pregnancies/1,000

Source: Central Statistical Bureau, *Befolknings-Förändringer 1983* (Stockholm: 1984), vol. 3 of *Swedish Official Statistics,* tables 3.16 and 3.24.

MARRIAGE AND COHABITATION

Sweden has been in the avant-garde of the decline in marriage rates seen in most developed countries. Beginning in 1966, the marriage rate declined more or less continuously and dramatically among women under 30 years of age. The rate dropped from 39 per 1,000 15–19-

year-olds in 1966 to 5 in 1981; among women 20–24, the decline was from 191 to 49; and among women 25–29, the rate fell from 172 to 78 (U.N., *Demographic Yearbook*, various years). Among older women, there is some evidence of higher rates in recent years, reflecting the postponement of legal marriage to later ages.

Marriage rates among young people have also declined in the United States, although the decline started a few years later and the level remains much higher than in Sweden. The rate for American teenage women of 44 per 1,000 in 1981, after a decade of decline, was higher than the rate for Swedish teenagers at the beginning of their decline in 1966 (NCHS, 1985, table 5).

In theory, this evidence of the decline in the rate of marriage among young women is consistent with the hypothesis that exposure to the risk of pregnancy may have been reduced. However, there has been a more than compensating increase in informal cohabitation among young Swedish women. Thus if women legally married are combined with those informally cohabiting, the proportion in a sexual union by age 20 has increased markedly. Results from the 1981 Swedish Fertility Survey indicate an increase in the percentage of women who by age 20 have ever lived with a man for at least one month from just under 30 percent for women born between 1936 and 1940 to nearly 60 percent for those born between 1956 and 1960 (International Statistical Institute, 1984). On the basis of the evidence in Sweden, it must be concluded that the amount of exposure to the risk of pregnancy has substantially increased rather than decreased. Compared with the United States in 1980 (figure 8.3), informal cohabitation is markedly higher in Sweden, but the overall proportion in a stable sexual union is fairly similar in the two countries (U.S. figures inferred from census data). Among 20–24-year-olds, there appear to be more Swedes (60 percent) than Americans (47 percent) in regular unions, but the older age groups are very similar.

AGE AT INITIATION OF SEX

The other possible explanation of the lower teenage pregnancy rate in Sweden is that the age at which sex is initiated may be increasing. The most reliable information about the age at which Swedes begin sexual intercourse is also based on the National Swedish Fertility Survey of 1981. It is clear from table 8.1 that the great majority of teenage women in the most recent cohort (1956–60) had had sexual intercourse before age 18. The estimated median age at first intercourse has decreased over time, from an estimated 19.0 for women born between 1936 and 1940 to 16.7 for those born between 1956 and 1960. This trend toward younger ages at initiation seems to have accelerated rapidly in recent

Fig. 8.3. *Sweden and the United States: Percentage of women cohabiting, married, or single, 1980*

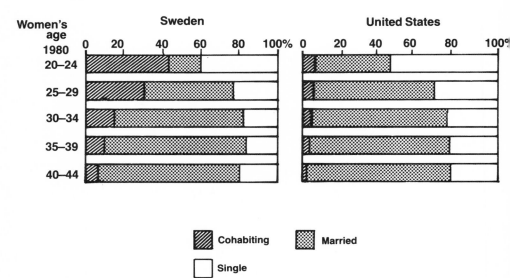

Sources: Sweden: International Statistical Institute, 1984, p. 9. United States: calculated from the microdata sample file of the 1980 census.

years.[2] These data are generally consistent with scattered results from other surveys cited by various individuals interviewed in Sweden.

A comparison of the data from the 1981 Swedish survey with estimates of the age at first intercourse for women in the United States (table 3.5) indicates that Swedish adolescent women in recent years have been exposed to the risk of pregnancy at an earlier age than Americans. This evidence makes the very low pregnancy rates among Swedish teenagers even more remarkable.

CONTRACEPTIVE PRACTICE

The explanation for Sweden's low and declining teenage pregnancy rate has to be the practice of contraception. There must be a very high level of use and fairly effective use of contraceptives among Swedish teenagers. Unfortunately, there are no national data on contraceptive practice for Swedish teenagers. The 1981 Swedish Fertility Survey did

2. The average age may be underestimated, however, especially for the earlier cohorts; see the second footnote to table 8.1.

Table 8.1. *Sweden: Cumulative percentage of women who have had sexual intercourse* before exact ages, and birth cohort*

	Age					
Birth cohort	16	18	20	22	25	Median†
1936–40	3.6	31.9	68.4	87.5	94.4	19.0
1941–45	6.4	39.9	74.5	89.8	97.5	18.6
1946–50	10.9	50.3	86.1	95.3	97.9	18.0
1951–55	14.7	62.3	89.9	95.5	98.5	17.5
1956–60	33.5	79.2	93.9	96.9‡	97.5‡	16.7

Source: Central Bureau of Statistics, unpublished tabulations from the 1981 Swedish Fertility Survey.

*Based on responses to the interview question: "At what age did you first have intercourse?" Women who could not remember or who refused to answer, about 4 percent across cohorts, were redistributed according to the age distribution of known responses.

†The medians estimated here are imprecise because the data were collected in two-year age intervals. In calculating the median, the somewhat unrealistic assumption was made that the experience of 16- and 17-year-olds was the same, an assumption that probably affects the estimate for the earlier cohorts.

‡Because women born after 1958 could not have reached age 23 in 1981, the base of the percentages for the 1956–60 cohort declines at the older ages.

not include women below age 20, and the questions asked do not permit a reconstruction of contraceptive practice for women aged 15–19. However, given the fact that 40 percent of Swedish women aged 20–24 are neither legally married nor cohabiting, the contraceptive experience of women in this age group may shed some light on the practices of younger women.

For women aged 20–24, 59.6 percent practiced contraception in the four weeks preceding the survey, a rate similar to that reported in the United States (Pratt et al., 1984, table 7); and 8.8 percent used no birth control method. The remaining 31.6 percent of women were either pregnant, sterile, or sexually inactive for that period. These statistics imply that 87.1 percent of those exposed to risk were practicing contraception—the same percentage as in the United States (Pratt et al., 1984, table 7, and Bachrach, 1984, table 3). The birth control pill is clearly the method of choice for these young women (table 8.2), accounting for 61 percent of their contraceptive practice, a level slightly higher than the 55 percent reported for the United States (Pratt et al., 1984, table 7). This pattern is in marked contrast with the preferences of women over age 24, who more often use barrier methods or the IUD.

How useful such information is for characterizing the contraceptive practices of teenagers is uncertain. It may be helpful in describing the practices of women aged 18 and 19, since about 60 percent of Swedish women are in some type of regular sexual union by age 20, but it is less

Table 8.2. *Sweden: Percentage distribution of women using a contraceptive method* during the past four weeks, 1981*

	Age in 1980	
Method	20–24	20–44
Rhythm	4	9
Barrier	23	33
Pill	61	31
IUD	12	27
Total	100	100

Source: International Statistical Institute, 1984; adapted from table on p. 15.
*Where several methods were used, the "most efficient" was noted.

helpful in describing the practices of younger teenagers for whom sexual relations tend to be episodic. The only direct information on the subject comes from special studies (usually involving very small samples), clinic data, and impressions of persons involved in programs serving youth.

A longitudinal study of persons born in the Stockholm area in 1955 showed that at age 18, 75 percent of sexually active young women and 84 percent of sexually active young men practiced contraception regularly, and the condom was used more than the pill (Klackenberg-Larsson, 1977). A 1980 study by Bo Lewin of 181 Uppsala school students, mostly 16 years of age and of both sexes, indicated that two-thirds of those who had had coital experience had used contraception at their first intercourse, mostly the condom. At the most recent experience, the level of use had increased to 81 percent; the pill was used at least as often as the condom. In a third study of a sample of 19-year-old women in the city of Göteborg in 1981, just under 9 percent had never used any method of contraception (Andersch and Milsom, 1982). Three-fourths of current users relied on the pill. Almost 13 percent of these women had previously been pregnant, and half of their pregnancies had been terminated by abortion.

Interviews with medical clinic personnel providing contraceptive services for young people tend to confirm this picture. Although many teenagers come to a clinic to obtain contraceptives in advance of their first sexual experience, a sizable proportion of new clients have had unprotected sex at least once before making such a visit. The pill is viewed as a highly acceptable method, both by service providers and by potential users. Although condoms are dispensed less often than are pills through clinics, they are readily available from other sources, and clinic personnel believe they are widely used by teenagers.

Thus, although the evidence is far from ideal, the general picture that emerges is that most adolescents in Sweden probably use the condom or pill, although the level and type of contraceptive practice does not entirely succeed in preventing unwanted pregnancies.

GENERAL ATTITUDES AND SOCIAL BACKGROUND

One very clear impression that emerges from the literature and from discussions with knowledgeable persons is that sexuality is accepted in Sweden as a perfectly natural part of life. Recently this acceptance has come to apply to adolescents as much as to older people. There does not seem to be the same degree of moral ambivalence surrounding the subject as in societies like the United States, where premarital sex is regarded by many as wrong, or even sinful. As Jan Trost has observed, "Premarital sexuality has never been an issue in Sweden" (1984).

Sweden and the Scandinavian countries in general seem to have evolved a largely secular view of sexual behavior in which the main concerns are that individuals know what they are doing and are sensitive to the needs and feelings of the other person and to the responsibilities involved. Of course, this demystification of sex also includes the right to say no. In fact, in this postliberation period, there is some evidence of a rejection of the ideology of casual sex and a renewed emphasis on the value of commitment. The whole system of sex education and contraceptive counseling is organized around those principles. Abortion is readily available if unwanted pregnancies do occur, but it is regarded as a highly undesirable alternative to the prevention of pregnancy.

Although premarital pregnancy is not regarded as a particularly problematical form of behavior, a teenage mother is considered deviant and teenage childbearing is in fact becoming increasingly uncommon. In other words, the age of the mother is considered more important than her marital status. Births out of wedlock now constitute about 40 percent of all births, largely because of the ever-growing popularity of informal cohabitation. Increasingly in the Nordic countries, and to a lesser extent in other western countries including the United States, informal cohabitation is becoming a substitute for engagement (Trost, 1979), "and in addition has taken on some of the role of the early period of marriage" (Hoem and Selmer, 1984).

Another set of circumstances is also relevant. In Sweden, although subsidies are paid to women who have children, there is evidently no strong economic incentive for a young woman to have a child. Perhaps more important, the father is held financially responsible for his child's upbringing, and paternal responsibility is rigorously enforced by the state. In a small population like that of Sweden, which has an accurate population register, it is not as easy as it is in the United States for fathers just to disappear. Of course, these circumstances are not particularly new, so that they could not explain the recent decline in teenage pregnancy, but they probably contribute in some part to the general picture of the low teenage birthrates.

The youth of Sweden spend a considerable amount of time in school, much more than in the past. Sixteen is the legal age to leave school, but apparently a large majority are still in school at ages 18–19 (Björklund and Persson-Tanimura, 1983). In the United States, only 48 percent are still in school at ages 18–19 (table 3.10). For boys, school is followed by universal military training. Most adolescent social life takes place in groups; going to parties starts around ages 14–16. Of those who completed the three-to-four-year secondary school course in 1977, 32 percent of young men and 43 percent of young women entered higher educational institutions. Women tend to be slightly more educated than men, but they typically follow different vocational tracks, with men in more technical fields and women on tracks that lead to office work or service jobs.

Most Swedish women now expect to work, and two incomes are regarded as essential for a family. Yet despite a feminist ideology and a strong egalitarian ethos, the labor market is still very segregated, with women concentrated in largely "female" jobs (Skard and Haavio-Mannila, 1984). Their earnings are around 63 percent of men's, slightly higher than in the United States (U.S. Bureau of the Census, 1984d, table 699). Although living conditions have improved greatly in recent decades, the relative status of men and women may have changed less than is commonly believed. A rather strong conclusion is reached by Skard and Haavio-Mannila in a review of sexual equality in the Nordic countries generally:

> Women have increased control over child-bearing, are better edu-
> cated than before, and participate more in the labor force and in
> politics. Yet, their education is still rather second-rate, they still
> carry the main burden of household chores, can find employment
> in only a limited number of low-wage, low-status occupations, and
> are a distinct minority in decision-making bodies. In spite of the
> improvements, the gender gap has not been closed. (p. 156)

With the slowing of economic growth in the 1970s, the rate of unemployment increased among teenagers and young adults, but not among persons aged 25–74. Teenagers' increasing difficulty in finding work has been widely publicized. In a 1980 study by Bo Lewin, covering six different areas in Sweden in which data were obtained from a sample of 1,208 adolescents mostly aged 13–15, more concern was expressed about unemployment than any of 13 other problems except pollution. The likelihood of being employed is about the same for young men and women (Björklund and Persson-Tanimura, 1983); and both face perhaps even worsening employment prospects as the baby-boom cohorts of 1964–67 move into the working ages.

The government maintains labor-market programs and provides financial aid to youth. Temporary jobs, which increased during the 1970s, are sponsored or arranged by the government. Labor-market training is provided in special centers and educational institutions. Unemployment insurance is available for youth who have been unemployed for at least three months. In 1980, some 35 percent of unemployed 16–24-year-olds were covered. In 1980, some two-thirds of young women who were out of school at 16 were gainfully employed; 14 percent were in government-created jobs, 10 percent were unemployed; 14 percent were in labor market training programs (Björklund and Persson-Tanimura, 1983). Only 2–3 percent of women who graduated from the upper secondary school system were unemployed.

In general, youth are facing more unemployment, and youth in temporary jobs are having a more difficult and prolonged transition into regular jobs. Yet parenthood is not viewed as an alternative path to fulfillment.

ABORTION LAWS

The Abortion Act of 1938 permitted abortion for medical, sociomedical, humanitarian, and eugenic reasons or upon injury to the fetus (the Swedish Institute, 1982). It required approval by two physicians up to the twentieth week, with more stringent requirements up to 24 weeks. Some minor liberalizing amendments were added in 1946 and in 1963, but the law was not basically altered until 1975. Until the late 1960s and early 1970s, the interpretation and enforcement of these laws were quite rigorous, and many Swedish women went abroad, mainly to Poland, to obtain abortions. Concern about this pattern, along with growing opposition to the law by women's groups and left-of-center politicians, led ultimately to a more liberal interpretation of the law; the abortion rate began to rise around 1970, and the number of illegal abortions virtually disappeared (Sundström-Feigenberg, 1984). A government committee was appointed in 1965 to consider future legislation; its report emerged in 1971. Publication of this report led to a spirited public debate. Finally, in 1974, the Swedish parliament enacted a liberalized abortion law that went into effect at the beginning of 1975.

The new law established some fresh legal principles: there is nothing criminal about abortion, and every woman has the right to decide whether or not to carry a pregnancy to term; the society can neither refuse a woman an abortion nor press her to obtain one (Sundström-Feigenberg, 1984); a teenager need not inform her parents in order to obtain an abortion, but discussion with the parents is encouraged.

Abortion is permitted on request up to the end of the eighteenth week of pregnancy. Through the twelfth week, a woman has only to consult a doctor; after that, she is also required to confer with a social worker. After 18 weeks, special grounds and additional approval are necessary. Some 95 percent of all abortions are performed by the twelfth week of pregnancy, according to reports of the 1980 Abortion Committee appointed to evaluate the new law (compared to 91 percent in the United States [Henshaw, 1985]) There is a small charge for the service, as for other minor gynecological operations. An abortion must be performed by a qualified medical practitioner, and the operation must be performed in a hospital or other approved institution. Most first-trimester abortions are done by vacuum aspiration or sharp curettage on an outpatient basis. Later abortions usually require a hospital stay of four to five days.

As noted above, the abortion rate among teenagers declined by slightly more than one-third between 1975 and 1982, while among women 20 and older it remained stable. Why should the teenage abortion rate have declined rather than increased after abortion was made more accessible?

CONTRACEPTIVE PROGRAMS

Although differences in views on abortion remain to some extent, all groups agree that abortion should be avoided insofar as possible. One of the political concerns at the time of the enactment of the new law was that an explosion of teenage abortions might ensue. A rise in the abortion rate for women 15–19 years old, from 12.7 per 1,000 in 1970 to 29.7 in 1975, increased this concern. Hence a major component of the 1974 Abortion Act involved contraceptive services, with a special emphasis on youth. In this sense, the liberalized abortion law might be called an abortion prevention measure.

Before the new law was enacted, it had actually been easier in some ways to obtain an abortion than to secure contraceptives, which were not considered part of the public health services and carried some cost. Since 1975, society has taken responsibility for the provision of contraceptives. Advisory services and some contraceptives are provided free. All contraceptives are offered without charge to young people. One of the interesting sidelights of the law is that a physician in Sweden is actually *prohibited* from informing parents that a young person has approached him or her for advice, a feature that presumably makes the program less threatening to younger teenagers.

A network of primary health care centers has been built up throughout the country. Family planning services are integrated into the maternal and child health care provided by these centers, which are the cornerstone of the whole health care system. A key step has been the training of midwives in maternal health care and the provision of contraceptive methods, including those methods formerly under physicians' control. The midwives, who are almost all women, take pride in their expertise and give individual attention to each patient. About 1,000 midwives are now trained to give pelvic examinations, insert IUDs, and, since 1978, to prescribe pills. In 1980, they provided 70 percent of the 450,000 public health consultations for contraception in Sweden (Swedish Institute, 1982).

While many young people, mostly women, utilize this primary health care network to obtain birth control services, it was recognized that such clinics would not necessarily be the best way to meet the needs of adolescents. Some young women are uncomfortable mingling with adults, pregnant women, and mothers with children—particularly if they feel they may run into their neighbors or their mothers' friends. One innovation of the 1974 Abortion Act was to finance a system of contraceptive clinics for youth. Since 1975, the number of such clinics has risen from 2 to 30, although they still do not cover the entire country. One in Stockholm is run directly by the school system, another by the National Association for Sexual Information, and a third by the Lutheran established church, but most are operated under the auspices of local government. These clinics provide contraceptive counseling and services to young people. As in the primary health care centers, the personnel consist largely of midwives; medical doctors act in a supervisory capacity and attend to special problems. Awareness of these facilities by teenagers is developed primarily in the school system through information given to teachers and school nurses and through pamphlets distributed to students.

The clients are mainly young women, although young men are more likely to attend if they have previously become acquainted with the clinic through a visit with their school class. The youth clinics are closed during school holidays; young people must either plan ahead for these periods or turn to other facilities in their communities. The clinics, moreover, are normally open only during the school day. A visit to a youth clinic is viewed as a valid reason for absence from school, and the school is often instrumental in making the arrangements.

Both types of clinic, the primary health care centers and the youth clinics, offer abortion counseling and care for sexually transmitted diseases, as well as contraceptive assistance. Care is taken to ensure that the realities of giving birth and child care are well understood. Although every client is free to make her own decision about abortion, abortion may be encouraged if the potential mother is known to have emotional problems. Many young people, particularly young men, come to the clinics initially with questions about sexually transmitted diseases. Medical personnel are particularly concerned about the recent rise in chlamydia among young women. Some clinics provide psychosexual counseling.

The clinics work closely with the school system. In addition to the midwife, the school nurse plays a crucial role in bringing birth control services to teenagers. Every school has a school nurse, who is prepared to make suggestions, discuss problems, and arrange referrals to clinics. School nurses are more likely than clinic personnel to have direct contact with male students; they are able to distribute condoms if necessary, although these are also available free from the clinics. Starting at around age 14, many students have an opportunity to become familiar with a clinic through a visit with their school class. (These are carried out in small groups, sometimes segregated by sex.) The clinics however, have not been able to fulfill all requests for such visits. One attempt to establish a medical contraceptive service directly in a school was not a great success; it was found that students prefer to go outside the school to obtain contraceptives, probably to assure anonymity.

There is now a considerable accumulation of experience in working with youth in Sweden. As noted above, the pill is widely accepted by the medical profession as the most appropriate method for young people. It is perceived to involve less risk and fewer complications than other methods and to be easy to manage. Pills may be prescribed as soon as a girl has menstruated regularly for one year, and a pelvic examination is not a necessary prerequisite, although it is always done soon after initiation of pill use. The IUD, which is used more widely in Sweden than in most other western countries, is also considered to be suitable for young people; it is believed that pelvic inflammatory disease can be dealt with satisfactorily and without risk to future fertility when there is a close relationship between the service and the client.

The morning-after pill is available on an experimental basis in a few places but is not yet permitted for general use. A few clients choose the diaphragm and, of course, many rely on condoms, which are available free from the clinics and are sold in gas stations, department stores, supermarkets, kiosks, and newspaper stands. Condoms and other contraceptives are widely advertised in the mass media.

Parallel to the provision of medical services, the Health Education Committee of the National Board of Health and Welfare has been working since 1974 on a long-term health education program to prevent unwanted pregnancies. It operates mainly through professionals in the public health and social welfare system and also through women's and youth organizations. Special information is directed to young people, through such means as notices posted in schools to publicize family planning services. Evidently this program has been successful. The rate of visits to the contraceptive advisory services increased by 41 percent between 1975 and 1981.

The public commission formed in 1980 to evaluate the implementation of the new abortion law reached the conclusion that the expanded contraceptive advisory services have prevented any increase in the abortion rate (*Family Planning and Abortion in Sweden,* 1983). The fact that the teenage pregnancy rate has fallen since 1975 was also interpreted to mean that abortion is not being used as an alternative to contraception. The team was told that, in the prevailing climate, pregnancies occur among the very young and immature and among those who are economically or emotionally deprived and do not use contraception effectively.

SEX EDUCATION

Sweden has been one of the world's leaders in promoting and institutionalizing sex education. The National Association for Sexual Information, which was founded in 1933, has spearheaded this effort. Sweden became the first country, in 1956, to make sex education a compulsory part of the school curriculum. There is evidently wide support now in the general population for such education.

The underlying philosophy of sex education in Sweden and the content of the curriculum have undergone several transformations. From a narrow biological emphasis, sex education has evolved to include the full context of human relationships. Even the label, "sex education," has been broadened, at first to "education in sex and life together," and then to "education in living together" (Trost, 1984). The word *sex* was not deleted for euphemistic reasons, but rather to indicate the changed orientation of the effort. Whereas in the early days stress had been laid on freedom and the presentation of all points of view, adult value judgments are now clearly stated for young people to accept or to reject. Responsible premarital sex is acceptable; sex is not to be regarded as an isolated event. Stress is placed on the importance of ethics, fidelity and equal rights, and on the responsibilities of parenthood.

Sex education is considered as part of an individual's education throughout the school years. Beginning at age seven, the child is taught about physical differences, sexual anatomy, menstruation, conception, contraception, and childbirth. These and many other topics of increasing complexity are covered during the entire period the individual is in school—typically from age 7 to age 19 (Boethius, 1984). Sexually transmitted diseases and abortion are included. The basic curriculum, which is part of the natural science program, is drawn up by the National Board of Education, but there is considerable latitude for interpretation by individual schools and teachers.

There has been concern over the years about the quality and training of the teachers who have the responsibility for transmitting this information and about underlying attitudes and values. A new handbook for teachers was published in 1977 following 10 years of research (National Swedish Board of Education, 1977). This manual describes the goals, questions and answers, methods, subject content, and the facts about sex education. Even though many of today's teachers were themselves exposed to sex education in school, not all are comfortable with the topic. It has been proven particularly difficult to train the teachers of teachers, and much reliance is still placed on in-service training when new teachers are already in the classroom.

Individual teachers may call upon a range of supplementary resources. The school nurse or a midwife from a nearby clinic may be brought in for assistance. The national educational television service has developed a series of programs designed to facilitate classroom discussion. Two examples for 15-year-olds, entitled "Get to Know Each Other First" and "You Can Get Pregnant," were found to be remarkably frank and open in their presentations. The latter included a conversation between a doctor and a young female patient during the course of a pelvic examination, a useful way to reduce possible apprehension about that procedure.

There is a considerable amount of communication between parents and their children; 58 percent of Swedish adolescents in Lewin's study (1980) of six localities reported having talked about sexuality with their mothers. But these same adolescents said that the best information concerning sexuality came from teachers. As Trost observed, "In fact most parents in Sweden as well as in the United States are not competent to give their children sex education" (Trost, 1984, p. 11). Recently there has been discussion of expanding the Swedish sex education program to provide for parents the same materials their children are receiving. Objections to sex education on the part of parents are expressed only occasionally by some new immigrant groups, who tend to be more traditional in their attitudes about sex.

The mass media appear to have played a minor role in changing sexual attitudes in Sweden. There is considerable portrayal of violence and of women as sex objects on television programs, which are largely imported from the United States. The sex education program attempts to counteract this kind of message. Video cassette recorders have recently become very popular, leading to a public debate about the showing of violence and pornography and, in 1981, to passage of an antipornography law. On the other hand, women's magazines do carry numerous articles on contraception, and a few special television programs have had some impact. One such program, "Peter's Baby," included the twin themes that it is difficult to have a baby when you are young and that it is all right for a young man to take care of a baby. The National Association for Sexual Information initiated a series of major publicity campaigns for particular purposes; following a 1970 campaign on gonorrhea the prevalence of this disease was reduced; a campaign on chlamydia was underway at this writing.

CAUSES OF THE RECENT DECLINE IN ADOLESCENT PREGNANCY

Given the close temporal correspondence in the decline of the teenage pregnancy rate and the expansion of contraceptive services that have been directed especially toward youth, it would seem reasonable to conclude that there is a direct causal connection. One possible method to evaluate this hypothesis might be to examine the changes in programs and in pregnancy rates on a county basis to determine how closely linked such changes were. The relative increase in the number of consultations about contraception in the first year of the new program, between 1975 and 1976, in relationship to the relative decline in teenage fertility during those two years, was examined for 11 counties (National Swedish Board of Education, 1977, p. 51). A moderate correlation (.53) in the expected direction was confirmed, but a more comprehensive analysis would be desirable.

There are two pieces of evidence, however, that raise at least some questions about this causal connection, although neither disqualifies it. The first is the fact that the teenage pregnancy rate in Denmark follows a very similar declining trend since 1975 (see figure 8.4); between 1977 and 1982, the rates in the two countries are virtually indistinguishable. The declines in pregnancy rates from 1975 for the age group 20–24 are also similar, but at ages 25 and over the rates show a decline in Denmark but no change in Sweden.

The difficulty in concluding that the special contraceptive and educational programs initiated in Sweden as part of the 1974 Abortion Act are responsible for the decline in teenage pregnancy in that country is that an identical trend in a neighboring country with many cultural and economic similarities suggests that more basic social changes may be occurring. The missing link in this analysis is the absence of information on teenage contraceptive practice and, in particular, whether

Fig. 8.4. *Sweden and Denmark: Births plus abortions per 1,000 women aged 15–19 and 20–24, 1970–82*

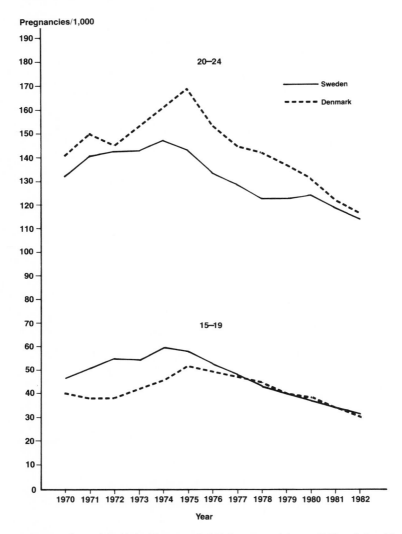

Sources: Central Statistical Bureau, *Befolknings-Förändringer, 1983*, vol. 3, tables 3.16 and 3.24; Statistics Denmark, *Befolkningens Bevaegelser, 1980* (Copenhagen: 1982).
Note: Data are unavailable for Denmark for 1973.

government programs relevant to teenage contraceptive behavior comparable to those in Sweden have also operated in Denmark.

The abortion law in Denmark was significantly liberalized in 1973, making the procedure available on request through the first trimester. Abortion is considered a medical procedure in Denmark and, like all other hospital care, is financed by the government. In 1974 and 1975, the abortion rate increased dramatically in all age groups. At the same time, the sales of oral contraceptives declined, but those of IUDs increased (Matthiessen, 1979; Somers and Gammeltoft, 1976). Since 1975, the sale of pills, a measure that is particularly indicative of the contraceptive use levels of younger women, has increased again, a trend that is consistent with the decline in the teenage pregnancy rate. Sex education has been compulsory in Danish schools since 1958 for children over 13 and, since the early 1970s, has been increasingly linked with contraceptive services. Thus the abortion, contraceptive, and sex education practices in Denmark appear quite similar to those in Sweden, though the government seems to have pushed harder in Sweden on all fronts.

During the researchers' collection of information about teenage pregnancy in Sweden, several different social trends were detected that might also be relevant to the teenage subculture in Sweden. The juvenile delinquency rate declined during the 1970s, especially among 15–17-year-olds and, to a lesser extent, among 18–20-year-olds; in contrast, the crime rate for adults continued to rise (Sarnecki, 1983). There is also evidence reported that alcohol consumption has declined among youth (Henriksson, 1983; Rehn, 1984). Rehn asserts that the consumption of alcohol "reached its peak in the early 1970s and has tended to decline — at least in Sweden, owing perhaps to the energetic dissemination of information in the schools about the harmful effects of alcohol" (p. 153). Evidently there is also some decline in drug use among 16-year-olds, and teenage smoking is reported to have declined (Henriksson, 1983, p. 186).

If whatever social forces that were contributing to increasing the alienation of youth were diminishing, this should be reflected in a reduction in teenage suicide rates. Indeed, World Health Organization statistics show a 21–percent decline between 1975 and 1979 in the suicide rate for 15–24-year-olds, while over the same period the suicide rates for persons over age 24 generally increased. In Denmark, however, the teenage suicide rate increased by 13 percent during the same time period, which is contrary to the more general theory of social change (WHO).

Without undertaking a more extensive study, this is about as far as these causal interpretations can be pushed. The most plausible reason for the decline in the teenage pregnancy rate in Sweden since the mid-1970s is the government-financed program of health education and contraceptive services to youth that was initiated following the liberalization of abortion in 1975, and the close integration of these services with the school sex education program. A demonstration program on the island of Gotland certainly indicated the potential of these programs for reducing teenage pregnancy (National Swedish Board of

Health and Welfare, 1978). However, there may be other social changes reducing the alienation of youth that may be significant. Moreover, the situation is not exactly parallel in Denmark, which shows the same decline of teenage pregnancy since 1975. Nevertheless, the most obvious explanation seems also in this instance to be the most reasonable one.

SWEDEN AND THE UNITED STATES

The principal objective of this review of Swedish teenage pregnancy was to learn what could possibly be exported from the Swedish experience to the United States in the interest of reducing U.S. teenage pregnancy rates. Even before the beginning of the decline in teenage pregnancy in Sweden—that is, in the 1960s and 1970s—the rates were much lower than in the United States.

It is not difficult to enumerate the important respects in which Sweden and the United States are different. Sweden is much smaller and much more ethnically homogeneous than the United States. There is nothing comparable in Sweden to the large American black and Hispanic minorities. The greater homogeneity of the Swedish population also extends to the socioeconomic class system, where the high tax rates greatly reduce income differences. There is no extensive poverty or large underclass in Sweden such as exists in the United States. The government in Sweden, in the context of a benign welfare state, plays a much more pervasive role in the lives of its citizens. Sweden is also more homogeneous in terms of religion. Most Swedes have a Lutheran background, but Sweden is, in fact, a highly secular society. The United States on the other hand, is highly relgious with a strong element of sexually conservative religious fundamentalism that influences sexual and reproductive behavior (chapter 3).

One important implication of these differences is that the Swedish attitude toward sexuality is more relaxed and less moralistic than is the American. This means that sex education, which is so institutionalized and comprehensive in Sweden, is still surrounded with controversy in the United States. For many years attitudes toward premarital sexuality in Swedish society have been less encumbered with ambivalence than in the United States. In the latter country, sex education is believed ideally to be transmitted in the home, but there is little evidence that much effective communication occurs there (chapter 3).

The differences between the two countries in population size and homogeneity also promote greater social control in Sweden, which affects not only paternal responsibilities, but also increases the potential for responses to new programs—for example, the noted redirection of the sex education curriculum to broader issues.

These contrasts between the societies are important, but the many basic similarities should not be overlooked. Both countries are democracies, have highly advanced economies, and are consumer societies. In both countries the educational process extends through the teenage years for most people, and young Swedish and American men and women entering the labor market face considerable difficulty in finding and keeping a satisfactory job (chapter 3). In both countries the populations are highly urbanized and widely exposed to the influence of mass media. Abortion is legal and contraception is widely available in Sweden and the United States, although differences exist in costs, ease of access, and advertising; and there is much more controversy about abortion in the United States. In both countries adult fertility is very low, the age at maternity is increasing, and similar patterns of differential fertility exist with later ages of childbearing and lower fertility among the more educated, white-collar classes. In both countries the status of women has advanced in recent decades.

What lessons can be learned from the Swedish experience about teenage pregnancy? The most obvious is that the provision of comprehensive sex education in the schools combined with contraceptive services oriented toward youth seem to yield results, at least in a society like Sweden's. This conclusion is the same as that reached by Prudence Brown on the basis of her impressions in Sweden (Brown, 1983, p. 95). But could these programs be adopted in America without fundamental changes in attitudes toward premarital sex? As seen in chapter 3, although approval of premarital sex has increased, not much more than half of Americans believe it is not wrong.

The Scandinavian societies, particularly those of Sweden and Denmark, have long been regarded as models of social change for other western nations, including the United States. The decline in marriage and the rise of informal cohabitation that began in Sweden and Denmark is being followed in the United States, France, Britain, the Netherlands, and other developed countries. One consequence of this change in Sweden, with so many children born out of wedlock, has been the rejection of the status of illegitimacy, a process that is beginning among the U.S. white population and is already well established among American blacks. These, as well as other changes, perhaps imply that the United States will be following suit eventually in adopting more relaxed attitudes toward adolescent sexuality.

"Eventually," however, could be a long time coming, and there may well be opportunities in the meantime for local demonstration projects of the potential effectiveness of sex education and contraceptive services in reducing teenage pregnancy. As in other areas of human behavior, perhaps behavior can be altered without having to wait for changes in basic social attitudes.

9

The Six Countries:
Some Conclusions

The six countries examined in the preceding chapters have much in common. All are highly developed and share the benefits and problems of urban industrial societies. All belong essentially to the cultural tradition of northwestern Europe. In each, life expectancy at birth is over 70 years, and fertility has declined to levels below that required for generational replacement.

Yet their experience with respect to the reproductive behavior of young women has been quite diverse. One element they have in common is that the birthrates for women below age 20 have declined in recent years. The trends in abortion rates, where they are known, vary markedly. The overall teenage pregnancy rate rose in the United States during the late 1970s, whereas the incidence of pregnancy fell in England and Wales and Sweden. Around 1980, the intercountry patterns of the birthrates and abortion rates and, hence, of the pregnancy rates, were very similar. The U.S. rates were highest by a considerable margin; all three rates were by far the lowest in the Netherlands. Canada, England and Wales, and France form an intermediate group. Sweden is the one anomaly, with a birthrate almost as low as the Netherlands but abortion and overall pregnancy rates nearer to the intermediate group of countries. The difference between the U.S. birthrate and those of the other countries was greater for women aged 17 and below than for those aged 18–19, whereas the differential in the abortion rate was similar for each age.

The similarity of the relative positions of the birthrate and abortion rate for the six countries points immediately to one important conclusion: adolescent birthrates are not lower in other countries than in the United States due to more frequent resort to abortion in those countries. On the contrary, where the birthrate is low, the abortion rate tends to be low as well. Thus the explanation of intercountry differences is best focused on the determinants of pregnancy as the antecedent of both births and abortions. At the same time, in every country, abortion does play a greater role in reducing the birthrates of younger teenagers than of older teenagers.[1]

The generalizations made below are based on information that varies widely with respect to precision and objectivity. The key quantitative data relevant to adolescent pregnancy that lend themselves to presentation in a reasonably comparable form are summarized first. Even some of these figures, although objectively derived, have a wide margin of error. The data on sexual activity and contraceptive use, especially, must be examined in the light of the comments and qualifications detailed in the individual country chapters. The inferences drawn in the latter part of this chapter represent the common threads emerging from interviews with individuals in the countries; much of the material is qualitative and could be interpreted in different ways. But given the dearth of hard data and the problems of intercountry comparability, it appears that only in this way can the range of issues most frequently raised in connection with adolescent pregnancy be addressed.

PREGNANCY INTENTIONS

One factor that is important for the evaluation of differences among countries in the incidence of teenage pregnancy is the extent to which these pregnancies are unintended. If the differences in pregnancy rates between the United States and the other countries were due mainly to the fact that more young American women choose to become pregnant, the implications for policy and program would be quite different than if the higher U.S. pregnancy rates were mainly the result of involuntary conceptions. Direct data on pregnancy intentions are not available for any country except the United States. However, the percentage distributions of pregnancies by several categories of outcome designed to shed some light on this point are shown in table 9.1. Figure 9.1 shows the same data weighted by the overall pregnancy rate for women 15–19 years old. No account has been taken of spontaneous fetal loss in these distributions, and age is defined as elsewhere in this book, as of the termination of the pregnancy rather than at conception.

1. When births and abortions are tabulated by age at conception rather than age at outcome, the contrast between 15–17-year-olds and 18–19-year-olds in the relative importance of abortion is reduced and in the United States it virtually disappears.

Table 9.1. *Percentage distribution of pregnancy outcomes, by age of woman at outcome*

Age and outcome	United States 1981	Canada 1981	England & Wales 1981	France* 1980	Netherlands 1980	Sweden 1980
Age and outcome						
15–17						
Marital births	18	—	15	17	32	—
Postmarital conceptions	(8)	—	(3)	—	—	—
Premarital conceptions†	(10)	—	(12)	—	—	—
Nonmarital births	32	—	32	22	15	—
Abortions	50	—	53‡	61	54	—
Total	100	100	100	100	100	—
18–19						
Marital births	34	—	43	39	55	—
Postmarital conceptions	(24)	—	(24)	—	—	—
Premarital conceptions†	(10)	—	(19)	—	—	—
Nonmarital births	24	—	27	20	15	—
Abortions	42	—	29‡	41	30	—
Total	100	100	100	100	100	—
15–19						
Marital births	28	24	33	34	48	8
Postmarital conceptions	(18)	—	(17)	—	—	—
Premarital conceptions†	(10)	—	(16)	—	—	—
Nonmarital births	27	35	29	20	15	35
Abortions	45	41	38	46	37	58
Total	100	100	100	100	100	100

Sources: Canada: Abortions—Statistics Canada, 1984; *Therapeutic Abortions, 1981,* 71. Births—Statistics Canada, 1983; *Vital Statistics,* vol. 1, "Births and Deaths," table 8. France: Abortions—Tietze, 1984; unpublished data from DAGSPR (deaging program) output (age at term) for *Induced Abortion: A World Review, 1983,* The Population Council, New York, 1984. Births—Les Collections d'INSEE [D94], table 18. England and Wales: Abortions and Births—OPCS, 1984; *Birth Statistics 1981, England and Wales,* Series FMI, No. 8, HMSO, London. Netherlands: Abortions—Tietze, 1984. Births—Central Bureau of Statistics, 1984, unpublished statistics, The Hague. Sweden: Abortions and total births—Tietze, 1984. Legitimate births—United Nations, 1982. *United Nations Demographic Yearbook 1982,* table 33. United States: Table 3.1.
*Age defined as that achieved during the calendar year.
†Defined as births occurring less than eight months after marriage.
‡Estimated from the total number of abortions to women aged 15–19 in 1981 and the distribution of abortions by single year of age in 1980.

It is probably safe to assume that the overwhelming majority of abortions follow unintended conceptions. Using abortion as a preliminary measure of unintended pregnancy, the highest proportion of pregnancies terminated by abortion occurs in Sweden, and the lowest proportions in England and Wales and the Netherlands.[2] A higher percentage of pregnancies occurring among women below age 17 than among women aged 18–19 are terminated by abortion and, in this

2. The same comparison, including complete data for age groups 15–17 and 18–19, can be made on the basis of the abortion rates and the pregnancy rates given in chapter 2.

Fig. 9.1. *Percentage distribution of pregnancies and pregnancy rates, by outcome, for women aged 15–19, 1980–81*

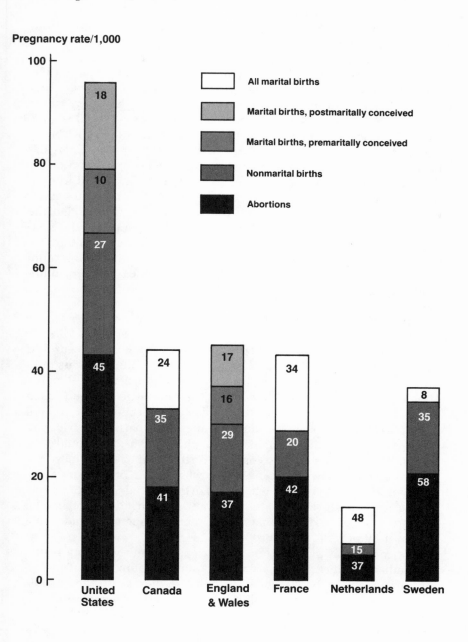

Sources: See sources in table 9.1.
Note: The numbers inside the bars represent the percentage distributions.

sense, are unintended in every country; but the difference between the two age groups is smaller in the United States than in the other four countries for which data are available.

The proportion of pregnancies resulting in births outside marriage is greatest in Sweden and Canada and least in the Netherlands. The overwhelming majority of such births have probably also been undesired. Such is probably not the case in Sweden, however, where premarital childbearing has traditionally been free of social stigma. There the fraction of all pregnancies resulting in out-of-wedlock births is as large as or larger than that of any of the other countries. There has been a growing acceptance of cohabitation in other countries as well—a situation that is thought to explain partially the rising trend in nonmarital birthrates. If it is assumed, nevertheless, that in the five countries outside Sweden, most births outside marriage are unintended, the combined fraction of pregnancies represented by abortions and nonmarital births is about three-fourths in the United States and Canada, close to two-thirds in England and Wales and France, and only around one-half in the Netherlands. According to this measure also, unintended pregnancy is considerably higher among younger than among older teenagers.

Thus, as a whole, marital births, the category most likely to be wanted, constitute the largest proportion of all pregnancies in the Netherlands (48 percent); if all births in Sweden are wanted regardless of the marital status of the mother—admittedly, an unlikely assumption—the percentage is nearly as high there (43 percent). For the United States and England and Wales, marital births can be broken down by the marital status of the mother at conception. Premarital conceptions are probably mainly unintended, particularly among young women, although the extent to which this is true could vary substantially from country to country. Births legitimated by marriage following conception represent a somewhat larger proportion of all pregnancies in England and Wales than in the United States, especially among women 18–19 years old; if these are included in the total proportion of pregnancies that are unintended, the total comes to a little over 80 percent in both countries.[3]

The conclusion that emerges most clearly from these data is that involuntary childbearing appears to be a smaller component of adolescent pregnancy in the Netherlands than elsewhere, with the possible exception of Sweden. A much higher proportion of pregnancies lead to abortions and nonmarital births, the categories most likely to be unintended, among younger than among older teenagers; but this dif-

3. Direct reporting of intention status for the United States yields a similar proportion unintended; see chapter 3.

ference by age may not apply to births legitimated by marriage following conception. The incidence of pregnancies, both intended and unintended, is far greater overall in the United States than in any of the other countries (figure 9.1). A dramatic illustration of the significance of the differential in unintended pregnancies between the United States and the other countries is that the rate of abortions in the United States is about as high as or higher than the *overall* teenage pregnancy rate in each of the other countries (figure 9.1).

A somewhat different view of essentially the same topic can be gained from the marital and nonmarital fertility rates presented in table 9.2. (Sweden is omitted from this table because Swedish women's marital status is less relevant for her childbearing intentions.) The number of births per 1,000 married women aged 15–19 ranges from around 250 in France and the Netherlands to about 350 in England and Wales and the United States.[4] The extent to which marital childbearing can be interpreted as intended depends on how many marriages are precipitated by accidental pregnancies. The relative differences among the countries in nonmarital fertility are much greater, although the absolute differences are very small. Again, France and the Netherlands have the lowest rates.[5] The U.S. rate is about double those of Canada and England and Wales. Thus in this perspective, too, unintended conception does appear to contribute disproportionately to the high teenage pregnancy rate in the United States.

The racial difference in teenage birthrates within the United States, to which reference has been made in chapters 2 and 3, revolves to a large extent around marital status. The marital birthrate for whites is the same as that for all U.S. women aged 15–19 and, thus, is only marginally higher than the marital rate for England and Wales; the nonmarital rate is very much lower than that for all U.S. women aged 15–19 and not a great deal above the nonmarital rates for Canada and England and Wales (see chapter 3). Hence the contrast between the United States and other countries with respect to unintended childbearing—but not unintended pregnancy—would be much less striking if only the white population were considered.

EXPOSURE TO THE RISK OF PREGNANCY

Another fundamental issue involves the comparative levels of exposure to the risk of pregnancy among adolescents in the six countries. Two

4. The French rate would be marginally lower if age were defined in the same way as it is for the other countries.

5. In this case, the French rate would be a little higher if age were defined in terms of completed years.

Table 9.2. *Number of marital and nonmarital births per 1,000 women aged 15–20*

Marital status and age	United States 1981	Canada 1981	England and Wales 1981	France† 1980	Netherlands 1980
Marital					
15	386	—	—	229	221
16	452	—	430	309	368
17	453	—	483	315	434
18	378	—	364	240	309
19	301	—	309	240	219
20	—	—	—	223	—
15–17	447	—	472	311	407
18–19	327	—	326	240	245
15–19	351	286	343	247	264
Nonmarital					
15	11	—	2	1	0
16	21	—	8	2	1
17	30	—	15	6	1
18	37	—	22	10	4
19	42	—	24	19	5
20	—	—	—	24	—
15–17	21	—	9	3	1
18–19	40	—	23	14	4
15–19	28	16	14	7	2

Sources: United States: Calculated from NCHS, 1983, tables 2 and 15; U.S. Bureau of the Census, 1984a, table 2, and 1982c, table 1; Westoff, 1984. Canada: Calculated from Statistics Canada, 1983, 1983b, and 1983c; J. A. Norland, *Common-Law Unions in Canada: Age Composition,* Interim Report No. 4, Statistics Canada, Ottawa, 1984. England and Wales: Calculated from OPCS, *Sex, Age, and Marital Status 1981,* HMSO, London, 1983. France: Calculated from Les Collections d'INSEE [D94], table 18 and [D90] table 2, 1982. Netherlands: Calculated from Central Bureau of Statistics, unpublished tables.

*Sweden is omitted because the traditional acceptance of nonmarital childbearing makes the situation noncomparable with other countries.

†Age defined as that achieved during the calendar year.

kinds of data are assembled here: those on marriage and cohabitation and those on sexual activity per se. The former give a minimum estimate of the prevalence of regular sexual relationships, in which exposure to the risk of pregnancy can be assumed to be high. The one piece of direct information on sexual activity that can be compared across countries is the proportion of teenagers who had ever had intercourse, a maximum estimate of those exposed to the risk of pregnancy. Thus the two sets of data form, in a sense, the probable upper and lower bounds of sexual experience.

Among women aged 15–19 the percentage who are married varies quite widely, from 1 percent in Sweden to 8 percent in the United States (table 9.3).[6] In the other four countries, the level is approximately half that of the United States. Although the absolute values are very small, the proportions married are greater in the United States than in other countries, even at age 17 and below. In all six countries, the percentages of women under age 20 who were married had been declining during the late 1970s, in conjunction with a general rise in the age at first marriage. The implications of data on marriage are somewhat uncertain because marriage is a consequence, as well as an antecedent, of pregnancy.

On the other hand, the proportions of women who were living with a man to whom they were not legally married had generally been rising during this period. The scattered data available suggest that around 1980, small but not negligible proportions of women aged 18–19 were currently in such relationships (table 9.3). The exception is Sweden, where in 1980 at least 18 percent of 18–19-year-old women were cohabiting, compensating for the very low proportion actually married. Elsewhere also, the proportions cohabiting seem to some extent to be an inverse function of the proportions married, with the result that the relative differences in the overall proportions living in a sexual union are not so large (table 9.3). U.S. women at ages 18–19 appear to be somewhat more likely than those in Canada and Great Britain to be living in some kind of sexual union, but by the time they reach their early twenties, this differential is no longer apparent.

Needless to say, not all sexual activity is confined to couples who live together, although intercourse is likely to be less frequent or more episodic for women who do not reside with a partner. The proportions of women who have ever had sexual intercourse are shown, cumulated by age, in table 9.4 and figure 9.2. These data come mainly from special surveys for some countries; they tend to suffer from small sample size, as well as noncomparability of various kinds, and they must therefore be interpreted with considerable caution.

The outstanding observation emerging from these comparisons is that sexual activity appears to be initiated at an appreciably earlier age in Sweden than in the other countries; by age 16 one-third of all Swedish women have had intercourse and by age 18 four-fifths have done so. Although data for Canada are not ideal, it seems that women have their first sexual experience later there than elsewhere; in 1976 only one out of five was sexually experienced at ages 16–17. However, data on contraceptive use from the Canadian Fertility Survey suggest that by 1984 sexual activity among Canadian and U.S. young women

6. The minimum legal age at marriage (with parental consent) is 15 in France, 16 in England and Wales and the Netherlands, and 18 in Sweden (Paxman, 1980, table E); in the United States and Canada it varies according to state and provincial law.

Table 9.3. *Percentages of women currently married, currently cohabiting, and total currently in a sexual union, by age*

Marital status and age	United States 1980	Canada 1981	Great Britain 1981	France 1980	France 1981	Netherlands 1980	Netherlands 1982	Sweden 1981†
Currently married								
15	1	0	—	0	—	0	0	—
16	2	1	0	0	—	0	0	—
17	5	2	2	2	—	1	‡	—
18	10	5	6	6	—		‡	—
19	20	11	14	15	—	9	1	—
18–19	15	8	10	10	—	6	5	1
15–19	8	4	4	5	—	3	2	1
							13*	
20–24	41	39	44	47	—	43	—	15
Currently cohabiting								
15	0	0	—	—		—		—
16	1	1	—	—		—		—
17	1	2	—	—		—		—
18	3	4	—	—		—		—
19	4	7	—	—		—		—
18–19	3	6	4	—				18
15–19	2	3	—		1			8
							9*	
20–24	5	9	6	8				44
Total in a sexual union								
15	1	0	—					—
16	3	1	—					—
17	6	3	—					—
18	13	9	—					—
19	24	18	—					—
18–19	18	13	14					19
15–19	10	7	—					9
							22*	
20–24	47	48	50	—				59

Sources: United States: See table 3.4; Canada: Statistics Canada, 1983b; Norland, 1983, table 1; Great Britain: Brown and Kiernan, 1981; United Nations, 1984, p. 502; France: Collections d'INSEE, [D90] 1982, Gokalp, 1981, tables 52 and 53. Netherlands: Central Bureau of Statistics, 1983, figures 1–3, and unpublished tabulations. Sweden: International Statistical Institute, 1984, p. 9.

*Data refer to ages 18–22.

†Estimates for teenagers based on the 1980 census, adjusted to the level of the 1981 survey using the results for older women.

‡<0.5 percent.

Table 9.4. *Percentages of women who ever had intercourse, by age and marital status*

Exact age	United States						Canada*	Great Britain		France	Netherlands		Sweden
	1976 T	1979 T	1982 T	1976 NM	1979 NM	1982 NM	1976 T	1976 T	1976 NM	1984† T	1981 NM	T	1981‡ T
15	19	22	19	18	21	19	8			4			
16	28	36	31	25	35	29	19	22	22		34	35	34
17	45	49	44	41	46	41		37	36	28			
18	54	59	58	45	53	53		60	54		62	64	81
19	68	71	72	55	65	65		68	57	70			
20													96
21							60§						

Sources: See tables 3.5, 4.1, 5.3, 7.2, 8.1; France: *Le Nouvel Observateur*, 1984.
Notes: See Chapters 3–8 for a discussion of the special characteristics and limitations of the data. T = all women; NM = never married women.
*Proportions shown may exclude women who had had intercourse but were having it less than "a few times a year" at the time of the survey.
†Retrospective data 1975–84.
‡Retrospective data 1971–79.
§Data refer to age group 18–23.

Fig. 9.2. *Percentage of women who ever had intercourse, by age*

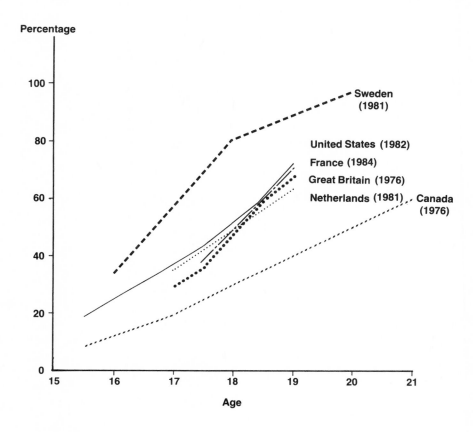

Source: Table 9.4.
Note: The year of the most recent information available for each country appears in parentheses.

aged 18–19 was comparable, since 50 percent of the Canadians in this age group were currently practicing contraception and another 3 percent were pregnant, postpartum, or seeking pregnancy—and are, therefore, by definition sexually active (table 4.2). Some, in addition, must have had intercourse but were not currently practicing contraception. In 1982, 65 percent of American women in that age group had ever had intercourse.

The median age at initiation of intercourse among U.S. teenage women appears to be slightly below age 18; in France, the Netherlands, and Great Britain, the median age is about age 18; in Sweden, it is below age 17; and in Canada, it is probably between ages 18 and 19.

In general, it would seem that Swedish teenage women initiate intercourse about one year earlier, and Canadian teens possibly as much as one year later, than their U.S. counterparts. However, U.S. teenagers appear to be more likely than those in the other countries, except Sweden, to have started intercourse at the youngest ages. This has implications for contraceptive use because contraceptive practice is generally more effective at the older ages. In both Great Britain and France, fewer women may initiate coitus at ages below 18 than in the United States, but they then seem to catch up rapidly, and in France, at least, the proportion who have had intercourse by age 19 could well be higher than in the United States. It would be a mistake to make too much of small differences, but the pattern is at least consistent with the age curves of the pregnancy rates, which show a greater excess among younger U.S. teenagers and a very steep rise in the French rate after age 16. The Dutch data on this point are weak in various respects; probably the most that can be said is that the levels seem to be roughly on a par with those in the United States.

From the information on exposure to the risk of pregnancy, it is obvious that the pattern of intercountry variation in adolescent pregnancy rates cannot be explained satisfactorily by differences in the level of sexual activity. The examples of the Netherlands and Sweden make it clear that the postponement of intercourse is not a necessary prerequisite for the avoidance of early pregnancy. Exposure seems, nevertheless, to play a noticeable role in certain instances. Whether measured by the proportions living in a sexual union or by the proportions ever having had intercourse, there appears to be somewhat more exposure at ages 17 and below in the United States than in the other countries except Sweden, which could contribute to the greater differential between the pregnancy rates observed for younger U.S. teenagers as compared to young teenagers in the other countries. It is tempting, moreover, to speculate whether the pregnancy rates in Sweden might be as low as those in the Netherlands were it not for the unusually early initiation of sex in Sweden. Finally, it seems probable that there is less sexual activity among younger Canadian teenagers than elsewhere and that reduced exposure might be partly responsible for keeping the pregnancy rates of young teenagers low in that country.

The only remaining opportunity for quantitative comparison among the six countries concerns contraceptive use. Figure 9.3 shows the proportions of sexually active women using any method of contraception and, among users, the proportions relying on the pill. Again, these data are taken from surveys that differ widely in their design and approach to the topic, and assembling them in a comparative format is, at the very least, a bold undertaking.

Use of any contraceptive method seems to be less common in France,

Fig. 9.3. *Percentage of sexually active women using any contraceptive method and, among users, percentage using the pill, by age and marital status of woman, and occasion of contraceptive use*

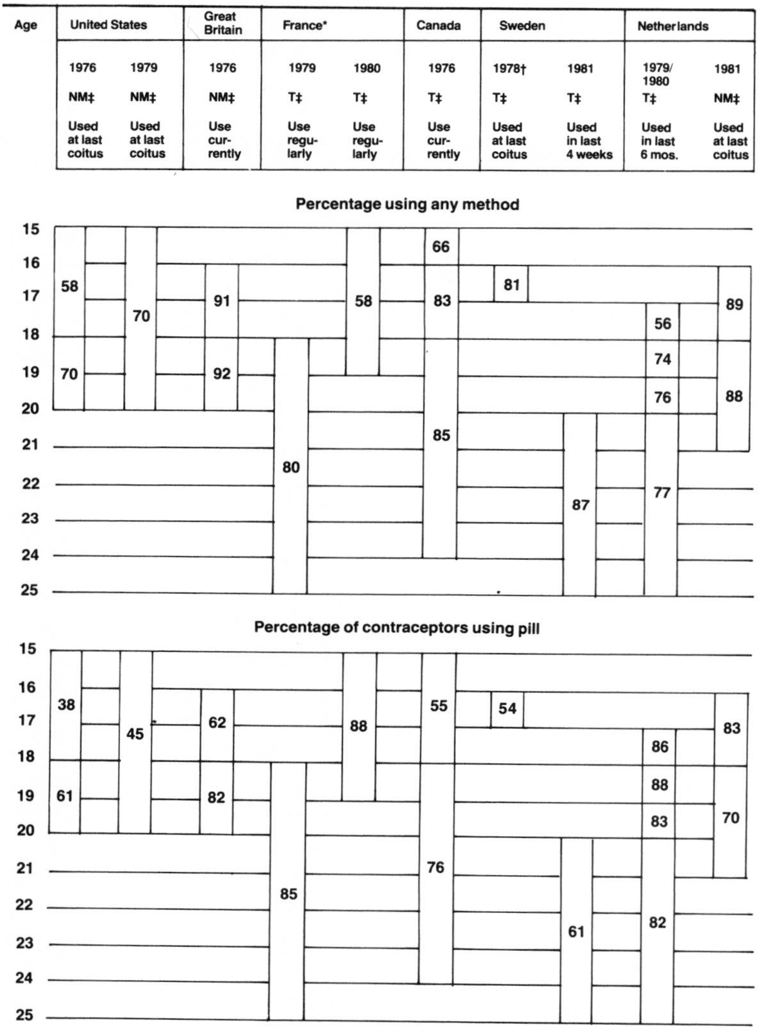

Age
United States
Great Britain
France*
Canada
Sweden
Netherlands
1976
1979
1976
1979
1980
1976
1978†
1981
1979/1980
1981
NM‡
NM‡
NM‡
T‡
T‡
T‡
T‡
T‡
T‡
NM‡
Used at last coitus
Used at last coitus
Use currently
Use regularly
Use regularly
Use currently
Used at last coitus
Used in last 4 weeks
Used in last 6 mos.
Used at last coitus
Percentage using any method
15
16
17
18
19
20
21
22
23
24
25
58
70
70
91
92
80
58
66
83
85
81
87
56
74
76
77
89
88
Percentage of contraceptors using pill
15
16
17
18
19
20
21
22
23
24
25
38
61
45
62
82
85
88
55
76
54
61
86
88
83
82
83
70

Sources: United States: Zelnik and Kantner, 1977, table 12; Dryfoos and Bourque-Scholl, 1981. Great Britain: table 5.4. France: table 6.3. Canada: table 4.3. Sweden: B. Lewin, 1980; table 8.2 and chapter 8, this work. Netherlands: table 7.5.

Notes: The data should be interpreted cautiously because of problems in their comparability and quality.

As an example of how to read this figure, the data for Canada indicate that among all the United States, and possibly the Netherlands than in the other three countries (figure 9.3). In France, the proportions shown are probably underestimated due to the omission of male methods. The low figures for the Netherlands come from one of two surveys, both of which had very small samples; the other Dutch survey suggests appreciably more use of contraceptives. More recent data from the 1984 Canadian Fertility Survey reinforces the impression that contraceptive use is higher than in the United States (table 4.2). Thus the United States could well have the lowest level of use of any of the six countries. The proportion of users who employ the pill, the most effective of the methods widely used by young people, also appears to be smaller in the United States than in the other countries (figure 9.3). The principal conclusion to emerge from this review is that less adequate practice of contraception contributes to the higher incidence of unintended pregnancy in the United States. The more detailed evidence presented in some of the country reports corroborates this view.

Sexual activity and contraceptive use among adolescents are critical issues in this study. This is the rationale for presenting the quantitative data that exist. Some relevant topics could not be covered due to lack of data. With respect to sexual activity, the omission of coital frequency is especially regrettable.[7] Even when the age at first intercourse is similar in two countries, actual exposure to the risk of pregnancy may not be the same due to substantial differences in the likelihood that intercourse will occur subsequently on a regular basis. Adolescent relationships are thought to be typically episodic in all of these countries, but insufficient data exist to address this question.

With respect to fertility control, no information was available concerning the efficacy of adolescent contraceptive practice. There are many reasons to believe that the regularity and care with which adolescents use a given method of contraception could vary widely from one society to another. Contraceptive use could also be affected by the type of relationship involved. For example, a casual encounter may be less likely than an ongoing relationship to involve a level of communication and respect for the other person that would encourage efforts to avoid

7. Data on coital frequency were available only for the United States and the Netherlands and are not directly comparable. The available information suggests, however, that in these two countries frequency is not very different; see chapters 3 and 7.

sexually active women, 66 percent of 15-year-olds, 83 percent of 16–17-year-olds, and 85 percent of 18–23-year-olds were using some method in 1976.

*Students only; condom use excluded.

†Students of both sexes in one city.

‡T=all women; NM=never-married women.

pregnancy. A few scattered pieces of information on the nature of relationships and number of partners were gathered, as were such additional data that could be indirectly relevant, such as differences in age at first intercourse by sex and prevalence of sexually transmitted disease and pelvic inflammatory disease; but there was not enough evidence on which to base intercountry comparisons. Finally, it should be noted that both postcoital contraception and menstrual extraction are practiced to some degree in most of these countries, but it seems unlikely that either is sufficiently widespread to have a substantial bearing on the pregnancy rate, except perhaps in the Netherlands.

CONTRACEPTIVE SERVICES, ABORTION SERVICES, AND SEX EDUCATION

Given the many types of providers of contraceptive services that exist in all of the countries, it would be difficult to obtain an objective measure of the physical accessibility of services, and no attempt was made to do so. The comments on this topic are based on the reports of knowledgeable people and on firsthand observation in the countries.

Contraceptive services appear to be most accessible in England and Wales, the Netherlands, and Sweden. Young people in these three countries almost always have more than one option. In England and Wales and the Netherlands, those seeking care may choose to go either to a general practitioner (in the Netherlands, their own family doctor) or to one of a reasonably dense network of clinics. The likelihood that a teenager would encounter a physician who was not receptive to her request is small in either of these countries (with the exception of women below age 16 in England and Wales, as noted below). The Dutch clinic system is less extensive than the English one, but it is directed largely toward meeting the special needs of youth; in England and Wales there are relatively few youth clinics. In Sweden, there are two parallel clinic systems, one consisting of the primary health care centers, which serve every community, and the other made up of a less complete network providing contraceptive care and related services specifically to the school-age population.

The impression gained is that contraceptive services tend to be less physically accessible in Canada, France, and the United States. Although all of these countries have an adequate supply of physicians who could be consulted, many doctors will not provide contraceptives to unmarried minors, especially without parental involvement. All three countries also have clinic systems, but they appear to be less well developed than those in the first group of countries. In France, this applies mainly to the period before 1981. The Canadian clinic system is uneven, with fairly complete coverage for adolescents in the provinces of Ontario and Quebec but scattered services elsewhere. The U.S. clinic network provides a local source of assistance in most communities and, thus, is reasonably accessible in a strictly geographic sense. Moreover, all U.S. family planning clinics that receive federal funds are required to serve adolescents. A basic drawback of the U.S. clinic system, however, is that it was developed primarily as a service for the poor and is avoided by many nonpoor teenagers.

The above considerations focus on medical services. Condoms are very widely available in Sweden, the Netherlands, and England and Wales. They are sold not only in family planning clinics and pharmacies, but in supermarkets, kiosks, and ubiquitous vending machines. In many parts of Canada, France, and the United States, condoms have been less freely available.

Contraceptive care, including supplies, is provided entirely free of charge to young people in England and Wales and Sweden. Elsewhere the possible costs depend partly on whether or not young people are willing to take advantage of public or private family health insurance, an option that often implies their parents will know what they are doing. Free services and supplies are available from clinics to French women under age 18, and for older teenagers most of these expenses are reimbursable under social security. Dutch family doctors are paid through the national health insurance scheme, but the clinics charge a small fee; until very recently no charge was made to have a prescription filled at a pharmacy. In Canada, doctors' services are also covered by national medical insurance; but all except those on welfare have to pay for supplies obtained from pharmacies. Clinic services are free in Ontario and some other parts of Canada. The potential expense of obtaining contraceptive services in the United States varies considerably. A small fraction of teenagers are able to get free care through Medicaid, the federal-state system of payments for health care to the very poor—mainly the old, the handicapped, and single indigent mothers. Some do not have to pay anything because of individual clinic policy; otherwise clinic fees are usually modest. On the other hand, consulting a private doctor usually entails appreciable expense, as does purchase of supplies at pharmacies.

Confidentiality was found to be an important issue in every country; even where attitudes about sex are very open, as in the Netherlands and Sweden, most young people prefer to keep their personal sex lives private. The need for confidential services is best met in Sweden where doctors are specifically forbidden to inform parents about an adolescent's request for contraceptives. Dutch physicians also are required to keep the visit confidential if the teenager requests it, and the services in Dutch clinics are entirely confidential. French official policy stipulates that clinic services for women under age 18 be absolutely confidential.

In Britain parental consent for prescription of contraceptives for women under age 16 is left to the doctor's discretion, a policy recently upheld by that country's highest court. In Canada and the United States, many individual doctors insist on parental consent before providing contraceptives to minors. However, clinics in the United States usually provide services to young women without any such restriction.

In sum, Sweden seems to have been the most successful of the six countries in providing contraceptive services for adolescents that are close at hand, inexpensive, and confidential. England and Wales and the Netherlands have also largely achieved this goal. The basis for high-quality services in France has been laid out in policy, but implementation has been proceeding slowly. By all three criteria, the United States and Canada lag behind.

An additional observation concerning contraceptive services for young people that emerged during the country visits is the central role of the pill everywhere outside the United States. In each country it was stressed that the medical profession accepts the pill as an appropriate—usually the most appropriate—method for use by adolescents. Teenagers themselves are also favorably disposed toward this method. Moreover, except in the United States, a pelvic exam is not necessarily required before the pill can be prescribed, although it is always performed within the first few months of pill use. Fear of the pelvic exam is thought to deter some young women from seeking contraceptive assistance. The emphasis on pill use emerged more clearly from the interviews than is apparent in the admittedly weak statistics on contraceptive use (figure 9.3). In contrast, there seems to be considerable ambivalence in the United States about use of the pill, among both doctors and young women. Whether justified or not, concerns about this method are likely to affect contraceptive practice profoundly since the pill is unquestionably a highly effective method.

Abortion is widely available in all six of the countries considered here, although the situation is different in each one. Physical proximity, cost, and regulations, such as those requiring parental consent, are again primary concerns in relation to abortion services. Illegal abortion is no longer considered a problem in any of these countries.

Abortion services are geographically readily accessible in the Netherlands and Sweden. In England and Wales and France services are theoretically available throughout the country, but substantial differences in the abortion rates for local areas have been attributed to variation in their actual availability. A relatively low incidence of abortion in some parts of the United States and Canada have similarly been attributed to a paucity of services. Abortion services are likely to be concentrated in cities in these four countries.

In Sweden and Canada charges for abortion represent only a small portion of the cost. In the Netherlands and, until 1982, in France, the cost of an abortion has been borne by the woman, but the expense does not appear to be prohibitive, even for a young person. Public-sector abortions are free in England and Wales, but many women choose to pay for an abortion in a private facility, mainly because of delays and bureaucracy in the national health system. Young women in the United States usually must pay to get an abortion, and the charges may be substantial.

Specific rules and practices hamper access to abortion to a greater or lesser extent in every country. In Sweden and the Netherlands, there are only very minor administrative obstacles. Grounds for abortion are broadly defined in Britain, but two physicians must agree that it is justified, and parental consent usually must be given for those under age 16; moreover, most abortions involve hospitalization. Many abortion providers in the United States require parental consent for unmarried women below age 18 to obtain an abortion, but otherwise there are virtually no restrictions, and most abortions are performed as outpatient procedures. In France, parental consent for abortion is required of all unmarried minors; abortion is strictly limited to the first trimester; there is an elaborate mandatory preabortion procedure involving two visits to a doctor, counseling, and a delay of at least nine days; finally, most abortion patients spend two or more nights in the hospital. Grounds for abortion are quite narrowly defined in Canada; in addition, abortions can only be performed in hospitals and require the approval of a committee of three doctors; they often involve at least an overnight stay, and some hospitals require young, unmarried women to obtain parental consent. (These requirements are not enforced in Quebec.)

Overall, it would seem that a teenager can get an abortion most easily in Sweden. There is only a minor obstacle of cost in the Netherlands, and services are quite readily available in England and Wales. Abortion laws are less restrictive in the United States than in other countries; but geographic accessibility, cost, and concerns about confidentiality limit access. The accessibility of abortion services in Canada varys greatly by geographical area; access is limited in France by numerous restrictions.

Sex education policies also differ among the six countries, especially with regard to teaching about contraception in sex education courses. (There appears to be a serious question as to whether sex education courses that do not incorporate instruction on specific methods of contraception can be expected to have any real impact on teenage pregnancy.) Sweden is renowned as the first country in the world to have established an official sex education curriculum. It is now compulsory and extends to all grade levels; special attention is given to contraception and the discussion of human relationships. Perhaps most important is the close link in Sweden between the schools and the clinic services. None of the other countries comes close to this model.

In Canada, England and Wales, and the United States, school sex education is a community option; it is essentially up to the local authorities, school principals, or individual teachers to determine how much is taught and at what age. In England and Wales, however, there is a national policy favoring the inclusion of topics related to sex and family life in the curriculum, whereas there is no such policy in Canada or the United States. French policy now mandates broad coverage of sexuality for all adolescents although, in practice, local decision makers are free to interpret this provision. The meager evidence available suggests that in these four countries a substantial proportion, probably a majority, of female students is currently learning about contraception in school.

The Netherlands is to some extent a case apart. Sex education in the school curriculum is generally limited to instruction about the facts of reproduction in natural science classes. The Dutch government, nevertheless, encourages teaching about contraception indirectly by subsidizing mobile educational teams that operate under the auspices of the private family planning association. At the same time, in recent years there has been an explosion of materials on contraception and other sex-related topics in the media, much of which is of a responsible and informative nature. In recent youth surveys, knowledge of how to avoid pregnancy appears to be virtually universal.

In Sweden, sex education is completely accepted by the vast majority of parents, most of whom have had school sex education courses themselves. Objections are confined to the immigrant community, for some of whom sex education represents a challenge to their own traditions. In other countries, parents remain a potential stumbling block for school sex education courses. British law requires that schools offering sex education notify the parents. In Canada, France, the Netherlands, and the United States the belief is often expressed that ideally sex education should be handled in the home, and there is much concern about potential parental reactions to inclusion of this topic in the curriculum. Nevertheless, in Canada and the United States, at least, public opinion polls show a large majority of people favoring sex ation, including instruction about contraception, in school.

her problem shared by most if not all of these countries is that of aining. Even in Sweden it was felt that the training courses for re seriously deficient on this topic. In France, the Nether- e United States, the difficulty of introducing sex and nto the training programs for the next generation of zed. Thus far a great deal of stress has been placed on and the development of special teaching materials designed to guide the teachers along with the students in discussion of these sensitive topics.

The above review of the services and programs generally thought to be most relevant to the reduction of teenage fertility demonstrates that there is no single route to success. Sweden is best known for its sex education program, but it is also a leader with respect to contraceptive and abortion services. The broad and well-integrated approach developed in Sweden in the late 1970s seems to be the main reason why its teenage pregnancy rates and birthrates are as low as they are, despite a high level of sexual activity. The Netherlands, the country with the lowest pregnancy rates, has very little formal sex education, but contraceptives and abortion are readily available. The situation in the United States tends to be unfavorable in many respects. The Canadian programs also appear to be less than adequate in most parts of the country.

SOCIAL, ECONOMIC, AND POLITICAL CONSIDERATIONS

The case-study format provides an unusual opportunity to identify relevant underlying conditions and to collect descriptive information, although it has not been possible to investigate such issues in a systematic way. In certain instances, the original hypotheses of the overall study have stimulated inquiry into specific areas. The main results are summarized here, not so much in the form of conclusions, but rather as observations that may point up areas for fruitful further research.

Role of government

In European countries and in Canada, the government is the principal, if not the only, significant funder and provider of basic health and social services. Governments tend to take the initiative in defining the needs of the population and in developing ways to meet these needs. Governmental recognition that unmarried adolescents are in need of birth control services and governmental commitment to take some kind of appropriate action have ipso facto created a positive climate, helping the public to perceive the realities of teenage sexuality and to react responsibly. This recognition and commitment have probably been important in keeping teenage pregnancy rates low in spite of high levels of sexual activity.

Adolescent use of health and medical services

In all of the countries studied except the United States, young people appear to have easy access to health and medical facilities and are accustomed to using them on their own initiative. Accessibility is partly a financial and partly a social and psychological issue. National health insurance schemes designed to provide care for all members of society help to resolve both aspects of the problem. For a young person who is familiar with this kind of arrangement, consulting a family planning service when the need arises is unlikely to appear to be a "big deal," whether or not the service is actually a part of the public health care system. In the United States, however, most public medical facilities serve only the poor. Teenagers cannot negotiate independently for payment of expenses by either public or private insurance.

Contraception as a means of reducing abortion

In France, the Netherlands, and Sweden, the decision to develop contraceptive services for teenagers was specifically linked to the desire to minimize resort to abortion among young people. Although it is recognized that safe and legal abortion should be available, prevention of the need for abortion is the primary goal. The provision of safe, effective, low-cost, and easily accessible contraceptives for young people is a direct response. The logical connection is most obvious in Sweden where the 1975 law liberalizing abortion also laid the groundwork for the development of contraceptive services for young people. But in France and the Netherlands also, conservative medical organizations were reluctant to endorse the provision of contraceptives to young, unmarried women, and it was the alternative of rising abortion rates that ultimately swayed their judgment. On the other hand, in the United States, there are many people who view the availability of contraception as provocation to premarital sexual activity and, thus, as a cause of increased recourse to abortion.

Acceptability of adolescent sexual activity

Public recognition of the responsibility to provide birth control services for young, unmarried people implies acceptance of the fact that they are sexually active without necessarily condoning such behavior. It is very uncertain whether early sexual activity in itself could be influenced by policy decisions, assuming that it is desirable to do so. The experience of England and Wales, France, the Netherlands, Sweden, and Canada's Quebec province shows clearly, however, that the reproductive consequences of sexual activity can be dealt with effectively. Acknowledgment that adolescents are sexually active was not a difficult step in Sweden because there have not been the same taboos against premarital sex that have existed elsewhere, although attitudes concerning the appropriate age for the initiation of sex have probably changed over the years. But such acknowledgment represents a substantial break with traditional standards of behavior in the other countries, as it does in the United States. One reason for the successful experience of these other countries is that public attention was never focused directly on this potentially divisive issue.

Attitudes toward sex

In the United States sex tends to be treated as a special topic, set apart from normal life. At the same time, there is much ambivalence: sex is romantic but also sinful and dirty; it is flaunted but also something to be hidden. This ambivalence is less apparent in the European countries, where matter-of-fact attitudes seem to be more prevalent. Again, Sweden is the outstanding example, but the contrast with the United States was perceptible in all of the countries visited. Survey results tend to bear out this impression although the questions asked have not been directly comparable from country to country. For instance, in 1981, 76 percent of Dutch adults agreed with the statement that "sex is natural—even outside marriage," whereas in 1985, 57 percent of Americans thought premarital sex was "not wrong." It stands to reason that where sexuality as a whole carries less emotional baggage, sex and pregnancy among teenagers are likely to be dealt with more realistically. Indeed, the results of the 37-country study suggest that a society's openness about sex may be an especially important factor influencing adolescent fertility and pregnancy (table 1.2 and Appendices 6 and 7).

Religiosity

The United States public prides itself on its religiosity. Although the U.S. Constitution provides for strict separation of church and state, and tolerance of the religious views of others is central to American traditions, studies have repeatedly shown that a higher proportion of the U.S. population attends religious services and more people in the United States feel that God is important in their lives than in other countries. Countries like England and Wales and Sweden, which have an established church and countries like France, that are predominantly Roman Catholic, are nevertheless more secular than the United States in outlook. Increasing secularization in the Netherlands and in Canada's Quebec province is thought to be intimately linked with recent social change. Not only is religion generally prominent in American life, but fundamentalist groups are very vocal. Such groups often have extreme views of a sort rarely encountered in Europe. Both the intensity and the nature of religious feeling in the United States serve to heighten the tension surrounding public activities having to do with teenage sexual activity and abortion. The 37–country study showed religiosity to be highly correlated with teenage fertility (table 1.2) and pregnancy (Appendix 6).

Political confrontation

All of the countries studied are parliamentary democracies but each has its own political institutions, and there is considerable variation in the process through which public policy is developed. The important point for this investigation is that the U.S. system appears to foster confrontation at many levels, a less common element in the political life of the other countries. The extensive use of private financing for political purposes in the United States enables an enormous variety of pressure groups to mount effective campaigns. Although confrontation no doubt has its uses, it makes the resolution of emotionally charged issues more difficult; positions become rigid and the possibilities for creative compromise are narrowed. The most interesting country to compare with the United States is probably the Netherlands. Like the United States, the Netherlands is a self-consciously pluralistic society, but, unlike the United States, a host of formal and informal conventions exist there for heading off and dealing with conflict before it emerges into the open. As a result, the Dutch have been able to meet the evident need for birth control services for adolescents to a great extent without arousing direct opposition from those segments of society that could not possibly go along with such activities.

Size and directness of communication

Tied in directly with political confrontation is the fact that the United States is a much larger country than any of the others, both in terms of population and geographic area.[8] Thus there is comparatively little possibility for direct communication between individuals. In countries like Sweden and the Netherlands, for instance, doctors tend to know one another. When a new idea comes up, such as the advisability of prescribing the pill for adolescents, the relevant arguments can be circulated quickly and easily and an understanding reached that will be accepted by virtually everyone. Lines of communication within the medical profession in the United States are more extended and, consequently, awareness, much less consensus, is more difficult to achieve. Such intangibles may affect not only the professional, political, and social groups that would be likely to take an interest in adolescent

8. Canada is obviously an exception in terms of territory, but its population is only one-tenth that of the United States, and the vast majority of Canadians live in a small portion of the country close to the southern border.

pregnancy and its prevention, but also the ability of individual citizens to perceive and accept the social message concerning reproductive responsibility.

Centralization of authority

Yet another closely related facet of national life is the extent to which political and administrative power is concentrated in the national government. France is often cited as the epitome of a centralized state, but even the existence of two "nations" within England and Wales is a simple arrangement compared to the arrangements in Canada and the United States. Both of the latter countries have three-tiered governmental structures, with some powers delegated to the national government and some reserved to the provinces or states. This division has two main consequences for the issues examined in this book. First, major differences can develop within the country in setting policy for adolescent reproductive behavior. The contrast between Quebec and the rest of Canada is an outstanding example. The situation also varies substantially among the U.S. states. Indeed, at several points in the course of the study, the question arose as to whether it would not be more appropriate to compare the European countries with one or more individual states than to compare them with the United States as a whole, although the national perspective was ultimately retained as more appropriate. Second, the task of giving form to social change in terms of public policies and programs becomes enormously complicated because of the many bureaucracies that must be dealt with and the sometimes indeterminate boundaries of their separate jurisdictions.

Welfare supports

It has often been claimed that in the United States the availability of public assistance for mothers with dependent children has offered a financial incentive for poor women, including very young women, to bear children outside of marriage. All of the other countries studied do provide extensive benefits related to childbearing, usually including health and medical care, food supplements, and housing as well as family allowances; in most cases the overall level of support is more generous than the average AFDC payments in a state in the United States. These benefits are usually available to everyone and do not depend on marital status or income for eligibility, although in England and Wales and in France, at least, there are special supplementary programs for poor, single mothers. Hence for these countries there is substantial material support for childbearing that is not associated with high adolescent birthrates. It should be noted, however, that public support is generally available in other countries to young people who do not have children as well, in the form of unemployment benefits, housing, and other allowances.

Paternal financial responsibility

A matter of particular interest is whether or not fathers are required to assume some financial responsibility for the upbringing of children born to unmarried women. In the United States, men can often evade supporting offspring born outside of marriage, even in states where they are legally required to pay. This fact has been cited as contributing to male indifference concerning pregnancy prevention. The evidence collected in this study is inconclusive. In the two countries where the pregnancy rates are lowest, policy is very different. In Sweden, all known fathers are held financially responsible; the mother is paid directly by the government, which independently collects funds from the father, so that the support realized does not depend on the effort that the woman is willing or able to expend. But in the Netherlands, a father has no legal responsibility toward a child born outside of marriage unless the mother herself takes action against him, which she seldom does.

Education and employment

It is said that if young people feel they lack prospects for the future and perceive that they do not have any real control over what happens to them, they will be less likely to think about the possible consequences of their sexual activity. During the country visits, information was collected on education and employment in order to explore this area. At a superficial level, educational opportunities in the United States appear to be as great as, or greater than, those in other countries. In Canada, France, and Sweden, most adolescents leave school after completion of the secondary level at around age 18, or in Sweden, 19; a smaller proportion go on to higher education than in the United States. In the Netherlands only about half of women aged 18 are still in school; in Engand and Wales, the majority of young people finish their education at age 16.

The employment situation is even more difficult to assess, since definitions of labor force participation and unemployment differ from country to country, and part-time work may not be counted in the same way. Perhaps the most that can be said is that youth unemployment is considered to be a serious problem everywhere, and young people are universally uneasy on this score. The chances of acquiring and keeping a satisfying job do not appear to be worse in the United States than in other countries. At the same time, however, all of these other countries provide assistance designed to ease the problem, in the form of youth training programs, unemployment benefits, and other kinds of support, to a greater extent than does the United States.

Poverty

One difference between the United States and the other countries in the study that may be relevant to teenage pregnancy concerns the extent and the nature of poverty. Poverty as it exists in the United States is essentially unknown in Europe. Whatever way the political winds are blowing, the European governments are committed to the philosophy of the welfare state and, thus, to the notion that everyone is entitled to a reasonable standard of living. The Dutch and the Swedes have been especially successful in achieving relatively egalitarian societies, but even in England and Wales and France, the contrast between those who are better off and those who are less well off is not nearly so great as it is in the United States. In every country, when pressed to describe the kind of young woman who would be most likely to bear a child, the answer was the same: those from emotionally as well as economically deprived backgrounds, who unrealistically seek gratification and fulfillment from having a child of their own. Such judgments are heard also in the United States, but they apply to a much larger proportion of people growing up in a culture of poverty. Again, the 37—country study showed that the extent of poverty in the country was an important determinant of fertility for younger teenagers (table 1.2 and Appendices 6 and 7).

10

Policy Implications for the United States

Both the large study of 37 countries described in chapter 1 and the case studies of individual countries (chapters 3–8) were undertaken to better understand the reasons why birthrates and pregnancy rates among teenagers in the United States are so much higher than they are in other developed countries, and to determine whether it is possible to learn from the experience of countries with low teenage pregnancy rates how to reduce those rates in the United States. As has been stated on numerous occasions throughout the preceding chapters, the data for many variables of interest leave much to be desired. Nevertheless, it is possible to draw some conclusions involving the policy and program implications of this study's findings. It is important to note that no attempt has been made to evaluate whether or not any of the policy or program interventions that appear to have affected teenage pregnancy in the study countries would be considered morally acceptable in the United States, but merely to assess the extent to which such efforts have been efficacious and whether or not any of them are theoretically transferable to the U.S. situation.

One of the most important policy implications to come from this study is the discrediting of certain beliefs, some widely held by social conservatives and others held by liberal reformers. Both sets of beliefs—each in its own way—have tended to paralyze efforts aimed at reducing the relatively high rates of pregnancy experienced by American adolescents. What are those beliefs?

• Adolescent pregnancy rates are higher in the United States than in Europe mainly because of the high pregnancy rate among U.S. blacks

228

• American adolescents begin sex much earlier and more of them are sexually active than their counterparts in other developed countries
• Teenagers are too immature to use contraceptives effectively
• Unwed adolescents want to have babies in order to obtain welfare assistance
• Making abortions and contraceptives available and providing sex education only encourages promiscuity and, therefore, increases teenage pregnancy
• As long as there is no clear path for unemployed teenagers to improve their economic condition they will continue to have high pregnancy rates because having babies is one of the few sources of satisfaction and accomplishment available to them

None of these beliefs explains the differences between teenage pregnancy rates in the United States and other developed countries.

LESSONS FROM THE 37–COUNTRY STUDY

The study of 37 countries was restricted to an examination of the factors affecting teenage birthrates rather than pregnancy rates (chapter 1). Of the 13 countries for which both abortion and birth data are available, however, those with high teenage birthrates also have high abortion rates, and vice versa. Thus it is reasonable to infer that factors affecting fertility differentials found to be significant in the 37–country study also apply to differences in pregnancy. It is notable that in those countries where abortion *and* fertility data are available, the gap between the United States and the other countries with regard to their pregnancy rates is at least the same as, or even greater than, the differentials for birthrates alone.

Six factors were found to be most important in their effect on teenage fertility (see chapter 1). Those associated with low teenage fertility rates are:

• High levels of socioeconomic modernization
• Openness about sex
• A relatively large proportion of household income distributed to the low-income population (important mainly for younger teenagers)
• A high minimum legal age at marriage (important for older teenagers only)

Factors associated with high teenage fertility are:

• Generous maternity leaves and benefits
• Overall pronatalist policies designed to raise fertility

The United States differs from most of the countries with comparably high adolescent fertility with regard to four of these factors. The position of the United States is anomalous, however, with regard to socioeconomic development, one of the most important factors associated with low teenage fertility. Although it is one of the most highly developed countries examined, the United States has a teenage fertility rate much higher than the rates observed in countries that are comparably modernized, and considerably higher than the rates found in a number of much less developed countries. The inconsonance applies particularly to fertility among younger teenagers, where the U.S. rate falls between that of Romania and Hungary (see chapter 1). The relatively high adolescent birthrate in the United States would suggest that it has a pronatalist fertility policy (which it does not), high levels of maternity leaves and benefits, and a low minimum age at marriage. Maternity benefit policies on average are less liberal than those in most European countries (Kamerman, Kahn, and Kingston, 1983), and in most states women can marry on their own consent by age 18, an age similar to that found in most of the countries studied.

The United States fits the pattern for high teenage fertility in that it ' is far less open about sexual matters than most countries with low teenage birthrates, and a smaller proportion of its income is distributed to families on the bottom rungs of the economic ladder. All of these findings suggest that two factors are key to the location of the United States with regard to high teenage fertility: an ambivalent, sometimes puritanical attitude about sex, and the existence of a large, economically deprived underclass.

With better or more complete information, it is likely that at least some of the factors found significantly correlated with adolescent fertility in the bivariate analysis in chapter 1 would have survived into the multivariate analysis (table 1.2 and Appendix 7). A number of these factors correlate highly with those found significant in the multivariate analysis and deserve special mention because of their policy significance and because they figure prominently in the case studies for which more detailed information was available (see chapters 2–9). These include the relationship between high levels of adolescent fertility and restrictions placed on teenagers' access to contraception and with high levels of religiosity in the country, and the association of low adolescent fertility with teaching about contraceptives in the schools. It is notable that government subsidy of abortions is not associated with teenage fertility.

In the 37–country study, the United States does not appear to be more restrictive than low-fertility countries in the provision of contraceptive services to teenagers; however, comparable data could not be obtained on the provision of contraceptives free of charge or at very low cost—a factor that appears to be very important in terms of accessibility in the case studies. In this respect, the United States is more restrictive than the other 5 countries studied in detail—all of which have much lower adolescent fertility and pregnancy rates than the United States. The very high levels of religiosity reported for the United States (the highest of any of the 13 countries for which there are data) is probably one, but certainly not the only, factor underlying the low rating of the United States on openness about sex. It is also noteworthy that the United States scores relatively low among the countries studied on the measures of availability of contraceptive education in the schools.

The results from the comparative study also indicate that intercountry differences in teenage fertility and in teenage pregnancy are *not* mainly due to the fact that these rates are much higher among U.S. black than white teenagers. The birthrates of white American teenagers are higher than those of teenagers in any Western European country (Westoff et al., 1983). (It is notable that many of these countries have substantial numbers of nonwhite inhabitants—who tend to be poorer and to have higher fertility than the general population—e.g., West Indians and Asians in England, Algerians in France, and Surinamese in the Netherlands.) Birthrates for adolescents under age 18 are higher than those reported in any developed country except Bulgaria, Cuba, and Hungary (see Appendix 3). Similarly, U.S. pregnancy rates for those young teenagers are higher than those in all developed countries for which there are data (see chapters 2 and 3).[1]

THE SIX COUNTRY CASE STUDIES

The individual country studies confirm the findings of the 37–country study, help explain some of the ambiguities in those study findings, and cast light on factors for which data were not available for the larger study. Two of the commonly held beliefs about teenage pregnancy that were noted earlier in this chapter are refuted in the case studies: teenagers are *not* precluded by their presumed immaturity from using contraceptives consistently and effectively; and teenagers in the United States are *not* more sexually experienced than adolescents in other countries with lower pregnancy rates.

With the possible exception of younger teenagers in Canada, national differences in the percentage of teenagers who have ever had intercourse appear to contribute little or nothing to the variations in teenage pregnancy rates. Disparities in age at initiation of sexual relations appear to be too small to play a large part in determining the

1. Canada, Czechoslovakia, Denmark, England and Wales, Finland, France, Hungary, the Netherlands, New Zealand, Norway, Scotland, Sweden.

pregnancy differentials between the United States and the other countries.

In the five countries other than the United States, contraceptive use, and particularly use of the pill, appears to be greater than it is in the United States—among younger as well as older teenagers. Physicians and clinics in these countries actively encourage pill use among teenagers; and in some of the countries, there have been active campaigns addressed to young men to encourage the use of condoms. There is not the same level of concern that pill use may involve serious health complications. In fact, the health risks to teenagers have been found to be exceedingly low and outweighed by the health benefits (Ory et al., 1983). IUD use is not especially high among teenagers in the five countries, but neither is it automatically considered to be contraindicated for teenagers—largely because pelvic inflammatory disease is less prevalent and tends to be treated more promptly than it is in the United States.

Does the availability of contraceptives, sex education, and abortion services in the United States encourage sexual promiscuity and thereby account for the higher teenage pregnancy rates in the United States? The findings from the case-study countries suggest that this cannot be the case, since availability is generally greater in countries with lower teenage pregnancy rates.

Teenagers who obtain contraceptives from *any* source are assured of confidentiality of services in Sweden, the Netherlands, and France. It is notable that in England the government went to the House of Lords asking that a previous court decision be reversed which would have required those under age 16 to have parental consent to obtain contraceptive services. The House of Lords law panel, Britain's highest court, agreed with the government that physicians may provide contraceptive services to minors under 16 on their own consent. Conversely, in the United States, the U.S. Justice Department went to court, unsuccessfully, to defend a Department of Health and Human Services regulation that would have *required* that the parents of all teenagers under 18 be notified if their children obtained a prescription contraceptive. (Another branch of government, the U.S. Congress, had rejected a proposal that parental consent or notification be mandated.)

Abortions are available free of charge in England and Wales and in France. The cost to the woman is low in Canada and Sweden and is small enough in the Netherlands not to be prohibitive. In more than two-thirds of U.S. states, the full price of an abortion must be paid by the woman, whether or not she can afford it; and, because abortion services tend to be concentrated in populous metropolitan areas, costs can include not only the fee for the abortion itself, but also travel and hotel expenses. Access to abortion in some of the countries studied, however, is more restrictive than in the United States with regard to parental consent, gestational age, required waiting period, legally required overnight hospital stays, and required approval by an additional doctor or doctors or a medical committee.

It is noteworthy that liberalization of abortion has often been accompanied by facilitating the access of teenagers to contraceptive services to minimize the need for abortions among women in this young age group.

Sex and contraceptive education in the schools differs widely among the case-study countries. Sweden has by far the most extensive program. In the Netherlands, although there is little formal school sex education beyond the facts of reproduction, widespread public education via all the media is superior to that of any of the countries studied except, possibly, Sweden.

In short, teenagers living in countries where contraceptive services, sex education in and out of the schools, and abortion services are widely available have lower rates of adolescent pregnancy and do not have appreciably higher levels of sexual experience than do teenagers in the United States.

The findings from the 37–country study suggest that generous maternity leaves and benefits—mostly in pronatalist countries of Eastern Europe—are associated with high fertility rates among older teenagers. The United States was not included in those comparisons because policies differ among the states and because such benefits are largely provided through private rather than government programs. Overall, however, the United States does not appear to have generous policies compared to other countries, even when private programs, as well as public subsidy, are taken into account (Kamerman, Kahn, and Kingston, 1983). Nevertheless, it has been suggested that U.S. Aid to Families with Dependent Children—a benefit that is largely limited to single mothers, a very high proportion of whom are teenagers—encourages out-of-wedlock fertility in the United States.

All of the countries in the case studies have more generous health and welfare provisions for the general population and for mothers than does the United States; and several of them, like the United States, provide special financial assistance for single mothers. Yet these countries all have lower teenage fertility rates than the United States. Differences in welfare assistance to mothers, or to single mothers, does not appear to explain the differentials in teenage birthrates between the United States and the other countries studied, and certainly they do not explain the differences in abortion rates. Although this study does not address the question of whether differential welfare payments can encourage adolescent fertility within individual countries, a number of American studies have failed to confirm this hypothesis (Cutright, 1970 and 1973; Moore, 1978; Moore and Caldwell, 1977; Placek and Hendershot, 1975; Hendershot and Placek, 1974; Presser and Salsberg, 1975; Cutright et al.,1974). Yet it continues to be put forward (Fuchs, 1983; Murray, 1984; Sklar and Berkov, 1974). One recent study finds that although welfare does not encourage out-of-wedlock fertility, it does infuence the decision of single parents to move out of the parents' home and, to a lesser extent, may encourage young married women to divorce or separate (Ellwood and Bane, 1984).

Teenagers' prospects for economic improvement do not appear to be appreciably greater in the five case-study countries than in the United States; nor is the educational achievement of young people greater. However, more extensive health, welfare, and unemployment benefits in the other countries keep poverty from being as deep or as widespread as it is in the United States. The findings from the 37–country study suggest that more equitable distribution of household income is associated with lower fertility among younger teenagers. The inequality of income distribution appears to be a contributing factor to the differences between teenage birthrates in the United States and those in other developed countries. Unfortunately, data are not available to compare teenage pregnancy rates by income between countries. However, it does not seem likely, given the fact that the U.S. white adolescent pregnancy rate is so much higher than those in the other countries, and that poverty, while not so extensive or so deep as in the United States, also exists in the other countries studied, that differentials in socioeconomic status can explain the differences in adolescent pregnancy between the United States and the other five countries. Differences in economic status among teenagers *within* individual countries, however, may very well contribute substantially to pregnancy and especially to fertility differentials.

To summarize, the 37–country study and the individual country studies provide convincing evidence that many widely held beliefs about teenage pregnancy cannot explain the large differences in adolescent pregnancy between the United States and other developed countries: teenagers in these other countries apparently are *not* too immature to use contraceptives consistently and effectively; the availability of welfare services does *not* seem correlated with higher adolescent fertility; teenage pregnancy rates are *lower* in countries where there is *greater* availability of contraceptive and abortion services and of sex education; adolescent sexual activity in the United States is not very different from what it is in countries that have much *lower* teenage pregnancy rates; although the pregnancy rate of American blacks is much higher than that of whites, the white rate is still much higher than the overall teenage pregnancy rates in the other case-study countries; teenage unemployment appears to be at least as serious a problem in all the countries studied as it is in the United States, and American teen-agers have more or at least as much schooling as those in most of the countries studied that have lower pregnancy rates. Because the other case-study countries have more extensive public health and welfare benefit systems, however, they do not have so extensive an economically deprived underclass as does the United States. However, the differences in teenage pregnancy rates would probably not be eliminated if socioeconomic status could be controlled.

Clearly, then, it *is* possible to achieve a lower teenage pregnancy rate than that experienced in the United States, and a number of countries with comparable levels of adolescent sexual activity have done so. Although no single factor has been found responsible for the differences in adolescent pregnancy rates between the United States and the other five countries, is there anything to be learned from these countries' experiences to improve the situation in the United States?

A number of factors affecting teenage pregnancy rates, of course, are not easily transferable or are not exportable at all to the United States. Each of the five case-study countries has a considerably smaller population, and all but Canada are geographically more compact than the United States — making rapid dissemination of innovations easier; their populations are less heterogenerous ethnically (though not so homogeneous as is commonly assumed, since most have substantial minority nonwhite populations, usually with higher-than-average fertility); religion and the influence of conservative religious bodies are less pervasive than they are in the United States, even in countries like Sweden and England that have officially established churches; governments tend to be more centralized; the provision of wide-ranging social and welfare benefits is firmly established, whether the country is led by parties labeled conservative or liberal; income distribution is more equal; there appears to be less of a tradition of political confrontation and, possibly, a more widespread respect for authority and for public order; and constituencies that oppose contraception, sex education, and legal abortion are not so powerful and well funded as they are in the United States.

Some other factors are, at least theoretically, transferable—and here, it is important to note that some of the factors associated with low pregnancy rates may differ between countries. For example, school sex education appears to be a much more important factor in Sweden than it is in the other countries; high levels of media exposure to contraceptive information and sex-related topics is more prominent in the Netherlands; condoms are more widely available in England, the Netherlands, and Sweden. Use of the pill by teenagers is most extensive in the Netherlands.

By and large, Sweden has been the most active of the countries studied in developing programs and policies to reduce teenage pregnancy. It is notable that Sweden has *lower* teenage pregnancy rates than have all of the countries examined, except for the Netherlands, although teenagers begin intercourse at earlier ages in Sweden. It is also notable that Sweden is the only one of the countries observed to show a rapid decline in teenage abortion rates in recent years, even after its abortion law was liberalized.

It is also noteworthy that none of the five case-study countries has developed government-sponsored programs designed to discourage teenagers from engaging in sexual relations—even at young ages—a program intervention officially advocated in the United States and rewarded through government subsidies. Although in Sweden committed relationships and responsible sexual behavior are advocated in the school sex education program, most of the countries have preferred to leave such matters to parents and churches.

Theoretically, universal health insurance, which would include contraceptive (and abortion) services, could be made available in the United States. Practically, there is little likelihood that legislation of this kind will be passed in the near future. Most persons, however, who are employed or who are students in higher educational institutions are covered by health insurance and, although most insurance policies do not now cover contraception, there is an increasing trend toward the inclusion of preventive health services, including contraception, in insurance contracts. It is possible that the American answer to national health insurance, at least for the forseeable future, is to supplement private insurance coverage for those who are unemployed or otherwise uninsured and to create or continue publicly supported programs to meet special needs and to reach specific population groups. (Coverage for abortion services in any publicly funded health program would require the reversal, at the federal and state levels, of prohibitions now in effect.) Even if this trend were to accelerate more rapidly than seems likely, the problem of teenagers' access to effective contraceptive services would not be solved. In addition to the problem of cost, many teenagers in the United States, as well as in the other countries studied, do not want their parents informed that they are obtaining contraceptive services. For young people who are not themselves employed or enrolled in an institution of higher learning, coverage under their parents' health insurance policy could violate their privacy and constitute a barrier to effective services.

POSSIBLE APPROACHES

Several U.S. communities have instituted school-based health clinics that provide contraceptive services—usually in partnership with health, youth-serving, or other nonprofit agencies. In many cases, parental consent is required to enroll in the health clinics (Dryfoos, 1985). Contraception, however, is only one of the many health services offered, so that the parent is not specifically informed when contraceptive services or advice are being obtained. The school, which has a continuing relationship with the young person, is in a position to monitor both continuation and any possible medical complications; the student is not lost to follow up because she has dropped out of the clinic.[2]

A complementary approach would be to enhance the current family planning clinic system, by increasing government subsidy, to provide free or low-cost contraceptive services to all teenagers who want them, not just to those from poor families. This is already permissible under federal law and, to some extent, the process has already begun. In 1982, 6 out of 10 contraceptive visits by U.S. teenagers were visits to family planning clinics; and 44 percent of teenagers using the pill, IUD or diaphragm (and 54 percent of those aged 15–17) first obtained their method at a family planning clinic (Pratt et al., 1984, tables 9 and 10). In point of fact, however, although the high unmet need for family planning services among teenagers in the United States is well documented, federal subsidies in real dollars have declined. Moreover, in many communities family planning clinics—especially those operated by hospitals and health departments—tend to be stigmatized by teenagers who have not actually been to such clinics; they are likely to avoid them in the belief that they are restricted to very poor patients, that services are not confidential, that the surroundings are shabby and unclean, the services poor, and the treatment of patients disrespectful (Kisker et al., 1985). Advertising that portrays the clinic services as inviting, professional, confidential, and available to all segments of the community can do much to counteract this negative image. In Planned Parenthood and some neighborhood health clinics, however, there is a trend toward charging a flat fee to all patients; such a fee policy is thought to be likely to discourage teenage enrollment.

The growing reliance on health maintenance organizations (HMOs) to increase health coverage while reducing health costs provides another opportunity to extend family planning services to teenagers. There is no reason why HMOs cannot establish special adolescent clinics on the Swedish model to provide contraceptive services confidentially as part of a general health-care service. Youth-serving agen-

2. It might also be feasible to develop demonstration sex education programs in local school districts that are closely integrated with teenage birth control clinics as has been done in Sweden. A pilot program of this nature was developed by Johns Hopkins University in Baltimore (Zabin, et al, 1984).

cies, the Society for Adolescent Medicine and physician groups might well consider developing models for the provision of adolescent health care in the United States that are not linked to poverty programs.

Unlike the governments of most of the countries in the case studies, the U.S. federal government does not mandate or even encourage the inclusion of sex education courses in public schools. Only two states and the District of Columbia require sex education, and hardly any encourage such courses. For the most part, state and even local governments leave the question of whether sex education should be offered at all to the nearly 16,000 local school districts. The extent to which contraception should be discussed—and at what grade—is entirely a matter for the local school district to decide. Although numerous public opinion polls show that American parents overwhelmingly approve of sex education in the schools, including education about contraception (see chapter 3), local school districts have tended to be timid about establishing courses because of fear of minority, but highly vocal, opposition. Although not all the countries studied put much emphasis on school sex education, the evidence from Sweden at least suggests that comprehensive sex education programs can help to reduce teenage pregnancy.

Local school districts in the United States can be encouraged to institute programs and experiment with new approaches. Open discussions of sexuality may also encourage more rational contraceptive decision making. Although sex education is usually left to the school districts, both the federal and state governments are in a position to influence the development and establishment of school sex education courses. Simply by asserting that sex education is desirable, they could help to legitimate the inclusion of sex education courses in the curricula. Congress, by providing subsidies for the development of curricula, for teacher-training programs, and perhaps for some demonstration programs could further encourage such instruction. State governments similarly can promote sex education efforts, as a few have by taking a clear position, offering selected subsidies, and providing practical help in curriculum development.

Openness about sex is increasing in the United States. (The days when even married couples in motion pictures could not be shown occupying the same bed are long past.) Cohabitation among unmarried couples is rising rapidly. Some restrictive laws relating to sexual information have been struck down by the Supreme Court. Sex, nevertheless, is treated far less openly and is surrounded by more ambivalence than it is in most of the countries in the case studies. In virtually all of the countries examined, for example, information about contraception and sexuality is far more available through the media than it is in the United States; condoms are more widely distributed; and advertisements for contraceptives are far more ubiquitous. Shops providing sex-related materials in other countries, such as the Netherlands, are not as sleazy as they are in the United States.

The self-imposed restrictions on contraceptive advertising in the media—especially on television—are incongruous in an era when virtually every other product, including vaginal douches, sanitary napkins, and hemorrhoid preparations, is advertised everywhere and without protest. At least one cable television network in the United States has begun to carry advertisements for spermicides; and sunbathers at New York area beaches during the summer of 1985 could look up and see a popular condom brand advertised via streamers from an airplane. It seems likely that if the restrictions on advertising were lifted, some aggressive manufacturers would develop and promulgate effective advertising campaigns. A recent study sponsored by the U.S. Food and Drug Administration suggests that such advertising may be feasible (Morris, 1984). Of course, governmental restrictions on advertising prescription drugs except in medical journals also preclude advertising the most widely used reversible contraceptive method—the pill.

There is also a need to disseminate more realistic information among the general public and health professionals about the health risks of the pill (which are minimal for teenagers) and about its extensive benefits (Ory et al., 1983). Most Americans are badly misinformed on this subject (Gallup, 1985). Although teenagers in other countries have experienced much lower pregnancy rates than U.S. adolescents while using currently available methods, it is probable that the development of new methods more appropriate for teenagers who have episodic sex—such as a once-a-month pill—could greatly reduce teenage pregnancies in the United States, and further reduce them in other countries, too. Yet funds for contraceptive development have declined in real terms in recent years in the United States (the major funder of contraceptive research); and research into a monthly pill is further hampered by governmental restrictions on abortion-related expenditures.

In general, American teenagers seem to have inherited the worst of all possible worlds insofar as their exposure to messages about sex are concerned: movies, music, radio, and television tell them that nonmarital sex is romantic, exciting, and titillating; premarital sex and cohabitation are visible ways of life among the adults they see and hear about; their own parents or their parents' friends are likely to be divorced or separated but involved in sexual relationships. Yet, at the same time, young people get the message (now subsidized by the federal government) that good girls should say no. Little that teenagers see or hear about sex informs them about contraception or the consequences of sexual activity. (They are much more likely to hear about abortions than contraception on the daily television soap opera.) Increased exposure to messages about sex has not meant more realistic exposure or exposure to messages about responsible sex. (Nonmarital sex, though it may be irresistible, is branded irresponsible.) Such mixed messages lead to the kind of ambivalence about sex that stifles communication between partners and exposes young people to increased risk of pregnancy, out-of-wedlock births, and abortions. Increasing the legitimacy and availability of contraception and of sex education in its broadest sense is likely to result in declining pregnancy rates, without raising teenage sexual activity rates to any great extent. That has been the experience of most countries of Western Europe, and there is no reason to think it would not also occur in the United States.

Application of any of the program and policy measures that appear to have been effective in other countries is admittedly more difficult in the United States where governmental authority is far more dispersed, but it may, in fact, be as easy or easier in some states and communities. Efforts need to be directed not just to the federal executive branch of government, but to Congress, the courts, state houses, state legislatures, local authorities, and school superintendents and principals—as well as to such private-sector and charitable enterprises as insurance companies, broadcast and publishing executives, church groups, and youth-serving agencies. Because of its complexity, the task may require considerable effort and ingenuity, but clearly it can be accomplished, and there is a broad consensus that the need to reduce teenage pregnancy in the United States is high on the social agenda.

Appendices
References
Index

Teenage Fertility
in Industrialized Countries:
1971–80

Country	(1) Teenage total fertility rate (14–19) per 1,000 women 1971	(2) Teenage total fertility rate (14–19) per 1,000 women 1979/80	(3) Teenage fertility rate <18 1979/80	(4) Percent of teenage fertility <18 1979/80	(5) Percent of TFR <20 1979/80	(6) Percent change <20 rate since 1971	(7) Percent change in TFR since 1971
Group A							
Australia	271	145	45	31	7	−47	−33
Austria	286	179	41	23	11	−38	−24
Canada	208	140	46	33	8	−33	−21
East Germany	309	253	39	15	13	−18	6
England	254	157	41	26	8	−38	−20
France	191	125	25	20	6	−34	−21
Iceland	372	289	88	30	12	−22	−15
New Zealand	351	194	64	33	9	−45	−35
Norway	232	128	29	23	7	−45	−31
Sweden	170	83	15	19	5	−51	−14
U.S. (White)	274	221	71	32	13	−19	−19
West Germany	228	102	21	23	7	−55	−25
Yugoslavia	273	241	59	24	11	−11	−11
Israel (Total)	202	179	32	18	6	−11	−21
U.S. (Total)	333	266	101	38	14	−20	−19
Group B							
Belgium	164	117	26	22	7	−29	−23
Denmark	145	84	16	19	5	−42	−24
Finland	149	94	18	19	6	−36	−3
Ireland	100	113	23	21	3	13	−19
Israel (Jewish)	144	132	18	14	5	−8	−21
Italy	143	117	28	24	7	−18	−28

(*continued*)

Appendix 1 (*Continued*)

Country	(1) Teenage total fertility rate (14–19) per 1,000 women 1971	(2) 1979/80	(3) Teenage fertility rate <18 1979/80	(4) Percent of teenage fertility <18 1979/80	(5) Percent of TFR <20 1979/80	(6) Percent change <20 rate since 1971	(7) Percent change in TFR since 1971
Japan	21	17	2	13	1	−17	−19
Luxembourg†	163	82	22	26	5	−50	−24
Netherlands	112	46	10	22	3	−59	−32
Switzerland	108	48	8	17	3	−55	−27
Group C							
Czechoslovakia	222	265	40	15	12	20	−2
Greece	185	269	80	30	12	45	−2
Hungary	267	342	103	30	18	28	−1
Poland	207	225	40	18	10	9	2
Portugal	162	210	59	28	10	30	−25
Romania	321	352	100	28	14	9	−9
Spain	78	133	37	28	5	70	−12
Group D							
Israel (Arab)	574	376	82	22	7	−35	−27
U.S. (Black)	715	515	237	46	23	−28	−22

Source: Charles F. Westoff, Gérard Calot, and Andrew D. Foster, "Teenage Fertility in Developed Nations: 1971–1980," *Family Planning Perspectives* 15:105. 1983.

*The most recent data for Belgium, Ireland, and Spain are for 1978.

†Rates for Luxembourg are estimated from reports for five-year age categories.

APPENDIX 2

External Data
Sources

The first source given is the primary one, covering all data not detailed in subsequent numbered items.

Abbreviations used in this appendix:
- ILO International Labour Organization
- INED Institut National d'Etudes Démographiques
- IPPF International Planned Parenthood Federation
- WHO World Health Organization

I. DEPENDENT VARIABLES

A. Birthrate for Women Aged 15–19

1. U.N., *Demographic Yearbook 1981*, 1983, table 24.
2. Argentina, Taiwan, USSR. U.S. Bureau of the Census, 1983f, table 14A.
3. Australia, France, F.R.G., Greece, Ireland, Italy, Netherlands, New Zealand, Poland, Spain, Switzerland, U.K., England and Wales, Yugoslavia. G. Calot, INED, unpublished data, Paris.
4. Cuba. P. Hollerbach and S. Diaz-Briquet, *Fertility Determinants in Cuba,* Panel on Fertility Determinants, Committee on Population and Demography, National Research Council, National Academy Press, 1983, table 19.

B. Cumulative Birth Rates

1. C. Westoff, G. Calot, and A. Foster, 1983.
2. Bulgaria, Chile, Cuba, Hong Kong, Singapore, Taiwan, USSR. Estimated from birthrate for women aged 15–19.
3. Puerto Rico. Numerators: Administración de Facilidades y Servicios de

245

Salud, *Informe Anual de Estadisticas Vitales, 1981,* Commonwealth of Puerto Rico, September 1982. Denominators: U.S. Bureau of the Census, *1980 Census of Population: Characteristics of the Population,* vol. 1, ch. B., part 53, May 1983, table 15.

    4. U.K., G.B., Scotland. G. Calot, op. cit.

C. *Pregnancy Rate for Women Aged 15–19 and Cumulative Pregnancy Rates*

    1. Numerators: C. Tietze, Population Council, unpublished data, New York. Denominators: G. Calot, op. cit.

    2. Canada. Numerators: C. Tietze, op. cit., and C. Tietze, 1983, p. 21.

    3. France. Numerators: G. Calot, op. cit.

    4. Netherlands. Numerators: G. Calot, op. cit., and correspondence from E. Ketting, Netherlands Institute for Social Sexological Research, Netherlands, December 12, 1983.

    5. U.S. Denominators: U.S. Bureau of the Census, 1982b, table 2.

II. INDEPENDENT VARIABLES

A. *Proportion of Females Married at Ages 15–19*

    1. U.N., 1984, table 40.

    2. Austria, Belgium, Bulgaria, Denmark, F.R.G., Greece, Hong Kong, Japan, Poland, Romania, Switzerland, Taiwan, U.S.S.R., Yugoslavia. U.S. Bureau of the Census, 1983f, table 10A.

    3. Cuba. P. Hollerbach and S. Diaz-Briquets, op. cit., table 19.

    4. U.K. Estimated from figures for England and Wales and Scotland.

    5. U.S. U.S. Bureau of the Census, 1981, table 1.

B. *Minimum Legal Age for Marriage Without Parental Consent*

    1. J. Paxman, *Law and Planned Parenthood,* IPPF, London, 1980, table E.

C. *Five-year Total Fertility Rate for Ages 20+*

    1. U.N., 1983, table 24.

    2. Argentina, Taiwan, USSR. U.S. Bureau of the Census, 1983f, table 14A.

    3. Australia, France, F.R.G., Greece, Ireland, Italy, Netherlands, New Zealand, Poland, Spain, Switzerland, U.K., England and Wales, Yugoslavia. G. Calot, op. cit.

    4. Cuba. P. Hollerbach and S. Diaz-Briquets, op. cit.

D. *Government Policy to Raise Fertility*

    1. IPPF, "Fertility and Family Planning," *A 1982 People Wallchart,* London, 1982.

E. *Liberal Policy on Maternity Leaves and Benefits*

    1. U.S. Department of Health and Human Services, *Social Security Programs throughout the World 1981,* Research Report No. 58, 1982.

F. *Percentage of Government Expenditure on Income Maintenance and Family Allowances*

1. U.N., *World Population Trends and Policies: 1981 Monitoring Report,* vol. II: Population Policies, New York, 1982, table 24.

G. *Percentage of All Currently Married Using the Pill*

1. A. Kols et al., "Oral Contraceptives in the 1980s," *Population Reports,* Series A, 6:195, 1982, table 3.

H. *Percentage of All Currently Married Using Condoms*

1. J. Berent, "Family Planning in Europe and USA in the 1970s," *Comparative Studies: ECE Analyses of WFS Surveys in Europe and USA,* No. 20, International Statistical Institute/World Fertility Survey, Voorburg, Netherlands, October 1982.

I. *Abortions per 1,000 Women Aged 15–44*

1. C. Tietze, *Induced Abortion,* 1983, table 2.
2. Australia. Correspondence from S. Siedlecky, Medical Services Adviser, Family Planning and Women's Health, Department of Health, Canberra, December 22, 1983.
3. Canada. C. Tietze, 1983, table 2, and p. 21.
4. F.R.G. E. Ketting and P. van Praag, *Schwangerschafsabbruch Gesetz und Praxis,* Stimezo, Netherlands, 1983, table IV.1, p. 272.
5. France. C. Tietze, 1983, table 2; and INED, "Neuvième Rapport sur la Situation Démographique de la France," *Population* 35:786, 1980; and INED, 1983.
6. Poland. M. Okolski, "Abortion and Contraception in Poland," *Studies in Family Planning* 14:263, 1983.

J. *Population Per Physician*

1. World Bank, *World Development Report 1982,* Oxford University Press, 1982, table 22.

K. *Maternal Mortality Per 1,000 Live Births*

1. WHO, *World Health Statistics Annual 1982,* Geneva, 1982, Annex III.

L. *Per Capita Government Expenditure on Health Care (1975 U.S. Dollars)*

1. World Bank, op. cit., table 24, p. 156.

M. *Percentage of Secondary-school-age Females Attending School*

1. World Bank, *World Tables,* 2d ed., Johns Hopkins University Press, Baltimore and London, 1980, table 4.

N. Percentage of Women Aged 15–19 Attending School

1. U.S. Bureau of the Census, 1983f, table 16c.
2. Czechoslovakia. U.N. Statistical office, unpublished data from the *Demographic Yearbook 1980,* census questionnaire, table 12.
3. Denmark. U.N. Statistical office, unpublished data from the *Demographic Yearbook 1978,* census questionnaire, table 12.
4. New Zealand. U.N. Statistical office, unpublished data from the *Demographic Yearbook 1976,* census questionnaire, table 12.
5. Norway. Numerator: U.N., *Demographic Yearbook 1979,* New York, 1980, table 34. Denominator: U.N., *Demographic Indicators of Countries: Estimates and Projections as Assessed in 1980,* New York: Oxford University Press, 1982.
6. Portugal. U.N., *Demographic Yearbook 1979,* New York, 1980, table 34.

O. Per Capita Government Expenditure on Education (1975 U.S. Dollars)

1. World Bank, *World Development Report 1982,* table 24.

P. Total Marital Divorce Rate

1. A. Monnier, "La conjoncture démographique: L'Europe et les pays développés d'outre-mer," *Population* 37:911, 1982.

Q. Mortality Rate from Liver Cirrhosis (Per 100,000 Population)

1. WHO, *World Health Statistics Annual 1982,* Geneva, 1982, tables 7A and 7B.
2. Czechoslovakia, G.D.R., U.S. WHO, *Sixth Report on the World Health Situation 1973–1977,* Geneva, 1980, table 15.

R. Incidence of Suicide, Ages 15–24 (Per 100,000)

1. WHO, *World Health Statistics Annual 1982,* tables 7A and 7B.

S. Proportion Foreign Born

1. U.N. *Demographic Yearbook 1977,* 29th issue, New York, 1978, table 32.

T. Log of Population Density (Per Square Mile)

1. U.N., *Demographic Indicators of Countries.*

U. Percentage in Cities ≥500,000

1. World Bank, *World Development Report 1982,* table 20.

V. Percentage of Labor Force in Agriculture

1. World Bank, *World Development Report 1982,* table 19.

W. Religiosity (Scale 1–10)

1. Center for Applied Research in the Apostolate, "Value Systems Study Group of the Americas," Washington, D.C., July 1982, table 8.

X. *Labor Force Participation Rate for Females Aged 15–19 (Percentage Working or Seeking Employment)*

  1. U.S. Bureau of the Census, 1983f, table 17c.

Y. *Labor Force Participation Rate for Males Aged 15–19*

  1. U.S. Bureau of the Census, 1983f, table 17c.

Z. *Percentage of Labor Force Female*

  1. World Bank, *World Tables,* table 5.
  2. U.S. U.S. Bureau of the Census, *Statistical Abstract of the United States, 1981,* 102d ed., Washington, D.C., 1981, table 635.

AA. *Labor Force Participation Rate for Women Aged 35–44*

  1. Numerators: U.S. Bureau of the Census, 1983f, table 17c. Denominators: G. Calot, op. cit.
  2. Bulgaria, Hong Kong, Japan. Denominators: U.N., *Demographic Indicators of Countries,* Annex II.
  3. Israel. U.S. Bureau of the Census, 1983f, table 17c.
  4. U.S. U.S. Bureau of the Census, *Statistical Abstract of the United States, 1981,* table 636.

BB. *Overall Unemployment Rate (Percentage of the Labor Force Unemployed, Excluding Puerto Rico)*

  1. ILO, *1982 Yearbook of Labour Statistics,* 42d issue, Geneva, 1982, table 9A.
  2. Cuba. P. Hollerbach and S. Diaz-Briquets, op. cit., table 46.
  3. U.S. U.S. Bureau of the Census, *Statistical Abstract of the United States, 1981,* table 635.

CC. *Gross National Product Per Capita (1975 U.S. Dollars)*

  1. World Bank, *World Development Report 1982,* table 1.

DD. *Average Annual Growth in Gross Domestic Product*

  1. World Bank, *World Tables,* table 11.

EE. *Percentage of Total Household Income to Top 10 Percent of Households*

  1. World Bank, *World Development Report 1982,* table 25.

FF. *Percentage of Total Household Income to Bottom 20 Percent of Households*

  1. World Bank, *World Development Report 1982,* table 25.
  2. Australia, Israel, New Zealand, Portugal, Taiwan. World Bank, *World Tables,* table 5.

File of Data Obtained from External Sources, 1980

Dependent variables	Australia	Austria	Belgium	Bulgaria	Canada	Chile	Cuba	Czechoslovakia
								Country
Birthrate for women aged 15–19	28	35	23	81	28	65	80	54
Cumulative birthrate for ages <20	145	179	117	402	140	321	397	265
Cumulative birthrate for ages <18	45	41	26	120	46	93	118	40
Cumulative birthrate for ages 18–19	100	138	91	282	94	228	278	225
Pregnancy rate for women aged 15–19	—	—	—	—	46	—	—	60
Cumulative pregnancy rate for ages <20	—	—	—	—	233	—	—	312
Cumulative pregnancy rate for ages <18	—	—	—	—	91	—	—	59
Cumulative pregnancy rate for ages 18–19	—	—	—	—	142	—	—	253
Independent variables								
Proportion of women married at ages 15–19 (per 1,000)	72	44	46	172	43	103	210	79
Minimum age for marriage without parental consent	18	19	—	18	—	—	18	18
5-year total fertility rate for ages ≥20 (per 1,000)	1,776	1,506	1,579	1,650	1,587	2,145	1,180	2,098
Government policy to influence fertility*	2	2	2	1	2	1	2	2
Policy on maternity leaves and benefits†	—	2	—	3	1	2	3	3
Percentage of government expenditure on income maintenance and family allowances	4.6	17.0	17.2	—	7.9	—	—	—
Percentage of all currently married using pill	—	—	—	2	27	—	—	14
Percentage of all currently married using condoms	—	—	—	2	—	—	—	13
Abortions per 1,000 women aged 15–44	14.1	—	—	69.6	13.2	—	47.1	31.1
Population per physician	650	430	440	440	560	1,930	1,100	390
Maternal mortality per 100,000 live births	9.8	7.7	10.7	21.1	6.4	73.1	45.6	18.3
Per capita government expenditure on health care (1975 U.S. $)	187	290	65	—	126	20	—	—
Percentage of secondary-school-age women attending school	73	78	89	87	95	51	—	47
Percentage of women aged 15–19 attending school	—	36.4	55.4	60.3	—	51.0	—	66.1
Per capita government expenditure on education (1975 U.S. $)	164	223	527	—	72	40	—	—
Total marital divorce rate	—	26.1	18.7	18.5	—	—	—	26.6

(*continued*)

Dependent variables	Den-mark	F.R.G.	Fin-land	France	G.D.R.	Greece	Hong Kong	Hun-gary
Birthrate for women aged 15–19	16	20	19	25	54	53	12	69
Cumulative birthrate for ages <20	84	102	94	125	253	269	62	342
Cumulative birthrate for ages <18	16	21	18	25	39	80	9	103
Cumulative birthrate for ages 18–19	68	81	76	100	214	189	53	239
Pregnancy rate for women aged 15–19	40	—	39	43	—	—	—	96
Cumulative pregnancy rate for ages <20	—	—	193	218	—	—	—	464
Cumulative pregnancy rate for ages <18	—	—	62	60	—	—	—	156
Cumulative pregnancy rate for ages 18–19	—	—	131	159	—	—	—	308
Independent variables								
Proportion of women married at ages 15–19 (per 1.000)	10	35	22	46	48	110	34	152
Minimum age for marriage without parental consent	18	18	18	18	18	—	21	18
5-year total fertility rate for ages ≥20 (per 1,000)	1,461	1,354	1,540	1,851	1,685	1,935	2,000	1,582
Government policy to influence fertility*	2	2	2	1	1	1	2	2
Policy on maternity leaves and benefits†	2	2	3	2	3	1	1	3
Percentage of government expenditure on income maintenance and family allowances	11.2	12.7	10.6	14.9	—	—	—	—
Percentage of all currently married using pill	25	—	11	27	42	—	23	36
Percentage of all currently married using condoms	—	—	32	6	—	—	—	4
Abortions per 1,000 women aged 15–44	21.4	11.4	13.9	22.3	22.5	—	8.6	36.3
Population per physician	510	490	630	610	530	460	1,180	430
Maternal mortality per 100,000 live births	1.7	20.6	3.1	15.5	22.0	14.2	4.7	20.9
Per capita government expenditure on health care (1975 U.S. $)	—	437	197	406	—	76	—	—
Percentage of secondary-school-age women attending school	75	—	101	88	86	72	49	58
Percentage of women aged 15–19 attending school	57.8	—	—	—	—	—	39.2	—
Per capita government expenditure on education (1975 U.S. $)	—	21	281	255	—	88	—	—
Total marital divorce rate	39.8	21.3	28.9	24.7	32.3	—	—	28.9

(continued)

| | Country | | | | | | | |
Dependent variables	Ireland	Israel	Italy	Japan	Nether-lands	New Zealand	Nor-way	Po-land
Birthrate for women aged 15–19	23	25	23	4	9	39	25	46
Cumulative birthrate for ages <20	113	179	117	17	46	194	128	225
Cumulative birthrate for ages <18	23	32	28	2	10	64	29	40
Cumulative birthrate for ages 18–19	90	147	89	15	36	130	99	185
Pregnancy rate for women aged 15–19	—	—	—	—	14	47	50	—
Cumulative pregnancy rate for ages <20	—	—	—	—	73	232	255	—
Cumulative pregnancy rate for ages <18	—	—	—	—	22	87	93	—
Cumulative pregnancy rate for ages 18–19	—	—	—	—	51	145	162	—
Independent variables								
Proportion of women married at ages 15–19 (per 1,000)	27	75	68	9	27	101	23	45
Minimum age for marriage without parental consent	21	—	18	—	21	—	20	18
5-year total fertility rate for ages ≥20 (per 1,000)	3,108	2,926	1,622	1,718	1,554	1,858	1,598	2,048
Government policy to influence fertility*	2	1	2	2	2	2	2	2
Policy on maternity leaves and benefits†	—	1	2	1	2	—	2	2
Percentage of government expenditure on income maintenance and family allowances	7.3	—	11.6	2.9	16.0	8.3	11.1	—
Percentage of all currently married using pill	—	—	14	—	—	—	16	8
Percentage of all currently married using condoms	—	—	13	—	—	—	16	14
Abortions per 1,000 women aged 15–44	—	—	18.5	84.2	6.2	8.6	16.3	49.0
Population per physician	830	310	490	850	580	740	540	610
Maternal mortality per 100,000 live births	17.1	5.4	17.1	20.4	8.8	11.5	11.8	11.7
Per capita government expenditure on health care (1975 U.S. $)	—	141	—	—	19	241	—	—
Percentage of secondary-school-age women attending school	95	42	67	93	89	85	90	62
Percentage of women aged 15–19 attending school	—	—	—	81.3	62.6	49.3	55.0	—
Per capita government expenditure on education (1975 U.S. $)	—	246	—	—	540	216	—	—
Total marital divorce rate	—	—	—	—	23.5	—	25.1	13.8

(*continued*)

	Country							
Dependent variables	Por-tugal	Puerto Rico	Ro-mania	Singa-pore	Spain	Swe-den	Swit-zerland	Tai-wan
Birthrate for women aged 15–19	41	78	73	12	27	16	10	33
Cumulative birthrate for ages <20	210	396	352	64	133	83	48	165
Cumulative birthrate for ages <18	59	158	100	9	37	15	8	42
Cumulative birthrate for ages 18–19	151	239	252	54	96	68	40	122
Pregnancy rate for women aged 15–19	—	—	—	—	—	37	—	—
Cumulative pregnancy rate for ages <20	—	—	—	—	—	195	—	—
Cumulative pregnancy rate for ages <18	—	—	—	—	—	69	—	—
Cumulative pregnancy rate for ages 18–19	—	—	—	—	—	126	—	—
Independent variables								
Proportion of women married at ages 15–19 (per 1,000)	72	110	142	23	47	7	36	49
Minimum age for marriage without parental consent	21	—	—	21	—	18	—	—
5-year total fertility rate for ages ≥20 (per 1,000)	1,966	2,326	2,088	1,677	2,171	1,598	1,499	2,350
Government policy to influence fertility*	2	—	2	2	2	2	2	3
Policy on maternity leaves and benefits†	2	—	2	1	2	3	—	1
Percentage of government expenditure on income maintenance and family allowances	—	—	—	—	—	10.4	—	—
Percentage of all currently married using pill	—	—	1	17	12	20	—	6
Percentage of all currently married using condoms	—	—	3	—	5	—	—	—
Abortions per 1,000 women aged 15–44	—	—	88.1	28.4	—	20.7	—	—
Population per physician	700	—	740	1,250	560	560	510	—
Maternal mortality per 100,000 live births	30.6	10.9	132.1	4.9	12.9	8.2	5.4	—
Per capita government expenditure on health care (1975 U.S. $)	—	—	—	47	7	92	208	—
Percentage of secondary-school-age women attending school	84	—	59	55	71	70	48	—
Percentage of women aged 15–19 attending school	18.2	—	—	—	27.8	59.7	—	—
Per capita government expenditure on education (1975 U.S. $)	—	—	—	100	65	412	65	—
Total marital divorce rate	—	—	20.9	—	—	42.7	27.4	—

(*continued*)

			Country			
Dependent variables	USSR	U.K. (G.B.)	England and Wales	Scot- land	U.S.	Yugo- slavia
Birthrate for women aged 15–19	41	31	31	33	54	48
Cumulative birthrate for ages <20	204	159	157	165	266	241
Cumulative birthrate for ages <18	55	43	41	45	101	59
Cumulative birthrate for ages 18–19	149	114	116	121	165	182
Pregnancy rate for women aged 15–19	—	—	48	44	96	—
Cumulative pregnancy rate for ages <20	—	—	248	—	488	—
Cumulative pregnancy rate for ages <18	—	—	87	—	201	—
Cumulative pregnancy rate for ages 18–19	—	—	161	—	287	—
Independent variables						
Proportion of women married at ages 15–19 (per 1,000)	100	52	51	56	80	158
Minimum age for marriage without parental consent	18	—	18	16	—	18
5-year total fertility rate for ages ≥20 (per 1,000)	2,055	1,727	1,742	1,676	1,582	1,899
Government policy to influence fertility*	2	2	—	—	2	2
Policy on maternity leaves and benefits†	2	—	—	—	—	2
Percentage of government expenditure on income maintenance and family allowances	—	8.3	—	—	8.0	—
Percentage of all currently married using pill	—	—	28	—	23	5
Percentage of all currently married using condoms	—	—	18	—	8	2
Abortions per 1,000 women aged 15–44	—	—	12.8	8.4	29.3	58.5
Population per physician	290	750	—	—	580	760
Maternal mortality per 100,000 live births	—	—	10.7	14.6	9.6	21.9
Per capita government expenditure on health care (1975 U.S. $)	—	219	—	—	183	101
Percentage of secondary-school-age women attending school	82	81	—	—	—	50
Percentage of women aged 15–19 attending school	—	—	—	—	—	—
Per capita government expenditure on education (1975 U.S. $)	—	45	—	—	51	—
Total marital divorce rate	37.4	—	36.7	21.0	—	—

(continued)

APPENDIX 3 (*Continued*)

Independent variables	Country							
	Aus-tralia	Aus-tria	Bel-gium	Bul-garia	Cana-da	Chile	Cuba	Czecho-slovakia
Mortality rate from liver cirrhosis (per 100,000)	84	304	133	102	121	296	—	177
Incidence of suicide ages 15–24 (per 100,000)	11.2	18.0	10.1	9.3	16.9	6.9	—	—
Proportion foreign born	.202	.081	.076	—	—	.010	.015	—
Log of population density (per sq. km.)	2	89	322	81	2	15	85	120
Percentage in cities ≥500,000	68	39	24	18	62	44	32	12
Percentage of labor force in agriculture	6	9	3	37	5	19	23	11
Religiosity‡	—	—	5.94	—	—	—	—	—
Labor force participation rate for women aged 15–19	50.3	—	24.8	35.0	42.6	—	—	—
Labor force participation rate for males aged 15–19	56.0	—	30.8	23.7	50.4	—	—	—
Percentage of labor force female	34.7	38.3	35.6	43.0	32.9	23.4	—	45.0
Labor force participation rate for women aged 35–44	57.9	—	41.5	93.4	53.7	—	—	—
Overall unemployment rate	6.1	1.9	9.4	—	7.5	10.4	1.3	—
Gross national product per capita	9,820	10,230	12,180	4,150	10,130	2,150	—	5,820
Average annual growth in gross domestic product	3.3	4.0	3.7	—	4.7	0.1	—	—
Percentage of total household income to top 10%	—	—	—	—	26.9	—	—	—
Percentage of total household income to bottom 20%	7.1	—	—	—	3.8	—	—	—

(*continued*)

APPENDIX 3 (*Continued*)

Independent variables	Country							
	Den- mark	F.R.G.	Fin- land	France	G.D.R.	Greece	Hong Kong	Hun- gary
Mortality rate from liver cirrhosis (per 100,000)	114	267	56	308	130	123	77	277
Incidence of suicide ages 15–24 (per 100,000)	12.1	12.5	20.7	9.7	—	2.2	7.8	20.0
Proportion foreign born	—	—	.007	—	—	—	.436	—
Log of population density (per sq. km.)	119	245	14	98	156	71	4,886	116
Percentage in cities ≥500,000	32	45	27	34	17	70	100	37
Percentage of labor force in agriculture	7	4	11	8	10	37	3	15
Religiosity‡	4.47	5.67	5.35	4.72	—	—	—	—
Labor force participation rate for women aged 15–19	34.0	41.4	26.5	—	—	—	42.6	—
Labor force participation rate for males aged 15–19	45.4	48.5	29.9	—	—	—	45.2	—
Percentage of labor force female	37.2	36.3	42.1	35.2	46.2	32.9	34.2	42.2
Labor force participation rate for women aged 35–44	82.0	54.7	87.3	50.1	—	—	53.5	—
Overall unemployment rate	7.0	3.8	4.8	6.3	—	2.4	3.8	—
Gross national product per capita	12,950	13,590	9,720	11,730	7,180	4,380	4,240	4,180
Average annual growth in gross domestic product	2.8	2.4	3.4	3.8	—	4.6	8.0	—
Percentage of total household income to top 10%	22.4	28.8	21.2	30.5	—	—	31.3	—
Percentage of total household income to bottom 20%	7.4	6.9	6.8	5.3	—	—	5.4	—

(*continued*)

APPENDIX 3 (*Continued*)

Independent variables	Country							
	Ireland	Israel	Italy	Japan	Nether-lands	New Zealand	Nor-way	Po-land
Mortality rate from liver cirrhosis (per 100,000)	37	78	347	141	47	53	61	123
Incidence of suicide ages 15–24 (per 100,000)	4.4	6.1	3.3	12.5	6.0	8.2	12.0	12.1
Proportion foreign born	.046	.449	—	.006	—	—	—	.064
Log of population density (per sq. km.)	47	190	189	313	345	12	13	115
Percentage in cities ≥500,000	48	35	52	42	24	30	32	47
Percentage of labor force in agriculture	19	7	11	12	6	9	7	31
Religiosity‡	8.02	—	6.96	4.49	5.33	—	—	—
Labor force participation rate for women aged 15–19	—	—	—	18.5	28.5	—	—	20.7
Labor force participation rate for males aged 15–19	—	—	—	20.2	24.6	—	—	28.9
Percentage of labor force female	27.0	29.7	27.8	39.6	25.6	30.4	28.1	46.1
Labor force participation rate for women aged 35–44	—	47.1	42.7	58.4	33.6	—	—	81.6
Overall unemployment rate	10.3	4.8	7.6	2.0	5.9	2.9	1.7	—
Gross national product per capita	4,880	4,500	6,480	9,890	11,470	7,090	12,650	3,900
Average annual growth in gross domestic product	3.4	5.0	2.9	5.0	3.2	2.9	4.8	—
Percentage of total household income to top 10%	—	—	28.1	—	22.1	—	22.2	—
Percentage of total household income to bottom 20%	—	7.8	6.2	—	8.1	3.9	6.3	—

(*continued*)

APPENDIX 3 (*Continued*)

	Country							
Independent variables	Por-tugal	Puerto Rico	Ro-mania	Singa-pore	Spain	Swe-den	Swit-zerland	Tai-wan
Mortality rate from liver cirrhosis (per 100,000)	264	245	288	51	225	122	133	—
Incidence of suicide ages 15–24 (per 100,000)	6.6	6.2	—	10.3	2.4	11.5	23.4	—
Proportion foreign born	—	.019	—	.255	.011	.067	—	—
Log of population density (per sq. km.)	107	413	94	4,114	74	18	157	—
Percentage in cities ≥500,000	44	—	17	100	44	35	22	—
Percentage of labor force in agriculture	24	—	29	2	15	5	5	—
Religiosity‡	—	—	—	—	6.39	3.99	—	—
Labor force participation rate for women aged 15–19	44.8	—	32.5	—	—	—	—	43.9
Labor force participation rate for males aged 15–19	79.0	—	37.8	—	—	—	—	47.1
Percentage of labor force female	25.5	—	44.6	32.2	20.6	36.6	33.7	—
Labor force participation rate for women aged 35–44	22.3	—	82.6	—	—	72.9	—	—
Overall unemployment rate	7.8	17.1	—	3.1	11.7	2.0	0.2	—
Gross national product per capita	2,370	—	2,340	4,430	5,400	13,520	16,440	—
Average annual growth in gross domestic product	4.6	3.6	—	8.6	4.7	1.7	0.2	7.7
Percentage of total household income to top 10%	—	—	—	—	26.7	21.2	—	—
Percentage of total household income to bottom 20%	7.3	—	—	—	6.0	7.2	—	8.7

(*continued*)

APPENDIX 3 (*Continued*)

Independent variables	Country					
	USSR	U.K. (G.B.)	England and Wales	Scotland	U.S.	Yugo-slavia
Mortality rate from liver cirrhosis (per 100,000)	—	48	45	79	144	186
Incidence of suicide ages 15–24 (per 100,000)	—	—	4.7	6.4	—	8.1
Proportion foreign born	—	—	.061	.026	.047	.008
Log of population density (per sq. km.)	12	229	—	—	24	87
Percentage in cities ≥500,000	33	55	—	—	77	23
Percentage of labor force in agriculture	14	2	—	—	2	29
Religiosity‡	—	5.72	—	—	8.21	—
Labor force participation rate for women aged 15–19	—	—	—	—	41.5	—
Labor force participation rate for males aged 15–19	—	—	—	—	45.8	—
Percentage of labor force female	49.7	36.7	—	—	41.9	36.3
Labor force participation rate for women aged 35–44	—	—	—	—	65.5	—
Overall unemployment rate	—	7.5	—	—	7.1	11.9
Gross national product per capita	4,550	7,920	—	—	11,360	2,620
Average annual growth in gross domestic product	—	1.9	—	—	2.8	6.2
Percentage of total household income to top 10%	—	23.8	—	—	26.6	22.9
Percentage of total household income to bottom 20%	—	7.3	—	—	4.5	6.6

*Codes: 1 = to raise, 2 = to maintain or no intervention, 3 = to reduce.

†Codes: 1 = *low benefits*, i.e., leave time and other benefits (birth grants, etc.) equivalent to 30–70 days; 2 = *medium benefits*, i.e., leave time and other benefits equivalent to 71–120 days; 3 = *high benefits*, i.e., leave time and other benefits equivalent to 121–200 days.

‡Scale: 1–10.

File of Data Derived from the Country Survey

Explanation of Codes for the Country Survey

Questionnaire number	*Explanation*
1.	1 = Usually possible
	0 = Usually not possible
2. a, b.	1 = Required
	2 = Varies
	3 = Not required
2. c.	1 = Not required
	2 = Varies or information incomplete
	3 = Required
	4 = Abortion is illegal
3.	1 = Yes
	2 = NA
	3 = No
5.	1 = Widely available
	2 = Availability limited
	7 = Limited only to users dependent on certain services
6.	0 = Yes
	1 = No
	7 = No commercial television

Questionnaire number	*Explanation*

7.
1 = Not permitted
2 = Officially discouraged
    but not prohibited
3 = No uniform policy—up
    to the individual
    school or school district
4 = Officially encouraged
    but not always done
5 = Compulsory

8.
2 = Less than 1/3
5 = At least 1/3
    but less than 2/3
7 = At least 2/3
    but less than 9/10
9 = 9/10 or more
NA = NA on Q. 7 or Q. 8

9.
Number = Years of age
V = It varies*
X = No instruction provided*

10.
2 = Less than 1/3
5 = At least 1/3
    but less than 2/3
8 = At least 2/3
    but less than 9/10
9 = 9/10 or more

11.
1 = To any woman
2 = To low-income women only
3 = To low-income women in some
    areas only
4 = Not to anyone
5 = Other

12.
0 = None
1 = Less than 1/10
2 = At least 1/10
    but less than 1/3
5 = At least 1/3
    but less than 2/3
8 = 2/3 or more
Y = Other*
I = Abortion is illegal*

Questionnaire number	Explanation

13.

1 = Less than 1/3
2 = At least 1/3
    but less than 2/3
3 = At least 2/3
    but less than 9/10
4 = 9/10 or more

14.

0 = Father not easily located
1 = Easily located

15.

Number = Years of age
V = It varies*
X = No legal age*

17.

1 = Yes
2 = No

18.

1 = ⌠All or most public beaches
    ⌡Some public beaches
3 = A very few specially
    designated beaches
5 = None

19.

2 = Legal
5 = Illegal

Indices

A   1 = Least support; 5 = most support
B   1 = Least favorable; 8 = most favorable
C   1 = Abortion illegal†
    2 = Most restrictions
    7 = Fewest restrictions
D   1 = Least open; 16 = most open

Computation of indices

A. Paternal financial support
    Sum of the two constituent items, questions (Q) 13 and 14.
        Range: 1 (least) to 5 (most)

B. Policy favoring provision of contraceptives for young unmarried women
    Sum of items (questions 1, 2a, 2b, and 3; in questions 2a and 2b, NA was
    given the value 2) minus 8.
        Range = 1 (least favorable) to 8 (most favorable)

C. Least restrictions regarding parental consent for abortion
   9 minus the sum of the two parts of question 2c.
      Range = 1–7

D. Open attitudes about sex
   22 minus the sum of questions 6, 17, 18, and 19. In question 6, a 7 is counted as 0 and NA is counted 1. If any of the parts of question 17 are NA, 4 is added for this question.
      Range: 1–16

Notes: For all items, a dash means "not ascertained"; values of NA, I, Y, X, and V were treated as missing data in the statistical analysis.
   *Excluded from statistical analysis.
   †In some countries where abortion is technically illegal, it is available in practice.

FILE OF DATA AND COMPOSITE INDICES DERIVED FROM THE COUNTRY SURVEY

Indices A–D and questionnaire items 1–19	Aus-tralia	Aus-tria	Bel-gium	Bul-garia	Cana-da	Chile	Cuba	Czecho-slovakia	Den-mark
A. *Paternal financial support*	1	4	—	5	1	1	5	5	5
Proportion of out-of-wedlock children receiving support from father (Q 13)	1	3	—	4	1	1	4	4	4
Ability of unwed mother to locate father of child if he moves (Q 14)	0	1	1	1	0	0	1	1	1
B. *Policy favoring provision of contraceptives for young unmarried women*	6	7	5	2	2	6	8	2	8
Purchase of non-prescription contraceptives by adolescents (Q 1)	1	1	1	1	0	1	1	1	1
Parental consent/notification required for single women <18 to obtain non-prescription contraceptives (Q 2a)									
policy	3	3	3	2	3	3	3	3	3
practice	3	3	3	1	—	3	3	3	3
Parental consent/notification required for single women <18 to obtain prescription contraceptives (Q 2b)									
policy	2	2	3	2	2	3	3	1	3
practice	2	3	2	1	—	3	3	1	3
Other restrictions on fertility control services to single women <18 (Q 3)	3	3	1	3	1	1	3	1	3
C. *Least restrictions regarding parental consent for abortion* (Q 2c)	5	6	4	4	5	3	7	3	3
policy	2	2	4	3	2	4	1	3	3
practice	2	1	1	2	2	2	1	3	3

(*continued*)

Appendix 4 (*Continued*)

Indices	Aus-tralia	Aus-tria	Bel-gium	Bul-garia	Cana-da	Chile	Cuba	Czecho-slovakia	Den-mark
D. *Open attitudes about sex*	10	10	5	3	10	1	1	1	14
Condom advertisement in (Q 6):									
television	1	1	1	1	1	1	1	1	7
mass circulation newspapers	1	1	1	1	1	1	1	1	0
general interest magazines	0	0	1	1	0	1	1	1	0
other magazines	0	0	1	1	0	1	1	1	0
billboards	1	1	1	1	1	1	1	1	0
Complete female nudity shown in (Q 17):									
mass circulation magazines	1	1	1	2	1	2	2	2	1
on television, prime time	2	2	—	2	2	2	2	2	2
on television, off hours	1	1	—	2	1	2	2	2	2
Proportion public beaches where complete nudity is common (Q 18)	3	3	3	3	3	5	5	5	1
Sale of sexually explicit literature in large cities (Q 19)	2	2	5	5	2	5	5	5	2
Individual variables									
Government policy favoring teaching about contraceptive methods in secondary schools (Q 7)	3	4	3	4	3	1	2	5	5
Proportion of female students taught about contraceptive methods by age 18 (Q 8)	5	—	2	5	5	—	—	9	9
Age students receive contraceptive instruction in schools (Q 9)	15	16	16	16	16	X	X	14	13
Percentage of 15–16-year-old girls in coed schools (Q 10)	8	8	5	9	9	5	9	9	9
Public subsidy of abortions (Q 12)	5	—	I	8	5	I	8	—	8

(*continued*)

Appendix 4 (*Continued*)

Indices	Aus-tralia	Aus-tria	Bel-gium	Bul-garia	Cana-da	Chile	Cuba	Czecho-slovakia	Den-mark
Minimum legal age for consensual intercourse for girls (Q 15)	16	14	16	18	16	16	16	16	15
Variables not used									
General availability of oral contraceptives (Q 5)	1	1	1	2	1	1	1	2	1
Availability of free maternal and child health services (Q 11)	5	1	4	1	1	2	1	1	1

(continued)

Appendix 4 (*Continued*)

Indices	F.R.G.	Fin-land	France	G.D.R.	Greece	Hong Kong	Hun-gary	Ireland	Isra-el
A. *Paternal financial support*	4	5	—	2	2	2	4	—	2
Proportion of out-of-wedlock children receiving support from father (Q 13)	3	4	—	1	1	1	3	—	1
Ability of unwed mother to locate father of child if he moves (Q 14)	1	1	1	1	1	1	1	0	1
B. *Policy favoring provision of contraceptives for young unmarried women*	8	8	8	4	3	6	1	6	8
Purchase of non-prescription contraceptives by adolescents (Q 1)	1	1	1	1	1	1	1	0	1
Parental consent/notification required for single women <18 to obtain non-prescription contraceptives (Q 2a)									
policy	3	3	3	3	3	3	2	3	3
practice	3	3	3	3	2	3	2	3	3
Parental consent/notification required for single women <18 to obtain prescription contraceptives (Q 2b)									
policy	3	3	3	1	2	3	1	3	3
practice	3	3	3	1	2	3	2	3	3
Other restrictions on fertility control services to single women <18 (Q 3)	3	3	3	3	1	1	1	2	3
C. *Least restrictions regarding parental consent for abortion* (Q 2c)	6	6	4	3	6	3	—	1	6
policy	2	2	3	3	1	3	—	4	1
practice	1	1	2	3	2	3	—	4	2

(*continued*)

Appendix 4 (*Continued*)

Indices	F.R.G.	Fin-land	France	G.D.R.	Greece	Hong Kong	Hun-gary	Ireland	Isra-el
D. *Open attitudes about sex*	12	10	11	11	4	4	3	1	4
Condom advertisement in (Q 6):									
television	1	0	1	1	1	1	1	1	1
mass circulation newspapers	—	0	0	0	1	0	1	1	1
general interest magazines	1	0	0	0	1	0	1	1	1
other magazines	0	0	0	0	0	0	1	1	1
billboards	0	0	1	1	1	1	1	1	1
Complete female nudity shown in (Q 17):									
mass circulation magazines	1	—	1	1	2	2	2	2	1
on television, prime time	2	—	2	1	2	2	2	2	2
on television, off hours	1	—	1	1	2	2	2	2	2
Proportion public beaches where complete nudity is common (Q 18)	1	3	3	1	3	5	3	5	3
Sale of sexually explicit literature in large cities (Q 19)	2	5	2	5	5	5	5	5	5
Individual variables									
Government policy favoring teaching about contraceptive methods in secondary schools (Q 7)	4	5	4	5	3	3	4	3	4
Proportion of female students taught about contraceptive methods by age 18 (Q 8)	7	9	7	9	2	2	7	—	7
Age students receive contraceptive instruction in schools (Q 9)	15	13	15	15	V	17	14	X	14
Percentage of 15–16-year-old girls in coed schools (Q 10)	8	9	9	9	5	8	9	5	8
Public subsidy of abortions (Q 12)	8	8	5	8	0	1	8	I	1

(*continued*)

Appendix 4 (*Continued*)

Indices	F.R.G.	Fin-land	France	G.D.R.	Greece	Hong Kong	Hun-gary	Ireland	Isra-el
Minimum legal age for consensual intercourse for girls (Q 15)	16	15	15	16	16	16	18	16	17
Variables not used									
General availability of oral contraceptives (Q 5)	1	1	1	1	1	1	1	2	1
Availability of free maternal and child health services (Q 11)	1	1	1	1	2	1	1	5	3

(*continued*)

Appendix 4 (*Continued*)

Indices	Italy	Ja-pan	Neth-er-lands	New Zea-land	Nor-way	Po-land	Por-tugal	Puerto Rico	Ro-ma-nia
A. *Paternal financial support*	1	2	3	—	5	5	2	4	—
Proportion of out-of-wedlock children receiving support from father (Q 13)	1	1	2	—	4	4	1	3	—
Ability of unwed mother to locate father of child if he moves (Q 14)	0	1	1	—	1	1	1	1	1
B. *Policy favoring provision of contraceptives for young unmarried women*	6	6	8	8	8	8	2	2	6
Purchase of non-prescription contraceptives by adolescents (Q 1)	1	1	1	1	1	1	1	1	1
Parental consent/notification required for single women <18 to obtain non-prescription contraceptives (Q 2a)									
policy	3	3	3	3	3	3	3	1	3
practice	3	3	3	3	3	3	1	3	3
Parental consent/notification required for single women <18 to obtain prescription contraceptives (Q 2b)									
policy	1	3	3	3	3	3	3	1	3
practice	3	1	3	3	3	3	1	1	2
Other restrictions on fertility control services to single women <18 (Q 3)	3	3	3	3	3	3	1	3	2
C. *Least restrictions regarding parental consent for abortion* (Q 2c)	3	3	4	6	7	7	2	4	4
policy	3	3	3	1	1	1	4	3	3
practice	3	3	2	2	1	1	3	2	2

(*continued*)

Appendix 4 (*Continued*)

Indices	Italy	Ja-pan	Neth-er-lands	New Zea-land	Nor-way	Po-land	Por-tugal	Puerto Rico	Ro-ma-nia
D. *Open attitudes about sex*	12	5	14	5	16	6	7	1	3
Condom advertisement in (Q 6):									
television	0	1	0	1	7	1	1	1	1
mass circulation newspapers	0	0	0	1	0	1	1	1	1
general interest magazines	0	0	0	0	0	1	1	1	1
other magazines	0	0	0	0	0	1	1	1	1
billboards	0	0	0	1	0	1	1	1	1
Complete female nudity shown in (Q 17):									
mass circulation magazines	2	2	1	2	1	1	2	2	2
on television, prime time	2	2	1	2	1	1	2	2	2
on television, off hours	1	2	1	2	1	1	1	2	2
Proportion public beaches where complete nudity is common (Q 18)	3	5	3	3	1	3	3	5	3
Sale of sexually explicit literature in large cities (Q 19)	2	5	2	5	2	5	2	5	5
Individual variables									
Government policy favoring teaching about contraceptive methods in secondary schools (Q 7)	2	3	3	2	4	4	3	4	2
Proportion of female students taught about contraceptive methods by age 18 (Q 8)	2	—	5	5	7	2	2	2	—
Age students receive contraceptive instruction in schools (Q 9)	16	X	15	14	14	15	V	14	X
Percentage of 15–16-year-old girls in coed schools (Q 10)	9	9	9	8	9	9	8	9	9

(*continued*)

Appendix 4 (*Continued*)

Indices	Italy	Ja-pan	Neth-er-lands	New Zea-land	Nor-way	Po-land	Por-tugal	Puerto Rico	Ro-ma-nia
Public subsidy of abortions (Q 12)	8	0	2	8	8	8	I	0	8
Minimum legal age for consensual in-tercourse for girls (Q 15)	18	18	14	16	16	16	X	21	16
Variables not used									
General availability of oral contracep-tives (Q 5)	1	2	1	1	1	2	1	7	2
Availability of free maternal and child health ser-vices (Q 11)	1	1	2	1	1	1	1	2	1

(*continued*)

Appendix 4 (*Continued*)

Indices	Singa-pore	Spain	Swe-den	Swit-zer-land	Tai-wan	USSR	United Kingdom		U.S.	Yu-go-sla-via
							En-gland & Wales	Scot-land		
A. *Paternal financial support*	—	1	3	4	4	3	2	2	1	2
Proportion of out-of-wedlock chil-dren receiving support from fa-ther (Q 13)	—	1	2	3	3	2	2	2	1	1
Ability of unwed mother to locate father of child if he moves (Q 14)	1	—	1	1	1	1	0	0	0	1
B. *Policy favoring provision of con-traceptives for young unmarried women*	8	5	8	7	8	5	8	8	6	—
Purchase of non-prescription contraceptives by adolescents (Q 1)	1	0	1	1	1	1	1	1	1	—
Parental con-sent/notification required for sin-gle women <18 to obtain non-prescription contraceptives (Q 2a)										
policy	3	3	3	3	3	—	3	3	3	—
practice	3	—	3	—	3	3	3	3	3	—
Parental con-sent/notification required for sin-gle women <18 to obtain pre-scription con-traceptives (Q 2b)										
policy	3	3	3	3	3	—	3	3	2	—
practice	3	—	3	3	3	3	3	3	3	—
Other restrictions on fertility con-trol services to single women <18 (Q 3)	3	3	3	3	3	2	3	3	2	2

(*continued*)

Appendix 4 (*Continued*)

Indices	Singapore	Spain	Sweden	Switzerland	Taiwan	USSR	England & Wales	Scotland	U.S.	Yugoslavia
							United Kingdom			
C. *Least restrictions regarding parental consent for abortion*										
(Q 2c)	7	1	7	6	5	5	7	6	6	—
policy	1	4	1	1	3	2	1	1	1	—
practice	1	4	1	2	1	2	1	2	2	—
D. *Open attitudes about sex*	1	11	16	9	1	3	9	6	7	7
Condom advertisement in (Q 6):										
television	1	1	7	1	1	1	1	1	1	1
mass circulation newspapers	1	1	0	1	1	1	0	0	1	1
general interest magazines	1	1	0	1	1	1	0	0	1	1
other magazines	1	0	0	1	1	1	0	0	0	1
billboards	1	1	0	1	1	1	0	1	1	1
Complete female nudity shown in (Q 17):										
mass circulation magazines	2	1	1	1	2	2	1	2	2	1
on television, prime time	2	2	1	1	2	2	2	2	2	2
on television, off hours	2	1	1	1	2	2	1	2	2	2
Proportion public beaches where complete nudity is common (Q 18)	5	1	1	3	5	3	3	3	3	3
Sale of sexually explicit literature in large cities (Q 19)	5	2	2	2	5	5	5	5	2	2
Individual variables										
Government policy favoring teaching about contraceptive methods in secondary schools (Q 7)	2	4	5	3	3	1	4	3	3	3
Proportion of female students taught about contraceptive methods by age 18 (Q 8)	—	2	9	9	2	—	7	5	5	2

(*continued*)

Appendix 4 (*Continued*)

Indices	Singa-pore	Spain	Swe-den	Swit-zer-land	Tai-wan	USSR	United Kingdom En-gland & Wales	Scot-land	U.S.	Yu go sla via
Age students receive contraceptive instruction in schools (Q 9)	X	13	10	14	14	X	13	15	15	18
Percentage of 15–16-year-old girls in coed schools (Q 10)	8	5	9	9	8	9	8	8	8	—
Public subsidy of abortions (Q 12)	0	I	8	Y	1	8	5	8	2	8
Minimum legal age for consensual intercourse for girls (Q 15)	16	18	15	16	18	18	16	16	V	18
Variables not used										
General availability of oral contraceptives (Q 5)	1	1	1	1	2	2	1	1	1	1
Availability of free maternal and child health services (Q 11)	1	1	1	1	1	1	1	1	2	1

Adolescent Fertility Questionnaire

(The Alan Guttmacher Institute, 1983)

Instructions:

Please circle the number by the most appropriate answer. Since the pre-defined answer categories may not fit the particular circumstances of your country, we encourage you to write in comments and explanations of your answers.

We do not expect you to do research to answer the questions. Where data are not readily available, please give the best estimate that is conveniently available from a knowledgeable person. We realize that the responses may be based on general impressions in some cases.

1. Is it usually possible for unmarried adolescents aged 15–17 to buy non-prescription contraceptives (condoms, spermicides) in pharmacies or other stores?

    1 — Yes   0 — No   (6)

2. Is parental consent or notification required for unmarried women under age 18 to obtain:

	By official policy			In practice		
	Yes	Varies	No	Yes	Varies	No
a. Nonprescription contraceptives	1	2	3	1	2	3 (7–8)
b. Prescription contraceptives	1	2	3	1	2	3 (9–10)
c. An abortion	3	2	1	3	2	1 (11–12)

3. Are there other restrictions on fertility control services to unmarried women under aged 18 that do not apply to older women? If so, please describe.

(13)

277

4. How much does a cycle (one-month supply) of birth control pills typically cost on the private retail market? (specify currency)

Approximate usual cost:_____   Range:_____ to_____   (14–16)
      Usually provided free through the national health plan
      Pills not usually available

5. Are oral contraceptives widely available, or is availability limited due to lack of supply or lack of government approval? (For example, some countries have import restrictions on oral contraceptives that severely limit the number of users.)

     1 — Widely available   2 — Availability is limited   (17)

6. Are specific brands of condoms advertised in the following media?

	Yes	No	
Television	0	1	(18)
Mass circulation newspapers	0	1	(19)
Mass circulation general interest magazines (such as *Time* magazine)	0	1	(20)
Any other magazines	0	1	(21)
Billboards	0	1	(22)

7. What is governmental policy regarding the teaching of the use of contraceptive methods in public secondary schools?

     5 — Always done   (23)
     4 — Officially encouraged but not always done
     3 — No uniform policy; up to the individual school or school district
     2 — Officially discouraged but not prohibited
     1 — Not permitted

8. About what proportion of girls have received formal instruction in school about contraceptive methods by the time they reach age 18?

     2 — Less than 1/3   (24)
     5 — At least 1/3 but less than 2/3
     7 — At least 2/3 but less than 9/10
     9 — 9/10 or more

     Is this information:

     1 — Based on statistical data
     2 — An impressionistic estimate   (25)

9. At what age are students usually exposed to instruction about contraception in the schools?_____   (26–27)

10. Of the 15–16-year-old girls in school, either public or private, what proportion attend coeducational schools (schools with boys and girls)?

    2 — Less than 1/3   (28)
    5 — At least 1/3 but less than 2/3
    8 — At least 2/3 but less than 9/10
    9 — 9/10 or more

11. Are maternal and child health services:

    1 — Available free for any woman   (29)
    2 — Free for low-income women only
    3 — Free for low-income women in some regions or cities but not others
    4 — Not free for anyone

12. What proportion of women obtaining legal induced abortions have their abortions provided free by a government program such as national health insurance or a government health facility?

    I — Abortion is illegal   (30)
    0 — None
    1 — Less than 1/10
    2 — At least 1/10 but less than 1/3
    5 — At least 1/3 but less than 2/3
    8 — 2/3 or more

13. Of children born out of wedlock living with their mothers but not their fathers, about what proportion are supported in part by their fathers?

    1 — Less than 1/3   (31)
    2 — At least 1/3 but less than 2/3
    3 — At least 2/3 but less than 9/10
    4 — 9/10 or more

Is this information:

    1 — Based on statistical data
    2 — An impressionistic estimate?   (32)

14. Can an unwed mother easily locate the father of her child if he moves to a different part of the country?

    1 — Yes   0 — No   (33)

15. What is the minimum legal age for consensual intercourse for girls?_____
                                                             (34–35)

16. Is prostitution legal?

    1 — Yes   2 — No   (36)

17. Is complete female nudity shown:

	Yes	No	
In mass circulation magazines	1	2	(37)
On television, prime time	1	2	(38)
On television, off hours	1	2	(39)

18. On what proportion of public beaches is complete nudity common?

    1 — All or most public beaches   (40)
    1 — Some public beaches
    3 — A very few specially designated beaches
    5 — No beaches

19. Is hard core pornographic literature legally for sale in stores in most large cities?

    2 — Yes   5 — No   (41)

Zero-Order Correlations for Countries Having Data on Abortions

ZERO-ORDER CORRELATIONS BETWEEN THE INDEPENDENT VARIABLES AND THE EIGHT MEASURES OF TEENAGE FERTILITY AND PREGNANCY FOR COUNTRIES HAVING DATA ON ABORTIONS, BY AGE OF WOMAN

	Measure									
Group and variable	Birthrate for women aged 15–19	Pregnancy rate for women aged 15–19	No. of countries for which data available	Cumulative birthrate for ages <20	<18	18–19	Cumulative pregnancy rate for ages <20	<18	18–19	No. of countries for which data available
Marriage										
Proportion of women married at ages 15–19	.91	.75	13	.90	.86	.85	.72	.59	.75	11
Minimum age for marriage without parental consent	–.34	–.35	10	–.46	–.36	–.48	–.53	–.40	–.56	8
Childbearing										
5-year total fertility rate for ages <20	.38	.07	13	.31	–.03	.45	.03	–.25	.22	11
Policy to raise fertility	.13	.12	11	.16	.21	.12	.13	.20	.08	10
Liberal policy on maternity leaves and benefits	.39	.36	9	.36	.15	.42	.35	.13	.43	8
Percentage of government expenditure on income maintenance and family allowances	–.65	–.64	9	–.68	–.68	–.65	–.63	–.68	–.58	8
Paternal financial support	–.08	–.14	11	.01	–.32	.17	–.15	–.39	.02	9
Contraception										
Percentage of all currently married using the pill	.36	.41	10	.44	.59	.32	.43	.46	.36	9
Percentage of all currently married using condoms	–.65	–.64	7	–.66	–.63	–.60	–.64	–.49	–.68	7
Policy favoring provision of contraceptives for young unmarried women	–.70	–.58	13	–.07	–.53	–.72	–.56	–.35	–.64	11
Policy favoring teaching contraception	.15	.06	13	.07	.39	–.09	.02	.24	–.12	11
Proportion of female students taught contraception	–.14	–.09	13	–.05	–.39	.13	–.06	–.30	.09	11

Age at which contraception taught	.25	.16	13	.21	.30	.15	.15	.17	.13	11
Abortion										
Abortions per 1,000 women aged 15–44	.70	.78	13	.79	.59	.82	.82	.59	.90	11
Least restriction regarding parental consent for abortion	.02	–.16	12	.17	–.12	.30	–.13	–.39	.07	10
Public subsidy of abortions	.01	–.03	12	.09	–.07	.18	.00	–.09	.06	10
Sex										
Open attitudes about sex	–.84	–.59	13	–.84	–.66	–.86	–.60	–.37	–.71	11
Minimum age for consensual intercourse	.78	.73	12	.77	.86	.68	.72	.73	.66	10
Proportion of female students in coeducational schools	–.28	–.25	13	–.27	–.48	–.15	–.31	–.46	–.19	11
Health										
Population per physician	–.42	–.37	11	–.49	–.18	–.61	–.42	–.14	–.56	10
Maternal mortality	.71	.48	13	.70	.44	.78	.50	.22	.64	11
Per capita government expenditure on health care	.35	.29	7	.36	.19	.48	.28	.14	.39	7
Education										
Percentage of secondary-school-age women attending school	–.67	–.59	10	–.72	–.44	–.79	–.63	–.30	–.73	9
Percentage of women aged 15–19 attending school	–.05	–.12	6	.02	–.59	.20	–.07	–.70	.18	5
Per capita government expenditure on education	–.82	–.81	7	–.83	–.79	–.84	–.80	–.78	–.80	7
Social Integration										
Total marital divorce rate	–.21	–.02	10	–.09	–.03	–.11	.04	.18	–.04	8
Mortality rate from liver cirrhosis	.49	.49	13	.50	.35	.53	.48	.28	.57	11
Incidence of suicide ages 15–24	.32	.50	11	.38	.34	.39	.51	.49	.50	9
Proportion foreign born	.09	.14	5	.15	.13	.16	.12	.14	.10	4

(continued)

Appendix 6 (*Continued*)

Group and variable	Measure									
	Birthrate for women aged 15–19	Pregnancy rate for women aged 15–19	No. of countries for which data available	Cumulative birth-rate for ages			Cumulative pregnancy rate for ages			No. of countries for which data available
				<20	<18	18–19	<20	<18	18–19	
General Social Conditions										
Log of population density	.07	−.05	11	.14	−.05	.22	−.01	−.21	.11	10
Percentage in cities >500,000	.22	.50	11	.21	.55	.02	.50	.74	.31	10
Percentage of labor force in agriculture	.42	.20	11	.42	.14	.52	.15	−.11	.31	10
Religiosity	.86	.78	6	.85	.90	.78	.80	.82	.76	5
Employment										
Labor force participation rate for females aged 15–19	.73	.68	5	.76	.79	.72	.69	.73	.66	4
Labor force participation rate for males aged 15–19	.58	.61	5	.74	.74	.74	.69	.71	.67	4
Percentage of labor force female	.59	.61	11	.62	.42	.68	.64	.42	.73	10
Labor force participation rate for females 35–44	.07	.26	7	.19	.10	.26	.32	.29	.35	6
Overall unemployment rate	.14	.19	9	.23	.32	.16	.23	.23	.22	8
General Economic Conditions										
Gross national product per capita	−.78	−.50	11	−.76	−.55	−.79	.45	−.21	−.57	10
Average annual growth in gross domestic product	.03	−.01	9	−.02	−.06	.02	−.04	−.06	−.02	8
Percentage of total household income to top 10% of population	.52	.40	8	.50	.44	.53	.38	.30	.44	7
Percentage of total household income to bottom 20% of population	−.79	−.60	9	−.79	−.76	−.79	−.59	−.58	−.59	8

Multivariate Analysis of the Cumulative Birthrates for Women under Age 18 and Women Aged 18–19

Ordinary least squares regression procedures were chosen for a multivariate analysis of the teenage birthrates. Some preliminary work with factor analysis provided useful insight into the interrelationship among the independent variables, but the results did not lend themselves readily to substantive interpretation, and the role of individual variables was largely obscured.

The approach taken was mainly determined by the necessity to minimize the problems associated with the very small sample size and the varying numbers of missing observations. Although multicollinearity was also a potential difficulty, none of the pair-wise correlations between the independent variables exceeded 0.7. In general terms, the strategy was as follows. First, the three most important factors affecting each of the two rates were identified. Then, the remaining variables were added one at a time to assess their impact on the birthrates after having taken into account the effects the three factors identified in the first step. Pair-wise deletion of missing data was used throughout. Where data for the United Kingdom existed only in the form of separate figures for England and Wales and Scotland, a single weighted figure was entered in order to maximize the number of matching observations.

An spss stepwise regression was used to select the most important factors influencing the cumulative birthrates based on the probabilities of significance of their F values. The next task was to add the remaining independent variables one by one to the two models (one for each of the two birthrates) in order to evaluate the importance of each individual variable beyond that of the first three variables in combination. Increase in the adjusted R-square was used as the criterion to identify the additional variables that individually contributed most to explanation of the remaining variation in the dependent variables. For example, in table A, adding minimum age for marriage without parental consent actually reduces the adjusted R-square by 7 points. The only variables that increase the adjusted R-square are open attitudes about sex (by 9 points)

285

and the gross national product per capita (by 1 point). Adjusted R-square was considered a better measure than R-square itself in this instance, not so much because of change in the number of variables in the equation (which was uniformly +1), but because it helped to overcome the fact that the proportion of missing observations was sufficiently high and uneven to affect the degrees of freedom and hence the computation of R-square.

The results are shown in table A for women younger than 18 years old and in table B for women aged 18–19. The variables are listed in the same order as presented in chapter 1 of the text and in table 1.2; the directions of the effects of all of the important variables are consistent with the bivariate analysis. The possible implications of these findings are discussed in chapter 1.

Table A. *Effects (standardized regression coefficients) of selected variables on the cumulative birthrate for women under age 18*

	Model										
Minimum age for marriage without parental consent	.33	.30	.34	.33	.41	.32	.31	.65	.39	.35	.38
Policy to raise fertility		-.05									
Liberal policy on maternity leaves and benefits			.12								
Policy to provide contraceptives for young unmarried women				-.01							
Open attitudes about sex					-.35						
Maternal mortality						.18					
Mortality rate from liver cirrhosis							.12				
Proportion foreign born								.52			
Proportion in cities >500,000									.10		
Proportion of labor force in agriculture	.62	.62	.66	.62	.46	.54	.59	.82	.63	.62	.44
Proportion of labor force female										-.06	
Gross national product per capita											-.26
Proportion of total household income to bottom 20% of population	-.55	-.54	-.58	-.54	-.52	-.54	-.53	-.69	-.52	-.56	-.53
Adjusted R^2	.63	.56	.61	.59	.72	.63	.61	.63	.60	.59	.64
Change in R^2		-.07	-.02	-.04	+.09	-.00	-.02	-.00	-.03	-.04	+.01

Table B. *Effects (standardized regression coefficients) of selected variables on the cumulative birthrate for women aged 18–19*

	Model									
Minimum age for marriage without parental consent										
Policy to raise fertility		-.22	.19							
Liberal policy on maternity leaves and benefits	.48	.35	.48	.46	.46	.46	.66	.55	.44	.51
Policy to provide contraceptives for young unmarried women				-.13						
Open attitudes about sex	-.43	-.45	-.45	-.40	-.40	-.44	-.34	-.42	-.41	-.29
Maternal mortality					.16					
Mortality rate from liver cirrhosis						.19				
Proportion foreign born							.34			
Proportion in cities >500,000								.10		
Proportion of labor force in agriculture	.40	.37	.34	.37	.35	.37	.56	.42	.41	.27
Proportion of labor force female									.08	
Gross national product per capita										-.29
Proportion of total household income to bottom 20% of population										-.25
Adjusted R^2	.68	.68	.71	.69	.69	.70	.64	.68	.67	.70
Change in R^2	-.00	-.00	+.03	+.01	+.01	+.02	-.04	-.00	-.01	+.01

References

Adler, M. W. 1980. "Trends for Gonorrhea and Pelvic Inflammatory Disease in England and Wales and for Gonorrhea in a Defined Population." *American Journal of Obstetrics and Gynecology* 138:901.

Alan Guttmacher Institute, The (AGI). 1975. *Provisional Estimates of Abortion Need and Services in the Year following the 1973 Supreme Court Decisions: United States, Each State and Metropolitan Area.* New York.

———. 1976. *Eleven Million Teenagers.* New York.

———. 1981. *Teenage Pregnancy: The Problem That Hasn't Gone Away.* New York.

———. 1982. "New Facts Clarify Issue of Parental Notification for Teenage Birth." News release. April 7, 1982.

———. 1983. *Current Functioning and Future Priorities in Family Planning Services Delivery.* New York.

———. 1984. "Should Government Squeal on Teens Seeking Contraception?" *Public Policy Issues in Brief.* Vol. 4, No. 3.

Andersch, B. and I. Milsom. 1982. "Contraception and Pregnancy among Young Women in an Urban Swedish Population." *Contraception* 26:211.

Ashton, John R. 1980a. "Components of Delay amongst Young Women Obtaining Terminations of Pregnancy." *Journal of Biosocial Science* 12:261.

———. 1980b. "Patterns of Discussion and Decision-Making amongst Abortion Patients." *Journal of Biosocial Science* 12:247.

Ashton, John R., K. J. Dennis, R. G. Rowe, W. E. Waters, and J. Wheeler. 1980. "The Wessex Abortion Studies: I, Interdistrict Variation in Provision of Abortion Services." *The Lancet*, Jan. 12, 1980, 82.

Bachrach, Christine A. 1984. "Contraceptive Practice among American Women, 1973–1982." *Family Planning Perspectives* 16:253.

Barrett, F. N. 1980. "Sexual Experience, Birth Control Usage and Sex Education of Unmarried Canadian University Students: Changes Between 1968 and 1978. *Archives of Sexual Behaviour* 9:367.

Berent, Jerzy. 1982. "Family Planning in Europe and the U.S.A. in the 1970's." *Comparative Studies.* No. 20. London: International Statistical Institute/ World Fertility Survey.

Björkland, Anders and Inga Persson-Tanimura. 1983. "Youth Employment in Sweden." In *Youth at Work: An International Survey,* ed. B. Reubens. Totawa, N.J.: Allanheld, Osmun and Company.

Blum, Robert and Michael Resnick. 1982. "Adolescent Sexual Decision-Making: Contraception, Pregnancy, Abortion, Motherhood." *Pediatric Annuals* 11:797.

Boethius, Carl G. 1984. "Swedish Sex Education and Its Results." *Current Sweden.* No. 315. Stockholm: Swedish Institute.

Boldt, Edward D., Lance W. Roberts, and Abdel H. Latif. 1982. "The Provision of Birth Control Services to Unwed Minors: A National Survey of Physician Attitudes and Practices." *Canadian Journal of Public Health.* 73 (Nov./Dec.): 392–95.

Bone, Margaret. 1978. *The Family Planning Services: Changes and Effects.* Office of Population Censuses and Surveys, Social Survey Division. London: Her Majesty's Stationery Office (HMSO).

————. 1984. *The Family Planning Services in Scotland—1982.* First Draft Report. Office of Population Censuses and Surveys, Social Survey Division. London: HMSO. Brook Advisory Centers. 1983. *Annual Report, 1982–83.* London.

Brook Advisory Centres. 1983. *Annual Report, 1982–83.* London.

Brown, Audrey and Kathleen Kiernan. 1981. "Cohabitation in Great Britain." *Population Trends* 25:4–10. London: HMSO.

Brown, Prudence. 1983. "The Swedish Approach to Sex Education and Adolescent Pregnancy: Some Impressions." *Family Planning Perspectives* 15:90.

Burnham, Drusilla. 1983. "Induced Termination of Pregnancy: Reporting States, 1980." *Monthly Vital Statistics Report.* Vol. 32, No. 8, Supplement. National Center for Health Statistics (NCHS).

Bury, Judith. 1984a. *Teenage Pregnancy in Britain.* London: Birth Control Trust.

————. 1984b. Updated version of 1980 Annual Report. Edinburgh Brook Advisory Center.

Campbell, Arthur. 1984. Unpublished tabulations from National Survey of Family Growth, Cycle III.

Canadian Institute of Public Opinion. 1977. "Sex Outside Marriage Always Wrong, Say 60%." Press release, Oct. 1, 1977.

Cates, Willard and Roger Rochat. 1976. "Illegal Abortions in the United States: 1972–1974." *Family Planning Perspectives* 8:86.

Central Bureau of Statistics. *Sociale Maandstatistiek.* The Hague. Dec. 1981; Jan 1983.

————. 1982. *Statistical Yearbook of the Netherlands, 1982.* The Hague.

————. 1982–84. *Maandstatistiek van de Bevolking.* The Hague. Nov. 1982; Apr.–May 1983; Nov. 1983; Dec. 1983; Jan. 1984.

Central Bureau of Statistics and Netherlands Institute for Social Sexological Research. 1979–80. Survey of the living conditions of young people. Unpublished tabulations provided by Evert Ketting of Netherlands Institute for Socio-Sexological Research (NISSO).

Central Bureau of Statistics and Ministry of Welfare, Health, and Culture. 1983. *Vademecum Gezondheidsstatistiek Nederland 1983*. The Hague.

Central Statistical Office. 1984. *Social Trends*. No. 14. London: HMSO.

Chambers, Joanna. 1984. "Condom Survey." In *Men, Sex and Contraception*, ed. Margaret Bernard. London: Birth Control Trust and Family Planning Association.

Chamie, Mary, Susan Eisman, Jacqueline D. Forrest, Margaret T. Orr, and Aida Torres. 1982. "Factors Affecting Adolescent Use of Family Planning Clinics." *Family Planning Perspectives* 14:126.

Chatterton, Saundra. 1982. *Adolescent School Health Services: The Role of the Public Health Nurse*. Ottawa: Health and Welfare Canada.

Chester, R. 1981. "Sex Education." *Woman's Own*. London.

Chilman, Catherine S. 1980. *Adolescent Sexuality in a Changing American Society*. Washington, D.C.: U.S. Department of Health, Education, and Welfare.

Chrétien, Odile. 1981. "Les Jeunes et la Contraception: l'Experience du MFPF." In *Les Jeunes et la Contraception: Quelle Politique pour une Réelle Information?* Actes du Colloque de la Mutuelle Nationale des Etudiants de France (3 Nov.): 27–28.

Clarke, L., C. Farrell, and B. Beaumont. 1983. *Camden Abortion Study*. West Midlands: British Pregnancy Advisory Service.

Collections d'INSEE, Les. 1981. *La Situation Démographique en 1981*. Paris.

———. 1982. *La Situation Démographique en 1982*. Paris.

Conseil Economique et Social. 1979. *La Situation Démographique de la France et Ses Implications Economiques et Sociales: Bilan et Perspectives*. No. 4003. Paris.

Conseil Supérieur de l'Information Sexuelle, de la Régulation des Naissances, et de l'Education Familiale (CSISRNEF). 1983. *Sexualité—Maternité—Adolescence*. (Nov.) Paris.

Cooper, Lynne. 1982. *The Selection and Preparation of Family Life Educators: A Review of the Literature*. San Diego: Network Publications, ETR Associates.

Cossey, Dilys. 1984. In *Men, Sex and Contraception*, ed. Margaret Bernard. London: Birth Control Trust and Family Planning Association.

Crépault, Claude and Robert Gemme. 1981. "La Sexualité Prémaritale en Québec." In *La Sexualité en Québec: Perspectives Contemporaines*, eds. J. J. Levy and A. Dupras. Québec: Editions IRIS.

Cutright, Phillips. 1970. "AFDC Family Allowances and Illegitimacy." *Family Planning Perspectives*. Vol. 2, No. 4:4–9.

———. 1971. "Illegitimacy: Myths, Causes and Cures." *Family Planning Perspectives* 3:25.

———. 1973. "Illegitimacy and Income Supplements" In *Studies in Public Welfare*, eds. R. Lerman and A. Townsend. Paper No. 12, Pt. I, 90. Joint Economic Committee of the Congress. Washington, D.C.: U.S. Government Printing Office.

Cutright, Phillips, Frank F. Furstenberg, Jr., June Sklar, and Beth Berkov. 1974. "Teenage Illegitimacy: An Exchange." *Family Planning Perspectives* 6:132.

Deiseach, Donal. 1977. *Family Life Education in Canadian Schools*. Toronto, Ontario: Canadian Education Association.

DeLamater, John and Patricia MacCorquodale. 1979. *Premarital Sexuality: Attitudes, Relationships, Behavior*. Madison: University of Wisconsin Press.

Donovan, Patricia. 1982. "Airing Contraceptive Commercials." *Family Planning Perspectives* 14:321.

———. 1983. "Challenging the Teenage Regulations: The Legal Battle." *Family Planning Perspectives* 15:126.

Dryfoos, Joy G. 1985. "School-based Health Clinics: A New Approach to Preventing Adolescent Pregnancy?" *Family Planning Perspectives* 17:70.

Dryfoos, Joy G. and Nancy Bourque-Scholl. 1981. *Factbook on Teenage Pregnancy.* New York: Alan Guttmacher Institute.

Dunnell, Karen. 1979. *Family Formation, 1976.* Office of Population Censuses and Surveys, Social Survey Division. London: HMSO.

Dupras, Andre and Joseph J. Levy. 1981. "La Sexualité et la Contraception Chez les Cegepiens." In *La Sexualité au Québec: Perspectives Contemporaines,* eds. J. J. Levy and A. Dupras, 43–54. Longueuil, Québec: Editions IRIS.

Ellwood, David T. and Mary Jo Bane. 1984. "The impact of AFDC on Family Structure and Living Arangements." Report to the U.S. Department of Health and Human Services. Cambridge, Mass.: Harvard University.

European Collaborative Committee for Child Health of the Children's Research Fund. 1983. "Teenage Mothers, London"; and U.S. National Center for Health Statistics. "Advance Report of Final Natality Statistics, 1982." *1984 Monthly Vital Statistics Report.* Vol. 33, No. 6, Supplement.

"Familje planering och abort. Erfarenheter ny lagstiftning." SOU. Stockholm.

Family Planning and Abortion in Sweden. 1983. Report of the Swedish Abortion Committee. Stockholm.

Family Planning Association. 1982a. *Fact Sheet No. A. 3.* London.

———. 1982b. *Fact Sheet No. D. 2.* London.

Family Planning Information Service (FPIS). 1983a. *Fact Sheet F-3.* "Sexually Transmitted Diseases and Contraception." London.

———. 1983b. "Parents Endorse Sex Education." *Family Planning Today* (First Quarter 1983). London.

Farrell, Christine. 1978. *My Mother Said.* London: Routledge and Kegan Paul Ltd.

Festy, Patrick. 1982. "Quelques Changements de Calendrier dans le Cycle de la Vie." In *Les Ages de la Vie.* Actes du VIIe Colloque National de Démographie, Strasbourg 5–7 Mai. Travaux et Documents de l'INED, Cahier No. 96. 183–200. Presses Universitaires de France.

Fogelman, Ken. 1976. *Britain's Sixteen-Year-Olds.* London: National Children's Bureau.

Ford, James and Michael Schwartz. 1979. "Birth Control for Teenagers: Diagram for Disaster." *Linacre Quarterly* (Feb.) 46:71.

Ford, Kathleen. 1978. "Contraceptive Use in the United States, 1973–1976." *Family Planning Perspectives* 10:264.

Forrest, Jacqueline Darroch. 1984. "The Impact of U.S. Family Planning Programs on Births, Abortions and Miscarriages, 1970–1979." *Social Science and Medicine* 18:461.

Forrest, Jacqueline Darroch and Stanley K. Henshaw. 1983. "What U.S. Women Think and Do about Contraception." *Family Planning Perspectives* 15:157.

Fox, Greer Litton. 1983. "The Family's Role in Adolescent Sexual Behavior."

In *Teenage Pregnancy in a Family Context,* ed. T. Ooms. Philadelphia: Temple University Press.

Francome, Colin. 1983. "Unwanted Pregnancies amongst Teenagers." *Journal of Biosocial Science* 15:139.

Fuchs, Victor. 1983. *How We Live: Economic Perspectives on Americans from Birth to Death.* Cambridge, Mass: Harvard University Press.

Gallup Organization, The. 1985. "Attitudes toward Contraception." Unpublished report to the American College of Obstetricians and Gynecologists. Princeton, N.J.

Gallup Poll. 1984a. "Religion in America—1984." *The Gallup Report.* No. 222 (Mar.). Princeton, N.J.

———. 1984b, 1985a. "The Gallup Poll of Teachers' Attitudes toward the Public Schools I and II." *Phi Delta Kappan* 66:97, 67:323.

———. 1985b. "Premarital Sex." *The Gallup Report.* No. 237 (June). Princeton, N.J.

———. 1985c. "Religion in America—50 Years: 1935–1985." *The Gallup Report.* No. 236 (May). Princeton, N.J.

Gendell, Murray. 1980. "Sweden Faces Zero Population Growth." *Population Bulletin* 35:2.

Gokalp, Catherine. 1981. *Quand Vient L'Age des Choix—Enquête Auprès des Jeunes de 18 à 25 Ans: Emploi, Résidence, Mariage.* Travaux et Documents de l'INED, Cahier No. 95. Presses Universitaires de France.

———. 1982. "Insertion Professionelle et Formation de la Famille." In *Les Ages de la Vie.* Actes du VIIᵉ Colloque National de Démographie, Strasbourg, 5–7 Mai. Travaux et Documents de l'INED, Cahier No. 96. 201–11. Presses Universitaires de France.

Goodchild, Romie. 1984. "The Influence of the Media." In *Men, Sex and Contraception,* ed. Margaret Bernard. London: Birth Control Trust and Family Planning Association.

Gourgues, Jules-Henri. 1975. "The Sexual Concerns of Young People: Quebec Commits Itself." *Bulletin de la Fédération pour la Planification Familiale du Canada.* Vol. 2, No. 3.

———. 1980. *"The Quebec Experience: Achievements in Perspective."* Quebec City.

Grant, W. V., and L. J. Eiden. 1982. *Digest of Education Statistics, 1982.* Washington, D.C.: National Center for Education Statistics.

Grimes, David. 1984. "Second Trimester Abortions in the United States." *Family Planning Perspectives* 16:260.

Guttmacher Institute. See Alan Guttmacher Institute.

Hayman, Suzie. 1977. *Advertising and Contraceptives.* London: Birth Control Trust.

Health Education Council. 1983. "Sex Education in Schools." London.

Helms, Jesse. 1984. Testimony before the U.S. Senate Commitee on Labor and Human Resources, Subcommittee on Family and Human Services, April 5.

Hendershot, Gerry E. and Paul J. Placek, 1974. "Use of Contraceptive Services in Periods of Receipt and Nonreceipt of AFDC." *Public Health Reports* 89:533.

Henriksson, Benny. 1983. *Not For Sale: Young People in Society.* Aberdeen: Aberdeen University Press.

Henripin, Jacques and Nicole Marcil-Gratton. 1981. "L'Avortement, la Contraception et la Fécondité au Québec et au Canada." In *La Sexualité au Québec: Perspectives Contemporaines,* eds. J. J. Levy and A. Dupras, 301–319. Longeueil, Québec: Editions IRIS.

Henshaw, Stanley K. 1984. Unpublished tabulations from AGI Abortion Provider Survey and data from Centers for Disease Control Abortion Surveillance.

———. 1985. "Characteristics of Abortion Patients." *Family Planning Perspectives* 17:90.

Henshaw, Stanley K. and Greg Martire. 1982. "Abortion and the Public Opinion Polls." *Family Planning Perspectives* 14:53.

Henshaw, Stanley K., Jacqueline D. Forrest, and Ellen Blaine. 1984. "Abortion Services in the United States, 1981 and 1982." *Family Planning Perspectives* 16:119.

Henshaw, Stanley K., Nancy J. Binkin, Ellen Blaine, and Jack C. Smith. 1985. "A Portrait of American Women Who Obtain Abortions." *Family Planning Perspectives* 17:90.

Herold, Edward S. 1984. *Sexual Behaviour of Canadian Young People.* Markham, Ontario: Fitzhenry and Whiteside.

Herold, Edward S. and Marilyn Shirley Goodwin. 1979. "Why Adolescents Go to Birth-Control Clinics Rather Than to Their Family Physicians." *Canadian Journal of Public Health* 70:317.

Heuser, Robert L. 1976. "Fertility Tables for Birth Cohorts by Color." Rockville, Md.: Department of Health, Education, and Welfare.

Hobart, Charles W. 1980. "The Courtship Process: Premarital Sexual Attitudes and Behavior." In *Courtship, Marriage and the Family in Canada,* ed. G. N. Ramu. Gage Publishing Limited. 37–58.

Hoem, Jan and Bo Rennermalm. 1982. "Cohabitation, Marriage, and First Birth among Never-Married Swedish Women in Cohorts Born 1936–1960." *Research Report,* No. 8. Department of Statistics, University of Stockholm.

Hoem, Jan M. and Randi Selmer. 1984. "The Negligible Influence of Premarital Cohabitation in Marital Fertility in Current Danish Cohorts, 1975." *Demography* 21:193.

Hogue, Carol, Willard Cates, and Christopher Tietze. 1982. "The Effects of Induced Abortion on Subsequent Reproduction." *Epidemiologic Reviews* 4:66.

Horn, Marjorie C. 1985. *Incidence and Correlates of Unintended Childbearing among Teenagers in the United States: Findings from the NSFG, Cycle III, 1982.* Paper presented at the 1985 Annual Meeting of the Population Association of America, Mar. 28–30, Boston.

Institut National d'Etudes Démographiques (INED). 1981. "Dixième Rapport sur la Situation Démographique de la France." *Population* 36:685.

———. 1982. "Onzième Rapport sur la Situation Démographique de la France." *Population* 37:729.

———. 1983. "Douzième Rapport sur la Situation Démographique de la France." *Population* 38:665.

International Statistical Institute. 1984. *Fertility Survey in Sweden: A Summary of Findings.* No. 43. Voorburg.

Johns Hopkins University, 1979. Survey of Young Men and Women: unpublished tabulations from M. Zelnik.

Johnson, Jeanette H. 1984. "Contraception—The Morning After." *Family Planning Perspectives* 16:266.

Jones, Elise, James Beniger, and Charles Westoff. 1980. "Pill and IUD Discontinuation in the United States, 1970–1975: The Influence of the Media." *Family Planning Perspectives* 12:293.

Journal Officiel de la République Française. 1983. *Interruption Volontaire de la Grossesse: Textes Législatifs et Réglementaires, Circulaires.* No. 1501. Paris.

Kahn, Alfred J. and Sheila B. Kamerman. 1983. *Income Transfers for Families with Children: An Eight-Country Study.* Philadelphia: Temple University Press.

Kamerman, Sheila B., Alfred J. Kahn, and P. Kingston. 1983. *Maternity Policies and Working Women.* New York: Columbia University Press.

Kenney, Asta, Jacqueline D. Forrest, and Aida Torres. 1982. "Storm Over Washington: The Parental Notification Proposal." *Family Planning Perspectives* 14:185.

Kenney, Asta and Margaret Terry Orr. 1983. "Addressing Teen Pregnancy: School Sex Education in Policy and Practice." AGI *Public Policy. Issues in Brief.* Vol. 3. No. 3.

Ketting, Evert. 1983. "Contraception and Fertility in the Netherlands." *Family Planning Perspectives.* Vol. 15, No. 1:19–25.

Ketting, Evert and Ferd Leliveld. 1983. *Abortus en anticonceptie anno 1982.* Den Haag: Stimezo Nederland.

Ketting, Evert and Paul Schnabel. 1980. "Induced Abortion in the Netherlands: A Decade of Experience." *Studies in Family Planning* 11:385.

Kiernan, Kathleen. 1980. "Teenage Motherhood: Association Factors and Consequences—The Experiences of a British Birth Cohort." *Journal of Biosocial Science* 12:393.

Kirby, Douglas. 1984. "The Effects of Selected Sexuality Education Programs: Toward a More Realistic View." *Journal of Sex Education Therapy.* Vol. 2, No. 1:28–37.

Kisker, Ellen. 1984a. Unpublished tabulations from survey of family planning clinic patients.

———. 1984b. "The Effectiveness of Family Planning Clinics in Serving Adolescents." *Family Planning Perspectives* 16:212.

Kisker, Ellen, Stanley K. Henshaw, Aida Torres, Margaret Terry Orr, and Jacqueline Darroch Forrest. 1985. "Teenagers Talk about Sex, Pregnancy and Contraception." *Family Planning Perspectives* 17:83.

Klackenberg-Larsson, Ingrid. 1977. Unpublished tabulations.

Koenig, Michael and Melvin Zelnik. 1982. "The Risk of Premarital First Pregnancy among Metropolitan-Area Teenagers: 1976 and 1979." *Family Planning Perspectives* 14:239.

Latif, Abdel H. and Edward D. Boldt. 1977. "A Survey of the Physician's Role in Family Planning: The Manitoba Case." *Canadian Journal of Public Health* 68:59–65.

Lazure, Denis. 1980. "The Child: His Development as a Sexual Being." In "Childhood and Sexuality." Proceedings of International Symposium. *Etudes Vivantes,* ed. Jean-Marc Samson. Montreal. 16–19.

LeClair, Maurice and A. W. Johnson. 1973. *Current Status of Family Planning in Canada.* Ottawa: Health and Welfare Canada.

Leliveld, Ferd and Evert Ketting. 1984. *Op de grens van volwassenheid; verslag van een onderzoek naar de intieme leefsituatie van 17 tot 24 jarigen.* NISSO Studies. Zeist: NISSO.

Le Nouvel Observateur. 1984. "Amour: La Première Fois" (Sondage SOFRES. *Le Nouvel Observateur*) 23–29 Mar. 46–53.

Les Dossiers de l'Etudiant. 1978. "120 questions aux étudiants et aux lycéens." *Guide Pratique 1978/1979.*

―――. 1980. "123 questions aux lycéens, lycéennes." Sept.

L'Etudiant. 1979. "Qui sont les étudiants?" *Guide de L'Etudiant 1979/80,* 12 Oct.

―――. 1980. "Qui sont les lycéens 80?" No. 16, Sept. 3–8.

―――. 1982. "Les étudiants en 1982." Extracted from "l'Almanach 82–83." Sept.

Lewin, Bo, ed. 1980. "Sexual Attitudes and Sexual Experiences Among Teenagers in a Swedish City." Uppsala: Uppsala University.

―――. 1982. "The Adolescent Boy and Girl: First and Other Early Experiences with Intercourse from a Representative Sample of Swedish School Adolescents. May 1981." *Archives of Sexual Behavior.* Vol.11, No. 5.

Lincoln, Richard. 1983. "Teenage Pregnancy and Childbearing: Why the Difference between Countries." *Family Planning Perspectives* 15:104.

Longourdeau, Annie. 1978. "Etude sur la Fréquentation des Centres de Planning Familial." Mouvement Français pour le Planning Familial (MFPF).

Makinson, Carolyn. 1985. "The Health Consequences of Teenage Fertility." *Family Planning Perspectives* 19:132.

Mascola, Laurence, Willard Cates, Gladys Reynolds, Joseph Blount, and William Albritton. 1983. "Gonorrhea and Salpingitis Among American Teenagers, 1960–1981." *Morbidity and Mortality Weekly Report.* Vol. 32, No. 3SS, 25SS–30SS.

Matthiessen, P. C. 1979. "The Interaction between Legalization of Abortion and Contraception in Denmark." *World Health Statistics* 32:246.

Maury, Isabelle. 1981–82. "Blocage des Idées." *La Mutu.* No. 5, (Dec.–Jan.): 12–14.

Meikle, Stewart, K. I. Pearce, J. Peitchinis, and F. Push. 1981. *An Investigation into the Sexual Attitudes, Knowledge and Behaviour of Teenage School Students.* Calgary, Alberta: unpublished report.

Minister of Supply and Services. 1977. *Report of the Committee on the Operation of the Abortion Law.* Ottawa.

Moore, Kristin A. 1978. "Teenage Childbirth and Welfare Dependency." *Family Planning Perspectives* 10:233.

Moore, Kristin A. and Steven B. Caldwell. 1977. "The Effect of Government Policies on Out-of-Wedlock Sex and Pregnancy." *Family Planning Perspectives* 9:164.

Morris, L. A. 1984. "Prescription Drug Advertising to Consumers: Brief Summary Format for Television and Magazine Advertising." Food and Drug Administration, U.S. Department of Health and Human Services.

Mosher, William. 1985. Unpublished tabulations from the 1982 National Survey of Family Growth: Cycle III.

Mouvement Français pour le Planning Familial (MFPF). 1983. *Colloque International sur la Contraception vue du Côté des Femmes.* Paris.

Murray, Charles. 1984. *Losing Ground.* New York: Basic Books.

National Center for Education Statistics (NCES). 1982. *Digest of Educational Statistics.* Washington, D.C.

National Center for Health Statistics (NCHS). 1975. *Vital Statistics of the United States 1971, Volume I—Natality.* Rockville, Md.: Department of Health, Education, and Welfare.

———. 1983. "Advance Report of Final Natality Statistics, 1981." *Monthly Vital Statistics Report.* Vol. 32, No. 9, Supplement.

———. 1984a. *Vital Statistics of the United States, 1979.* Vol. 1, Natality.

———. 1984b. "Advance Report of Final Natality Statistics, 1982." *Monthly Vital Statistics Report.* Vol. 33, No. 6, Supplement.

———. 1985. "Advance Report of Final Marriage Statistics, 1982." *Monthly Vital Statistics Report.* Vol. 34, No. 3, Supplement.

National Council for One Parent Families. 1979. *Pregnant at School.* London: Community Development Trust.

National Institute for Mental Health (NIMH). 1982. *Television and Behavior: Ten Years of Scientific Progress and Implications for the Eighties, Vol. I.: Summary Report.* Washington D.C.: Department of Health and Human Services.

National Swedish Board of Education. 1977. *Instruction Concerning Interpersonal Relations 1977.* (Translated into English, 1981.)

National Swedish Board of Health and Welfare. 1978. *Living Together: A Family Planning Project on Gotland, Sweden 1973–1976.*

Netherlands Information Service. 1983. *The Netherlands in Brief.* The Hague: Ministry of Foreign Affairs.

Newcomer, Susan F. and J. Richard Udry. 1985. "Parent-Child Communication and Adolescent Sexual Behavior." *Family Planning Perspectives* 17:169.

Nolte, Judith. 1984. "Sex Education in Canadian Classrooms." *Tellus* (Sept. 30) 13. Ottawa: Planned Parenthood Federation of Canada.

Norland, J. A. 1983. *Common-Law Unions in Canada: Age Composition.* Statistics Canada, Interim Report No. 4.

O'Connell, Martin and Maurice J. Moore. 1980. "The Legitimacy Status of First Births to U.S. Women Aged 15–24, 1939–1978." *Family Planning Perspectives* 12:17.

O'Connell, Martin and Carolyn Rogers. 1984. "Out-of-Wedlock Births, Premarital Pregnancies and Their Effect on Family Formation and Dissolution." *Family Planning Perspectives* 16:157.

Office of Population Censuses and Surveys (OPCS), Immigration Statistics Unit. 1978. "Marriage and Birth Patterns among the New Commonwealth and Pakistani Population." *Population Trends* 11:5. London: HMSO.

———. 1982. Editorial, "Sources of Statistics on Ethnic Minorities." *Population Trends* 28:1.

———. 1983a. *Abortion Statistics 1981, England and Wales.* Series AB No. 8. London: HMSO.

———. 1983b. *General Household Survey 1981.* London: HMSO.

———. 1984a. *Birth Statistics 1981, England and Wales.* Series FMI No. 8. London: HMSO.

————. 1984b. "Conceptions Inside and Outside Marriage." *OPCS Monitor*. FM I84/6. London: HMSO.

Ontario Ministry of Health. 1981. *Family Planning Ontario Yearly Report, 1980* Feb. 23.

Orr, Margaret Terry. 1982. "Sex Education and Contraceptive Education in U.S. Public High Schools." *Family Planning Perspectives* 14:304.

————. 1984a. "Private Physicians and the Provision of Contraceptives to Adolescents." *Family Planning Perspectives* 16:83.

————. 1984b. "The Media and Sex Education: A Review of the Literature." Unpublished paper.

Orr, Margaret Terry and Jacqueline Darroch Forrest. 1985. "The Availability of Reproduction Health Services from U.S. Private Physicians," *Family Planning Perspectives* 17:63.

Orton, Maureen Jessop and Ellen Rosenblatt. 1981. *Adolescent Birth Planning Needs: Ontario in the Eighties*. Hamilton: Planned Parenthood Ontario.

Ory, Howard W., Jacqueline Darroch Forrest, and Richard Lincoln. 1983. *Making Choices: Evaluating the Health Risks and Benefits of Birth Control Methods*. New York: Alan Guttmacher Institute.

Parents. 1982. "15–18 Ans: Eux et la Virginité." (Sondage *Parents*, Ifop), (May): 74–79.

Paxman, John M. 1980. "Young People, Fertility and the Law." *People*. Vol. 17, No. 3.

Perrson, Rune and Anita Dahlgren. 1975. "Some Observations on Swedish Youth." In "Community and Youth Education in Europe," *Paedagogica Europaea*. Vol 10, No. 2:75–78.

Placek, Paul J. and Gerry E. Hendershot. 1975. "Public Welfare and Family Planning: An Empirical Study of the 'Brood Sow' Myth." *Social Problems* 23:226.

Planned Parenthood Federation of America. 1984 (revision). *Manual of Medical Standards and Guidelines*. New York.

Pool, Janet Sceats and D. Ian Pool. 1978. *Contraception and Health Care among Young Canadian Women*. Ottawa: Carleton University Department of Sociology and Anthropology.

Pratt, William F. and Gerry E. Hendershot. 1984. "The Use of Family Planning Services by Sexually Active Teenage Women." Paper delivered at the 1984 Annual Meeting of the Population Association of America, May 3–5, Minneapolis.

Pratt, William F., William D. Mosher, Christine A. Bachrach, and Marjorie C. Horn. 1984. "Understanding U.S. Fertility: Findings from the National Survey of Family Growth, Cycle III." *Population Bulletin*. Vol. 39, No. 5.

Presser, Harriet B. and L. S. Salsberg. 1975. "Public Assistance and Early Family Formation: Is There a Pronatalist Effect?" *Social Problems* 23:226.

Reese, B. and S. Zimmerman. 1974. "The Effects of Formal Sex Education on the Sexual Behaviors and Attitudes of College Students." *Journal of the American College Health Association* 22:370.

Rehn, Gösta. 1984. "The Wages of Success." *Daedalus*. Vol. 113, No. 2:137

Reid, Donald. 1982. "School Sex Education and the Causes of Unintended Pregnancies—A Review." *Health Education Journal* 41:4.

Report of the Royal Commission on the Status of Woman in Canada. 1974. In *Family Planning in Canada,* ed. Benjamin Schlesinger. Toronto: University of Toronto Press. 101–10.

Réquillart, Marie-Alix. 1983. "Une Enquête sur le Recours des Adolescents à la Contraception." *Revue Française de Sociologie* 24:81.

Reynoldson, F. 1982. *Grapevine.* London: Family Planning Association.

Robinson, Ira and Davor Jedlicka. 1982. "Change in Sex Attitudes and Behavior of College Students, 1965–1980." *Journal of Marriage and the Family* 44:237.

Royal Commission on the Status of Women in Canada. See *Report of.*

Sarnecki, Jerzy. 1983. "Some Mechanisms of the Growth of Crime in Sweden." Stockholm: Institute for Crime Prevention. Unpublished paper.

Savary, A., Ministre de l'Education Nationale. 1981. *Note de Service No. 81–502.* Dec. 8.

Schofield, Michael. 1965. *The Sexual Behavior of Young People.* London: Longmans, Green.

———. 1973. *The Sexual Behavior of Young Adults.* Boston: Little Brown.

Schwartz, Michael and James Ford. 1982. "Family Planning Clinics: Cure or Cause of Teenage Pregnancy?" *Linacre Quarterly* 49:143.

Sex in Nederland. 1981. Survey carried out by Interact b.v. for *Nieuwe Revu.* Unpublished tabulations provided by Hein Moors of N.I.D.I.

———. 1983. Utrecht/Antwerpen: Het Spectrum.

Sharma, Raghubar D. 1982. "Premarital and Ex-Nuptial Fertility (Illegitimacy) in Canada, 1921–1972." *Canadian Studies in Population* 9:1–15.

Singh, B. K. 1980. "Trends in Attitudes Towards Premarital Sexual Relations." *Journal of Marriage and the Family* 42:387.

Skard, Torild and Elina Haavio-Mannila. 1984. "Equality between the Sexes— Myth or Reality in Norden?" In "The Nordic Enigma," *Daedalus.* Vol. 113, No. 1:141.

Skinner, C. 1984. *Teenage Pregnancy in South London.* Unpublished manuscript.

Sklar, Jane and Beth Berkov. 1974. "Teenage Family Formation in Postwar America." *Family Planning Perspectives* 6:80.

Somers, R. L. and M. Gammeltoft. 1976. "The Impact of Liberalized Abortion Legislation on Contraceptive Practice in Denmark." *Studies in Family Planning* 7:218.

Sonenstein, Freya and Karen Pittman. 1984. "The Availability of Sex Education in Large City School Districts." *Family Planning Perspectives* 16:19.

Statistics Canada. 1978. *Vital Statistics.* Vol. 1, *Births 1975–76.* Ottawa.

———. 1981a. *Canada Year Book 1980–1981.* Ottawa.

———. 1981b. *The Health of Canadians: Report of the Canada Health Survey.* Catalogue 82–538E. Ottawa.

———. 1983a. *Therapeutic Abortions, 1981.* Ottawa.

———. 1983b. *Intercensal Annual Estimates of Population by Marital Status, Age and Sex for Canada and the Provinces, 1976–1981.* Ottawa.

———. 1983c. *Vital Statistics.* Vol. 1, *Births and Deaths, 1981.* Ottawa.

———. 1983d. *Historical Labour Force Statistics: Actual Data, Seasonal Factors, Seasonally Adjusted Data, 1982.* Ottawa.

———. 1983e. *Education in Canada: A Statistical Review for 1982–1983.* Ottawa.

————. 1983f. *1981 Census of Canada, Population* (Vol. 1, National Series), Nuptiality and Fertility (Catalogue 92–906). Ottawa.

————. 1984. *Therapeutic Abortions, 1982.* Ottawa.

————. 1984b. *Vital Statistics.* Vol. 1, *Births and Deaths, 1982.* Ottawa.

Statistics Sweden. 1984. Demographic Section. Unpublished data. Stockholm.

Stimezo Nederland. 1983. *Persbericht.* SN. 83.137/EK/MP, May.

Sundström-Feigenberg, Kajsa. 1984. "Induced Abortion in Sweden." Unpublished manuscript.

Swedish Institute, The. 1982. "Legislation on Family Planning." Fact sheet. Aug. Stockholm.

Sweet, James A. and Larry L. Bumpass. 1984. *Progress Report on Census Monograph of Families and Households, with Special Attention to the Increase in Cohabiting.* Paper presented at the Annual Meeting of the Population Association of America, May 3–5, Minneapolis.

Tanfer, Koray and Marjorie C. Horn. 1985. "Contraceptive Use, Pregnancy and Fertility Patterns among Single Women in their 20s." *Family Planning Perspectives* 17:10.

Thompson, Dennis N. 1983. "Sex Education Curricula in Teacher Education Institutions: A Survey." *Journal of Research and Development in Education* 16:2.

Tietze, Christopher. 1979. *Induced Abortion: 1979.* New York: Population Council Factbook.

————. 1983. *Induced Abortion: A World Review, 1983.* 5th edition. New York: Population Council.

Tietze, Christopher and Marjorie Murstein. 1975. "Induced Abortion: A Factbook, 1975." *Reports on Population/Family Planning.* No. 14. New York: Population Council.

Title IX. 1975. Educational Amendments of 1972. *Federal Register* 40:24142.

Tomasson, Richard F. 1970. *Sweden: Prototype of Modern Society.* New York: Random House.

Torres, Aida. 1984. "The Effects of Federal Funding Cuts on Family Planning Services, 1980–1983." *Family Planning Perspectives* 16:134.

Torres, Aida, Jacqueline Darroch Forrest, and Susan Eisman. 1980. "Telling Parents: Clinic Policies and Adolescent Behavior." *Family Planning Perspectives* 12:284.

Torres, Aida and Jacqueline Darroch Forrest. 1983a. "The Costs of Contraception." *Family Planning Perspectives* 15:70.

————. 1983b. "Family Planning Clinic Services in the United States, 1981." *Family Planning Perspectives* 15:272.

————. 1985. "Family Planning Clinic Services in the United States, 1983." *Family Planning Perspectives* 17:30.

Trost, Jan. 1979. *Unmarried Cohabitation.* Vaesteràs, International Library.

————. 1984. "Teenage Contraception and Pregnancies: Sweden and the USA." Paper presented at the 1984 annual meeting of the American Association for the Advancement of Science, New York.

United Nations. 1979. *Demographic Yearbook. Special Issue: Historical Supplement.* ST/ESA/STAT/SER.R/8. New York.

————. 1983. *Demographic Yearbook 1981.* New York.

————. 1984. *Demographic Yearbook 1982.* New York.

———. Various years. *Demographic Yearbook*. New York.

U.S. Bureau of the Census. 1969. "Marital Status and Family Status." *Current Population Reports*. Series P–20, No. 187.

———. 1970. "Marital Status and Family Status: March 1969." *Current Population Reports*. Series P–20, No. 198.

———. 1971. "Marital Status and Family Status: March 1970." *Current Population Reports*. Series P–20, No. 212.

———. 1972a. "Marital Status and Living Arrangements, 1971." *Current Population Reports*. Series P–20, No. 225.

———. 1972b. *1970 Census Subject Reports: Marital Status*. PC(2)–4c.

———. 1973. "Marital Status and Living Arrangements." *Current Population Reports*. Series P–20, No. 242.

———. 1974a. "Marital Status and Living Arrangements, 1973." *Current Population Reports*. Series P–20, No. 255.

———. 1974b. "Population Estimates and Projections." *Current Population Reports*. Series P–25, No. 519.

———. 1975. "Marital Status and Living Arrangements, 1974." *Current Population Reports*. Series P–20, No. 271.

———. 1976. "Marital Status and Living Arrangements, March 1975." *Current Population Reports*. Series P–20, No. 287.

———. 1977. "Marital Status and Living Arrangements, 1976." *Current Population Reports*. Series P–20, No. 306.

———. 1978. "Marital Status and Living Arrangements, 1977." *Current Population Reports*. Series P–20, No. 323.

———. 1979a. "Marital Status and Living Arrangements, 1978." *Current Population Reports*. Series P–20, No. 338.

———. 1979b. "School Enrollment: Social and Economic Characteristics of Students." *Current Population Reports*. Special Studies, P–20, No. 360.

———. 1980. "Marital Status and Living Arrangements, 1979." *Current Population Reports*. Series P–20, No. 349.

———. 1981. "Marital Status and Living Arrangements, 1980." *Current Population Reports*. Series P–20, No. 365.

———. 1982a. Unpublished tabulations from the June 1981 Current Population Survey.

———. 1982b. "Preliminary Estimates of the Population of The U.S., by Age, Sex, and Race, 1970–1981." *Current Population Reports*. Series P–25, No. 917.

———. 1982c. "Marital Status and Living Arrangements, 1981." *Current Population Reports*. Series P–20, No. 372.

———. 1982d. "Money Income of Households, Families and Persons in the United States: 1980." *Current Population Reports*. Series P–60, No. 132.

———. 1982e. "Population Profile of the United States: 1982." *Current Population Reports*. Special Studies P–23, table 21.

———. 1982f. *Statistical Abstract of the United States: 1982–83* (103rd edition). Washington, D.C.

———. 1983a. "Marital Status and Living Arrangements, March 1982." *Current Population Reports*. Series P–20, No. 380.

———. 1983b. "Estimates of the Population of the United States, by Age, Sex and Race, 1980–1982." *Current Population Reports*. Series P–25, No. 929.

———. 1983c. "Fertility of American Women: June 1981." *Current Population Reports*. Series P–20, No. 378.

———. 1983d. *Statistical Abstract of the United States, 1984*. Washington, D.C.

———. 1983e. "Population Profile of the U.S.: 1982." *Current Population Reports*. Series P–23, No. 130.

———. 1983f. *"Women in Development IV*. Washington, D.C.

———. 1984a. "Estimates of the Population of the United States, by Age, Sex and Race: 1980–1983." *Current Population Reports*. Series P–25, No. 949.

———. 1984b. "Fertility of American Women, June 1982." *Current Population Reports*. Series P–20, No. 387.

———. 1984c. "Childspacing among Birth Cohorts of American Women: 1905–1959," *Current Population Reports*. Series P–20, No. 385.

———. 1984d. *Statistical Abstract of the United States: 1985*. Washington, D.C.

———. 1985. "Child Support and Alimony: 1981." *Current Population Reports*. Series P–23, No. 140.

van de Kaa, Dirk J. 1975. "Law and Fertility in the Netherlands." In *Law and Fertility in Europe*, eds. Maurice Kirk, Massino Livi Bacci, and Egon Szabady. Dolhain: Ordina Editions.

———. 1983. "Population: Asymmetric Tolerance or Politics of Accommodation." *Population and Family in the Low Countries III*. Netherlands Interuniversity Demographic Institute: 1–26.

Wafelbakker, Fritz. 1974. "Sexual Guidance for Young People in a Monthly Magazine." Paper presented at the Eighth Symposium of the International Union of School and University Health and Medicine, Stockholm.

Wallace, Helen, John Weeks, and Antonio Medina. 1982. "Services for and Needs of Pregnant Teenagers in Large Cities of the United States, 1979–80." *Public Health Reports* 97:6.

Westoff, Charles F. 1984. Unpublished tabulations from a 1–percent sample of the 1980 U.S. census of population.

Westoff, Charles F. and Elise F. Jones. 1977. "The Secularization of U.S. Catholic Birth Control Practices." *Family Planning Perspectives* 9:203.

Westoff, Charles F., Gérard Calot, and Andrew D. Foster. 1983. "Teenage Fertility in Developed Nations: 1971–1980." *Family Planning Perspectives* 15:105.

Weston, Jarianne. 1980. "Youth Health and Lifestyles." *Review of Child and Youth Health*. Regina, Saskatchewan: Saskatchewan Health.

White, Mary. 1984. Tabulations from the 1980 National Health Interview Survey. Personal communication.

World Health Organization (WHO). Various years. "Vital Statistics and Causes of Death." *World Health Statistics*. Geneva.

Zabin, Laurie S. and Samuel Clark. 1981. "Why They Delay: A Study of Teenage Family Planning Clinic Patients." *Family Planning Perspectives* 13:205.

Zabin, Laurie S., J. B. Hardy, R. Street, and Theodore M. King. 1984. "A School, Hospital and University-Based Adolescent Pregnancy Prevention

Program: A Cooperative Design for Service and Research." *Journal of Reproductive Medicine* 29:421.

Zabin, Laurie S., Marilyn Hirsch, Edward Smith, and Janet Hardy. 1984. "Adolescent Sexual Attitudes and Behavior: Are They Consistent?" *Family Planning Perspectives* 16:181.

Zelnik, Melvin. 1976. Unpublished data from John Hopkins' Survey of Young Women.

————. 1983. "Sexual Activity among Adolescents: Perspectives of a Decade." In *Premature Adolescent Pregnancy and Parenthood,* ed. Elizabeth R. McAnarney. New York: Grune and Stratton.

Zelnik, Melvin and John F. Kantner. 1977. Sexual and Contraceptive Experience of Young Unmarried Women in the United States, 1976 and 1971." *Family Planning Perspectives* 9:55.

————. 1978. "Contraceptive Patterns and Premarital Pregnancy among Women Aged 15–19 in 1976." *Family Planning Perspectives* 10:135.

————. 1979. "Reasons for Nonuse of Contraception by Sexually Active Women Aged 15–19." *Family Planning Perspectives* 11:289.

————. 1980. "Sexual Activity, Contraceptive Use and Pregnancy among Metropolitan-Area Teenagers: 1971–1979." *Family Planning Perspectives* 12:230.

Zelnik, Melvin and Young J. Kim. 1982. "Sex Education and Its Association with Teenage Sexual Activity, Pregnancy and Contraceptive Use." *Family Planning Perspectives* 14:117.

Zelnik, Melvin and Farida Shah. 1983. "First Intercourse among Young Americans." *Family Planning Perspectives* 15:64.

Zelnik, Melvin, Michael Koenig, and Young J. Kim. 1984. "Sources of Prescription Contraception and Subsequent Pregnancy among Young Women." *Family Planning Perspectives* 16:6.

Index

Abortion: rates of, intercountry comparisons, 1, 26–29, 30–32, 90, 182; as correlated with birth rate or pregnancy rate, 4, 8, 10, 16, 21, 29, 283; public funding for, 8, 18, 56–57, 230; illegal, 11, 40–41, 68, 129, 141, 191; and socioeconomic status, 43, 142; services, 56–57, 112–13, 117, 171–72; clinics, 56–58, 112, 139, 171–72; opposition to, 65, 123; restrictions on, 68, 140–41; delays in obtaining, 113, 141–42; parental consent, 218, 219; law and policy, 218–19; reduction of need for, 222, 223; and media, 239–40

—availability: 22; U.S., 56–57, 65; Canada, 68–70, 81; France, 138–39; Netherlands, 167–72; comparative, 218–19

—cost of: U.S., 56–57, 123; Canada, 70; Britain, 112–13; France, 141, 149–50; Netherlands, 171; Sweden, 192; comparative, 219, 232–33

—*See also* under specific countries

Abortion Law, Committee on the Operation of. *See* Badgley Report

Advertising: sex in, 58, 116, 145, 174, 239; and family planning services, 117, 145, 237

—of contraceptives, 11; United States, 58; Canada, 84, 88; England and Wales, 111, 116–17; France, 145; Sweden, 194, 197; Netherlands, 235; comparative, 238–39

Age of consent, 7, 10, 98, 109, 230, 267–76 passim

Agony Aunties, 117, 123

Aid to Families with Dependent Children (AFDC) (United States), 62, 233–34

Alcohol abuse, 12, 199

Argentina, 2

Australia, 3, 243, 251–67 passim

Austria, 3, 243, 251–67 passim

Badgley Report, 73, 75, 77, 78

Belgium, 3, 243, 251–67 passim

Birth:

—rates: as fertility measure, 3–4; by age, 3–4, 24–25, 26, 27; intercountry comparison of, 23–26, 30–32; black-white differential (U.S.), 25, 32–36, 38, 43–44; regional variations in Canada, 67, 71–72, 90–92. *See also* under specific countries

—nonmarital: U.S., 38, 42; Canada, 86; England and Wales, 98, 99, 118; France, 127–28; Nether-

304